COMMENTARY

ON A

HARMONY OF THE EVANGELISTS,

MATTHEW, MARK, AND LUKE

VOL. II

COMMENTARY

ON A

HARMONY OF THE EVANGELISTS,

MATTHEW, MARK, AND LUKE

BY JOHN CALVIN

TRANSLATED FROM THE ORIGINAL LATIN, AND COLLATED WITH
THE AUTHOR'S FRENCH VERSION,

BY THE REV. WILLIAM PRINGLE

VOLUME SECOND

WIPF & STOCK · Eugene, Oregon

Wipf and Stock Publishers
199 W 8th Ave, Suite 3
Eugene, OR 97401

Commentary on a Harmony of the Evangelists, Matthew, Mark, and Luke, Volume 2
By Calvin, John and Pringle, William
Softcover ISBN-13: 979-8-3852-1627-7
Hardcover ISBN-13: 979-8-3852-1628-4
eBook ISBN-13: 979-8-3852-1629-1
Publication date 2/13/2024
Previously published by Baker Book House, 2005

This edition is a scanned facsimile of the original edition published in 2005.

COMMENTARY

ON A

HARMONY OF THE EVANGELISTS.

MARK.

VI. 12. And they departed, and preached[1] that men should repent. 13. And they cast out many devils, and anointed with oil many diseased persons, and healed them.

LUKE.

IX. And they departed, and went round about through the villages[2] preaching the Gospel, and healing everywhere.

Mark VI. 12. *And they departed, and preached.* Matthew silently passes over what the Apostles did. Mark and Luke relate that they proceeded to execute the commission which they had received; and from their statements it appears more clearly, that the office which Christ at that time bestowed upon them, as I have formerly mentioned, was temporary, and indeed lasted but a few days. They tell us that the Apostles went through the cities and villages: and they unquestionably returned in a short time to their Master, as we shall find to be stated in another passage.

The only matter that requires exposition here is the fact related by Mark, that they *anointed with oil many diseased*

---

[1] "Eux donc estans partis prescherent;"—"they then having set out, preached."

[2] "Eux donc estans partis alloyent de village en village à l'entour;"—"they then having set out, went from village to village round about."

persons. Christ having conferred on them the power of healing, it is asked, why did they apply *oil?* Some learned persons suppose that it was a sort of medicine; and I acknowledge that in these countries the use of *oil* was very common. But nothing is more unreasonable than to imagine, that the Apostles employed ordinary and natural remedies, which would have the effect of obscuring the miracles of Christ. They were not instructed by our Lord in the art and science of healing, but, on the contrary, were enjoined to perform miracles which would arouse all Judea. I think, therefore, that this *anointing* was a visible token of spiritual grace, by which the healing that was administered by them was declared to proceed from the secret power of God; for under the Law *oil* was employed to represent the grace of the Spirit. The absurdity of an attempt to imitate the Apostles, by making the *anointing* of the sick a perpetual ordinance of the Church, appears from the fact, that Christ bestowed on the Apostles the gift of healing, not as an inheritance which they should hand down to posterity, but as a temporary seal of the doctrine of the Gospel. In our own day, the ignorance of the Papists is exceedingly ridiculous in maintaining that their nasty *unction*,[1] by which they hurry to the grave persons who are fast dying, is a Sacrament.

MATTHEW.	LUKE.
XI. 1. And it happened that when Jesus had made an end of commanding his twelve disciples,[2] he departed thence to teach and to preach in their cities. 2. Now when John had heard in the prison the works of Christ, he sent two of his disciples, 3. And said to him, Art thou he who was to come, or do we look for another? 4. And Jesus answering said to them, Go and relate to John	VII. 18. And the disciples of John informed him of all these things; 19. And John called to him two of his disciples, and sent them to Jesus, saying, Art thou he who was to come, or do we look for another? (*Shortly afterwards.*) 21. And in the same hour he cured many of diseases and plagues, and evil spirits, and to many who were blind he gave sight. 22. And

---

[1] The allusion is to *extreme unction*, (or *last anointing*,) which is one of the Seven Sacraments recognized by the Church of Rome.—*Ed.*

[2] " Quand Iesus eut achevé de donner mandemens a ses douze disciples ;"—" when Jesus had finished giving injunctions to his twelve disciples."

MATTHEW.	LUKE.
those things which you hear and see. 5. The blind receive their sight, and the lame walk; the lepers are cleansed, and the deaf hear; the dead are raised up, and the poor receive the message of the Gospel.[1] 6. And blessed is he who shall not be offended at me.	he answering said to them, Go and relate to John those things which you have heard and seen, that the blind see, the lame walk, the lepers are cleansed, the deaf hear, the dead rise again, to the poor the Gospel is preached. 23. And blessed is he who shall not be offended at me.[2]

Matthew XI. 1. *And it happened that when Jesus had made an end.* In this passage Matthew means nothing more than that Christ did not desist from the exercise of his office, while the Apostles were labouring in another direction. As soon, therefore, as he sent them away, with the necessary instructions, to perambulate Judea, he performed the duties of a teacher in Galilee. The word *commanding,* which Matthew employs, is emphatic; for he means that they did not receive a commission to do what they pleased, but were restricted and enjoined as to the statements which they should make, and the manner in which they should conduct themselves.

2. *Now when John had heard.* The Evangelists do not mean that John was excited by the miracles to acknowledge Christ at that time as Mediator; but, perceiving that Christ had acquired great reputation, and concluding that this was a fit and seasonable time for putting to the test his own declaration concerning him, he sent to him his disciples. The opinion entertained by some, that he sent them partly on his own account, is exceedingly foolish; as if he had not been fully convinced, or obtained distinct information, that Jesus is the Christ. Equally absurd is the speculation of those who imagine that the Baptist was near death, and therefore inquired what message he should carry, from Christ's mouth as it were, to the deceased fathers. It is

---

[1] "Et l'Evangile est annoncé aux poures;"—"and the Gospel is preached to the poor."

[2] "Qui ne sera point scandalizé, *ou offensé,* en moy;"—"who shall not be scandalized, *or offended,* at me."

very evident that the holy herald of Christ, perceiving that he was not far from the end of his journey, and that his disciples, though he had bestowed great pains in instructing them, still remained in a state of hesitation, resorted to this last expedient for curing their weakness. He had faithfully laboured, as I have said, that his disciples should embrace Christ without delay. His continued entreaties had produced so little effect, that he had good reason for dreading that, after his death, they would entirely fall away; and therefore he earnestly attempted to arouse them from their sloth by sending them to Christ. Besides, the pastors of the Church are here reminded of their duty. They ought not to endeavour to bind and attach disciples to themselves, but to direct them to Christ, who is the only Teacher. From the beginning, John had openly avowed that he was not *the bridegroom*, (John iii. 39.) As the faithful *friend of the bridegroom*, he presents the bride chaste and uncontaminated to Christ, who alone is *the bridegroom* of the Church. Paul tells us that he kept the same object in view, (2 Cor. xi. 2,) and the example of both is held out for imitation to all the ministers of the Gospel.

3. *Art thou he who was to come?* John takes for granted what the disciples had known from their childhood; for it was the first lesson of religion, and common among all the Jews, that Christ *was to come*, bringing salvation and perfect happiness. On this point, accordingly, he does not raise a doubt, but only inquires if Jesus be that promised Redeemer; for, having been persuaded of the redemption promised in the Law and the Prophets, they were bound to receive it when exhibited in the person of Christ. He adds, *Do we look for another?* By this expression, he indirectly glances at their sloth, which allowed them, after having been distinctly informed, to remain so long in doubt and hesitation. At the same time, he shows what is the nature and power of faith. Resting on the truth of God, it does not gaze on all sides, does not vary, but is satisfied with Christ alone, and will not be turned to another.

4. *Go and relate to John.* As John had assumed for the time a new character, so Christ enjoins them to carry to him that message, which more properly ought to have been addressed to his disciples. He gives an indirect reply, and for two reasons: first, because it was better that the thing should speak for itself; and, secondly, because he thus afforded to his herald a larger subject of instruction. Nor does he merely supply him with bare and rough materials in the miracles, but adapts the miracles to his purpose by quotations from the Prophets. He notices more particularly one passage from the 35th, and another from the 61st, chapter of Isaiah, for the purpose of informing John's disciples, that what the Prophets declared respecting the reign of Christ was accomplished and fulfilled. The former passage contains a description of Christ's reign, under which God promises that he will be so kind and gracious as to grant relief and assistance for every kind of disease. He speaks, no doubt, of spiritual deliverance from all diseases and remedies; but under outward symbols, as has been already mentioned, Christ shows that he came as a spiritual physician to cure souls. The disciples would consequently go away without any hesitation, having obtained a reply which was clear and free from all ambiguity.

The latter passage resembles the former in this respect. It shows that the treasures of the grace of God would be exhibited to the world in Christ, and declares that Christ is expressly set apart for the poor and afflicted. This passage is purposely quoted by Christ, partly to teach all his followers the first lesson of humility, and partly to remove the offence which the flesh and sense might be apt to raise against his despicable flock. We are by nature proud, and scarcely anything is much valued by us, if it is not attended by a great degree of outward show. But the Church of Christ is composed of poor men, and nothing could be farther removed from dazzling or imposing ornament. Hence many are led to despise the Gospel, because it is not embraced by many persons of eminent station and exalted rank. How perverse and unjust that opinion is, Christ shows from the very nature of the Gospel, since it was designed only for the poor and despised. Hence it follows, that it is no new occurrence, or one that ought to disturb our minds, if the Gospel is despised by all the great, who, puffed up with their wealth, have no room to spare for the grace of God. Nay, if it is rejected by the greater part of men, there is no reason to wonder; for there is scarcely one person in a hundred who does not swell with wicked confidence. As Christ here guards his Gospel against contempt, he likewise reminds us who they are that are qualified to appreciate the grace of salvation which it offers to them; and in this manner, kindly inviting wretched sinners to the hope of salvation, raises them to full confidence.

5. *The poor receive the message of the Gospel.* By *the poor* are undoubtedly meant those whose condition is wretched and despicable, and who are held in no estimation. However mean any person may be, his poverty is so far from being a ground of despair, that it ought rather to animate him with courage to seek Christ. But let us remember that none are accounted *poor* but those who are really such, or, in other words, who lie low and overwhelmed by a conviction of their poverty.

6. *And blessed is he who shall not be offended in me.* By this concluding statement Christ intended to remind them, that he who would adhere firmly and stedfastly to the faith of the Gospel must encounter *offences,* which will tend to interrupt the progress of faith. This is said by way of anticipation, to fortify us against offences; for we shall never want reasons for rejecting it, until our minds are raised above every offence. The first lesson, therefore, to be learned is, that we must contend with *offences,* if we would continue in the faith of Christ; for Christ himself is justly denominated *a rock of offence and stone of stumbling, by which many fall,* (1 Pet. ii. 8.) This happens, no doubt, through our own fault, but that very fault is remedied, when he pronounces those to be *blessed who shall not be offended in him;* from which too we infer, that unbelievers have no excuse, though

they plead the existence of innumerable offences. For what hinders them from coming to Christ? Or what drives them to revolt from Christ? It is because he appears with his cross, disfigured and despised, and exposed to the reproaches of the world; because he calls us to share in his afflictions; because his glory and majesty, being spiritual, are despised by the world; and in a word, because his doctrine is totally at variance with our senses. Again, it is because, through the stratagems of Satan, many disturbances arise, with the view of slandering and rendering hateful the name of Christ and the Gospel; and because every one, as if on purpose, rears up a mass of *offences*, being instigated by not less malignity than zeal to withdraw from Christ.[1]

MATTHEW.

XI. 7. And as they were departing, Jesus began to say to the multitudes concerning John, What went you out into the wilderness to see? A reed, which is shaken by the wind? 8. But what went you out to see? A man clothed in soft raiment?[2] Lo, they who wear soft clothing are in the houses of kings. 9. But what went you out to see? A Prophet? Yea, I say to you, and higher than a Prophet. 10. For this is he of whom it is written, Lo, I send my messenger before thy face, who will prepare the way before thee. 11. Verily, I say to you, Among those who are born of women, there hath not arisen a greater than John the Baptist: yet he who is least in the kingdom of heaven is greater than he. 12. And from the days of John the Baptist to this day, the kingdom of heaven suffereth violence, and the violent take it by force. 13. For all the Prophets and the Law itself pro-

LUKE.

VII. 24. And when the messengers of John had departed, he began to say to the multitudes concerning John, What went you out into the wilderness to see? A reed, which is shaken by the wind? 25. But what went you out to see? A man clothed with soft garments?[3] Lo, they that live in magnificent attire, and in delicacies, are in the courts of kings. 26. But what went you out to see? A Prophet? Yea, I say to you, and more than a Prophet. 27. It is he of whom it is written, Lo, I send my messenger[4] before my face, who will prepare the way before thee. 28. For I say to you, Among those who are born of women, there is not a greater Prophet than John the Baptist; yet he that is least in the kingdom of God is greater than he.

---

[1] " Pource que tous non seulement sont bien aises de se retirer de Christ, mais aussi tachent malicieusement d'entrouver les moyens ;"— " because not only are all strongly disposed to withdraw from Christ, but they even endeavour maliciously to discover the means of doing so."
[2] " Un homme vestu de precieux vestemens ?"—" A man clothed with costly garments ?"
[3] " Vestu de precieux vestemens ?"—" clothed with costly garments ? "
[4] " Mon messager, *ou, Ange ;*"—" my messenger, or, Angel."

MATTHEW.	LUKE.
phesied until John. 14. And if you are willing to receive it,[1] he is Elijah, who was to come. 15. He that hath ears to hear, let him hear.	XVI. 16. The Law and the Prophets (were) till John : since that time the kingdom of God is preached, and all press violently into it.

Matthew XI. 7. *And while they were departing.* Christ praises John before the people, in order that they may state from recollection what they have heard from him, and may give credit to his testimony. For his name was widely celebrated, and men spoke of him in lofty terms : but his doctrine was held in less estimation, and there were even few that waited on his ministrations. Christ reminds them, that those who *went out to see him in the wilderness* lost their pains, if they did not devoutly apply their minds and faculties to his doctrine. The meaning of the words, *you went out into the wilderness,* is this: "Your journey would have been an act of foolish and ridiculous levity, if you had not a fixed object in view. But it was neither worldly splendour nor any sort of amusement[2] that you were in quest of: your design was, to hear the voice of God from the mouth of the Prophet. If therefore you would reap advantage from your undertaking, it is necessary that what he spoke should remain fixed in your memory."

8. *Clothed with soft garments.* Those who think that Christ here condemns the extravagance of a court are mistaken. There are many other passages in which luxury of dress, and excessive attention to outward appearance, are censured. But this passage simply means, that there was nothing in the wilderness to attract the people from every quarter; that every thing there was rude and unpolished, and fitted only to inspire disgust ; and that such elegance of dress as delights the eyes is rather to be looked for in the courts of kings.[3]

[1] "Si vous le voulez recevoir, *ou, et si vous voulez recevoir* mon dire;" —"if you are willing to receive it, *or, and if you are willing to receive* my saying."
[2] "Ni autre passe-temps et amusement vain ;"—"nor other pastime nor vain amusement."
[3] "Que pour voir de beaux vestemens et autres choses agencees bien proprement il faut plustost aller és Cours des Rois ;"—"that in order to see fine dresses, and other things very neatly arranged, we must rather go to the courts of kings."

11. *Verily I say to you.* These words not only maintain the authority of John, but elevate his doctrine above the ancient prophets, that the people may keep in view the right end of his ministry; for they mistook the design of his mission, and, in consequence of this, derived almost no advantage from his discourses. Accordingly, Christ extols and places him above the rank of the prophets, and gives the people to understand that he had received a special and more excellent commission. When he elsewhere says respecting himself that he was *not a Prophet,* (John i. 21,) this is not inconsistent with the designation here bestowed upon him by Christ. He was, no doubt, a Prophet, like others whom God had appointed in his Church to be expounders of the Law, and messengers of his will; but he was *more excellent* than the Prophets in this respect, that he did not, like them, make known redemption at a distance and obscurely under shadows, but proclaimed that the time of redemption was now manifest and at hand. Such too is the import of Malachi's prediction, (iii. 1,) which is immediately added, that the pre-eminence of John consisted in his being the herald and forerunner of Christ;[1] for although the ancient Prophets spoke of his kingdom, they were not, like John, placed *before his face,* to point him out as present. As to the other parts of the passage, the reader may consult what has been said on the first chapter of Luke's Gospel.[2]

There hath not arisen. Our Lord proceeds farther, and declares that the ministers of the Gospel will be as far superior to John as John was superior to the Prophets. Those who think that Christ draws a comparison between himself and John have fallen into a strange blunder; for nothing is said here about personal rank, but commendation is bestowed on the pre-eminence of office. This appears more clearly from the words employed by Luke, *there is not a greater Prophet;* for they expressly restrict his eminence to the office of teaching. In a word, this magnificent eulogium is be-

---

[1] "Pource qu'il est le Heraut marchant devant Christ pour luy faire honneur;"—"because he is the Herald marching before Christ to do him honour."
[2] Harmony, vol. i. p. 20.

stowed on John, that the Jews may observe more attentively the commission which he bore. Again, the teachers who were afterwards to follow are placed above him, to show the surpassing majesty of the Gospel above the Law, and above that preaching which came between them. Now, as Christ intended to prepare the Jews for receiving the Gospel, we ought also, in the present day, to be aroused to listen with reverence to Christ speaking to us from the lofty throne of his heavenly glory; lest he take revenge for our contempt of him by that fearful curse which he pronounces on unbelievers by Malachi in the same passage.

The kingdom of heaven and *the kingdom of God* denote the new condition of the Church, as in other passages which have already occurred; for it was promised that at the coming of Christ all things would be restored. *He that is least in the kingdom.* The Greek word $\mu\iota\kappa\rho\delta\tau\epsilon\rho\varsigma$, which I have rendered *least*, is in the comparative degree, and signifies *less;* but the meaning is more clearly brought out, that all the ministers of the Gospel are included. Many of them undoubtedly have received a small portion of faith, and are therefore greatly inferior to John; but this does not prevent their preaching from being superior to his, because it holds out Christ as having rendered complete and eternal satisfaction by his one sacrifice, as the conqueror of death and the Lord of life, and because it withdraws the vail, and elevates believers to the heavenly sanctuary.

12. *Since the days of John.* I have no doubt that Christ speaks honourably of the majesty of the Gospel on this ground, that many sought after it with warm affection; for as God had raised up John to be the herald of the kingdom of his Son, so the Spirit infused such efficacy into his doctrine, that it entered deeply into the hearts of men and kindled that zeal. It appears, therefore, that the Gospel, which comes forward in a manner so sudden and extraordinary,[1] and

---

[1] "Laquelle tant soudainement gaigne les cœurs des hommes d'une façon non accoustumee, et y cause des mouvemens merveilleux;"—"which so suddenly gains the hearts of men in an unusual manner, and excites in them wonderful emotions."

awakens powerful emotions, must have proceeded from God. But in the second clause is added this restriction, that *the violent take it by force.* The greater part of men were no more excited than if the Prophets had never uttered a word about Christ, or if John had never appeared as his witness; and therefore Christ reminds them, that the *violence,* of which he had spoken, existed only in men of a particular class. The meaning therefore is, A vast assembly of men is now collected, as if men were rushing *violently* forward to seize *the kingdom of God;* for, aroused by the voice of one man, they come together in crowds, and receive, not only with eagerness, but with vehement impetuosity, the grace which is offered to them. Although very many are asleep, and are no more affected than if John in the wilderness were acting a play which had no reference to them, yet many flock to him with ardent zeal. The tendency of our Lord's statement is to show, that those who pass by in a contemptuous manner, and as it were with closed eyes, the power of God, which manifestly appears both in the teacher and in the hearers, are inexcusable. Let us also learn from these words, what is the true nature and operation of faith. It leads men not only to give a cold and indifferent assent when God speaks, but to cherish warm affection towards Him, and to rush forward as it were with a violent struggle.

Luke XVI. 6. *The Law and the Prophets were till John.* Our Lord had said that the earnestness of the people was a prelude to those things which *the Prophets* had foretold as to the future renovation of the Church. He now compares the ministry of John to *the Law and the Prophets.* "It is not wonderful," he tells us, "that God should now act so powerfully on the minds of men; for he is not, as formerly, seen at a distance under dark shadows, but appears openly and at hand for the establishment of his kingdom." Hence it follows, that those who obstinately reject *John's* doctrine are less excusable than those who despised *the Law and the Prophets.*

Matthew XI. 13. *All the Prophets and the Law itself*

PROPHESIED. The word *prophesied* is emphatic; for *the Law and the Prophets* did not present God before the eyes of men, but represented him under figures and shadows as absent. The comparison, we now perceive, is intended to show, that it is highly criminal in men to remain indifferent, when they have obtained a manifestation of the presence of God, who held his ancient people in suspense by predictions. Christ does not class *John* with the ministers of the Gospel, though he formerly assigned to him an intermediate station between them and *the Prophets.* But there is no inconsistency here: for although John's preaching was a part of the Gospel, it was little more than a first lesson.

14. *And if you are willing to receive it.* He now explains more clearly in what manner John began to preach *the kingdom of God.* It was in the character of that *Elijah*, who was to be sent before the face of God, (Mal. iv. 5.) Our Lord's meaning therefore is, that *the great and dreadful day of the Lord,* which Malachi described, is now beheld by the Jews, when *Elijah*, who was there promised, discharges his office as a herald. Again, by this exception, *if you are willing to receive it,* he glances at their hardened obstinacy, in maliciously shutting their eyes against the clearest light. But will he cease to be *Elijah,* if he shall not be *received?* Christ does not mean that John's official character[1] depends on their approbation; but having declared that he is *Elijah,* he charges them with carelessness and ingratitude, if he does not obtain that respect to which he is entitled.

15. *He that hath ears to hear, let him hear.* We know that it is customary with Christ to introduce this sentence, whenever he treats of subjects which are highly important, and which deserve no ordinary attention.[2] He reminds us, at the same time, of the reason why the mysteries of which he speaks are not received by all. It is because many of

---

[1] "L'estat et la commission de Iean;"—"John's rank and commission."

[2] "Et qui ne doit pas estre escoutee par acquit;"—"and which ought not to be listened to in an indifferent manner."

his hearers are deaf, or at least have their ears closed. But now, as every man is hindered not only by his own unbelief, but by the mutual influence which men exercise on each other, Christ here exhorts the elect of God, whose ears have been pierced, to consider attentively this remarkable secret of God, and not to remain deaf with unbelievers.

MATTHEW.	LUKE.
XI. 16. But to what shall I compare this generation? It is like children, who sit in the market-place, and call out to their companions, 17. And say, We have played on the flute to you, and you have not danced; we have sung mournful airs to you, and you have not lamented. 18. For John came neither eating nor drinking, and they say, He hath a devil. 19. The Son of man came eating and drinking, and they say, Lo, a man who is a glutton and a wine-bibber,[1] a friend to publicans and sinners; and Wisdom is justified by her children.	VII. 29. And all the people hearing, and the publicans, justified God, having been baptized with the baptism of John.[2] 30. But the Pharisees and Lawyers[3] despised[4] the counsel of God in themselves,[5] having not been baptized by him. 31. And the Lord said, To what then shall I compare the men of this generation? and to what are they like? 32. They are like children sitting in the market-place, and calling out to each other, and saying, We have played on the flute to you, and you have not danced; we have sung mournful airs to you, and you have not wept. 33. For John the Baptist came neither eating bread nor drinking wine, and you say, He hath a devil. 34. The Son of man came eating and drinking, and you say, Lo, a man gluttonous and a wine-bibber, a friend to publicans and sinners.[6] 35. And Wisdom is justified by all her children.

Luke VII. 29. *And all the people hearing.* This part is left out by Matthew, though it throws no small light on the connection of the words; for it was this circumstance which gave rise to Christ's expostulation, when he perceived that the scribes persisted so obstinately in despising God. The substance of this passage is, that the common *people* and the

---

[1] "Gourmand et yvrongne;"—"a glutton and a drunkard."
[2] "Et tout le peuple qui oyoit cela, et les Peagers qui estoyent baptizez du baptesme de Iean, iustifierent Dieu."—"And all the people who heard that, and the publicans who were baptized with the baptism of John, justified God."
[3] "Les Docteurs de la Loy;"—"the Doctors of the Law."
[4] "Reietterent le conseil de Dieu;"—"rejected the counsel of God."
[5] "En eux-mesmes, *ou, à l'encontre d'eux-mesmes*;"—"in themselves, *or, against themselves.*"
[6] "Ami des Peagers et gens du mauvaise vie;"—"a friend of publicans and persons of wicked life."

publicans gave glory to God; while *the Scribes,* flattering themselves with confidence in their own knowledge, cared little for what Christ said. At first sight, this tends only to obscure, and even to disfigure, the glory of the Gospel, that Christ could not gather disciples to himself, except from the dregs and offscourings of the people; while he was rejected by those who had any reputation for holiness or learning. But the Lord intended, from the beginning, to hold out this example, that neither the men of that age, nor even posterity, might judge of the Gospel by the approbation of men; for we are all by nature inclined to this vice. And yet nothing is more unreasonable than to submit the truth of God to the judgment of men, whose acuteness and sagacity amounts to nothing more than mere vanity. Accordingly, as Paul says, " God hath chosen that part which is weak and foolish in the eyes of the world, that he may cast down from its height whatever appears to be mighty and wise," (1 Cor. i. 27.) Our duty is to prefer this *foolishness of God*, to use Paul's expression, (1 Cor. i. 25,) to all the display of human wisdom.

Justified God. This is a very remarkable expression. Those who respectfully embrace the Son of God, and assent to the doctrine which he has brought, are said to ascribe righteousness to God. We need not therefore wonder, if the Holy Spirit everywhere honours faith with remarkable commendations, assigns to it the highest rank in the worship of God, and declares that it is a very acceptable service. For what duty can be deemed more sacred than to vindicate God's righteousness? The word *justify* applies generally, no doubt, to every thing connected with the praises of God, and conveys the idea, that God is beheld with approbation, and crowned with glory, by the people who embrace that doctrine of which He is the author. Now, since faith *justifies* God, it is impossible, on the other hand, but that unbelief must be blasphemy against him, and a disdainful withholding of that praise which is due to his name. This expression also teaches us, that men are never brought into complete subjection to the faith until, disregarding the flesh and sense, they conclude that every thing which comes from God is just and holy, and do not permit themselves to murmur against his word or his works.

Having been baptized with the baptism of John. Luke means that the fruits of *the baptism* which they had received were then beginning to appear; for it was a useful preparation to them for receiving the doctrine of Christ. It was already an evidence of their piety that they presented themselves to be *baptized.* Our Lord now leads them forward from that slender instruction to a higher degree of progress, as the scribes, in despising the baptism of John, shut against themselves, through their pride, the gate of faith. If, therefore, we desire to rise to full perfection, let us first guard against despising the very least of God's invitations,[1] and be prepared in humility to commence with small and elementary instructions. Secondly, let us endeavour that, if our faith shall have a feeble beginning, it may regularly and gradually increase.

30. *Despised the counsel of God within themselves.* The *counsel of God* is mentioned by way of respect, as contrasted with the wicked pride of the scribes; for the term *counsel* carries along with it a dignity, which protects the doctrine of God against the contempt of men. Literally, Luke says, that they *despised* AGAINST THEMSELVES: and indeed I do not disapprove of the meaning which is preferred by some, that the scribes were rebellious to their own destruction. But as Luke's narrative is simple, and as the preposition εἰς is often used in the sense of ἐν, I have chosen rather to translate it, *within themselves;* as meaning, that although they did not openly and expressly contradict, yet as they inwardly swelled with hidden pride, they *despised within themselves.*

31. *To what shall I compare?* He does not include all the men of his age, but speaks particularly of the scribes and their followers. He charges them with this reproach, that while the Lord endeavoured, by various methods, to draw

---

[1] "Gardons premierement de mespriser un seul moyen par lequel Dieu nous convie;"—"let us first guard against despising a single method by which God invites us."

them to himself, they repelled his grace with incorrigible obstinacy. He employs a comparison, which was probably taken from a common amusement of children; for there is probability in the conjecture, that the children divided themselves into two bands, and sang in that manner. And, indeed, I think that, in order to abase the pride of the scribes, Christ intentionally borrowed from children the materials of his reproof: thus declaring that, however distinguished they were, nothing more was necessary to condemn them than a song which children were wont to sing in the market-place for their amusement.

33. *For John the Baptist came.* Leading an austere life, he thundered out repentance and severe reproofs, and sung, as it were, a plaintive song; while the Lord endeavoured, by a cheerful and sprightly song, to draw them more gently to the Father. Neither of those methods had any success, and what reason could be assigned except their hardened obstinacy? This passage also shows us, why so wide a difference existed, as to outward life, between Christ and the Baptist, though both had the same object in view. Our Lord intended, by this diversity, and by assuming as it were a variety of characters, to convict unbelievers more fully; since, while he yielded and accommodated himself to their manners, he did not bend them to himself. But if the men of that age are deprived of every excuse for repelling, with inveterate malice, a twofold invitation which God had given them, we too are held guilty in their persons; for God leaves not untried any sort of pleasing melody, or of plaintive and harsh music, to draw us to himself, and yet we remain hard as stones. They called John a *demoniac,* just as persons of unsound mind, or whose brain is disturbed, are usually called *madmen.*

34. *The Son of man came.* To *eat and drink* means here nothing more than to live in the customary way; as Christ says that John *came neither eating nor drinking,* because he confined himself to a peculiar diet, and even abstained from ordinary food. This is more fully expressed by the words of Luke, *neither eating bread nor drinking wine.* Those who

think that the highest perfection consists in outward austerity of life, and who pronounce it to be an angelical life when a person is abstemious,[1] or mortifies himself by fasting, ought to attend to this passage. On this principle John would rank higher than the Son of God; but, on the contrary, we ought to maintain, that *bodily exercise profiteth little, but godliness is profitable to all things,* (1 Tim. iv. 8.) And yet we must not make this a pretence for giving a loose rein to the flesh, by indulging in luxuries and effeminacy: only we must beware of superstition, lest foolish men, imagining that perfection lies in matters of a purely elementary nature, neglect the spiritual worship of God. Besides, while Christ accommodated himself to the usages of ordinary life, he maintained a sobriety truly divine, and did not encourage the excesses of others by his dissimulation or by his example.

35. *And Wisdom is justified.* This passage is variously explained by commentators. Some maintain that *Wisdom* was *acquitted* by the Jews, because, conscious of guilt, and judges of their own unbelief, they were compelled to acknowledge, that the doctrine which they rejected was good and holy. By *the children of Wisdom* they understand the Jews who boasted of that title. Others think that it was spoken in irony: "It is in this manner that you approve of the *Wisdom* of God, of which you boast that you are the *children?*" But as the Greek preposition ἀπό[2] does not properly relate to an agent, some explain it, that *Wisdom is acquitted by her children,* and is no longer under obligation to them, in the same manner as when an inheritance is transferred to another. Thus Paul says, that Christ *was justified* (δεδικαίωται) *from sin,* (Rom. vi. 7,) because the curse of sin had no longer any power over him.

Some interpret it more harshly, and with greater excess of freedom, to mean that *Wisdom is estranged from her children.* But granting that this were the import of the Greek preposi-

---

[1] "Quand un homme ne boira point de vin;"—"when a person will drink no wine."
[2] "Le mot Grec que nous avons rendu par *De;*"—"the Greek word which we have translated *by.*"

tion, I look upon the other meaning as more appropriate, that *Wisdom*, however wickedly she may be slandered by her own sons, loses nothing of her worth or rank, but remains unimpaired. The Jews, and particularly the scribes, gave themselves out as *children* of the *Wisdom* of God; and yet, when they trod their mother under their feet, they not only flattered themselves amidst such heinous sacrilege, but desired that Christ should fall by their decision. Christ maintains, on the contrary, that, however wicked and depraved her *children* may be, *Wisdom* remains entire, and that the malice of those who wickedly and malignantly slander her takes nothing from her authority.

I have not yet brought forward that meaning which appears to my own mind the most appropriate and natural. First, the words of Christ contain an implied contrast between true *children* and bastards, who hold but an empty title without the reality; and they amount to this: "Let those who haughtily boast of being the *children* of *Wisdom* proceed in their obstinacy: she will, notwithstanding, retain the praise and support of her own *children*. Accordingly, Luke adds a term of universality, *by all her children;* which means, that the reluctance of the scribes will not prevent all the elect of God from remaining stedfast in the faith of the Gospel. With respect to the Greek word ἀπό, it undoubtedly has sometimes the same meaning as ὑπό. Not to mention other instances, there is a passage in Luke's Gospel, (xvii. 25,) where Christ says, that *he must suffer many things,* καὶ ἀποδοκιμασθῆναι ἀπὸ τῆς γενεᾶς ταύτης, *and be rejected* BY *this generation.* Everybody will admit, that the form of expression is the same as in the corresponding clause.[1] Besides, Chrysostom, whose native language was Greek, passes over this matter, as if there were no room for debate. Not only is this meaning more appropriate, but it corresponds to a former clause, in which it was said, that God was *justified* by *the people,* (v. 29.) Although many apostates may revolt from the Church of

---

[1] "On void bien que là ce mot *De* se rapporte à la personne qui fait, et non pas à celuy qui souffre;"—"It is very evident that the word *By* relates to the person that acts, and not to him who suffers."

God, yet, among all the elect, who truly belong to the flock, the faith of the Gospel will always remain uninjured."

LUKE.

X. 1. And after these things the Lord appointed other seventy also, and sent them by two and two before his face into every city and place, to which he was to come. 2. He said therefore to them, The harvest is indeed abundant, but the labourers are few: pray ye, therefore, the Lord of the harvest to send out labourers into his harvest. 3. Go: behold, I send you as lambs among wolves. 4. Carry neither purse, nor bag, nor shoes, and salute no man by the way. 5. Into whatsoever house you shall enter, first say, Peace be to this house. 6. And if the son of peace be there, your peace will remain upon it: but if not, it will return to you. 7. And remain in the same house, eating and drinking those things which shall be given by them;[1] for the labourer is worthy of his hire. Go not from house to house. 8. And into whatsoever city you shall enter, and they shall receive you, eat those things which are set before you: 9. And cure the diseased who are in it, and say to them, The kingdom of God is nigh to you. 10. And into whatsoever city you shall enter, and they shall not receive you, go out into its streets, and say, 11. Even the dust, which has cleaved to us from your city, we wipe off against you: yet know this, that the kingdom of God is nigh to you. 12. I say to you, That in that day it will be more tolerable for Sodom than for that city.

Luke X. 1. *And after these things the Lord appointed.* That the Apostles had returned to Christ before these *seventy* were substituted in their room, may be inferred from many circumstances. The twelve, therefore, were sent to awaken in the Jews the hope of an approaching salvation. After their return, as it was necessary that higher expectation should be excited, others were sent in greater numbers, as secondary heralds, to spread universally in every place the report of Christ's coming. Strictly speaking, they received no commission, but were only sent by Christ as heralds, to prepare the minds of the people for receiving his doctrine. As to the number *seventy*, he appears to have followed that order to which the people had already been long accustomed. We must bear in mind what has been already said about the *twelve* Apostles,[2] that as this was the number of the tribes when the people were in a flourishing condition, so an equal number of apostles or patriarchs was chosen, to reassemble

---

[1] "Mangeans et beuvans de ce qui sera mis devant vous;"—"eating and drinking of what shall be set before you."

[2] Harmony, vol. i. p. 438.

the members of the lacerated body, that the restoration of the Church might thus be complete.

There was a similar reason for these *seventy*. We know that Moses, finding himself insufficient for the burden, took *seventy* judges to be associated with him in governing the people, (Ex. xviii. 22; xxiv. 1.) But when the Jews returned from the Babylonish captivity, they had a council or συνέδριον —which was corrupted into *Sanedrin*[1]—consisting of seventy-two judges. As usually happens with such numbers, when they spoke of the council, they called them only the *seventy* judges; and Philo assures us, that they were chosen out of the posterity of David, that there might be some remaining authority in the royal line. After various calamities, this was the finishing stroke, when Herod abolished that council, and thus deprived the people of a legitimate share in the government. Now as the return from Babylon prefigured a true and complete redemption, the reason why our Lord chooses *seventy* heralds of his coming appears to be, to hold out the restoration of their fallen state; and as the people were to be united under one head, he does not give them authority as judges, but only commands them to go before him, that he may possess the sole power. *And sent them by two and two.* He appears to have done so on account of their weakness. There was reason to fear, that individually they would not have the boldness necessary for the vigorous discharge of their office; and therefore, that they may encourage one another, they are sent *by two and two*.

2. *The harvest is indeed abundant.* I have explained this passage under the ninth chapter of Matthew;[2] but it was proper to insert it again in this place, because it is related for a different purpose. In order to stimulate his disciples the more powerfully to apply with diligence to their work, he declares that *the harvest is abundant:* and hence it follows, that their labour will not be fruitless, but that they will find,

---

[1] " Lequel les Grecs nomment *Synedrion*, et eux l'appeloyent par une prononciation corrompue *Sanedrin*;"—" which the Greeks denominate *Synedrion*, and which they, by a corrupt pronunciation, called *Sanedrin*."

[2] Harmony, vol. i. p. 421.

in abundance, opportunities of employment, and means of usefulness. He afterwards reminds them of dangers, contests, and annoyances, and bids them go and prepare themselves for traversing with speed the whole of Judea.[1] In short, he repeats the same injunctions which he had given to the Apostles; and, therefore, it would serve no good purpose to trouble the reader here with many words, since a full exposition of all these matters may be found in the passage already quoted. We may notice briefly, however, the meaning of that expression, *salute no man by the way.* It indicates extreme haste, when, on meeting a person in *the way,* we pass on without speaking to him, lest he should detain us even for a short time. Thus, when Elisha sent his servant to the Shunamite woman, he charged him not to salute any person whom he met: *if thou meet any man, salute him not; and if any salute thee, answer not again,* (2 Kings iv. 31.) Christ does not intend that his disciples shall be so unkind[2] as not to deign to salute persons whom they meet, but bids them hasten forward, so as to pass by every thing that would detain them.

7. *Eating and drinking those things which they shall give you.* This is another circumstance expressly mentioned by Luke. By these words Christ not only enjoins them to be satisfied with ordinary and plain food, but allows them to eat at another man's table. Their plain and natural meaning is: "you will be at liberty to live at the expense of others, so long as you shall be on this journey; for it is proper that those for whose benefit you labour should supply you with food." Some think that they were intended to remove scruples of conscience, that the disciples might not find fault with any kind of food.[3] But nothing of this kind was intended, and

---

[1] " Et leur commande d'aller alaigrement et en diligence, à fin que bien tost ils ayent fait une course par tout le pays de Iudee;"—" and commands them to go with alacrity and diligence, that they may soon have performed a circuit through the whole country of Judea."
[2] " Si inhumains et mal-gracieux;"—" so barbarous and uncivil."
[3] " A fin que les disciples ne facent conscience d'aucune sorte de viande;"—" in order that the disciples may not make conscience of any kind of food."

it was not even his object to enjoin frugality, but merely to permit them to accept of a reward, by living, during this commission, at the expense of those by whom they were entertained.

MATTHEW.

XI. 20. Then he began to upbraid the cities, in which most of his mighty works were done, because they had not repented of crimes: 21. Woe to thee, Chorazin! woe to thee, Bethsaida! for if the mighty works, which have been done in you, had been done in Tyre and Sidon, they would have repented of their crimes long ago in sackcloth and ashes. 22. But I say to you, It will be more tolerable for Tyre and Sidon[1] in the day of judgment than for you. 23. And thou, Capernaum, which art exalted even to heaven, shall be cast down even to hell; for if the mighty works, which have been done in thee, had been done in Sodom, it would have remained until this day. 24. But I say to you, That it will be more tolerable for the land of Sodom[2] in the day of judgment than for thee.

LUKE.

X. 13. Woe to thee, Chorazin! woe to thee, Bethsaida! for if the mighty works, which have been done in you, had been done in Tyre and Sidon, they would long ago have repented, sitting in sackcloth and ashes. 14. But it will be more tolerable for Tyre and Sidon in the judgment than for you.[3] 15. And thou, Capernaum, which art exalted even to heaven, shall be cast down even to hell. 16. He that heareth you heareth me; and he that despiseth you despiseth me; and he that despiseth me despiseth him that sent me.

Matthew XI. 20. *Then he began to upbraid.* Luke states the time when, and the reason why, Christ uttered such invectives against those cities. It was while he was sending the disciples away into various parts of Judea, to proclaim, as they passed along, that the kingdom of God was at hand. Reflecting on the ingratitude of those among whom he had long discharged the office of a prophet, and performed many wonderful works, without any good result, he broke out into these words, announcing that the time was now come, when he should depart to other cities, having learned, by experience, that the inhabitants of the country adjoining that lake, among whom he had begun to preach the Gospel and perform

---

[1] " Que Tyr et Sidon seront plus doucement traittez ;"—" that Tyre and Sidon will be treated more gently."

[2] " Que ceux de Sodome seront traittez plus doucement ;"—" that those of Sodom will be treated more gently."

[3] " Pourtant Tyr et Sidon seront plus doucement traittez au Iugement que vous ;"—" therefore Tyre and Sidon will be more gently treated in the Judgment than you."

miracles, were full of obstinacy and of desperate malice. But he says nothing about the doctrine, and reproaches them that his miracles had not led them to repent.[1] The object which our Lord had in view, in exhibiting those manifestations of his power, undoubtedly was to invite men to himself; but as all are by nature averse to him, it is necessary to begin with repentance. *Chorazin* and *Bethsaida* are well known to have been cities which were situated on the lake of Gennesareth.

21. *If those mighty works had been done in Tyre and Sidon.* As *Tyre and Sidon*, in consequence of their proximity, were at that time abhorred for their ungodliness, pride, debauchery, and other vices, Christ employs this comparison for the express purpose of making a deeper and more painful impression on his Jewish countrymen. There was not one of them who did not look upon the inhabitants of *Tyre and Sidon* as abominable despisers of God. It is, therefore, no small heightening of his curse, when Christ says, that there would have been more hope of reformation from those places in which there was no religion, than is to be seen in Judea itself.

Lest any should raise thorny questions[2] about the secret decrees of God, we must remember, that this discourse of our Lord is accommodated to the ordinary capacity of the human mind.[3] Comparing the citizens of *Bethsaida*, and their neighbours, with the inhabitants of *Tyre and Sidon*, he reasons, not of what God foresaw would be done either by the one or by the other, but of what both parties would have done, so far as could be judged from the facts. The exceedingly corrupt morals and unrestrained debauchery of those cities might be ascribed to ignorance; for there the voice of God had never been heard, nor had miracles been performed, to warn

---

[1] " Que par les miracles ils n'ont point esmeus pour se convertir à repentance ;"—" that by the miracles they were not moved to be converted to repentance."

[2] " Des questions curieuses et difficiles ;"—" curious and difficult questions."

[3] " A la capacité et apprehension commune de l'entendement humain ;" —" to the ordinary capacity and apprehension of the human understanding."

them to repent. But in the cities of Galilee, which Christ *upbraids*, there was a display of very hardened obstinacy in despising miracles, of which they had seen a vast number without reaping any advantage. In short, the words of Christ convey nothing more than that the inhabitants of *Chorazin* and *Bethsaida* go beyond those of *Tyre and Sidon* in malice and incurable contempt of God.

And yet we have no right to contend with God, for having passed by others of whom better hopes might have been entertained, and displaying his power before some who were extremely wicked and altogether desperate. Those on whom he does not bestow his mercy are justly appointed to perdition. If he withhold his word from some, and allow them to perish, while, in order to render others more inexcusable, he entreats and exhorts them, in a variety of ways, to repentance, who shall charge him, on this account, with injustice? Let us, therefore, aware of our own weakness, learn to contemplate this height and depth[1] with reverence; for it is intolerable fretfulness and pride that is manifested by those who cannot endure to ascribe praise to the righteousness of God, except so far as it comes within the reach of their senses, and who disdainfully reject those mysteries, which it was their duty to adore, simply because the reason of them is not fully evident.

If the mighty works had been done. We have said that these words inform us concerning the right use of miracles, though they likewise include doctrine; for Christ did not remain silent,[2] while he was holding out to their view the power of the Father; but, on the contrary, miracles were added to the Gospel, that they might attend to what was spoken by Christ.

In sackcloth and ashes. Repentance is here described by outward signs, the use of which was at that time common in the Church of God: not that Christ attaches importance to that matter, but because he accommodates himself to the

---

[1] "Ceste hautesse et profondeur des iugemens de Dieu;"—"this height and depth of the judgments of God."

[2] "N'a pas eu cependant sa bouche close;"—"did not in the meantime keep his mouth shut."

capacity of the common people. We know that believers are not only required to exercise repentance for a few days, but to cherish it incessantly till death. But there is no necessity, in the present day, for being clothed with *sackcloth*, and sprinkled with *ashes;* and, therefore, there is not always occasion for that outward profession of repentance, but only when, after some aggravated revolt, men turn to God. *Sackcloth and ashes* are, no doubt, indications of guilt, for the purpose of turning away the wrath of the Judge;[1] and therefore relate strictly to the beginning of conversion. But as men testify by this ceremony their sorrow and grief, it must be preceded by hatred of sin, fear of God, and mortification of the flesh, according to the words of Joel, (ii. 13,) *Rend your hearts and not your garments.* We now see the reason why *sackcloth and ashes* are mentioned by Christ along with *repentance,* when he speaks of *Tyre and Sidon,* to the inhabitants of which the Gospel could not have been preached, without condemning their past life, leaving nothing for them, but to betake themselves to the wretched apparel of criminals for the sake of humbly beseeching pardon. Such, too, is the reference of the word *sitting,* which is employed by Luke, SITTING *in sackcloth and ashes;* for it denotes "lying prostrate on the ground,"—a posture adapted to express the grief of wretched persons, as is evident from many passages of the Prophets.

23. *And thou, Capernaum.* He expressly addresses the city of *Capernaum,* in which he had resided so constantly, that many supposed it to be his native place. It was indeed an inestimable honour, that the Son of God, when about to commence his reign and priesthood, had chosen *Capernaum* for the seat of his palace and sanctuary. And yet it was as deeply plunged in its filth, as if there had never been poured upon it a drop of Divine grace. On this account, Christ declares, that the punishment awaiting it will be the more dreadful, in proportion to the higher favours which it had received from God. It deserves our earnest attention in

[1] "A fin d'adoucir le Iuge, et destourner son iuste courroux;"—"in order to pacify the Judge, and to turn away his just wrath."

this passage, that the profanation of the gifts of God, as it involves sacrilege, will never pass unpunished; and that the more eminent any one is, he will be punished with the greater severity, if he shall basely pollute the gifts which God has bestowed upon him; and above all, an awful vengeance awaits us, if, after having received the spiritual gifts of Christ, we treat him and his Gospel with contempt.

If they had been done in Sodom. We have already hinted, that Christ speaks after the manner of men, and does not bring forth, as from the heavenly sanctuary,[1] what God foresaw would happen if he had sent a Prophet to the inhabitants of *Sodom.* But if quarrelsome persons are not satisfied with this answer, every ground of objection is removed by this single consideration, that although God had a remedy in his power for saving the inhabitants of *Sodom*, yet in destroying them he was a just avenger.[2]

Luke X. 16. *He that heareth you heareth me.* It is a mistake to suppose that this passage is a repetition of what we formerly met with in the Gospel of Matthew, (x. 40,) *he that receiveth you receiveth me.*[3] *Then*, Christ was speaking of persons, but *now*, of doctrine. The former *receiving* had a reference to offices of kindness; but *now* he recommends faith, which receives God in his Word. The general meaning is, that the godliness of men is ascertained by the obedience of faith;[4] and that those who reject the Gospel, though they may boast of being the most eminent of the worshippers of God, give evidence that they wickedly despise him.

We must now attend to the design of Christ. As a considerable portion of the world foolishly estimates the Gospel

---

[1] "Il ne veut point ici amener le conseil secret de Dieu;"—"he does not intend here to exhibit the secret purpose of God."

[2] "Que toutesfois, en les destruisant et damnant, il n'a rien fait qui empesche qu'il ne soit tousiours recognue iuste en sa punition et sa vengeance;"—"that notwithstanding, in destroying and condemning them, He has done nothing to prevent Him from being always acknowledged to be righteous in His punishment and in His vengeance."

[3] Harmony, vol. i. p. 475.

[4] "Que la crainte de Dieu qui est és hommes, se monstre par l'obeissance de la foy;"—"that the fear of God which is in men is manifested by the obedience of faith."

according to the rank of men, and despises it because it is professed by persons of mean and despicable condition, our Lord here contradicts so perverse a judgment. Again, almost all are so proud, that they do not willingly submit to their equals, or to those whom they look down upon as inferior to them. God has determined, on the other hand, to govern his Church by the ministry of men, and indeed frequently selects the ministers of the Word from among the lowest dregs of the people. It was, therefore, necessary to support the majesty of the Gospel, that it might not appear to be degraded by proceeding from the lips of men.

This is a remarkable commendation[1] of the outward ministry, when Christ declares, that whatever honour and respect is rendered to the preaching of men, provided that the preaching be faithful, God acknowledges as done to Himself. In two points of view, this recommendation is useful. Nothing ought to be a stronger encouragement to us to embrace the doctrine of the Gospel, than to learn that this is the highest worship of God, and a sacrifice of the sweetest odour, to hear him speaking by human lips, and to yield subjection to his word, which is brought to us by men, in the same manner as if he were descending from heaven or making known his will to us by angels. Again, our confidence is established, and all doubt is removed, when we learn, that the testimony of our salvation, when delivered to us by men whom God has sent, is not less worthy of credit, than if His voice resounded from heaven. To deter us, on the other hand, from despising the Gospel, he adds a severe threatening:

He that despiseth you despiseth me; and he that despiseth me despiseth him that sent me. Those who disdain to listen to ministers, however mean and contemptible they may be, offer an insult, not to men only, but to Christ himself, and to God the Father. While a magnificent eulogium is here pronounced on the rank of pastors, who honestly and faithfully discharge their office, it is absurd in the Pope and his

---

[1] " C'est donc une louange et recommendation singuliere ; "—" it is then a singular praise and recommendation."

clergy to take this as a pretence for cloaking their tyranny. Assuredly, Christ does not speak in such a manner, as to surrender into the hands of men the power which the Father has given him, but only to protect his Gospel against contempt. Hence it follows, that he does not transfer to the persons of men the honour which is due to himself, but only maintains that it cannot be separated from his Word. If the Pope wishes to be *received*, let him bring forward the doctrine by which he may be recognized as a minister of Christ; but so long as he continues to be what he now is, a mortal enemy of Christ, and destitute of all resemblance to the Apostles, let him cease to deck himself with borrowed feathers.

LUKE.

X. 17. And the seventy returned with joy, saying, Lord, even the devils are subject to us in thy name.[1] 18. And he said to them, I beheld Satan falling from heaven like lightning. 19. Lo, I give you power to tread on serpents and scorpions, and on all the power of the enemy, and nothing shall hurt you. 20. Nevertheless, rejoice not in this, that the spirits are subject to you; but rejoice, because your names are written in heaven.

17. *And the seventy returned.* It is evident, that the faith of the *seventy* disciples in the words of Christ had not been full and complete, when they *returned*, exulting over it as a thing new and unexpected, that they had cast out *devils* by the power of Christ. Nay, they had received this power accompanied by a command. At the same time, I have no doubt that, when they departed, they were convinced that nothing which the Master had said to them would fail of its accomplishment; but afterwards, when the matter proceeded to an extent which surpassed their expectations, they were astonished at the sight.[2] And this is frequently the case with believers, that they receive from the word but a slight perception of the Divine power, and are afterwards excited to admiration by actual experience. What was the

[1] "Par ton Nom;"—"by thy Name."
[2] "Ils furent esmerveillez et esbahis de voir cela advenir;"—"they were astonished and overwhelmed at seeing that happen."

nature of that joy will more clearly appear from Christ's reply.

18. *I beheld Satan.* From one instance Christ leads them to the whole class; for he commanded his Gospel to be published for the very purpose of overturning Satan's kingdom.[1] So then, while the disciples rested solely on that demonstration which they had obtained from experience, Christ reminds them, that the power and efficacy of their doctrine extends farther, and that its tendency is to extirpate the tyranny which Satan exercises over the whole human race. We have now ascertained the meaning of the words. When Christ commanded that his Gospel should be preached, he did not at all attempt a matter of doubtful result, but foresaw the approaching ruin of Satan.[2] Now, since the Son of God cannot be deceived, and this exercise of his foresight relates to the whole course of the Gospel, we have no reason to doubt, that whenever he raises up faithful teachers, he will crown their labour with prosperous success.

Hence we infer, that our deliverance from the bondage of Satan is effected in no other way than through the Gospel; and that those only make actual proficiency in the Gospel, in whom Satan loses his power, so that sin is destroyed, and they begin to live to the righteousness of God. We ought also to attend to the comparison which he employs, that the thunder of the Gospel makes *Satan fall like lightning;* for it expresses the divine and astonishing power of the doctrine, which throws down, in a manner so sudden and violent, the prince of the world armed with such abundant forces. It expresses also the wretched condition of men, on whose heads fall the darts of Satan, who rules in the air, and holds the world in subjection under his feet, till Christ appear as a Deliverer.

[1] " A ceste fin de renverser et destruire;"—"for the very purpose of overthrowing and destroying."

[2] " Christ n'a point entreprins, ou essayé une chose à l'aventure, et de laquelle l'issue fust incertaine: mais a veu que la ruine de Satan s'en ensuyvroit;"—" Christ did not undertake or attempt a thing at random, and the result of which was uncertain; but saw that the ruin of Satan would follow from it.'

19. *Lo, I give you power.* This is said by way of admission. Christ does not affirm that the gift of which they now boast is not illustrious, but reminds them, that they ought to keep their eye chiefly on something loftier still, and not remain satisfied with outward miracles. He does not altogether condemn their joy, as if it were groundless, but shows it to be faulty in this respect, that they were immoderately delighted with a temporal favour, and did not elevate their minds higher. To this disease even the godly are almost all liable. Though the goodness of God is received by them with gratitude, yet the acts of the Divine kindness do not assist them, as they ought to do, by becoming ladders for ascending to heaven. This makes it necessary that the Lord should, as it were, stretch out his hand to raise them up, that they may not rest satisfied with the earth, but may aspire to heavenly renovation. *The power of the enemy* is the name given by him to every kind of annoyance; for all that is hostile to us is wielded against us by Satan. I do not mean that every thing which tends to injure men is placed at his disposal; but that, being armed with the curse of God, he endeavours to turn to our destruction all his chastisements, and seizes them as weapons for the purpose of wounding us.

20. *Your names are written.* As it was the design of Christ to withdraw his disciples from a transitory joy, that they might glory in eternal life, he leads them to its origin and source, which is, that they were chosen by God and adopted as his children. He might indeed have commanded them to rejoice that they had been regenerated by the Spirit of God, (Titus iii. 5,) and become *new creatures in Christ*, (2 Cor. v. 17;) that they had been *enlightened* (Eph. i. 18) in the hope of salvation, and had received *the earnest of the inheritance*, (Eph. i. 14.) But he intended to point out, that the source from which all these benefits had flowed was the free election of God, that they might not claim any thing for themselves. Reasons for praising God are no doubt furnished by those acts of his kindness which we feel *within* us; but eternal election, which is *without* us, shows more clearly

that our salvation rests on the pure goodness[1] of God. The metaphorical expression, *your names are written in heaven,* means, that they were acknowledged by God as His children and heirs, as if they had been inscribed in a register.[2]

MATTHEW.	LUKE.
XI. 25. At that time Jesus answering said, I acknowledge to thee,[3] O Father, Lord of heaven and earth, that thou hast hid these things from the wise and prudent, and hast revealed them to little children. 26. Undoubtedly, O Father, such was thy good pleasure.[4] 27. All things have been delivered to me by my Father; and none knoweth the Son but the Father, and none knoweth the Father but the Son, and he to whom the Son has chosen to reveal him.[5] 28. Come to me, all that labour and are burdened, and I will relieve you. 29. Take my yoke upon you, and learn of me, that I am meek and lowly in heart, and you shall find rest in your souls. 30. For my yoke is easy, and my burden is light.	X. 21. In the same hour Jesus rejoiced in spirit, and said, I acknowledge to thee,[6] O Father, Lord of heaven and earth, that thou hast hid these things from the wise and prudent, and hast revealed them to little children: certainly, O Father, it is because such was thy good pleasure. 22. All things have been delivered to me by my Father, and none knoweth who the Son is but the Father, and who the Father is but the Son, and he to whom the Son shall choose to reveal him.

Matthew XI. 25. *Jesus answering.* Though the Hebrew verb, *answer,* (עָנָה,) is frequently employed even in the commencement of a discourse, yet in this passage I consider it to be emphatic; for it was from the present occurrence that Christ took occasion to speak. This is more fully confirmed by the words of Luke, that *in the same hour Jesus rejoiced in spirit.* Whence came that *rejoicing?* Was it not because the Church, composed of poor and despised persons, was viewed by him as not less precious and valuable than if all the nobility and high rank in the world had lent to it their brilliancy? Let it be observed, also, that the discourse is

---

[1] "La pure et simple bonté;"—"the pure and simple goodness."
[2] "Comme s'ils estoyent escrits en une rolle, ou enregistrez en quelque livre;"—"as if they were written in a roll, or registered in some book."
[3] "Ie te ren graces;"—"I give thee thanks."
[4] "Il est ainsi, Pere, pourtant que ton bon plaisir a esté tel;"—"it is so, O Father, because thy good pleasure was such."
[5] "Le Fils le veut reveler, *ou, donner à cognoistre ;*"—"the Son chooses to reveal him, *or, to make him known.*"
[6] "Ie te ren graces;"—"I give thee thanks."

addressed to the *Father*, and consequently is marked by greater energy than if he had spoken to his disciples. It was on their behalf, no doubt, and for their sake, that he *gave thanks to the Father*, that they might not be displeased with the low and mean aspect of his Church.

We are constantly looking for splendour; and nothing appears to us more incongruous, than that the heavenly kingdom of the Son of God, whose glory is so magnificently celebrated by the prophets, should consist of the dregs and offscourings of the common people. And truly it is a wonderful purpose of God, that though he has the whole world at his command, he chooses rather to select a peculiar people to himself from among the contemptible vulgar, than from the nobility, whose high rank would have been a greater ornament to the name of Christ. But here Christ withdraws his disciples from a proud and haughty imagination, that they may not venture to despise that mean and obscure condition of his Church, in which he delights and *rejoices*. To restrain more fully that curiosity which is constantly springing up in the minds of men, he rises above the world, and contemplates the secret decrees of God, that he may lead others to unite with him in admiring them. And certainly, though this appointment of God contradicts our senses, we discover not only blind arrogance, but excessive madness, if we murmur against it, while Christ our Head adores it with reverence.

I acknowledge to thee, O Father.[1] By these words he declares his acquiescence in that decree of the *Father*, which is so greatly at variance with human senses. There is an implied contrast between this praise, which he ascribes to the Father, and the malicious slanders, or even the impudent barkings, of the world. We must now inquire in what respect he glorifies the *Father*. It is because, while he was Lord of the whole world, he preferred *children and ignorant persons to the wise*. It has no small weight, as connected with this subject, that he calls the *Father Lord of heaven and earth;* for in this manner he declares that it is a distinction which

---

[1] "Ie te ren graces, que tu as caché;"—"I thank thee, that thou hast concealed."

depends entirely on the will of God,[1] that the *wise* remain blind, while the ignorant and unlearned receive the mysteries of the Gospel. There are many other passages of a similar nature, in which God points out to us, that those who arrive at salvation have been freely chosen by him, because he is the Creator and Governor of the world, and all nations are his.

This expression implies two things. First, that all do not obey the Gospel arises from no want of power on the part of God, who could easily have brought all the creatures into subjection to his government. Secondly, that some arrive at faith, while others remain hardened and obstinate, is accomplished by his free election; for, drawing some, and passing by others, he alone makes a distinction among men, whose condition by nature is alike.[2] In choosing *little children* rather than the *wise*, he has a regard to his glory; for the flesh is too apt to rise, and if able and learned men had led the way, it would soon have come to be the general conviction, that men obtain faith by their skill, or industry, or learning. In no other way can the mercy of God be so fully known as it ought to be, than by making such a choice, from which it is evident, that whatever men bring from themselves is nothing; and therefore human wisdom is justly thrown down, that it may not obscure the praise of divine grace.

But it is asked, whom does Christ denominate *wise?* And whom does he denominate *little children?* For experience plainly shows, that not all the ignorant and unlearned on the one hand are enlightened to believe, and that not all the *wise* or *learned* are left in their blindness. It follows, that those are called *wise and prudent,* who, swelled with diabolical pride, cannot endure to hear Christ speaking to them from above. And yet it does not always happen that God reprobates those who have a higher opinion of themselves than

---

[1] " Qu'il n'y a que le bon plaisir et vouloir de Dieu qui soit cause de ceste diversité;"—" that it is only the good pleasure and will of God that is the cause of this diversity."

[2] " Desquels tous la condition est semblable de nature;"—" of all of whom the condition by nature is alike."

they ought to have; as we learn from the instance of Paul, whose fierceness Christ subdued. If we come down to the ignorant multitude, the majority of whom display envenomed malice, we perceive that they are left to their destruction equally with the nobles and great men. I do acknowledge, that all unbelievers swell with a wicked confidence in themselves, whether their pride be nourished by their wisdom, or by a reputation for integrity, or by honours, or by riches. But I consider that Christ here includes all who are eminent for abilities and learning, without charging them with any fault; as, on the other hand, he does not represent it to be an excellence in any one that he is a *little* child. True, humble persons have Christ for their master, and the first lesson of faith is, Let no man presume on his wisdom. But Christ does not speak here as to voluntary childhood. He magnifies the grace of the Father on this ground, that he does not disdain to descend even to the lowest and most abominable, that he may raise up the poor out of filth.

But here a question arises. As *prudence* is a gift of God, how comes it that it hinders us from perceiving the brightness of God, which shines in the Gospel? We ought, indeed, to remember what I have already said, that unbelievers corrupt all the *prudence* which they possess, and that men of distinguished abilities are often hindered in this respect, that they cannot submit to be taught. But with respect to the present passage I reply: Though the sagacity of the *prudent* does not stand in their way, they may notwithstanding be deprived of the light of the Gospel. Since the condition of all is the same or alike, why may not God take this or that person according to his pleasure? The reason why he passes by the *wise* and the *great* is declared by Paul to be, that *God hath chosen the weak and foolish things of the world to confound the glory of the flesh*, (1 Cor. i. 27.)

Hence also we infer, that the statement made by Christ is not universal, when he says, that the mysteries of the Gospel are *hidden from the wise*. If out of five *wise men* four reject the Gospel and one embraces it, and if, out of an equal number of unlearned persons, two or three become disciples of Christ, this statement is fulfilled. This is also confirmed by that passage in Paul's writings, which I lately quoted; for he does not exclude from the kingdom of God all the *wise,* and *noble,* and *mighty,* but only declares that it does not contain *many* of them.

The question is now solved. *Prudence* is not condemned as far as it is a gift of God, but Christ merely declares that it has no influence in procuring faith. On the other hand, he does not recommend ignorance, as if it rendered men acceptable to God, but affirms that it does not hinder mercy from enlightening ignorant and unlearned men with heavenly wisdom. It now remains to explain what is meant by *revealing* and *hiding.* That Christ does not speak of the outward preaching may be inferred with certainty from this circumstance, that he presented himself as a Teacher to all without distinction, and enjoined his Apostles to do the same. The meaning therefore is, that no man can obtain faith by his own acuteness, but only by the secret illumination of the Spirit.

26. *Undoubtedly, O Father.* This expression removes every pretence for that licentiousness of inquiry, to which we are continually excited. There is nothing which we yield to God with greater difficulty, than that his will shall be regarded by us as the highest reason and justice.[1] He frequently repeats, that his *judgments are a deep abyss,* (Ps. xxxvi. 6;) but we plunge with headlong violence into that depth,[2] and if there is any thing that does not please us, we gnash our teeth, or murmur against him, and many even break out into open blasphemies. On the contrary, our Lord lays down to us this rule, that whatever God has determined must be regarded by us as right.[3] This is sober wisdom, to acquiesce in the good pleasure of God as alone equal to a thousand arguments.[4] Christ might indeed have

---

[1] "Pour la derniere et souveraine raison, et pour iustice parfaite;"—"for the last and supreme reason, and for perfect justice."
[2] "Pour sonder ce qui y est;"—"to sound what is in it."
[3] "Que tout ce que Dieu a determiné est bon et droict;"—"that all that God has determined is good and right."
[4] "Et cela est estre sage à sobrieté, d'acquiescer au seul bon plaisir de Dieu, et nous y arrester paisiblement, plus que s'il y avoit dix mille raisons

brought forward the causes of that distinction, if there were any; but he is satisfied with the good pleasure of God, and inquires no farther why he calls to salvation *little children* rather than others, and composes his kingdom out of an obscure flock.[1] Hence it is evident, that men direct their fury against Christ, when, on learning that some are freely chosen, and others are reprobated, by the will of God, they storm because they find it unpleasant to yield to God.[2]

27. *All things have been delivered to me.* The connection of this sentence with the preceding one is not correctly understood by those commentators who think that Christ intends nothing more than to strengthen the confidence of his disciples for preaching the Gospel. My opinion is, that Christ spoke these words for another reason, and with another object in view. Having formerly asserted that the Church proceeds from the secret source of God's free election, he now shows in what manner the grace of salvation comes to men. Many persons, as soon as they learn that none are heirs of eternal life but those whom God *chose before the foundation of the world*, (Eph. i. 4,) begin to inquire anxiously how they may be assured of God's secret purpose, and thus plunge into a labyrinth, from which they will find no escape. Christ enjoins them to come direct to himself, in order to obtain certainty of salvation. The meaning therefore is, that life is exhibited to us in Christ himself, and that no man will partake of it who does not enter by the gate of faith. We now see that he connects faith with the eternal predestination of God,—two things which men foolishly and wickedly hold to be inconsistent with each other. Though our salvation was always hidden with God, yet Christ is the channel through which it flows

---

devant nos yeux;"—" and this is to be wise to sobriety, to acquiesce in the good pleasure of God, and to rest calmly upon it, more than if there were ten thousand arguments before our eyes."

[1] " D'une troupe de gens incognus, et de petite estime;"—" from a flock of persons unknown and little esteemed."

[2] " Vienent incontinent à tempester, pource quil leur fasche que Dieu ait le dernier mot;"—" come immediately to storm, because it gives them uneasiness that God should have the last word."

to us, and we receive it by faith, that it may be secure and ratified in our hearts. We are not at liberty then to turn away from Christ, unless we choose to reject the salvation which he offers to us.

None knoweth the Son. He says this, that we may not be guided by the judgment of men, and thus form an erroneous estimate of his majesty. The meaning therefore is, that if we wish to know what is the character of Christ, we must abide by the testimony of *the Father,* who alone can truly and certainly inform us what authority he hath bestowed upon him. And, indeed, by imagining him to be what our mind, according to its capacity, conceives of him, we deprive him of a great part of his excellence, so that we cannot know him aright but from the voice of *the Father.* That voice alone would undoubtedly be insufficient without the guidance of the Spirit; for the power of Christ is too deep and hidden to be attained by men, until they have been enlightened by *the Father.* We must understand him to mean, not that *the Father knoweth* for himself, but that He *knoweth* for us to reveal him to us.

But the sentence appears to be incomplete, for the two clauses do not correspond to each other. Of *the Son* it is said, that *none knoweth the Father except himself, and he to whom he shall be pleased to reveal him.* Of *the Father* nothing more is said than this, that He alone *knoweth the Son.* Nothing is said about revelation. I reply, that it was unnecessary to repeat what he had already said; for what else is contained in the previous thanksgiving, than that the Father hath revealed the Son to those who approve of him? When it is now added that He alone *knoweth the Son,* it appears to be the assigning of a reason; for this thought might have occurred, What necessity was there that *the Son,* who had openly exhibited himself to the view of men, should be *revealed by the Father?* We now perceive the reason why it was said, that *none knoweth the Son but the Father only.* It now remains that we attend to the latter clause:

None knoweth the Father except the Son, and he to whom the Son shall be pleased to reveal him. This is a different kind of knowledge from the former; for the Son is said to *know the*

Father, not because he reveals Him by his Spirit, but because, being the lively image of Him, he represents Him visibly in his own person. At the same time, I do not exclude the Spirit, but explain the *revelation* here mentioned as referring to the manner of communicating information. This agrees most completely with the context; for Christ confirms what he had formerly said, *that all things had been delivered to him by his Father*, by informing us that *the fulness of the Godhead dwelleth in him*, (Col. ii. 9.) The passage may be thus summed up:[1] First, it is the gift of *the Father*, that *the Son is known*, because by his Spirit he opens the eyes of our mind to discern the glory of Christ, which otherwise would have been hidden from us. Secondly, *the Father*, who dwells in inaccessible light, and is in himself incomprehensible, is revealed to us by the Son, because he is the lively image of Him, so that it is in vain to seek for Him elsewhere.[2]

28. *Come to me all that labour.* He now kindly invites to himself those whom he acknowledges to be fit for becoming his disciples. Though he is ready to reveal the Father to all, yet the greater part are careless about coming to him, because they are not affected by a conviction of their necessities. Hypocrites give themselves no concern about Christ, because they are intoxicated with their own righteousness, and neither *hunger* nor *thirst* (Matth. v. 6) for his grace. Those who are devoted to the world set no value on a heavenly life. It would be in vain, therefore, for Christ to invite either of these classes, and therefore he turns to the wretched and afflicted. He speaks of them as *labouring*, or groaning under a *burden*, and does not mean generally those who are oppressed with grief and vexations, but those who are overwhelmed by their sins, who are filled with alarm at the wrath of God, and are ready to sink under so weighty a *burden*. There are various methods, indeed, by which God

---

[1] " Tout ce passage revient à ces deux points;"—" the whole of this passage amounts to these two points."

[2] " En sorte que c'est temps perdu de le chercher ailleurs;"—" so that it is lost time to seek him elsewhere."

humbles his elect; but as the greater part of those who are loaded with afflictions still remain obstinate and rebellious, Christ means by persons *labouring and burdened,* those whose consciences are distressed by their exposure to eternal death, and who are inwardly so pressed down by their miseries that they faint; for this very fainting prepares them for receiving his grace. He tells us that the reason why most men despise his grace is, that they are not sensible of their poverty; but that there is no reason why their pride or folly should keep back afflicted souls that long for relief.

Let us therefore bid adieu to all who, entangled by the snares of Satan, either are persuaded that they possess a righteousness out of Christ, or imagine that they are happy in this world. Let our miseries drive us to seek Christ; and as he admits none to the enjoyment of his rest but those who sink under the burden, let us learn, that there is no venom more deadly than that slothfulness which is produced in us, either by earthly happiness, or by a false and deceitful opinion of our own righteousness and virtue. Let each of us labour earnestly to arouse himself, first, by vigorously shaking off the luxuries of the world; and, secondly, by laying aside every false confidence. Now though this preparation for coming to Christ makes them as dead men,[1] yet it ought to be observed, that it is the gift of the Holy Spirit, because it is the commencement of repentance, to which no man aspires in his own strength. Christ did not intend to show what man can do of himself, but only to inform us what must be the feelings of those who come to him.

They who limit the *burden* and the *labour* to ceremonies of the Law, take a very narrow view of Christ's meaning. I do acknowledge, that the Law was intolerably burdensome, and overwhelmed the souls of worshippers; but we must bear in mind what I have said, that Christ stretches out his hand to all the afflicted, and thus lays down a dis-

---

[1] "Combien que ceste preparation à recevoir la grace de Christ despouille desia entierement les hommes, et monstre qu'ils sont du tout vuides de vertu;"—"though this preparation for receiving the grace of Christ already strips men entirely, and shows that they are wholly devoid of virtue."

tinction between his disciples and those who despise the Gospel. But we must attend to the universality of the expression; for Christ included all, without exception, who *labour and are burdened*, that no man may shut the gate against himself by wicked doubts.[1] And yet all such persons are few in number; for, among the innumerable multitude of those that perish, few are aware that they are perishing. The *relief* which he promises consists in the free pardon of sins, which alone gives us peace.

29. *Take my yoke upon you.* Many persons, we perceive, abuse the grace of Christ by turning it into an indulgence of the flesh; and therefore Christ, after promising joyful rest to wretchedly distressed consciences, reminds them, at the same time, that he is their Deliverer on condition of their submitting to his yoke. He does not, he tells us, absolve men from their sins in such a manner, that, restored to the favour of God, they may sin with greater freedom, but that, raised up by his grace, they may also *take his yoke upon them*, and that, being free in spirit, they may restrain the licentiousness of their flesh. And hence we obtain a definition of that rest of which he had spoken. It is not at all intended to exempt the disciples of Christ from the warfare of the flesh, that they may enjoy themselves at their ease, but to train them under the burden of discipline, and keep them under the yoke.

Learn of me. It is a mistake, I think, to suppose that Christ here assures us of his *meekness*, lest his disciples, under the influence of that fear which is usually experienced in approaching persons of distinction, should remain at a distance from him on account of his Divine glory. It is rather his design to form us to the imitation of himself, because the obstinacy of the flesh leads us to shrink from his *yoke* as harsh and uneasy. Shortly afterwards, he adds, (ver. 30,) *my yoke is easy.* But how shall any man be brought willingly and gently to bend his neck, unless, by putting on

---

[1] "Par une desfiance et façon perverse de douter;"—"by a distrust and wicked manner of doubting."

meekness, he be conformed to Christ? That this is the meaning of the words is plain; for Christ, after exhorting his disciples to bear his *yoke,* and desirous to prevent them from being deterred by its difficulty, immediately adds, *Learn of me;* thus declaring that, when his example shall have accustomed us to *meekness* and humility, we shall no longer feel his *yoke* to be troublesome. To the same purpose he adds, *I will relieve you.* So long as the flesh kicks, we rebel; and those who refuse the yoke of Christ, and endeavour to appease God in any other manner, distress and waste themselves in vain. In this manner, we see the Papists wretchedly torturing themselves, and silently enduring the dreadful tyranny under which they groan, that they may not bow to the *yoke* of Christ.

MATTHEW.	MARK.	LUKE.
XII. 1. At that time Jesus was passing through the corn-fields on the Sabbath;[1] and his disciples were hungry, and began to pluck the ears of corn, and to eat. 2. But when the Pharisees saw it, they said to him, Lo, thy disciples do what it is not lawful to do on the Sabbath. 3. But he said to them, Have you not read what David did, when he was hungry, and those who were with him? 4. How he entered into the house of God, and ate the shew-bread, which it was not lawful for him to eat, nor for those who were with him, but for the priests alone? 5. Or have you not read in the Law, that on the Sabbath the priests in the temple profane the temple, and are free from blame?[2] 6. But I say to	II. 23. And it happened, that he was passing through the corn-fields, and his disciples began to pluck the ears of corn as they went along. 24. And the Pharisees said to him, Lo, why do they on the Sabbath what is not lawful? 25. And he said to them, Have you not read what David did, when he had need, and was hungry, and those who were with him? 26. How he entered into the house of God in the time of Abiathar, the high-priest, and ate the shew-bread, which it is not lawful to eat but for the priests, and gave also[3] to those who	VI. 1. And it happened that, on the second-first Sabbath, he was passing through the corn-fields; and his disciples were plucking ears of corn, and were eating, rubbing them in their hands. 2. And some of the Pharisees said to them, Why do you do what it is not lawful to do on the Sabbath? 3. And Jesus answering saith to them, Have you not read even this which David did when he was hungry, and those who were with him? 4. How he entered into the house of God, and took the shew-bread, and ate it, and gave also to those who

[1] " Un iour du Sabbath ;"—" on a Sabbath-day."
[2] " Et n'en sont point reprehensibles ;"—" and are not blameable for it."
[3] " Et en donna aussi ;"—" and gave of it also."

MATTHEW.	MARK.	LUKE.
you, That one greater than the temple is in this place. 7. But if you knew what that is, I choose mercy, and not sacrifice, you would not have condemned the innocent. 8. For the Son of man is Lord even of the Sabbath.	were with him? 27. And he said to them, The Sabbath was made for man, and not man for the Sabbath. 28. Therefore the Son of man is Lord even of the Sabbath.	were with him, which it is not lawful to eat but only for the priests? 5. And he said to them, The Son of man is Lord even of the Sabbath.

Matthew XII. 1. *Jesus was walking on the Sabbath.* It was the design of the Evangelists, in this history, to show partly what a malicious disposition the Pharisees had, and partly how superstitiously they were attached to outward and slight matters, so as to make holiness to consist in them entirely. They blame the disciples of Christ for *plucking the ears of corn on the Sabbath*, during their journey, when they were pressed with hunger, as if, by so doing, they were violating the *Sabbath*. The keeping of the *Sabbath* was, indeed, a holy thing, but not such a manner of keeping it as they imagined, so that one could scarcely move a finger without making the conscience to tremble.[1] It was hypocrisy, therefore, that made them so exact in trifling matters, while they spared themselves in gross superstitions; as Christ elsewhere upbraids them with *paying tithe of mint and anise, and neglecting the important matters of the Law*, (Mat. xxiii. 23.) It is the invariable practice of hypocrites to allow themselves liberty in matters of the greatest consequence, and to pay close attention to ceremonial observances. Another reason why they demand that outward rites should be more rigorously observed is, that they wish to make their duty toward God to consist only in carnal worship. But it was malevolence and envy, still more than superstition, that led them to this act of censure; for towards others they would not have been equally stern. It is proper for us to observe the feelings by which they were animated, lest any one should be distressed by the fact, that the very Doctors of the Law were so hostile to Christ.

---

[1] "Avec tremblement et incertitude de conscience;"—" with trembling and uncertainty of conscience."

Luke VI. 1. *On the second-first Sabbath.* It is beyond all question that this Sabbath belonged to some one of the festival-days which the Law enjoined to be observed once every year. Some have thought that there were two festival-days in immediate succession; but as the Jews had arranged their festival-days after the Babylonish captivity so that one day always intervened between them, that opinion is set aside. Others maintain with greater probability, that it was the last day of the solemnity, which was as numerously attended as the first. I am more inclined to favour those who understand by it the second festivity in the year; and this agrees exceedingly well with the name given to it, *the second-first Sabbath,* because, among the great Sabbaths which were annually observed, it was the second in the order of time. Now the *first* was the Passover, and it is therefore probable that this was *the feast of first-fruits,* (Ex. xxiii. 15, 16.)

Mark II. 24. *Why do they on the Sabbath what is not lawful?* The Pharisees do not blame the disciples of Christ for *plucking ears of corn* from a field that was not their own, but for violating *the Sabbath;* as if there had been a precept to this effect, that famishing men ought rather to die than to satisfy their hunger. Now the only reason for keeping the Sabbath was, that the people, by sanctifying themselves to God, might be employed in true and spiritual worship; and next, that, being free from all worldly occupations, they might be more at liberty to attend the holy assemblies. The lawful observation of it, therefore, must have a reference to this object; for the Law ought to be interpreted according to the design of the Legislator. But this shows clearly the malicious and implacable nature of superstition, and particularly the proud and cruel dispositions of hypocrites, when ambition is joined to hatred of the person. It was not the mere affectation of pretended holiness, as I have said, that made the Pharisees so stern and rigorous; but as they expressly wished to carp at every thing that Christ said or did, they could not do otherwise than put a wrong meaning in cases where there was nothing to blame, as usually happens with prejudiced interpreters. The accusation was brought—according to Matthew and Mark—against our Lord, and—according to Luke—against his disciples. But there is no inconsistency here; for the disciples were in all probability so harassed, that the charge was directed chiefly against the Master himself. It is even possible that the Pharisees first wrangled with the disciples, and afterwards with Christ, and that, in the rage of their malice, they blamed him for remaining silent, and permitting his disciples to break the Sabbath.

Matthew XII. 3. *Have you not read what David did?* Christ employs five arguments to refute their calumny. *First,* he apologizes for his disciples by pleading the example of *David,* (1 Sam. xxi. 6.) While David was fleeing from the rage of Saul, he applied for provisions to the high-priest Ahimelech; and there being no ordinary food at hand, he succeeded in obtaining a part of the holy bread. If David's necessity excused him, the same argument ought to be admitted in the case of others. Hence it follows, that the ceremonies of the Law are not violated where there is no infringement of godliness.[1] Now Christ takes for granted, that David was free from blame, because the Holy Spirit bestows commendation on the priest who allowed him to partake of the holy bread. When he says, that *it was not lawful to eat* that bread *but for the priests alone,* we must understand him to refer to the ordinary law: *they shall eat those things wherewith the atonement was made, to consecrate and to sanctify them; but a stranger shall not eat thereof, because they are holy,* (Ex. xxix. 33.) If David had attempted to do what was contrary to law, it would have been in vain for Christ to plead his example; for what had been prohibited for a particular end no necessity could make lawful.

5. *That on the Sabbaths the priests profane the Sabbath.* This is the *second* argument by which Christ proves that the violation of the Sabbath, of which the Pharisees complained,

[1] " Quand on ne derogue rien à la reverence deuë à Dieu;"—" when nothing is taken away from the reverence that is due to God."

was free from all blame; because *on the Sabbaths* it is lawful to slay beasts for sacrifice, to circumcise infants, and to do other things relating to the worship of God. Hence it follows, that the duties of piety are in no degree inconsistent with each other.[1] But if *the temple* sanctifies manual operations connected with sacrifices, and with the whole of the outward service, the holiness of the true and spiritual *temple* has greater efficacy, in exempting its worshippers from all blame, while they are discharging the duties of godliness.[2] Now the object which the disciples had in view was, to present to God souls which were consecrated by the Gospel.

Matthew alone glances at this argument. When Christ says, that *the priests* PROFANE *the Sabbath*, the expression is not strictly accurate, and is accommodated to his hearers; for when the Law enjoins men to abstain from their employments, it does not forbid them to perform the services of religion. But Christ admits that to be true which might appear to be so in the eye of ignorant persons,[3] and rests satisfied with proving, that the labours performed in the temple are not offensive to God.

7. *But if you knew.* This *Third* argument is also mentioned by Matthew alone. Christ conveys an indirect reproof to the Pharisees, for not considering why ceremonies were appointed, and to what object they are directed. This has been a common fault in almost every age; and therefore the prophet Hosea (vi. 6) exclaims against the men of his own age for being too much attached to ceremonies, and caring little about the duties of kindness. But God declares aloud, that he sets a higher value on *mercy* than on sacrifice, employing the word *mercy*, by a figure of speech, for offices of

---

[1] " Que les exercices de pieté ne sont point contraires les uns aux autres, mais s'accordent bien ensemble;"—" that the exercises of godliness are not opposed to each other, but agree well together."
[2] " Quand ils s'employent à œuvres qui tendent à l'honneur de Dieu;" —" when they are employed in works which tend to the honour of God."
[3] " Ainsi Christ accorde estre vray, ce qui ne l'est pas de faict, mais qui pourroit sembler l'estre en apparence à gens qui ne scavent pas bien iuger et discerner les choses;"—" thus Christ admits that to be true which is not so in reality, but which might appear to be so to persons who do not know how to judge and distinguish matters properly."

kindness, as *sacrifices* include the outward service of the Law. This statement Christ applies to his own time, and charges the Pharisees with wickedly torturing the Law of God out of its true meaning, with disregarding the second table, and being entirely occupied with ceremonies.

But a question arises: Why does God declare that he is indifferent about ceremonies, when he strictly enjoined in his Law that they should be observed? The answer is easy. External rites are of no value in themselves, and are demanded by God in so far only as they are directed to their proper object. Besides, God does not absolutely reject them, but, by a comparison with deeds of kindness, pronounces that they are inferior to the latter in actual value. Nor is it inconsistent with this to say, that in the perfection of righteousness the highest rank belongs to the worship of God, and the duties which men owe to each other occupy the second rank. For, though piety is justly reckoned to be as much superior to charity as God is higher than men, yet as believers, by practising justice towards each other, prove that their service of God is sincere, it is not without reason that this subject is brought under the notice of hypocrites, who imitate piety by outward signs, and yet pervert it by confining their laborious efforts to the carnal worship alone.[1] From the testimony of the Prophet, Christ justly infers that no blame attaches to his disciples; for while God trained his people in the rudiments of the Law, it was far from being his design to kill wretched men with famine.

8. *For the Son of man is Lord even of the Sabbath.* Some connect this sentence with a preceding statement, *that one greater than the temple is in this place,* (ver. 6;) but I look upon them as different. In the former case, Christ, by an allusion to *the temple,* affirmed that whatever was connected with his personal holiness was not a transgression of the Law; but now, he declares that he has received authority to exempt

---

[1] " Et cependant neantmoins la renversent et falsifient, s'arrestans au seul service charnel, auquel ils prenent grande peine;"—" and yet nevertheless overthrow and falsify it, confining themselves to the carnal service alone, on which they bestow great pains."

his followers from the necessity of observing the Sabbath. *The Son of man,* (he says,) in the exercise of his authority, can relax the Sabbath in the same manner as other legal ceremonies. And certainly out of Christ the bondage of the Law is wretched, from which he alone delivers those on whom he bestows the free *Spirit of adoption,*[1] (Rom. viii. 15.)

Mark II. 27. *The Sabbath was made for man.* This *Fifth* argument is related by Mark alone. The general meaning is, that those persons judge amiss who turn to man's destruction,[2] the Sabbath which God appointed for his benefit. The Pharisees saw the disciples of Christ employed in a holy work; they saw them worn out with the fatigue of the journey, and partly with want of food; and yet are offended that, when they are hungry, they take a few grains of corn for the support of their wearied bodies. Is not this a foolish attempt to overturn the purpose of God, when they demand to the injury of men that observation of the Sabbath which he intended to be advantageous? But they are mistaken, I think, who suppose that in this passage the Sabbath is entirely abolished; for Christ simply informs us what is the proper use of it. Though he asserted, a little before, that he is *Lord of the Sabbath,* yet the full time for its abolition[3] was not yet come, because *the veil of the temple was not yet rent,* (Matth. xxvii. 51.)

MATTHEW.	MARK.	LUKE.
XII. 9. And having departed thence, he came into their synagogue: 10. And, lo, there was a man having a withered hand, and they asked him, saying, Is it lawful to heal on the Sabbaths? that they	III. 1. And he entered again into the synagogue, and there was a man there having a withered hand. 2. And they watched him, if he would heal that man on the Sabbath, that they might accuse him.	VI. 6. And it happened also on another Sabbath, that he entered into the synagogue, and taught; and there was a man there whose right hand was withered. 7. And the scribes and Pharisees watched him, if he would heal on the Sabbath, that

[1] " Ausquels il donne l'Esprit d'adoption, qui est l'Esprit de la liberté ;"
— " to whom he gives the Spirit of adoption, which is the Spirit of liberty."
[2] " Lesquels convertissent au dommage et à la ruine de l'homme ;"—
" who turn to the injury and to the ruin of man."
[3] " La vraye saison et le temps opportun de l'abolissement d'iceluy ;"—
" the true season and appropriate time for the abolition of it."

MATTHEW.	MARK.	LUKE.
might accuse him. 11. But he said to them, What man shall there be among you who shall have one sheep, and if it fall on the Sabbath into a ditch, will not lay hold on it, and lift it out? 12. How much more then is a man better than a sheep? Therefore it is lawful to do well on the Sabbaths. 13. Then he saith to the man, Stretch out thy hand. And he stretched it out, and it was restored to soundness like the other.	3. And he said to the man having the withered hand, Rise up in the midst. 4. And he saith to them, Whether is it lawful on the Sabbath to do good or to do evil? to save life or to kill? But they were silent. 5. And when he had looked round upon them with indignation, grieving on account of the blindness of their heart, he saith to the man, Stretch out thy hand; and he stretched it out, and his hand was restored to soundness like the other.	they might find an opportunity of accusing him. 8. But he knew their thoughts, and said to the man that had the withered hand, Rise up, and stand in the midst. And he rose up and stood. 9. Jesus therefore saith to them, I will ask you, Whether is it lawful on the Sabbaths to do good or to do evil? to save life or to destroy it? 10. And when he had looked round about upon them all, he said to the man, Stretch out thy hand. And he did so: and his hand was restored sound like the other.

Matthew XII. 9. *And having departed thence.* This narrative and that which immediately precedes it have the same object; which is to show, that the scribes watched with a malicious eye for the purpose of turning into slander every thing that Christ did, and consequently that we need not wonder if men, whose minds were so depraved, were his implacable enemies. We see also, that it is usual with hypocrites to pursue what is nothing more than a shadow of the righteousness of the Law, and as the common saying is, to stickle more about the form than about the substance. First, then, let us learn from this passage to keep our minds pure, and free from every wicked disposition, when we are about to form a decision on any question; for if hatred, or pride, or any thing of that description, reign within us, we will not only do injury to men, but will insult God himself, and turn light into darkness. No man, who was free from malice, would have refused to acknowledge that it was a Divine work, which those good teachers do not scruple to condemn.[1] Whence comes such fury, but because all their senses are

---

[1] "N'ont point de honte de condamner;"—"are not ashamed to condemn."

affected by a wicked hatred of Christ, so that they are blind amidst the full brightness of the sun? We learn also, that we ought to beware lest, by attaching undue importance to ceremonial observances, we allow other things to be neglected, which are of far higher value in the sight of God, and which Christ in another passage calls *the more important matters of the Law*, (Matth. xxiii. 23.) For so strongly are we inclined to outward rites, that we shall never preserve moderation in this respect, unless we constantly remember, that whatever is enjoined respecting the worship of God is, in the first place, spiritual; and, secondly, ought to be regulated by the rule which Christ has laid down to us in this passage.

10. *They asked him, saying*. Mark and Luke say only that they *watched* what our Lord would do; but Matthew states more clearly that they also attacked him by words. It is probable, that some others had been previously cured on Sabbath-days; and hence they take occasion to ask if he believes it to be *lawful* for him to do again what he had formerly done. They ought to have considered whether it was a work of God, or of man, to restore a withered hand by a mere touch, or by a single word. When God appointed the Sabbath, he did not lay down a law for himself, or impose upon himself any restraint from performing operations on the Sabbath, when he saw it to be proper, in the same manner as on other days. It was excessive folly, therefore, to call this in question, and thus to prescribe rules for God himself, and to restrain the freedom of his operations.

11. *What man shall there be among you who shall have a sheep?* Christ again points out what is the true way of keeping the Sabbath; and, at the same time, reproves them for slander, in bringing as a charge against him what was a universal custom. For if any man's *sheep had fallen into a ditch*, no person would have hindered it from being taken out: but in proportion as *a man is of more value than a sheep*, so much the more are we at liberty to assist him. It is plain, therefore, that if any man should relieve the necessity of brethren, he did not, in any degree, violate the rest which

the Lord has enjoined. Mark and Luke take no notice of this comparison, but only state that Christ inquired, *Is it lawful on the Sabbath to do good or to do evil?*

He who takes away the life of a man is held to be a criminal; and there is little difference between manslaughter and the conduct of him who does not concern himself about relieving a person in distress. So then Christ indirectly charges them with endeavouring, under the pretence of a holy act, to compel him *to do evil;* for sin is committed, as we have already said, not only by him who does any thing contrary to the Law, but also by him who neglects his duty. Hence also we perceive, that Christ did not always employ the same arguments in refuting this slander; for he does not reason here about his divinity as he does in the case mentioned by John, (v. 18.) Nor was there any necessity for doing so; since the Pharisees were completely refuted by this single defence, that nothing could be more unreasonable than to pronounce a man, who imitated God, to be a transgressor of the Sabbath.

Luke XII. 8. *But he knew their thoughts.* If Matthew states the truth, they had openly declared by their language what was in their minds; and therefore Christ replies not to *their secret thoughts,* but to express words. But both may be true, that they spoke plainly, and yet that Christ discerned their secret *thoughts;* for they did not openly avow their designs, and Matthew himself tells us that their question was intended to take Christ by surprise; and, consequently, Luke means nothing more than that Christ was aware of their insidious designs, though not expressed in words.

Mark III. 5. *And when he had looked around upon them with indignation.* To convince us that this was a just and holy anger, Mark explains the reason of it to be, that he was *grieved on account of the blindness of their hearts.* First, then, Christ *is grieved,* because men who have been instructed in the Law of God are so grossly *blind;* but as it was malice that *blinded* them, his *grief* is accompanied by *indignation.* This is the true moderation of zeal, to be distressed about the destruction of wicked men, and, at the same time, to be filled with wrath at their ungodliness. Again, as this passage assures us, that Christ was not free from human passions, we infer from it, that the passions themselves are not sinful, provided there be no excess. In consequence of the corruption of our nature, we do not preserve moderation; and our anger, even when it rests on proper grounds, is never free from sin. With Christ the case was different; for not only did his nature retain its original purity, but he was a perfect pattern of righteousness. We ought therefore to implore from heaven the Spirit of God to correct our excesses.

MATTHEW.	MARK.	LUKE.
XII. 14. Then the Pharisees went out, and took counsel against him, how they might destroy him.[1] 15. But when Jesus knew this, he withdrew from that place; and great multitudes followed him, and he cured them all. 16. And he threatened them,[2] that they should not make him known: 17. That it might be fulfilled which was spoken by Isaiah the Prophet, who says, 18. Lo, my servant, whom I have chosen, my beloved, in whom my soul is well pleased: I will put my Spirit upon him, and he shall proclaim judgment to the Gentiles. 19. He shall not strive, nor cry, nor shall any man hear his voice in the streets. 20. The bruised reed he will not break, and the smoking flax he will not quench, till he send forth judgment into victory. 21. And in his name the Gentiles will trust.	III. 6. And the Pharisees went out, and immediately took counsel with the Herodians against him, to destroy him. 7. And Jesus withdrew with his disciples to the sea, and a vast multitude followed him from Galilee, and from Judea, 8. And from Jerusalem, and from Idumea, and from beyond Jordan; and a great multitude (*of men*) who dwelt around Tyre and Sidon, who, when they had heard what he was doing, came to him. 9. And he commanded his disciples, that a small ship should wait upon him on account of the multitude, that they might not press upon him. 10. For he had cured many; so that as many as were afflicted pressed upon him to touch him. 11. And unclean spirits, when they saw him, fell down before him, and cried out, saying, Thou art the Son of God. 12. And he vehemently threatened them that they should not make him known.	VI. 11. And they were filled with madness, and talked with each other what they should do to Jesus.

Matthew XII. 14. *Then the Pharisees took counsel.* How

[1] " Comment ils le mettroyent à mort;"—" how they should put him to death."

[2] " Et aveques menaces leur defendit;"—" and with threatenings prohibited them."

obstinate is the rage which drives the wicked to oppose God! Even after having been convinced, they pour out their venom more and more. It is truly monstrous and shocking, that the most distinguished teachers of the Law, who were entrusted with the government of the Church, are engaged, like robbers, in contriving murder. But this must happen, whenever the malice of men reaches such a height, that they wish to destroy every thing that is opposed to their fancy, even though it may be from God.

The circumstance of Christ's making his escape by flight must not be ascribed to fear; for he did not become more courageous by the lapse of time, but was endued with the same fortitude of the Spirit at the time when he fled, as when, at a later period, he voluntarily presented himself to die. And this was a part of that *emptying of himself* which Paul mentions, (Phil. ii. 7,) that when he could easily have protected his life by a miracle, he chose rather to submit to our weakness by taking flight. The only reason why he delayed to die was, that the seasonable time, which had been appointed by the Father, *was not yet come*, (John vii. 30; viii. 20.) And yet it is manifest, that he was preserved by heavenly power rather than by flight; for it would not have been difficult for his enemies to find out the place to which he had retired, and so far was he from shrouding himself in darkness, that he carried a great company along with him, and rendered that place illustrious by his miracles. He withdrew from their presence for the sole purpose of not aggravating their rage.

Mark III. 6. *The Pharisees took counsel with the Herodians.* Now they regarded *the Herodians* with the fiercest hatred; for their eagerness to be considered the guardians and protectors of public liberty made it necessary for them to make an open profession of mortal hatred to the ministers of that tyrant. And yet this aversion is counteracted by their hatred and fury against Christ,[1] which makes them not only enter into a

---

[1] "Toutesfois la haine enragee qu'ils ont contre Christ, surmonte toutes leurs autres meschantes affections;"—"and yet the enraged hatred which they have against Christ rises above all their other wicked dispositions."

conspiracy with foreigners, but insinuate themselves into the good graces of those with whom, on other occasions, they would have shrunk from intercourse. While ungodliness hurries men in various directions, and drives them to different courses, it engages them, with one consent, in a contest with God. No hostilities prevent them from giving their hand to each other for opposing the truth of God.

16. *And he threatened them.* The expression used by *Mark* conveys, in a still more pointed manner, that he restrained the *unclean spirits*,[1] who were exclaiming, *Thou art the Son of God.* We have formerly explained the reason why he did not choose to have such witnesses.[2] And yet there is no room to doubt, that divine power extorted from the devils this confession; but having made it evident that they were subject to his dominion, Christ properly rejected their testimony. But *Matthew* goes farther, and states, that Christ discharged them from spreading the fame of the miracles which he was performing. Not that he wished that fame to be wholly repressed, (as we have pointed out on other occasions,[3]) but to allow it to strike root, that it might bring forth abundant fruit at the proper season. We know that Christ did not perform miracles for the purpose of amusement, but had a distinct object in view, which was to prove that he was the Son of God, and the appointed Redeemer of the world. But he was manifested gradually, and by regular steps, and was not revealed in his true character "until the time appointed by the Father," (Gal. iv. 2.) At the same time, it deserves our attention, that when wicked men do their utmost to extinguish the glory of God, they are so far from gaining their wish, that, on the contrary, God turns their rebellious designs in an opposite direction. Though Christ withdrew from a populous district, yet in this very concealment[4]

---

[1] "A scavoir qu'il menaçoit et faisoit taire les esprits immondes;"— "namely, that he threatened and silenced the unclean spirits."
[2] Harmony, vol. i. p. 246.
[3] Harmony, vol. i. pp. 374, 418.
[4] "Toutesfois mesmes en ceste cachete, (par maniere de dire;")– "yet even in this hiding place, (so to speak.")

his glory continues to shine, and even bursts forth magnificently into its full splendour.

17. *That it might be fulfilled which was spoken.* Matthew does not mean that this prediction was entirely fulfilled by Christ's prohibiting loud and general reports to be circulated respecting his power,[1] but that this was an exhibition of that mildness which Isaiah describes in the person of the Messiah. Those wonderful works which Christ performed in presence of a few, and which he did not wish to be announced in pompous terms, were fitted to *shake heaven and earth*, (Heb. xii. 26.) It was, therefore, no ordinary proof, how widely he was removed from the pomp and ostentation of the world.

But it will be proper for us to examine more closely the design of Matthew. By this circumstance he intended to show, that the glory of Christ's divinity ought not to be the less admired, because it appeared under a vail of infirmity. This is unquestionably the very object to which the Holy Spirit directed the eyes of the prophet. The flesh is constantly longing for outward display, and to guard believers against seeking any thing of this description in the Messiah, the Spirit of God declared that he would be totally different from earthly kings, who, in order to draw admiration upon themselves, produce great noises wherever they go, and fill cities and towns with commotion.[2] We now perceive how appropriately Matthew applies the prediction of the prophet to the case in hand. God appointed for his Son a low and mean appearance, and that ignorant persons may not take offence at an aspect which has no attraction, and is fitted to awaken contempt, both the prophet and Matthew come forward to declare, that it is not by accident, but in consequence of a decree of Heaven, that he assumes such a character.[3] Hence it follows, that deep blame attaches to all who despise

---

[1] "Les miracles et signes qu'il faisoit par sa vertu Divine;"—"the miracles and signs which he performed by his Divine power."

[2] "Ils font faire de grans bruits: il semble que les villes et citez doyvent tourner ce que dessus dessous, tant y a grande esmotion;"—"they cause great noises to be made; and so great is the commotion, that it would seem as if towns and cities were to be turned upside down."

[3] "Quand Christ vient au monde sans pompe exterieure;"—"when Christ comes into the world without external pomp."

Christ, because his outward condition does not correspond to the wishes of the flesh. We are not at liberty to imagine to ourselves a Christ that corresponds to our fancy, but ought simply to embrace him as he is offered by the Father. He who is offended by the low condition of Christ, which God declares to be agreeable to his will, is unworthy of salvation. I now come to examine the words of the prophet, (Isa. xlii. 1.)

18. *Lo, my servant, whom I have chosen.* To fix our attention more closely on his will, God points out by the finger, as it were, the person whom he is about to send; and this is the design of the exclamation, *Lo!* A similar reason may be assigned for the epithets that follow, when God calls him *his servant, his elect in whom his soul is well pleased.* For whence comes it, that men venture to measure Christ by their own sense, but because they do not consider that their redemption depends exclusively on the grace of God? When God offers to us an invaluable treasure, it is excessive and wicked presumption to regulate our estimation of it by the disdainful views of our flesh. He is called a *servant*, not as if he were of the ordinary rank, but by way of eminence, and as the person to whom God has committed the charge and office of redeeming his Church. As *no man taketh this honour to himself, but he who is called of God* (Heb. v. 6) is justly entitled to this rank, God declares that he who comes forward in this character was *elected* by his decree.[1] Hence it follows, that men are not at liberty to reject him; because, by doing so, they would be guilty of contempt and rebellion against God. And, indeed, it were the height of absurdity that our choice or our pride should set aside that calling of God which ought to be regarded as sacred and inviolable.

My beloved, in whom my soul is well pleased. There is a still wider import in this statement, which God next makes by the prophet, that the delight of his soul dwells in

---

[1] "Dieu prononce que par son ordonnance il a eleu celuy qu'on verra venir ayant les marques qu'il met là;"—"God declares that, by his decree, he hath elected him who will be seen coming, attended by the marks which he there describes."

Christ; for though the calling of each of us proceeds from the free favour of God as its only source, yet in Christ there is this remarkable peculiarity, that in his person God the Father embraces in his love the whole Church. As we are all by nature enemies of God, his love will never come to us till it first begin with the Head; which we have seen on a former occasion, and will see again under another passage, (Matt. xvii. 5.)

He will proclaim judgment to the Gentiles. The prophet gives a brief description of Christ's office, when he foretells that *he will proclaim judgment to the Gentiles.* By the word *judgment* the Jews understand a government which is correctly and properly arranged, in which order and justice prevail. The design of the prophet is to inform us, that a person will come who will restore justice that had fallen, who will be the governor not of one nation only, but will also bring under subjection to God the Gentiles, among whom dreadful confusion formerly prevailed. And this is the import of the word *bring forth,* which the prophet employs; for it was the office of Christ to spread throughout the whole world the kingdom of God, which was at that time confined to the corner of Judea;[1] as it is said in another passage, *The Lord will send forth the sceptre of thy power out of Zion,* (Psa. cx. 2.)

I will put my Spirit upon him. This explains the manner in which *judgment* shall be *brought forth.* It is no doubt true, that there never was any portion whatever of *righteousness* in the world that did not proceed from the Spirit of God, and that was not maintained by his heavenly power; as none of the kings of the earth can frame or defend good order, except so far as he shall be assisted by the same Spirit. But in *bringing forth judgment* Christ is greatly superior to all others, for he has received the Spirit from the Father, that he may pour it out on all his people; for not only does he by word or writing prescribe what is proper, but inwardly forms the hearts of men, by the grace of his Spirit, to preserve the rule of righteousness.

---

[1] "Qui estoit pour lors comme enclos en un anglet au pays de Iudee;"—"which was then shut up, as it were in a corner, in the country of Judea."

19. *He will not strive.* The general meaning is, that the coming of Christ will not be attended by noise, will have nothing of royal splendour and magnificence. He presently adds, that this will turn to the advantage of men, by inducing them to love that mildness which the world everywhere despises. And certainly it is an astonishing display of the folly of men, that their sentiments with regard to Christ are less respectful, because he mildly and voluntarily accommodates himself to their capacity. Were Christ to appear in his glory, what else could be expected, but that it would altogether swallow us up ? What wickedness then is it to be less willing to receive him, when on our account he descends from his elevation ?

That the gentleness of Christ may awaken reverence in believers, Isaiah reminds them how advantageous, and even how necessary that gentleness must be. Each of us is conscious of his own weakness ; and therefore we ought to consider of what importance it is that Christ should treat us with kindness. I speak not of unbelievers, who are entirely destitute of all the graces of the Spirit ; but with respect to those whom God has already called, are they not like *a half-broken reed* and a *smoking lamp*, till God kindle them to full brightness, and supply them with perfect strength ? When Christ is thus pleased to condescend to our weakness, let his unspeakable goodness be embraced by us with joy. Meanwhile, let none flatter himself in his vices, but let each of us labour to make greater proficiency, that we may not be *tossed about* (Eph. iv. 14) through our whole life, or bend, like *reeds*, to the slightest gale. Let us grow to the stature of perfect men, that we may remain firm against the diversified attacks of Satan, that our faith may not only emit slight sparks encompassed by thick smoke, but may send out bright rays.

The example of Christ instructs all his ministers in what manner they ought to conduct themselves. But as there are some who falsely and absurdly maintain that mildness ought to be exercised indiscriminately towards all, we must attend to the distinction which the prophet expressly makes between *weak* and *wicked* persons. Those who are too stubborn need to have their hardness beaten violently with a hammer; and those who endeavour to spread darkness in every direction, or who act as torches to kindle conflagrations, must have their smoke dispelled and their flame extinguished. While the faithful ministers of the Word ought to endeavour to spare the weak, and thus to cherish and increase that portion of the grace of God, however small, which they possess, they must also exercise prudent caution, lest they encourage the obstinate malice of those who have no resemblance to the *smoking lamp* or *bruised reed.*

20. *Till he send out judgment into victory.* The words of the prophet are a little different, *he will bring forth the judgment unto truth.* But the term employed by Matthew is very emphatic, and is intended to inform us, that *justice* is not established in the world without a great struggle and exertion. The devil throws all possible difficulties in the way, which cannot be removed without violent opposition. This is confirmed by the word *victory,* for victory is not obtained in any other way than by fighting.

21. *And in his name shall the Gentiles trust.* Instead of these words the prophet has, *The isles shall wait for his law.* But though Matthew has changed the words, the meaning is the same, that the grace of Christ will be shared by the Gentiles.

MATTHEW.	MARK.	LUKE.
XII. 22. Then was brought to him one who was tormented by a devil, blind and dumb; and he cured him, so that the blind and dumb person both spoke and saw. 23. And all the multitudes were astonished, and said,	III. 20. And they come into the house, and immediately a multitude assembled, so that they could not even eat bread.[1] 21. And when those who were related to him heard it, they went out to lay hands on him;[2] for they	XI. 14. And he was casting out a devil, and it was dumb.[3] And when he had cast out the devil, the dumb person spoke, and the multitudes

[1] "Ils ne pouvoyent pas mesme prendre leur repas;"—"they could not even take their meal."
[2] "Ils sortirent pour le saisir;"—"they went out to seize him."
[3] "Un diable qui estoit muet;"—"a devil which was dumb."

MATTHEW.	MARK.	LUKE.
Is not this the son of David? 24. But when the Pharisees heard it, they said, This man doth not cast out devils but by Beelzebub prince of the devils.	said, He is gone mad.[1] 22. And the Scribes, who had come down from Jerusalem, said, He hath Beelzebub, and by the prince of the devils he casteth out devils.	wondered.[2] 15. And some of them said, By Beelzebub, the prince of the devils, he casteth out devils.[3]

Mark III. 20. *And they come into the house.* Mark undoubtedly takes in a somewhat extended period of time, when he passes from the miracles to that wicked conspiracy which the relatives of Christ formed with each other, to bind him as if he had been a *madman.* Matthew and *Luke* mention not more than a single miracle, as having given to the Pharisees an opportunity of slander; but as all the three agree in this last clause which is contained in Mark's narrative, I have thought it proper to insert it here.

It is wonderful that such wickedness should have been found among the relatives of Christ, who ought to have been the first to aid him in advancing the kingdom of God. When they see that he has already obtained some reputation, their ambition leads them to desire that he should be admired in Jerusalem; for they exhort him to go up to that city, *that he may show himself more openly,* (John vii. 3, 4.) But now that they perceive him to be hated on one side by the rulers, exposed on another to numerous slanders, and even despised by the great body of the people—to prevent any injury, or envy, or dishonour, from arising to the whole family, they form the design of *laying hands on him,* and binding him at home, as if he had been a person who laboured under mental derangement; and, as appears from the words of the Evangelist, such was their actual belief.

Hence we learn, first, how great is the blindness of the human mind, in forming such perverse judgments about the

[1] "Car ils disoyent qu'il estoit hors du sens;"—"for they said that he was out of his senses."
[2] "Dont les troupes s'emerveillerent;"—"at which the multitudes wondered."
[3] "C'est par Beel-zebub, prince des diables, qu'il iette hors les diables;"—"it is by Beelzebub, prince of the devils, that he casteth out devils."

glory of God when openly displayed. Certainly, in all that Christ said and did, the power of the Holy Spirit shone magnificently; and if others had not clearly perceived it, how could it be unknown to his relatives, who were intimately acquainted with him? But because Christ's manner of acting does not please the world, and is so far from gaining its good graces that it exposes him to the resentments of many, they give out that he is deranged. Let us learn, in the second place, that the light of faith does not proceed from flesh and blood, but from heavenly grace, that no man may glory in any thing else than in the regeneration of the Spirit; as Paul tells us, *If any man wishes to be considered to be in Christ, let him be a new creature,* (2 Cor. v. 17.)

Matthew XII. 22. *Then was brought to him.* Luke explains from the effect, that the devil by which the man was possessed was *dumb;* but Matthew says, that a twofold plague had been inflicted on the man. Many persons, no doubt, are blind and deaf on account of natural defects; but it is evident, that this man had become blind, and had been deprived of the use of speech, though there was no defect in his optical nerves,[1] or in the proportion of his tongue. We need not wonder that so much liberty should be allowed to Satan in injuring the bodily senses, when God justly permits him to corrupt or pervert all the faculties of the soul.

23. *And all the people were astonished.* Hence we infer, that there was a visible display of the power of God, which drew upon him the admiration of the great body of the people, who were not at all actuated by any wicked disposition. For how came it that all admired, but because the fact compelled them to do so? And certainly there is not one of us, who does not see in this narrative, as in a mirror, an unwonted power of God: and hence it follows, that a diabolical venom must have seized the minds of the scribes, who were not ashamed to slander so remarkable a work of

---

[1] "Aux nerfs appelez Optiques, qui sont les conduits de la veuë;"—"in what are called the Optical nerves, which are the conductors of vision."

God. But we must attend to the result of the miracle. Moved with admiration, those who saw it ask each other, *Is not Jesus the Christ?* Acknowledging the power of God, they are led, as it were by the hand, to faith. Not that they suddenly profited as much as they ought to have done, (for they speak doubtfully;) but yet it is no small proficiency to be aroused to consider more attentively the glory of Christ. Some look upon this as a full affirmation, but the words convey no such meaning; and the fact itself shows, that an unexpected occurrence had struck them forcibly, and that they did not form a decided opinion, but only that it occurred to them that he might be the Christ.

24. *But when the Pharisees heard it.* The scribes cannot withhold the acknowledgment of a fact so open and manifest, and yet they maliciously carp[1] at what Christ did by Divine power. Not only do they obscure the praise of the miracle, but endeavour to turn it into a reproach, as if it were performed by magical enchantment; and that work, which could not be ascribed to a man, is alleged by them to have the devil for its author. Of the word *Beelzebub* I have spoken under the Tenth Chapter,[2] and of *the prince of the devils* I have said a little under the Ninth Chapter.[3] The opinion expressed by the scribes, that there is a *prince* among wicked spirits, did not arise from a mistake of the common

---

[1] "Ils ne laissent pas toutesfois de ronger, comme par despit et d'un vouloir malicieux;"—"and yet they do not fail to carp as with spite, and with a wicked disposition."

[2] Harmony, vol. i. p. 459.

[3] Harmony, vol. i. p. 419. The reader must have observed that, when our Author has explained a phrase or illustrated a fact, he seldom repeats what he had said, but refers to the earlier portions of his work, in which the information may be found. It is not improbable that this may have been his leading motive for adopting the plan of a *Harmony,* instead of writing a separate Commentary on each Gospel. He had made some observations on Matth. ix. 34, *But the Pharisees said, He casteth out devils by the prince of the devils;* and takes for granted, that the terms which occur in that passage require no farther elucidation. But it would appear to have escaped his recollection that, on the occasion alluded to, he satisfied himself with general remarks on the "wicked slander" of the Pharisees, and took no notice of the phrase, *prince of the devils.* The deficiency is partly supplied by an explanation which he now makes. —*Ed.*

people, or from supposition, but from a conviction entertained among the godly, that the reprobate have a head, in the same manner as Christ is the Head of the Church.

MATTHEW.	MARK.	LUKE.
XII. 25. But as Jesus knew their thoughts, he said to them,[1] Every kingdom divided against itself shall be laid waste; and every city or house divided against itself shall not stand. 26. And if Satan casteth out Satan, he is divided against himself, and how then shall his kingdom stand? 27. And if I, by the assistance of Beelzebub, cast out devils, by whose assistance do your children cast them out? therefore they shall judge concerning you.[2] 28. But if by the Spirit of God I cast out devils, then the kingdom of God has come to you. 29. Otherwise, how can a man enter into the house of a strong man, and pillage his property, unless he first bind the strong man, and then he will pillage his house? 30. He that is not with me is against me; and he that gathereth not with me scattereth. 31. Therefore I say to you, All sin and blasphemy[3] shall be	III. 23. And having called them to him, he spoke in parables, How can Satan cast out Satan? 24. And if a kingdom be divided against itself, that kingdom cannot stand. 25. And if a house be divided against itself, that house cannot stand. 26. And if Satan hath risen up against himself, and is divided, he cannot stand, but hath an end.[4] 27. No man can enter into the house of a strong man, and pillage his property, unless he first bind the strong man, and then he will pillage his house. 28. Verily I say to you, All sins shall be forgiven to the sons of men, and blasphemies with	XI. 16. And others tempting him sought from him a sign from heaven. 17. But as he knew their thoughts,[5] he said to them, Every kingdom divided against itself is laid waste, and a house against a house falleth.[6] 18. But if Satan also is divided against himself, how shall his kingdom stand? for you say that by Beelzebub I cast out devils. 19. But if I cast out devils by Beelzebub, by whom do your children cast them out? therefore they shall be your judges. 20. But if I cast out devils by the finger of God, truly has the kingdom of God come to you. 21. When a strong man armed keepeth his palace, his property is at peace; 22. But when a stronger than he cometh upon him, and overcometh him, he taketh from him all his armour, in which he trusted, and divideth his spoils. 23. He that is not with me is against

---

[1] "Mais Iesus, cognoissant leurs pensees, leur dit;"—"but Jesus, knowing their thoughts, said to them."

[2] "Parquoy iceux seront vos iuges;"—"therefore they shall be your judges."

[3] "Toute sorte de peché et blaspheme;"—"every description of sin and blasphemy."

[4] "Ains il prend fin;"—"and so he comes to an end."

[5] "Mais luy cognoissant leurs pensees;"—"but he knowing their thoughts."

[6] "Et 'toute' maison 'divisee' contre soy-mesme dechet;"—"and every house divided against itself falleth."

MATTHEW.	MARK.	LUKE.
forgiven to men; but the blasphemy against the Spirit shall not be forgiven to men. 32. And whosoever shall speak a word against the Son of man, it shall be forgiven him; but he who shall speak against the Holy Spirit, it shall not be forgiven him, neither in the present life nor in the future.	which they shall blaspheme : 29. But he who shall speak blasphemy against the Holy Spirit hath no forgiveness to eternity,[1] but is exposed to eternal judgment. 30. For they said, He hath an unclean spirit.[2]	me, and he that gathereth not with me scattereth. XII. 10. And whosoever speaketh a word against the Son of man, it shall be forgiven him; but he who shall blaspheme against the Holy Spirit, it shall not be forgiven him.

Matthew XII. 25. *But as Jesus knew their thoughts.* Though Christ knew sufficiently well, and had often learned by experience, that the scribes, in the exercise of their malice,[3] were in the habit of putting an unfavourable construction on every thing that he did, yet Matthew and Luke, I have no doubt, mean that Christ was a discerner of their hearts.[4] And indeed it is probable, that they spoke so openly against Christ, that their calumnies reached his ears; but Christ knew by his Divine Spirit the dispositions which led them to slander him. For it frequently happens that erroneous judgments are formed by men who do not intentionally, after all, oppose what is right, but err through ignorance; who do not cherish a hidden and concealed venom, but whose rashness carries them headlong.[5] The meaning therefore is, that Christ reproved them with the greater severity, because he was a witness and judge of their inward malice.

Every kingdom divided against itself. In refuting the calumny alleged against him, he first quotes a common

---

[1] " N'aura point de remission eternellement;"—" will have no forgiveness eternally."
[2] " Il a l'esprit immonde;"—" he hath the unclean spirit."
[3] " Comme c'estoyent gens tout pleins d'un malin vouloir;"—" as they were people entirely full of a wicked disposition."
[4] " Que Christ a cognu ce qui estoit caché dedans leur cœurs;"—" that Christ knew what was concealed within their hearts."
[5] " Mais se laissent trop aisément transporter d'une temerité ne voyans pas le mal qu'ils font;"—" but allow themselves too easily to be carried away by rashness, not perceiving the evil that they do."

proverb. This refutation may appear to be not quite satisfactory. We know what subtle methods Satan sometimes employs, presenting all the while an appearance of discord, in order to entrap the minds of men by superstitions. Thus, for example, the exorcisms of Popery are nothing else than feats of dexterity, in which Satan pretends to fight with himself. But no suspicion of this nature fell on Christ; for he cast out devils in such a manner, as to restore to God the men in whom they dwelt sound and whole. Whenever Satan enters into a collusion with himself, he pretends to be vanquished, and yet it is himself that triumphs. But Christ attacked Satan in open combat, threw him down, and left him nothing remaining. He did not lay him low in one respect, that he might give him greater stability in another, but stripped him completely of all his armour. Christ therefore reasons justly, that there is no community of interest between him and Satan, because that father of cunning[1] keeps one object in view, the preservation of his kingdom.

But perhaps it will be objected, that the devils are often hurried along, by giddiness and blind madness, to destroy themselves. The answer is easy. The words of Christ mean nothing more than that it was absurd in the scribes to maintain, that the devil, who endeavours by every method to make men his slaves, should, of his own accord, destroy the power which he possessed over them. Besides, it ought to be remembered, that common proverbs were employed by Christ in such a manner, as to be merely probable conjectures, and not solid arguments; and that, when he speaks of what is known and well attested, he finds it easier to reach the conscience of his adversaries.[2] Everybody knew that Christ had driven Satan from his possession, and nothing was plainer than that all his miracles tended to this object; and hence it was easy to conclude, that his power, which was so much opposed to Satan, was divine.

---

[1] "Ce pere de toute finesse et malice;"—"that father of all dexterity and malice."
[2] "Il ne va pas chercher fort loin les choses pour poindre les consciences de ses adversaires;"—"he does not go far to seek things fitted to affect the consciences of his adversaries."

27. *By whom do your children cast them out?* He charges them with passing an unjust and malicious decision, because in the same case they did not decide in a similar manner, but as they were affected towards the persons. Now this inequality shows, that their prevailing motive was not a regard to what is just and right, but blind love or hatred; and that it was even an evidence of wicked self-love (φιλαυτίας) and envy, to condemn in Christ what they praised in their own *children.* By *your children* some understand the children of the whole nation; and some think that the Apostles are so called, because they were acknowledged to be *children,* while Christ was treated as if he had been a foreigner.[1] Others refer it to the ancient Prophets. I have no doubt that he means the *Exorcists,* who were at that time generally employed among the Jews, as is evident from the Acts of the Apostles, (xix. 19.) There is reason to believe, that no greater kindness would be exercised in judging of the disciples of Christ than of their Master; and to apply these words to the dead is a forced construction, when they manifestly denote a comparison of the present time.

There was indeed no statute of the Law for having *Exorcists* among the Jews; but we know that God, in order to maintain their fidelity to his covenant, and their purity of worship, often testified his presence among them by a variety of miracles. It is even possible that there were persons who cast out devils by calling on the name of the Lord; and the people, having experienced such a display of the power of God, rashly concluded that it was an ordinary office.[2] The Papists afterwards, resolving not to occupy a lower rank, imitated them by creating *Exorcists;* and in this way were apes of apes. Besides, it was not necessary that Christ should approve of those *exorcisms,* in order to point out the malice of those who wished to have them regarded as sacred, and as authorized by the name of God; for the objection was, as we say, of a personal nature.[3]

[1] "Et cependant les scribes tenoyent Christ pour estranger;"—" and yet the scribes held Christ to be a foreigner."
[2] "Le peuple en a fait un office ordinaire sans regarder comment;"— "the people made it to be an ordinary office, without considering in what manner."
[3] "Car l'objection s'addresse à la personne, comme on dit, et non pas

Therefore they shall judge concerning you. These words are not to be taken literally, but the meaning is: "We need not go far to seek your condemnation. You attribute to Beelzebub the miracles which I have performed, and you praise the same things in your own children. You have at home what is sufficient to condemn you." But if any one prefer to understand them differently, as reproaching them with the grace of God, which was sometimes exhibited through the Exorcists, I do not greatly object to that view. Though they were greatly degenerated, yet the Lord was pleased not to leave them altogether without evidences of his power, that there might be some testimony to authorize the priesthood in general, and the service of the temple; for it was of the highest importance that there should be evident marks to distinguish them from the superstitions of the Gentiles. I look upon the former view, however, as the natural one.

28. *But if I cast out devils by the Spirit of God.* Luke says, *if I cast out devils by* THE FINGER *of God;* employing the word *Finger* metaphorically instead of the *Spirit.* As God works, and exerts his power, by his Spirit, it is with propriety that the word *Finger* is applied to him. And this mode of expression was common among the Jews, as Moses relates that Pharaoh's magicians said, *This is the finger of God.* Now Christ infers from what he has already stated, that the scribes prove themselves to be ungrateful to God, by being unwilling that He should reign among them. Hitherto, he replied to their idle calumny; but now, he treats them as convicted persons, and charges them not to make ungodly opposition to the kingdom of God. He does not confine himself to a single miracle, but takes occasion from it to discourse on the object of his coming, reminds them that they ought not merely to look at one remarkable fact, but at a far

à la chose: c'est à dire, Christ ne regarde point ce qu'à la verité il falloit dire de ces Exorcistes, mais ce qu'en pensoyent les scribes;"—"for the objection is addressed to the person, as we say, and not to the thing: that is to say, Christ does not consider what in truth ought to be said of these Exorcistes, but what the Jews thought of them."

more important truth, that it was the will of God, by revealing His Messiah, to raise up their salvation which was fallen, and to restore his kingdom among them. Thus we see that Christ complains of their ingratitude, in madly rejecting from the midst of them the inestimable grace of God. *The kingdom of God hath come to you.* The word *come* is emphatic, and implies that, without any request from them, God appears as their Redeemer, while they do everything that is in their power to drive him away, and, when he is present and prepared for their salvation, refuse to give him a place.

29. *How can any one enter into the house of a strong man?* Though the Evangelists differ a little as to words, there is a perfect agreement among them as to the substance of this discourse. Christ is pursuing the subject, on which he had lately touched, about *the kingdom of God,* and declares it to be necessary that Satan be violently driven out, in order that God may establish his *kingdom* among men. What he now states is nothing else than a confirmation of the preceding statement. But to ascertain more fully the intention of Christ, we must call to our recollection that analogy which Matthew (viii. 17) traces between the visible and the spiritual favours which Christ bestows.[1] Every benefit which the bodies of men received from Christ was intended to have a reference to their souls. Thus, in rescuing the bodily senses of men from the tyranny of the devil, he proclaimed that the Father had sent him as a Deliverer, to destroy his spiritual tyranny over their souls.

I now return to his words. He maintains that a *strong* and powerful tyrant cannot be deprived of his dominion, *till he is stripped of his armour;* for if he is not met by a force superior to his own, he will never yield of his own accord. Why is this asserted? First, we know that the devil is everywhere called *the prince of the world.* Now the tyranny which he exercises is defended on every side by strong ramparts. His snares for entrapping men are beyond all calculation; nay, men are already his slaves, and so firmly bound by a

[1] Harmony, vol. i. p. 251.

variety of fetters, that they rather cherish the slavery, to which they are devoted, than make any aspirations after freedom. There are also innumerable evils which he inflicts upon them, by which he holds them in wretched oppression under his feet. In short, there is nothing to prevent him from tyrannizing over the world without control. Not that he can do anything without the permission of the Creator, but because Adam, having withdrawn from the dominion of God, has subjected all his posterity to this foreign sway.

Now though it is contrary to nature that the devil reigns, and though it is by a just punishment of God, on account of sin, that men are subjected to his tyranny, yet he remains in quiet possession of his kingdom, and may insult us at his pleasure, till *a stronger than he* shall rise up against him. But this *stronger* person is not to be found on earth, for men have not sufficient power to relieve themselves; and therefore it was promised that a Redeemer would come from heaven. Now this kind of redemption Christ shows to be necessary, in order to wrench from the devil, by main force, what he will never quit till he is compelled. By these words he informs us, that it is in vain for men to expect deliverance, till Satan has been subdued by a violent struggle.[1]

He expressly accuses the scribes of ignorance, in not understanding the principles of the kingdom of God. But this reproof applies almost equally to all, for all are chargeable with the same folly. There is no man who does not loudly boast that he desires the kingdom of God; and yet we do not permit Christ to fight boldly, as the occasion requires, in order to rescue us from the power of our tyrant; just as if a sick man were to entreat the aid of a physician, and then to refuse every remedy. We now see the reason why Christ introduced this parable. It was to show, that the scribes were hostile to the kingdom of God, the beginnings of which they maliciously resisted. Let us also learn that, as we are all subject to the tyranny of Satan, there is no

---

[1] "Que c'est folie aux hommes d'attendre deliverance, si Satan n'est premierement mis bas en choquant à bon escient contre luy;"—"that it is folly in men to expect deliverance, if Satan is not first put down by encountering him in good earnest."

other way in which he commences his reign within us, than when he rescues us, by the powerful and victorious arm of Christ, from that wretched and accursed bondage.

30. *He that is not with me.* There are two ways of explaining this passage. Some suppose that it is an argument drawn from contraries, and that Christ's meaning is: "I cannot reign till the devil is overthrown; for the object of all his attempts is, to *scatter* whatever I *gather*." And certainly we see abundant evidence of the earnestness with which that enemy labours to destroy the kingdom of Christ. But I rather agree in opinion with those who explain it to denote, that the scribes are declared to be, in two respects, opposed to the kingdom of God, because they intentionally hinder its progress. "It was your duty to assist me, and to give me your hand in establishing the kingdom of God; for whoever does not assist is, in some measure, opposed to me, or, at least, deserves to be reckoned among enemies. What then shall be said of you, whose furious rage drives you into avowed opposition?"[1]

And he that gathereth not with me scattereth. The truth of this is abundantly manifest from what has been already said; for so strong is our propensity to evil, that the justice of God can have no place but in those who apply to it in good earnest. This doctrine has a still more extensive bearing, and implies that they are unworthy to be considered as belonging to the flock of Christ, who do not apply to it all the means that are in their power; because their indolence tends to retard and ruin the kingdom of God, which all of us are called to advance.

31. *Therefore I say to you.* This inference ought not to be confined to the clause immediately preceding, but depends on the whole discourse. Having proved that the scribes could not blame him for casting out devils, without opposing the kingdom of God, he at length concludes that it is no light or ordinary offence, but an atrocious crime, knowingly

[1] "A batailler ouvertement contre Dieu;"—"to fight openly against God."

and willingly to pour contempt on the Spirit of God. We have already said, that Christ did not pronounce this decision on the mere words which they uttered, but on their base and wicked thought.

All sin and blasphemy. As our Lord declares *blasphemy against the Holy Ghost* to be more heinous than all other sins, it is of importance to inquire what is the meaning of that term. Those who define it to be *impenitence*[1] may be refuted without any difficulty; for it would have been in vain and to no purpose for Christ to say, that *it is not forgiven in the present life.* Besides, the word *blasphemy* cannot be extended indiscriminately to every sort of crimes; but from the comparison which Christ makes, we shall easily obtain the true definition. Why is it said that he who *blasphemes against the Spirit* is a more heinous sinner than he who *blasphemes against Christ?* Is it because the majesty of the Spirit is greater, that a crime committed against him must be punished with greater severity? Certainly that is not the reason; for as *the fulness of the Godhead* (Col. ii. 9) shines in Christ, he who pours contempt upon him overturns and destroys, as far as it lies in his power, the whole glory of God. Now in what manner shall Christ be separated from his Spirit, so that those who treat the Spirit with contempt offer no injury or insult to Christ?

Already we begin to perceive, that the reason why *blasphemy against the Spirit* exceeds other sins, is not that the Spirit is higher than Christ, but that those who rebel, after that the power of God has been revealed, cannot be excused on the plea of ignorance. Besides, it must be observed, that what is here said about *blasphemy* does not refer merely to the essence of *the Spirit*, but to the grace which He has bestowed upon us. Those who are destitute of the light of the Spirit, however much they may detract from the glory of the Spirit, will not be held guilty of this crime.[2] We do not

---

[1] "Quant à ceux qui disent que c'est un endurcissement jusqu'à la mort;"—"as to those who say that it is hardened obstinacy even to death."

[2] "Ne seront pas toutesfois tenus coulpables de ce grand crime duquel il est ici parlé;"—"will not, on that account, be held guilty of the great crime here spoken of."

maintain, that those persons are said to pour contempt on the Spirit of God, who oppose his grace and power by hardened malice; and farther we maintain, that this kind of sacrilege is committed only when we knowingly endeavour to extinguish the Spirit who dwells in us.

The reason why contempt is said to be poured on the Spirit, rather than on the Son or the Father, is this. By detracting from the grace and power of God, we make a direct attack on *the Spirit*, from whom they proceed, and in whom they are revealed to us. Shall any unbeliever curse God? It is as if a blind man were dashing against a wall. But no man curses the Spirit who is not enlightened by him, and conscious of ungodly rebellion against him; for it is not a superfluous distinction, that all other *blasphemies* shall be forgiven, except that one *blasphemy* which is directed against the Spirit. If a man shall simply blaspheme against God, he is not declared to be beyond the hope of pardon; but of those who have offered outrage to *the Spirit*, it is said that God will never forgive them. Why is this, but because those only are *blasphemers* against the Spirit, who slander his gifts and power, contrary to the conviction of their own mind? Such also is the import of the reason assigned by Mark for the extreme severity of Christ's threatening against the Pharisees; *because they had said that he had the unclean spirit;* for in this manner they purposely and maliciously turned light into darkness; and, indeed, it is in the manner of the *giants*,[1] as the phrase is, to make war against God.

But here a question arises. Do men proceed to such a pitch of madness as not to hesitate, knowingly and wilfully, to rush against God? for this appears to be monstrous and incredible. I reply: Such audacity does indeed proceed from mad blindness, in which, at the same time, malice and virulent rage predominate. Nor is it without reason that Paul says, that though he was *a blasphemer, he obtained*

---

[1] "Et cela c'est desfier Dieu, et luy faire la guerre, comme les Géans des Poëtes, ainsi que porte le proverbe Latin;"—"and that is to defy God, and make war with him, like the Giants of the Poets, as the Latin proverb bears."

pardon, because he had done it ignorantly in his unbelief, (1 Tim. i. 13;) for this term draws a distinction between his sin and voluntary rebellion. This passage refutes also the error of those who imagine that every sin which is voluntary, or which is committed in opposition to the conscience, is unpardonable. On the contrary, Paul expressly limits that sin to the First Table of the Law;[1] and our Lord not less plainly applies the word *blasphemy* to a single description of sin, and at the same time shows, that it is of a kind which is directly opposed to the glory of God.[2]

From all that has been said, we may conclude that those persons sin and blaspheme against the Holy Spirit, who maliciously turn to his dishonour the perfections of God, which have been revealed to him by the Spirit, in which His glory ought to be celebrated, and who, with Satan, their leader, are avowed enemies of the glory of God. We need not then wonder, if for such sacrilege there is no hope of pardon; for they must be desperate who turn the only medicine of salvation into a deadly venom. Some consider this to be too harsh, and betake themselves to the childish expedient, that it is said to be unpardonable, because the pardon of it is rare and difficult to be obtained. But the words of Christ are too precise to admit of so silly an evasion. It is excessively foolish to argue that God will be cruel if he never pardon a sin, the atrocity of which ought to excite in us astonishment and horror.[3] Those who reason in that manner do not sufficiently consider what a monstrous crime it is, not only to profane intentionally the sacred name of God, but to spit in his face when he shines evidently before us. It shows equal ignorance to object, that it would be absurd if even repentance could not obtain pardon; for *blasphemy against the Spirit* is a token of reprobation, and hence it follows, that whoever have

---

[1] "Restreint nommément à la Premiere Table de la Loy ce peché contre l'Esprit;"—"expressly limits to the First Table of the Law this sin against the Spirit."

[2] "Que c'est un peché qui battaille directement contre la gloire de Dieu;"—"that it is a sin which fights directly against the glory of God."

[3] "Veu que l'horreur d'iceluy nous devroit à tous faire dresser les cheveux en la teste;"—"since the horror at it ought to have such an effect on all of us, as to make the hair stand on our head."

fallen into it, have been *delivered over to a reprobate mind*, (Rom. i. 28.) As we maintain, that he who has been truly regenerated by the Spirit cannot possibly fall into so horrid a crime, so, on the other hand, we must believe that those who have fallen into it never rise again; nay, that in this manner God punishes contempt of his grace, by hardening the hearts of the reprobate, so that they never have any desire towards repentance.

32. *Neither in the present life.* What these words mean, Mark briefly explains by saying, that *those who have spoken against the Spirit are exposed to eternal judgment.* Every day we ask from God the forgiveness of sins, and every day he reconciles us to Him; and, finally, at death, he takes away all our sins, and declares that he is gracious to us. The fruit of this mercy will appear at the last day. The meaning therefore is:—" There is no reason to expect that those who shall have blasphemed against the Spirit will obtain pardon in this life, or will be acquitted in the last judgment."

With regard to the inference drawn by the Papists, that the sins of men are forgiven after death, there is no difficulty in refuting their slander. First, they act foolishly in torturing the expression, *future life,* to mean an intermediate period, while any one may perceive that it denotes " the last judgment." But it is likewise a proof of their dishonesty; for the objection which they sophistically urge is inconsistent with their own doctrine. Who knows not their distinction, that sins are freely pardoned in respect of guilt, but that punishment and satisfaction are demanded? This is an acknowledgment, that there is no hope of salvation to any one whose guilt is not pardoned before death. To the dead, therefore, there remains no forgiveness, except as regards punishment; and surely they will not venture to deny that the subject of this discourse is guilt. Let them now go and light their fire of purgatory with these cold materials, if ice can kindle a flame.[1]

---

[1] " Voire s'il est possible de tant souffler la glace, qu'on la face flamber ;"—" that is, if it be possible to blow upon the ice in such a manner as to produce a flame."

MATTHEW.

XII. 33. Either make the tree good, and its fruit good: or make the tree bad, and its fruit bad; for the tree is known by the fruit. 34. Offspring of vipers, how can you speak what is good, when you are bad? for out of the abundance of the heart the mouth speaketh. 35. A good man, out of the good treasure of his heart, bringeth forth what is good, and a bad man, out of the bad treasure, bringeth forth what is evil. 36. But I say to you, That men will give account, at the day of judgment, for every idle word which they shall have spoken. 37. For by thy words thou shalt be justified, and by thy words thou shalt be condemned.

33. *Either make the tree good.* It might look like absurdity, that men should be allowed a choice of being *either good or bad;* but if we consider what sort of persons Christ is addressing, the difficulty will be speedily resolved. We know what opinion was generally entertained about the Pharisees; for their pretended sanctity had so blinded the minds of the common people, that no one ventured to pass sentence on their vices.[1] Wishing to remove this mask, Christ desires them to be *either good or bad;* or, in other words, declares that nothing is more inconsistent with honesty than hypocrisy, and that it is in vain for men to boast of pretensions to righteousness who are not sincere and upright.[2] So then he puts nothing at their disposal, and withdraws no restraint from them, but only reminds them that their empty professions will avail them nothing so long as they are double, because they must be *either good or bad.*

From the expression, *make the tree,* some foolishly infer, that it is in every man's power to regulate his own life and conduct. It is a rhetorical mode of speaking, by which Christ points out the scribes, dispels—so to speak—the smoke of their hypocrisy, and recalls them to pure and genuine uprightness. He afterwards explains the way and manner in which they may show that they are *good or bad trees;* which is by yielding *good or bad fruit:* so that there is no ambiguity in the meaning. The life of the scribes was not rendered infamous among men by gross vices. Pride, ambition,

---

[1] " Que nul n'osoit parler de leurs vices, et les condamner;"—" that none dared to speak of their vices, or to condemn them."
[2] " Lesquels ne vont point rondement, et n'ont une affection droite;" —" who do not go straight forward, and have not an upright disposition."

and envy, displayed their venom in the slanders which they uttered; but as that venom was not perceived by ignorant people, Christ brings the concealed evil from its lurking-place, and drags it forth to light.

But perhaps it will be objected that, in consequence of the corruption of our nature, it is impossible to find any man who is altogether upright, and free from every vice. The answer is ready. Christ does not demand absolute and entire perfection, but only a sincere and unfeigned disposition, which the Pharisees whom he addresses were far from possessing. As Scripture applies the terms, *bad and wicked*, to those who are completely given up to Satan, so the sincere worshippers of God, though they are encompassed by the infirmity of their flesh and by many sins, and groan under the burden, are called *good*. This arises from the undeserved kindness of God, who bestows so honourable a designation on those who aim at goodness.

34. *Offspring of vipers.* The similarity between *the tree* and *the fruit* is here applied by Christ to nothing more than speech, because this afforded an opportunity of detecting the inward and concealed malice of the scribes; and that is the reason why he dwells so much on this one kind of sin. It is because their falsehood and slanders betrayed what was not so visible in the rest of their life, that Christ attacks them with such severity. "There is no reason to wonder," he says, "that you vomit out wicked words; for your heart is full of malice." Nor are we to suppose that he ought to have treated them with greater gentleness, because some might regard this reproof as excessively severe. There are other sins, no doubt, that call for harsh reproofs; but when hypocritical persons pervert what is right, or put a false colouring on what is sinful, such wickedness renders it necessary that God should thunder against it in a more terrible manner than against other sins.

Now the design of Christ, suggested by the present occurrence, was to condemn the wicked sophistry which turns light into darkness. This passage shows how highly valuable in the sight of the Lord truth is, since he maintains and defends it with such rigour. Would that this were earnestly considered by those persons, whose ingenuity is too ready to be employed in defending any cause, and whose venal tongue disguises impostures! In a particular manner, Christ waxes wroth against those whom ambition, or envy, or some other fraudulent design, prompts to slander, even when there is nothing that their conscience condemns. Against the Pharisees, too, as his custom was, Christ used greater harshness, because they were so captivated by an unfounded conviction of their righteousness, that an ordinary warning had no effect upon them. And till hypocrites are sharply pierced,[1] all that is said to them is treated with scorn and contempt.

How can you speak what is good? We have formerly hinted, that proverbial sayings ought not to be rigidly interpreted as an invariable rule, for they state nothing more than the ordinary fact. Sometimes, no doubt, a cruel man will deceive the simple by honied flatteries, a cunning man will cheat under the garb of simplicity, and a man of very wicked thoughts will breathe almost angelical purity of language.[2] But the ordinary practice demonstrates the truth of what Christ here says, that *out of the abundance of the heart the mouth speaketh;* agreeably to the old proverb, which declared the tongue to be the index of the mind.[3] And, indeed, whatever hidden and crooked recesses may exist in the heart of man, and whatever may be the amazing contrivances by which every man conceals his vices, yet the Lord extorts from each of them some kind of confession, so that they discover by the tongue their natural disposition and hidden feelings. We must also observe the purpose for which Christ employs those parables; for he reproaches the Pharisees with having manifested by words the malice which they had inwardly conceived. Besides, knowing them

---

[1] " Iusques à ce qu'ils sentent qu'on le poigne à bon escient ;"—" till they feel that they are pierced in good earnest."

[2] " Il semblera, à l'ouir parler, qu'il ait une pureté Angelique ;"—" to hear him speak, you would imagine that he has the purity of an Angel."

[3] " Comme aussi le proverbe ancien portoit, Que la langue est le charactere ou pourtrait du cœur ;"—" as also the old proverb bore, That the tongue is the type or portrait of the heart."

to be sworn enemies, he takes occasion from a single calumny to expose their whole life, and to destroy their credit with the people, which gave them too great influence in deceiving and in doing mischief. Though *good* speeches do not always proceed from the inmost heart, but originate (as the phrase is) on the tip of the tongue, yet it is an invariable truth, that bad speeches are indications of a bad heart.

36. *Of every idle word.* This is an argument from the less to the greater; for if *every idle word* is to be called in question, how would God spare the open blasphemies and sacrilegious insolence of those who bark against his glory?[1] An *idle word* means one that is useless, or that yields no edification or advantage. Many look upon this as too severe;[2] but if we consider the purpose for which our tongues were made, we will acknowledge, that those men are justly held guilty who unthinkingly devote them to trifling fooleries, and prostitute them to such a purpose. It is no light fault to abuse, for frivolous purposes, the *time*, which Paul enjoins us to be careful to *redeem*, (Eph. v. 16; Col. iv. 5.)

Now since no man is so cautious in speech, or maintains such a wise restraint upon himself, as never to allow some *idle words* to escape him, there remains for all of us absolute despair, if the Lord should treat us with rigour. But as the confident hope of our salvation rests on the assurance that God will *not enter into judgment* with us, (Ps. cxliii. 2,) but will bury in gracious forgetfulness the sins which deserve innumerable deaths,[3] we entertain no doubt that, when he removes the condemnation of our whole life, he will likewise pardon the guilt of idle talking. When the judgment of God is mentioned in Scripture, it does not in any way set aside the forgiveness of sins. And yet let no man indulge himself, but let every man earnestly endeavour to

[1] "Qui abbayent contre sa gloire, comme chiens mastins;"—"who bark against his glory, like mastiff-dogs."
[2] "Ceci semble à plusieurs estre trop extreme et rigoureux;"—"this appears to many to be too extreme and rigorous."
[3] "Qui meritent dix mille morts;"—"which deserve ten thousand deaths."

bridle his tongue, (James i. 26.) First, let us speak of the sacred mysteries of God with the utmost reverence and sobriety; secondly, let us abstain from talkativeness, buffoonery, and vain jests, and much more from slanderous attacks; and, lastly, let us endeavour to have *our speech seasoned with salt,* (Col. iv. 6.)

37. *By thy words thou shalt be justified.* This was a common proverb, which he applied to the present subject; for I have no doubt that this was a saying which the people had frequently in their mouths, that " every man is condemned or acquitted by his own acknowledgment." But Christ turns it to a meaning somewhat different, that a wicked speech, being the indication of concealed malice, is enough to condemn a man. The attempt which the Papists make to torture this passage, so as to set aside the righteousness of faith, is childish. A man is *justified by his words,* not because his *speech* is the ground of his justification, (for we obtain by faith the favour of God, so that he reckons us to be righteous persons;) but because pure *speech*[1] absolves us in such a manner, that we are not condemned as wicked persons by our tongue. Is it not absurd to infer from this, that men deserve a single drop of righteousness in the sight of God? On the contrary, this passage upholds our doctrine; for, although Christ does not here treat of the ground of our justification, yet the contrast between the two words points out the meaning of the word *justify.* The Papists reckon it absurd in us to say, that a man is justified by faith, because they explain the word *justified* to mean, that he becomes, and is, actually righteous; while we understand it to mean, that he is accounted righteous, and is *acquitted* before the tribunal of God, as is evident from numerous passages of Scripture. And is not the same thing confirmed by Christ, when he draws a contrast between *justified* and *condemned?*

[1] " La parole pure, droite, et honneste;"—" pure, upright, and becoming speech."

MATTHEW.	LUKE.
XII. 43. But when the unclean spirit hath gone out of a man, he walketh through dry places, seeking rest, and findeth it not. 44. Then he saith, I will return to my house, whence I came out; and coming, he findeth it empty, and swept, and embellished. 45. Then he goeth away, and taketh with him seven other spirits more wicked than himself; and entering, he dwelleth there: and the last state of that man is worse than the first.[1] So shall it be also to this wicked generation.	XI. 24. When the unclean spirit hath gone out of a man, he walketh through dry places, seeking rest; and not finding it, he saith, I will return to my house, whence I came out. 25. And when he is come, he findeth it swept and embellished. 26. Then he goeth, and taketh with him seven other spirits more wicked than himself; and entering, they dwell there: and the last state of that man is worse than the first.

43. *But when the unclean spirit hath gone out.* He speaks of scribes and hypocrites of a similar character, who, despising the grace of God, enter into a conspiracy with the devil. Against such persons he pronounces that punishment which their ingratitude deserves. To make his doctrine more extensively useful, he points out, in a general manner, the condemnation that awaits those who, despising the grace offered to them, again open the door to the devil. But as almost every particle has great weight, there are some points that must be noticed in their order, before we come to treat the substance of the parable.

What Christ says about the *going out* of the devil is intended to magnify the power and efficacy of the grace of God. Whenever God draws near to us, and, above all, when he approaches us in the person of his Son, the design is, to rescue us from the tyranny of the devil, and to receive us into his favour. This had been openly declared by Christ in the miracle which he had lately performed. As it is the peculiar office of Christ to banish wicked spirits, that they may no longer reign over men, the devil is justly said to *go out of* those men to whom Christ exhibits himself as a Redeemer. Though the presence of Christ is not efficacious to all, because unbelievers render it useless to them, yet he intended to point out why he visits us, what is implied in his coming, and how it is regarded by wicked spirits; for in

[1] "La fin de cest homme est pire que le commencement;"—"the end of that man is worse than the beginning."

every case in which Christ operates on men, the devils are drawn into a contest with him, and sink beneath his power. Let us, therefore, hold it to be a settled point, that the devil is cast out of us, whenever Christ shines upon us, and displays his grace towards us by some manifestation.

Secondly, the wretched condition of the whole human race is here described to us ; for it follows that the devil has a residence within man, since he is driven from it by the Son of God. Now what is here said relates not to one individual or to another, but to the whole posterity of Adam. And this is the glory of our nature, that the devil has his seat within us, and inhabits both the body and the soul. So much the more illustrious is the display of the mercy of God, when we, who were the loathsome dens of the devil, are made temples to Himself, and consecrated for a habitation of His Spirit.

Thirdly, we have here a description of Satan's nature. He never ceases to do us injury, but is continually busy, and moves from one place to another. In a word, he directs all his efforts to accomplish our destruction ; and above all, when he has been vanquished and put to flight by Christ, it only tends more to whet his rage and keenness to do us injury.[1] Before Christ makes us partakers of his energy, it seems as if it were in sport and amusement that this enemy reigns over us ;[2] but when he has been driven out, he conceives resentment at having lost his prey, collects new forces, and arouses all his senses to attack us anew.

He walketh through dry places. This is a metaphorical expression, and denotes that to dwell out of men is to him a wretched banishment, and resembles a barren wilderness. Such, too, is the import of the phrase, *seeking rest,* so long as he dwells out of men ; for then he is displeased and tormented, and ceases not to labour by one means or by another, till he recover what he has lost.[3] Let us, therefore, learn that,

[1] " Il aiguise tant plus son appetit enragé de nous mal-faire ;"—" so much the more does it whet his enraged appetite to do us injury."
[2] " Ce mal-heureux ennemi nous manie tout a son aise, et regne en nous comme en se iouant ;"—" this unhappy foe governs us altogether at his ease, and reigns over us, as it were, in sport."
[3] " Iusques à ce qu'il retrouve la proye qu'on luy a ostee d'entre

as soon as Christ calls us, a sharper and fiercer contest is prepared for us. Though he meditates the destruction of all, and though the words of Peter apply to all without exception, that he *goeth about as a roaring lion, and seeketh whom he may devour,* (1 Pet. v. 8,) yet we are plainly taught by these words of Christ, that Satan views with deeper hatred, and attacks with greater fierceness and rage, those who have been rescued from his snares. Such an admonition, however, ought not to inspire us with terror, but to arouse us to keep diligent watch, and to put on the spiritual armour, that we may make a brave resistance.

44. *He findeth it empty.* Christ is unquestionably describing those who, being destitute of the Spirit of God, are prepared for receiving the devil; for believers, in whom the Spirit of God efficaciously dwells, are fortified on all sides, so that no opening is left for Satan. The metaphor of *a house swept and embellished* is taken from men who find pleasure in the cleanness and neatness of their apartments; for to Satan no sight is beautiful but deformity itself, and no smell is sweet but filth and nastiness. The meaning therefore is, that Satan never finds a more appropriate habitation within us, than when, having parted with Christ, we receive Satan as a guest.[1] His highest delight is in that *emptiness* by which the neglect of divine grace is followed.[2]

45. *He taketh with him seven other spirits.* The number *seven* is here used indefinitely, as in many other passages. By these words Christ shows that if we fall from his grace, our subjection to Satan is doubled, so that he treats us with

mains;"—" till he recover the prey that has been snatched out of his hands."

[1] " Que quand, laissans Christ, et nous esloignans de luy, nous attirons cest hoste à nous;"—" that when leaving Christ, and withdrawing from him, we entice this guest."

[2] " Ce qu'il aime donc le plus, et ou il prend un souverain plaisir, c'est ceste place vuide qui se fait quand l'homme ne tient conte de la grace de Dieu, et est nonchalant d'en bien user;"—" that which he loves most, and in which he takes a supreme pleasure, is the emptiness which is produced, when man sets no value on the grace of God, and is indifferent about making a good use of it."

greater cruelty than before, and that this is the just punishment of our slothfulness.¹ Let us not then suppose that the devil has been vanquished by a single combat, because he has once gone out of us. On the contrary, let us remember that, as his lodgment within us was of old standing, ever since we were born, he has knowledge and experience of all the approaches by which he may reach us; and that, if there be no open and direct entrance, he has dexterity enough to creep in by small holes or winding crevices.² We must, therefore, endeavour that Christ, holding his reign within us, may block up all the entrances of his adversary. Whatever may be the fierceness or violence of Satan's attacks, they ought not to intimidate the sons of God, whom the invincible power of the Holy Spirit preserves in safety. We know that the punishment which is here threatened is addressed to none but those who despise the grace of God, and who, by extinguishing the light of faith, and banishing the desire of godliness,³ become profane.

MATTHEW.	MARK.	LUKE.
XII. 46. And while he was still talking to the multitudes, lo, his mother and his brethren stood without, desiring to speak to him. 47. And one said to him, Lo, thy mother and thy brethren stand without, desiring to speak to thee. 48. But he	III. 31. And his mother and brethren came, and standing without, sent to him to call him.⁴ 32. And the multitude was sitting around him, and they say to him, Lo, thy mother and thy brethren without seek thee. 33. And	XI. 27. And it happened while he was saying these things, a certain woman from among the multitude, raising her voice, said to him, Blessed is the womb that bore thee, and the breasts which thou hast sucked. 28. But he said, Nay, rather, blessed are they that hear the word of God, and keep it.

¹ "En sorte qu'il nous tient le pied sur la gorge plus estroitement que devant : et qu'en cela nous recevons une iuste recompense et punition de nostre nonchalance ;"—" so that he holds his foot upon our throat more straitly than before ; and that in this we have a just reward of our indifference."
² "Et s'il n'y peut entrer de front et apertement, il est assez fin pour s'y fourrer secretement par dessous terre, ou par quelque fente à costé ;"— " and if he cannot enter it in front and openly, he is cunning enough to dig into it secretly below ground, or by some chink in the side."
³ " Et effaçans l'amour de la crainte de Dieu ;"—" and effacing the love of the fear of God."
⁴ "Et estans dehors envoyerent quelques uns vers luy pour l'appeler ;" —" and being without, sent some persons to him to call him."

MATTHEW.	MARK.	LUKE.
answering said to him who had told him, Who is my mother, or who are my brethren? 49. And stretching out his hand toward his disciples, he said, Lo, my mother and my brethren. 50. For whosoever shall do the will of my Father who is in heaven, he is my brother, and sister, and mother.	he answered, saying to them, Who is my mother and my brethren? 34. And when he had looked all around on the disciples sitting around him, he said, Lo, my mother and my brethren. 35. For he who shall do the will of God is my brother, and my sister, and mother.	VIII. 19. And his mother and his brethren came to him, and could not reach him on account of the crowd. 20. And it was related and told him, Thy mother and thy brethren stand without, desiring to see thee. 21. Who answering said to them, My mother and my brethren are those who hear the word of God, and do it.[1]

Luke XI. 27. *Blessed is the womb.* By this eulogium the woman intended to magnify the excellence of Christ; for she had no reference to Mary,[2] whom, perhaps, she had never seen. And yet it tends in a high degree to illustrate the glory of Christ, that she pronounces *the womb that bore him* to be noble and *blessed.* Nor was the blessing inappropriate, but in strict accordance with the manner of Scripture; for we know that offspring, and particularly when endued with distinguished virtues, is declared to be a remarkable gift of God, preferable to all others. It cannot even be denied that God conferred the highest honour on Mary, by choosing and appointing her to be the mother of his Son. And yet Christ's reply is so far from assenting to this female voice, that it contains an indirect reproof.

Nay, rather, blessed are they that hear the word of God. We see that Christ treats almost as a matter of indifference that point on which the woman had set a high value. And undoubtedly what she supposed to be Mary's highest honour was far inferior to the other favours which she had received; for it was of vastly greater importance to be regenerated by the Spirit of God than to conceive Christ, according to the

---

[1] "Mais luy respondant leur dit, Ceux-la sont ma mere et mes freres, qui oyent la parole de Dieu, et la mettent en effect;"—"but he answering said to them, Those are my mother and my brethren, who hear the word of God, and put it in practice."

[2] "Il ne faut pas penser qu'elle eust regard a Marie;"—"we must not suppose that she had reference to Mary."

flesh, in her womb; to have Christ living spiritually within her than to suckle him with her breasts. In a word, the highest happiness and glory of the holy Virgin consisted in her being a member of his Son, so that the heavenly Father reckoned her in the number of new creatures.

In my opinion, however, it was for another reason, and with a view to another object, that Christ now corrected the saying of the woman. It was because men are commonly chargeable with neglecting even those gifts of God, on which they gaze with astonishment, and bestow the highest praise. This woman, in applauding Christ, had left out what was of the very highest consequence, that in him salvation is exhibited to all; and, therefore, it was a feeble commendation, that made no mention of his grace and power, which is extended to all. Christ justly claims for himself another kind of praise, not that his mother alone is reckoned *blessed*, but that he brings to us all perfect and eternal happiness. We never form a just estimate of the excellence of Christ, till we consider for what purpose he was given to us by the Father, and perceive the benefits which he has brought to us, so that we who are wretched in ourselves may become happy in him. But why does he say nothing about himself, and mention only the word of God? It is because in this way he opens to us all his treasures; for without the word he has no intercourse with us, nor we with him. Communicating himself to us by *the word*, he rightly and properly calls us to *hear and keep it*, that by faith he may become ours.

We now see the difference between Christ's reply and the woman's commendation; for the *blessedness*, which she had limited to his own relatives, is a favour which he offers freely to all. He shows that we ought to entertain no ordinary esteem for him, because he has all *the treasures* of life, *blessedness*, and glory, *hidden in him*, (Col. ii. 3,) which he dispenses by the word, that they may be communicated to those who embrace *the word* by faith; for God's free adoption of us, which we obtain by faith, is the key to the kingdom of heaven. The connection between the two things must also be observed. We must first *hear*, and then *keep;* for as *faith cometh by hearing*, (Rom. x. 17,) it is in this way that the spiritual life must be commenced. Now as the simple hearing is like a transitory *looking into a mirror*,[1] as James says, (i. 23,) he likewise adds, *the keeping of the word*, which means the effectual reception of it, when it strikes its roots deep into our hearts, and yields its fruit. The forgetful hearer, whose ears alone are struck by the outward doctrine, gains no advantage. On the other hand, they who boast that they are satisfied with the secret inspiration, and on this ground disregard the outward preaching, shut themselves out from the heavenly life. What the Son of God *hath joined let not men*, with wicked rashness, *put asunder*, (Matth. xix. 6.) The Papists discover amazing stupidity by singing, in honour of Mary, those very words by which their superstition is expressly condemned, and who, in giving thanks, detach the woman's saying, and leave out the correction.[2] But it was proper that such a universal stupefaction should come upon those who intentionally profane, at their pleasure, the sacred word of God.

Luke VIII. 19. *And his mother and his brethren came to him.* There is an apparent discrepancy here between Luke and the other two Evangelists; for, according to their arrangement of the narrative, they represent Christ's mother and cousins as having come, while he was discoursing about *the unclean spirit*, while he refers to a different occasion, and mentions only the woman's exclamation, which we have just now explained. But we know that the Evangelists were not very exact as to the order of dates, or even in detailing minutely every thing that Christ did or said, so that the difficulty is soon removed. Luke does not state at what precise time Christ's mother came to him; but what the other two Evangelists relate before the parable of the sower

---

[1] " Autant que l'ouye simple est comme quand on regarde en un mirroir, et que la memoire s'en escoule incontinent;"—" since the simple hearing is as when we look into a mirror, and the remembrance of it immediately passes away."

[2] " Et en leurs graces apres le repas, ils prenent le dire de la femme, laissans la correction qui estoit le principal;"—" and in their thanksgivings after a meal, they employ the woman's saying, leaving out the correction, which was the most important matter."

he introduces after it. The account which he gives of the exclamation of the woman from among the multitude bears some resemblance to this narrative; for inconsiderate zeal may have led her to exalt to the highest pitch what she imagined that Christ had unduly lowered.

All the three Evangelists agree in stating, that while Christ was discoursing in the midst of a crowd of people, his *mother and brethren came to him.* The reason must have been either that they were anxious about him, or that they were desirous of instruction; for it is not without some good reason that they endeavour to approach him, and it is not probable that those who accompanied the holy mother were unbelievers. Ambrose and Chrysostom accuse Mary of ambition, but without any probability. What necessity is there for such a conjecture, when the testimony of the Spirit everywhere bestows commendation on her distinguished piety and modesty? The warmth of natural affection may have carried them beyond the bounds of propriety: this I do not deny, but I have no doubt that they were led by pious zeal to seek his society. Matthew relates that the message respecting their arrival was brought by *one* individual: Mark and Luke say that he was informed by many persons. But there is no inconsistency here; for the message which his mother sent to call him would be communicated, as usually happens, from one hand to another, till at length it reached him.

Matthew XII. 48. *Who is my mother?* These words were unquestionably intended to reprove Mary's eagerness, and she certainly acted improperly in attempting to interrupt the progress of his discourse.[1] At the same time, by disparaging the relationship of flesh and blood, our Lord teaches a very useful doctrine; for he admits all his disciples and all believers to the same honourable rank, as if they were his nearest relatives, or rather he places them in the room of his *mother and brethren.* Now this statement is closely connected with the office of Christ; for he tells us

---

[1] "Et de faict, c'estoit mal avisé à elle de vouloir ainsi rompre son propos, lors qu'il enseignoit;"—" and in fact, it was foolish in her to wish to break off his discourse in this manner, while he was teaching."

that he has been given, not to a small number of individuals, but to all the godly, who are united in one body with him by faith. He tells us also, that there is no tie of relationship more sacred than spiritual relationship, because we ought not to think of him according to the flesh, but according to the power of his Spirit which he has received from the Father to renew men, so that those who are by nature the polluted and accursed seed of Abraham begin to be by grace the holy and heavenly sons of God. In like manner, Paul affirms that to *know Christ after the flesh* is not to know him properly, (2 Cor. v. 16,) because we ought rather to consider that renovation of the world, which far exceeds human power, and which takes place when he forms us anew by his Spirit to the image of God. To sum up the whole, this passage, first, teaches us to behold Christ with the eyes of faith; and, secondly, it informs us, that every one who is regenerated by the Spirit, and gives himself up entirely to God for true justification, is thus admitted to the closest union with Christ, and becomes one with him.

50. *For whosoever shall do the will of my Father who is in heaven.* When he says that they *do the will of his Father*, he does not mean that they fulfil, in a perfect manner, the whole righteousness of the law; for in that sense the name *brother*, which is here given by him to his disciples, would not apply to any man.[1] But his design is, to bestow the highest commendation on faith, which is the source and origin of holy obedience, and at the same time covers the defects and sins of the flesh, that they may not be imputed. *This*, says Christ in a well-known passage, *is the will of my Father, that whosoever seeth the Son, and believeth in him, may not perish, but have eternal life,* (John vi. 40.) Although these words seem to imply that Christ has no regard to the ties of blood, yet we know that in reality he paid the strictest attention to human order,[2] and discharged his lawful

[1] " Ne conviendroit à homme vivant ;"—" would not apply to any man living."
[2] " Qu'à la verité il a observé et entretenu en toute saincteté l'ordre qui est entre les hommes ;"—" that in reality he observed and maintained, with all holiness, the order which exists among men."

duties towards relatives; but points out that, in comparison of spiritual relationship, no regard, or very little, is due to the relationship of the flesh. Let us therefore attend to this comparison, so as to perform all that nature can justly claim, and, at the same time, not to be too strongly attached to flesh and blood. Again, as Christ bestows on the disciples of his Gospel the inestimable honour of being reckoned as his brethren, we must be held guilty of the basest ingratitude, if we do not disregard all the desires of the flesh, and direct every effort towards this object.

MATTHEW.	LUKE.
XII. 38. Then some of the scribes and Pharisees asked him, saying, Master, we desire to see a sign from thee. 39. But he answering said to them, A wicked and adulterous generation seeketh a sign,[1] and a sign shall not be given to it, except the sign of Jonah the prophet. 40. For as Jonah was in the belly of the whale three days and three nights, so will the Son of man be three days and three nights in the heart of the earth. 41. The men of Nineveh will rise in judgment with this generation, and will condemn it: for they repented at the preaching of Jonah; and, lo, a greater than Jonah is here.[2] 42. The queen of the south will rise in judgment with this generation, and will condemn it: for she came from the ends of the earth to hear the wisdom of Solomon; and, lo, a greater than Solomon is here.[3]	XI. 16. And others tempting sought from him a sign from heaven.—(*A little after*,) 29. And while the multitudes were crowding together, he began to say, This is a wicked generation: it seeketh a sign, and a sign shall not be given to it, except the sign of Jonah the prophet. 30. For as Jonah was a sign to the Ninevites, so shall the Son of man be also to this nation. 31. The queen of the south will rise in judgment with the men of this nation, and will condemn them: for she came from the ends of the earth to hear the wisdom of Solomon; and, lo, a greater than Solomon is here. 32. The men of Nineveh will rise in judgment with this nation, and will condemn it: for they were brought to repentance by the preaching of Jonah; and, lo, a greater than Jonah is here.

Luke XI. 16. *And others tempting sought from him a sign.* Something similar to this is afterwards related by Matthew, (xvi. 4,) and by Mark, (viii. 11, 12.) Hence it is evident,

---

[1] " Ausquels il respondit, et leur dit, La nation meschante et adultere (*ou, bastarde*) requiert un signe;"—" to whom he answered, and said to them, The wicked and adulterous (*or, bastard*) nation demandeth a sign."

[2] " Et voyci, il y a ici plus que Ionas;"—" and, lo, there is here a greater than Jonah."

[3] " Et voyci, il y a ici plus que Salomon;"—" and, lo, there is here a greater than Solomon."

that Christ repeatedly attacked them on this subject, so that there was no end to the wickedness of those men who had once resolved[1] to oppose the truth. There can be no doubt that they ask a sign, in order to plead, as a plausible pretence for their unbelief, that Christ's calling has not been duly attested. They do not express such submissiveness as to be prepared to yield to two or three miracles, and still less to be satisfied with a single miracle; but as I hinted a little before, they apologize for not believing the Gospel on this pretence, that Christ shows no sign of it from heaven.[2] He had already performed miracles before their eyes sufficiently numerous and manifest; but as if these were not enough for the confirmation of doctrine, they wish to have something exhibited from heaven, by which God will, as it were, make a visible appearance. They call him *Master*, according to custom; for such was the appellation given at that time to all scribes and expounders of the law. But they do not acknowledge him to be a prophet of God, till he produce a testimony from heaven. The meaning therefore is: "Since thou professest to be a teacher and Master, if thou desirest that we should be thy disciples, let God declare from heaven that He is the Author of thy teaching, and let Him confirm thy calling by a miracle."

Matthew XII. 39. *A wicked generation.* He does not merely charge that age with malice, but pronounces the Jews—or at least the scribes, and those who resembled them—to be a *wicked nation;* thus declaring that they laboured under a hereditary disease of obstinacy. The word γενεά sometimes denotes an *age*, and sometimes a *people* or *nation*. He calls them *adulterous*, that is, spurious or illegitimate,[3] because they were degenerated from the holy fathers; as the prophets reproach the men of their age with being

[1] " Qui une fois s'estoyent endurcis;"—"who had once become hardened."
[2] " Que Christ ne leur monstre aucun signe d'enhaut qui soit pour seeler ceste doctrine;"—"that Christ shows them no sign from above that is sufficient to seal this doctrine."
[3] " Il entend qu'ils sont enfans bastars;"—"he means that they are bastard children."

not the descendants of Abraham, but the ungodly seed of Canaan.

Seeks a sign. This leads to the inquiry, Does Christ address them with such harshness of language, because they wished to have a sign given them? for on other occasions God manifests that He is not so much displeased on this account. Gideon asks *a sign,* (Judges vi. 17,) and God is not angry, but grants his request; and though Gideon becomes importunate and asks another sign, yet God condescends to his weakness. Hezekiah does not ask a *sign,* and it is offered to him, though unsolicited, (Isa. xxxviii. 7, 8.) Ahaz is severely blamed for refusing to ask a sign, as the prophet had enjoined him to do, (Isa. vii. 11.) It is not solely, therefore, because they *ask a sign,* that Christ makes this attack upon the scribes, but because they are ungrateful to God, wickedly despise so many of his wonderful works, and try to find a subterfuge for not obeying his word. What a display was this, I do not say of indifference, but of malice, in shutting their eyes against so many *signs!* There was, therefore, no proper ground for this annoyance; and they had no other object in view than to appear to have a good reason for rejecting Christ. Paul condemns their posterity for the same crime, when he says that the Jews *require a sign,* (1 Cor. i. 22.)

A sign shall not be given to it. They had already been convicted by various miracles, and Christ does not abstain from exerting his power among them, for the purpose of rendering them inexcusable, but only means that *one sign* would stand for all, because they were unworthy of having their ungodly desire granted. "Let them rest satisfied," says he, " with this sign, that as Jonah, brought up from the bottom of the sea, preached to the Ninevites, so they will hear the voice of a prophet risen from the dead." The most of commentators, I am aware, display greater ingenuity in expounding this passage; but as the resemblance between Christ and Jonah does not hold at every point, we must inquire in what respect Christ compares himself to Jonah. For my own part, leaving the speculations of other men, I think that Christ intends to mark out that single point of resemblance which I have already hinted, that he will be their prophet after that he is risen from the dead. "You despise," he says, "the Son of God, who has come down to you from heaven: but I am yet to die, and to rise from the grave, and to speak to you after my resurrection, as Jonah came from the bottom of the sea to Nineveh." In this manner our Lord cuts off every pretence for their wicked demands, by threatening that he will be their Prophet after his resurrection, since they do not receive him while clothed with mortal flesh.

Luke XI. 30. *As Jonah was a sign to the Ninevites.* He declares that he will be *a sign* to them, as *Jonah* was to the inhabitants of Nineveh. But the word *sign* is not taken in its ordinary sense, as pointing out something, but as denoting what is widely removed from the ordinary course of nature. In this sense Jonah's mission was miraculous, when he was brought out of the belly of the fish, as if from the grave, to call *the Ninevites* to repentance. *Three days and three nights.* This is in accordance with a well-known figure of speech.[1] As the *night* is an appendage to the *day*, or rather, as the day consists of two parts, light and darkness, he expresses a day by a day and a night, and where there was half a day, he puts down a whole day.

Matthew XII. 41. *The men of Nineveh will rise in judgment.* Having spoken of the Ninevites, Christ takes occasion to show that the scribes and others, by whom his doctrine is rejected, are worse than the Ninevites were. "Ungodly men," he says, "who never had heard a word of the true God, repented at the voice of an unknown and foreign person who came to them; while this country, which is the sanctuary of heavenly doctrine, hears not the Son of God, and the promised Redeemer." Here lies the contrast which is implied in the comparison. We know who the Ninevites

---

[1] " Quant aux *trois nuits*, il y a ici (comme on scait bien) une figure que les Grecs et Latins appellent Synecdoche ;"—" as to the *three nights*, there is here (as is well known) a figure which the Greek and Latin writers call Synecdoche."

were, men altogether unaccustomed to hear prophets, and destitute of the true doctrine. *Jonah* had no rank to secure their respect, but was likely to be rejected as a foreigner. The Jews, on the other hand, boasted that among them the Word of God had its seat and habitation. If they had beheld Christ with pure eyes,[1] they must have acknowledged, not only that he was a teacher sent from heaven, but that he was the Messiah, and the promised Author of Salvation. But if that nation was convicted of desperate ungodliness, for despising Christ while he spoke to them on earth, we are worse than all the unbelievers that ever existed, if the Son of God, now that he inhabits his sanctuary in heaven, and addresses us with a heavenly voice, does not bring us to obey him. Whether *the men of Nineveh* were truly and perfectly turned to God I judge it unnecessary to inquire. It is enough for the present purpose that they were so deeply affected by the teaching of Jonah, as to have their minds directed to repentance.

42. *The queen of the south.* As Ethiopia lies in a southerly direction from Judea, I willingly concur with Josephus and other writers, who assert that she was the queen of Ethiopia. In sacred history she is called *the queen of Sheba,* (2 Chron. ix. 1.) We must not suppose this *Sheba* to be the country of *Saba,* which rather lay toward the east, but a town situated in Meroë, an island on the Nile, which was the metropolis of the kingdom. Here, too, we must attend to the points of contrast. A woman who had not been at all educated in the school of God, was induced, by the desire of instruction, to come from a distant region to Solomon, an earthly king; while the Jews, who had been instructed in the divine law, reject their highest and only teacher, the Prince of all the prophets. The word *condemn* relates not to the persons, but to the fact itself, and the example which it yields.

---

[1] " D'un œil pur, et sans mauvaise affection ;"—" with a pure eye, and without evil disposition.'

MATTHEW.	MARK.	LUKE.
XIII. 1. And on the same day Jesus went out of the house, and sat down near the sea. 2. And great multitudes were gathered to him, so that he entered into a ship, and sat down, and the whole multitude was standing on the shore. 3. And he said many things to them by parables, saying, Lo, one who was sowing went out to sow. 4. And while he was sowing, some seeds fell near the road, and the birds came and devoured them. 5. And some fell on stony places, where they had not much earth, and immediately they sprang up, because they had not depth of earth. 6. But when the sun rose, they were burnt up, and because they had not a root, they withered away. 7. Others again fell on thorns, and the thorns grew up, and choked them. 8. And others fell on good soil, and yielded fruit: some a hundred-fold, some sixty-fold, some thirty-fold. 9. He that hath ears to hear, let him hear. 10. And the disciples approaching said to him, Why dost thou speak to them by parables? 11. But he answering, said to them, To you it is given to know the mysteries[1] of the kingdom of heaven, but to them it is not given. 12. For whosoever hath, it shall be given to him, and he shall be rendered more wealthy;[2] and whosoever	IV. 1. And again he began to teach near the sea, and a great multitude was gathered to him, so that, entering into a ship, he sat on the sea, and the whole multitude was near the sea on land. 2. And he taught them many things by parables, and said to them in his doctrine: 3. Hear, lo, a sower went out to sow. 4. And it happened while he was sowing, some fell close to the road; and the fowls of heaven came and ate them up. 5. And some fell on stony places, where it had not much earth, and immediately it sprang up, because it had not depth of earth. 6. And when the sun had risen, it was scorched; and because it had not a root, it withered. 7. And some fell among thorns; and the thorns grew, and choked it, and it did not yield fruit. 8. And some fell on good soil, and yielded fruit springing up and growing, and produced some thirty, and some sixty, and some a hundred. 9. And he	VIII. 1. And it happened afterwards, and he was travelling through each city and village,[3] preaching and proclaiming the glad tidings of the kingdom of God; and the twelve were with him, 2. And likewise some women, who had been cured of evil spirits and diseases, Mary, who is called Magdalene, out of whom had gone seven devils, 3. And Joanna, the wife of Chuza, Herod's steward, and Susanna, and many others, who assisted him out of their property 4. And while a very great multitude was assembling, and while they were crowding to him out of each city, he said by a parable: 5. One who sowed went out to sow his seed, and while he was sowing, some fell near the road, and was trodden down, and the fowls of heaven ate it up. 6. And some fell on a rock, and when it was sprung up, it withered, because it had not moisture. 7. And some fell among thorns, and the thorns springing up along with it, choked it. 8. And some fell on a

[1] " De cognoistre les secrets ;"—" to know the secrets."
[2] " Et en aura tant plus ;"—" and he shall have so much the more of it."
[3] " Il alloit de ville en ville, et de village en village ;"—" he was going from town to town, and from village to village."

MATTHEW.	MARK.	LUKE.
hath not, even that which he hath shall be taken from him. 13. For this reason I speak to them in parables, because seeing, they do not see, and hearing, they do not hear nor understand. 14. And in them is fulfilled the prophecy of Isaiah, which saith, With the ears you shall hear, and shall not understand, and seeing, you shall see, and shall not perceive. 15. For the heart of this people hath become gross, and with their ears they have heard heavily, and their eyes they have shut, lest at any time they should see with their eyes, and hear with their ears, and understand with the heart, and be converted, and I should heal them. 16. But your eyes are blessed, for they see; and your ears, for they hear. 17. Verily, I say to you, That many prophets and righteous men have desired to see the things which you see, and have not seen them, and to hear the things which you hear, and have not heard them.	said to them, He that hath ears to hear, let him hear. 10. And when he began to be alone, those who were around him, with the twelve, asked him about the parable. 11. And he said to them, To you it is given to know the mystery¹ of the kingdom of God, but to those who are without all things are done by parables: 12. That seeing, they may see and may not perceive, and hearing, they may hear and may not understand, lest at any time they may be converted, and their sins may be forgiven them.—(*A little after*,) 24. And he said to them, Observe what you hear: with what measure you measure, the same admeasurement shall be made to you, and it shall be added to you who shall hear. 25. For to him who hath it shall be given; and he that hath not, even that which he hath shall be taken away from him.	good soil, and, springing up, produced fruit a hundred-fold. Saying these things, he exclaimed, He that hath ears to hear, let him hear. 9. And his disciples asked him, saying, What was this parable?² 10. But he said, To you it is given to know the mysteries³ of the kingdom of God, but to the rest by parables; that seeing, they may not see, and hearing, they may not understand.—(*A little after*,) 18. Consider then how you hear. For whosoever hath, it shall be given to him; and whosoever hath not, even that which he thinketh that he hath shall be taken from him. X. 23. And turning to his disciples, he said to them privately, Blessed are the eyes that see the things which you see. 24. For I say to you, That many prophets and kings have desired to see the things which you see, and have not seen them; and to hear the things which you hear, and have not heard them.

What I have here introduced from Luke belongs, perhaps, to another time; but I saw no necessity for separating what

---

¹ "De cognoistre le secret;"—"to know the secret."
² "Et ses disciples l'interroguerent, dema, dans quelle estoit ceste similitude;"—"and his disciples interrogated him, asking what was this parable."
³ "De cognoistre les secrets;"—"to know the secrets."

he has placed in immediate connection. First, he says that the *twelve* apostles *preached the kingdom of God* along with Christ; from which we infer that, though the ordinary office of teaching had not yet been committed to them, they constantly attended as heralds to procure an audience for their Master; and, therefore, though they held an inferior rank, they are said to have been Christ's assistants. Next, he adds, that among those who accompanied Christ were *certain women, who had been cured of evil spirits and diseases,* such as *Mary Magdalene,* who had been tormented by *seven devils.* To be associated with such persons might be thought dishonourable; for what could be more unworthy of the Son of God than to lead about with him women who were marked with infamy? But this enables us more clearly to perceive that the crimes with which we were loaded before we believed, are so far from diminishing the glory of Christ, that they tend rather to raise it to a higher pitch. And, certainly, it is not said, that the Church which he elected was found by him to be without spot and blemish, but that he cleansed it with his blood, and made it pure and fair.

The wretched and disgraceful condition of those women, now that they had been delivered from it, redounded greatly to the glory of Christ, by holding out public manifestations of his power and grace. At the same time, Luke applauds their gratitude in following their Deliverer, and disregarding the ridicule of the world.[1] Beyond all question, they were pointed at with the finger on every side, and the presence of Christ served for a platform to exhibit them; but they do not refuse to have their own shame made generally known, provided that the grace of Christ be not concealed. On the contrary, they willingly endure to be humbled, in order to become a mirror, by which he may be illustriously displayed.

In *Mary,* the boundless goodness of Christ was displayed in an astonishing manner. A woman, who had been possessed by *seven devils,* and might be said to have been the meanest

[1] " D'autant qu'elles ont suyvi leur Liberateur, nonobstant l'ignominie du monde qu'il leur faloit endurer en ce faisant ;"—" because they followed their Deliverer, notwithstanding the ignominy of the world which they must endure by so doing."

slave of Satan, was not merely honoured to be his disciple, but admitted to enjoy his society. Luke adds the surname *Magdalene*, to distinguish her from the sister of Martha, and other persons of the name of *Mary*, who are mentioned in other passages, (John xi. 1; xix. 25.)

Luke VIII. 3. *Joanna, the wife of Chuza.* It is uncertain whether or not Luke intended his statement to be applied to those women in the same manner as to *Mary*. To me it appears probable that she is placed first in order, as a person in whom Christ had given a signal display of his power; and that *the wife of Chuza, and Susanna*, matrons of respectability and of spotless reputation, are mentioned afterwards, because they had only been cured of ordinary diseases. Those matrons being wealthy and of high rank, it reflects higher commendation on their pious zeal, that they supply Christ's expenses out of their own property, and, not satisfied with so doing, leave the care of their household affairs, and choose to follow him, attended by reproach and many other inconveniences, through various and uncertain habitations, instead of living quietly and at ease in their own houses. It is even possible, that *Chuza, Herod's steward*, being too like his master, was strongly opposed to what his wife did in this matter, but that the pious woman overcame this opposition by the ardour and constancy of her zeal.

Matthew XIII. 2. *And great multitudes were gathered together to him.* It is not without good reason that the Evangelists begin with informing us that a vast multitude had assembled, and that when Christ beheld them, he was led to compare his doctrine to *seed*. That *multitude* had been collected from various places: all were held in suspense; all were alike eager to hear, but not equally desirous to receive instruction. The design of the parable was to inform them, that the *seed* of doctrine, which is scattered far and wide, is not everywhere productive; because it does not always find a fertile and well cultivated soil. Christ declared that he was there in the capacity of a husbandman, who was going out *to sow seed*, but that many of his hearers resembled an uncultivated and parched soil, while others resembled a thorny soil; so that the labour and the very seed were thrown away. I forbear to make any farther inquiry into the meaning of the parable, till we come to the explanation of it; which, as we shall find, is shortly afterwards given by our Lord. It may only be necessary, for the present, to remind the reader, that if those who ran from distant places to Christ, like hungry persons, are compared to an unproductive and barren soil, we need not wonder if, in our own day, the Gospel does not yield fruit in many, of whom some are lazy and sluggish, others hear with indifference, and others are scarcely drawn even to hear.

9. *He that hath ears to hear, let him hear.* These words were intended partly to show, that all were not endued with true understanding to comprehend what he said, and partly to arouse his disciples to consider attentively that doctrine which is not readily and easily understood by all. Indeed, he makes a distinction among the hearers, by pronouncing some to have ears, and others to be deaf. If it is next inquired, how it comes to pass that the former have ears, Scripture testifies in other passages, that it is the Lord who *pierces the ears,* (Psalm xl. 7,) and that no man obtains or accomplishes this by his own industry.

10. *The disciples approaching said to him.* From the words of Matthew it is evident, that the disciples did not merely look to themselves, but wished also to consult the benefit of others. Being unable to comprehend the parable, they concluded that it would be as little understood by the people; and, therefore, they complain that Christ employed language from which his hearers could derive no profit. Now though parables are generally found to illustrate the subject of which they treat, yet the uninterrupted course of a metaphor may lead to obscurity.[1] So then Christ, in delivering this parable,

---

[1] "Si est-ce toutesfois qu'elles sont obscures et enveloppees, quand on continue tousiours la metaphore sans rien y entremesler;"—"yet they are obscure and involved, when the metaphor is constantly pursued, without any thing being intermingled with it."

intended to wrap up, in an allegory, what he might have said more plainly and fully, without a figure.[1] But now that the exposition is added, the figurative discourse has greater energy and force than if it had been simple: by which is meant, that it is not only fitted to produce a more powerful impression on the mind, but is also more clear. So highly important is the manner in which any thing is said.[2]

11. *To you it is given to know the mysteries*[3] *of the kingdom of heaven.* From this reply of Christ we learn, that the doctrine of salvation is proclaimed by God to men for various purposes; for Christ declares that he intentionally spoke obscurely, in order that his discourse might be a riddle to many, and might only strike their ears with a confused and doubtful sound. It will perhaps be objected, that this is inconsistent with that prophecy, *I have not spoken in secret, nor in a dark corner: I said not in vain to the seed of Jacob, Seek me,* (Isa. xlv. 19;) or with the commendations which David pronounces on the Law, that it *is a lamp to the feet,* and that it *giveth wisdom to little children* (Ps. cxix. 105, 130.) But the answer is easy: the word of God, in its own nature, is always bright,[4] but its light is choked by the darkness of men. Though the Law was concealed, as it were, by a kind of veil, yet the truth of God shone brightly in it, if the eyes of many had not been blinded. With respect to the Gospel, Paul affirms with truth, that it is *hidden* to none but to the reprobate, and to those who are devoted to destruction, *whose minds Satan hath blinded,* (2 Cor. iv. 3, 4.) Besides, it ought to be understood, that the power of enlightening which David mentions, and the familiar manner of teaching which Isaiah predicts, refer exclusively to the elect people.

Still it remains a fixed principle, that the word of God is

---

[1] " En usant de termes communs ;"—" by using ordinary terms."
[2] " Voyla comme il y a bien à regarder comment on couche ou on deduit un propos ;"—" this shows us the great attention that is due to the manner in which a discourse is expressed or conveyed."
[3] " De cognoistre les secrets ;"—" to know the secrets."
[4] " La parole de Dieu de sa nature est tousiours pleine de lumiere et clairté ;"—" the word of God in its own nature is always full of light and brightness."

not obscure, except so far as the world darkens it by its own blindness. And yet the Lord conceals its mysteries, so that the perception of them may not reach the reprobate.[1] There are two ways in which he deprives them of the light of his doctrine. Sometimes he states, in a dark manner, what might be more clearly expressed; and sometimes he explains his mind fully, without ambiguity and without metaphor, but strikes their senses with dulness and their minds with stupidity, so that they are blind amidst bright sunshine.

Such is the import of those dreadful threatenings, in which Isaiah forewarns, that he will be to the people a barbarian, speaking in a foreign and unknown language; that the prophetical visions will be to the learned a shut and sealed book, in which they cannot read; and that when the book shall be opened, all will be *unlearned,* and will remain in amazement, through inability to read, (Isa. xxviii. 11; xxix. 11.) Now since Christ has purposely dispensed his doctrine in such a manner, that it might be profitable only to a small number, being firmly seated in their minds, and might hold others in suspense and perplexity, it follows that, by divine appointment, the doctrine of salvation is not proclaimed to all for the same end, but is so regulated by his wonderful purpose, that it is not less *a savour of death to death* to the reprobate than *a life-giving savour* to the elect, (2 Cor. ii. 15, 16.) And that no one may dare to murmur, Paul declares, in that passage, that whatever may be the effect of the Gospel, its *savour,* though deadly, is always *a sweet savour* to God.

To ascertain fully the meaning of the present passage, we must examine more closely the design of Christ, the reason why, and the purpose for which, these words were spoken. First, the comparison is undoubtedly intended by Christ to exhibit the magnitude of the grace bestowed on his disciples, in having specially received what was not given indiscriminately to all. If it is asked, why this privilege was peculiar

---

[1] " Cependant neantmoins il ne laisse point d'estre vray, que le Seigneur tient ses secrets cachez, à fin que le goust et la fruition d'iceux ne parviene aux reprouvez ;"—" yet, nevertheless, it does not cease to be true, that the Lord keeps its secrets hidden, in order that the relish and enjoyment of them may not reach the reprobate."

to the apostles,[1] the reason certainly will not be found in themselves, and Christ, by declaring that it was *given* to them, excludes all merit.[2] Christ declares that there are certain and elect men, on whom God specially bestows this honour of revealing to them his *secrets*, and that others are deprived of this grace. No other reason will be found for this distinction, except that God calls to himself those whom he has gratuitously elected.

12. *For whosoever hath, it shall be given to him.* Christ pursues the subject which I have just mentioned; for he reminds his disciples how kindly God acts towards them, that they may more highly prize his grace, and may acknowledge themselves to be under deeper obligations to his kindness. The same words he afterwards repeats, but in a different sense, (Matt. xxv. 29;) for on that occasion the discourse relates to the lawful use of gifts.[3] But here he simply teaches, that more is *given* to the apostles than to the generality of men, because the heavenly Father is pleased to display in perfection his kindness towards them. *He does not forsake the work of his own hand,* (Ps. cxxxviii. 8.) Those whom he has once begun to form are continually polished more and more, till they are at length brought to the highest perfection. The multiplied favours which are continually flowing from him to us, and the joyful progress which we make, spring from God's contemplation of his own liberality, which prompts him to an uninterrupted course of bounty. And as his riches are inexhaustible,[4] so he is never wearied with enriching his children. Whenever he advances us to a higher degree, let us remember that every increase of the favours which we daily receive from him flows from this source, that it is his purpose to

---

[1] " Si on demande d'ou venoit un tel privilege et honneur aux Apostres plustost aux autres ;"—" if it is asked, whence came such a privilege and honour to the Apostles rather than to the others."

[2] " Exclud toute merite de sa part ;"—" excludes all merit on their part."

[3] " Car là le propos sera touchant le droict et legitime usage des dons de Dieu ;"—" for there the discourse will relate to the right and lawful use of the gifts of God."

[4] " Et comme ses richesses sont infinies, et ne se peuvent espuiser ;"— " and as his riches are infinite, and cannot be exhausted."

complete the work of our salvation already commenced. On the other hand, Christ declares that the reprobate are continually proceeding from bad to worse, till, at length exhausted, they waste away in their own poverty.

And he that hath not, even that which he hath shall be taken from him. This may appear to be a harsh expression; but instead of saying, that *what* the ungodly *have not is taken from them,* Luke softens the harshness and removes the ambiguity by a slight change of the words: *and whosever hath not, even that which he thinketh that he hath shall be taken from him.* And indeed it frequently happens, that the reprobate are endued with eminent gifts, and appear to resemble the children of God: but there is nothing of real value about them; for their mind is destitute of piety, and has only the glitter of an empty show. *Matthew* is therefore justified in saying that they *have nothing;* for what they have is of no value in the sight of God, and has no permanency within. Equally appropriate is the statement of *Luke,* that the gifts, with which they have been endued, are corrupted by them, so that they shine only in the eyes of men, but have nothing more than splendour and empty display. Hence, also, let us learn to aim at progress throughout our whole life; for God grants to us the taste of his heavenly doctrine on the express condition, that we feed on it abundantly from day to day, till we come to be fully satiated with it.

The manner in which *Mark* introduces this sentence has some appearance of confusion. *Consider,* says our Lord, *what you hear;* and then, if they make due progress, he holds out the expectation of more plentiful grace: *it shall be added to you that hear.* Lastly, follows the clause which agrees with the words of *Matthew,* but is inserted in the middle of a sentence which I expounded under the seventh chapter of *Matthew*;[1] for it is not probable that they are here placed in their proper order. The Evangelists, as we have remarked on former occasions, were not very exact in arranging Christ's discourses, but frequently throw together a variety of sayings uttered by him. *Luke* mixes this sentence with other

[1] Harmony, vol. i. p. 315.

discourses of Christ spoken at different times, and likewise points out a different purpose for which Christ used these words. It was that they might be attentive to his doctrine, and not permit the seed of life to pass away unimproved, which ought to be cordially received, and take root in their minds. " Beware," he says, " lest what has been given be taken away from you, if it yield no fruit."

13. *For this reason I speak by parables.* He says that he speaks to the multitude in an obscure manner, because they are not partakers of the true light. And yet, while he declares that a veil is spread over the blind, that they may remain in their darkness, he does not ascribe the blame of this to themselves, but takes occasion to commend more highly the grace bestowed on the Apostles, because it is not equally communicated to all. He assigns no cause for it, except the secret purpose of God; for which, as we shall afterwards see more fully, there is a good reason, though it has been concealed from us. It is not the only design of a *parable* to state, in an obscure manner, what God is not pleased to reveal clearly; but we have said that the *parable* now under our consideration was delivered by Christ, in order that the form of an allegory might present a doubtful riddle.

14. *And in them is fulfilled the prophecy of Isaiah.* He confirms his statement by a prediction of *Isaiah*, that it is far from being a new thing, if many persons derive no advantage from the word of God, which was formerly appointed to the ancient people, for the purpose of inducing greater blindness. This passage of the Prophet is quoted, in a variety of ways, in the New Testament. Paul quotes it (Acts xxviii. 26) to charge the Jews with obstinate malice, and says that they were blinded by the light of the Gospel, because they were bitter and rebellious against God. There he points out the immediate cause, which appeared in the men themselves. But in the Epistle to the Romans (xi. 7) he draws the distinction from a deeper and more hidden source; for he tells us, that *the remnant was saved according to the election of grace,* and that *the rest were blinded,*

according as it is written. The contrast must there be observed; for if it is *the election* of God, and an undeserved *election*, which alone saves any remnant of the people, it follows that all others perish by a hidden, though just, judgment of God. Who are the *rest*, whom Paul contrasts with the *elect remnant*, but those on whom God has not bestowed a special salvation?

Similar reasoning may be applied to the passage in John, (xii. 38;) for he says that *many believed not*, because no man believes, except he to whom God *reveals his arm*, and immediately adds, that *they could not believe, because it is again written, Blind the heart of this people.* Such, too, is the object which Christ has in view, when he ascribes it to the secret purpose of God, that the truth of the Gospel is not revealed indiscriminately to all, but is exhibited at a distance under obscure forms, so as to have no other effect than to overspread the minds of the people with grosser darkness.[1] In all cases, I admit, those whom God blinds will be found to deserve this condemnation; but as the immediate cause is not always obvious in the persons of men, let it be held as a fixed principle, that God enlightens to salvation, and that by a peculiar gift, those whom He has freely chosen; and that all the reprobate are deprived of the light of life, whether God withholds his word from them, or keeps their eyes and ears closed, that they do not hear or see.

Hearing, you shall hear. We now perceive the manner in which Christ applies the prediction of the prophet to the present occasion. He does not quote the prophet's words, nor was it necessary; for Christ reckoned it enough to show, that it was no new or uncommon occurrence, if many were hardened by the word of God. The words of the prophet were, *Go, blind their minds, and harden their hearts*, (Isa. vi. 10.) Matthew ascribes this to the hearers, that they may endure the blame of their own blindness and hardness; for the one cannot be separated from the other. All who have been *given over to a reprobate mind* (Rom. i. 28) do voluntarily, and from

---

[1] " En sorte que c'estoit tousiours pour esblouir de plus en plus les yeux de l entendement du peuple ;"—" so that it was always to dazzle more and more the eyes of the understanding of the people."

inward malice, blind and harden themselves. Nor can it be otherwise, wherever the Spirit of God does not reign, by whom the elect alone are governed. Let us, therefore, attend to this connection, that all whom God does not enlighten with the Spirit of adoption are men of unsound mind; and that, while they are more and more blinded by the word of God, the blame rests wholly on themselves, because this blindness is voluntary. Again, the ministers of the word ought to seek consolation from this passage, if the success of their labours does not always correspond to their wish. Many are so far from profiting by their instruction, that they are rendered worse by it. What has befallen them was experienced by a Prophet,[1] to whom they are not superior. It were, indeed, to be wished, that they should bring all under subjection to God; and they ought to labour and strive for that end. But let them not wonder if that judgment, which God anciently displayed through the ministration of the Prophet, is likewise fulfilled at the present day. At the same time, we ought to be extremely careful, that the fruit of the Gospel be not lost through our negligence.

Mark IV. 12. *That seeing, they may see, and not perceive.* Here it may suffice to state briefly what has already been fully explained, that the doctrine is not, strictly speaking, or by itself, or in its own nature, but by accident, the cause of blindness. When persons of a weak sight come out into sunshine, their eyes become dimmer than before, and that defect is in no way attributed to the sun, but to their eyes. In like manner, when the word of God blinds and hardens the reprobate, as this takes place through their own depravity, it belongs truly and naturally to themselves, but is accidental, as respects the word.

Lest at any time they should be converted. This clause points out the advantage that is gained by *seeing and understanding.* It is, that men, having been *converted* to God, are restored to his favour, and, being reconciled to him, enjoy prosperity and happiness. The true end for which

---

[1] "Il leur advient ce que le Prophete Isaie a experimenté;"—"it happens to them what the Prophet Isaiah experienced."

God desires that his word should be preached is, to reconcile men to himself by renewing their minds and hearts. With respect to the reprobate, on the other hand, Isaiah here declares that the stony hardness remains in them, so that they do not obtain mercy, and that the word fails to produce its effect upon them, so as to soften their minds to repentance.

Matthew XIII. 15. *Lest I should heal them.* In the word *healing*, Matthew, as well as the Prophet, includes deliverance from every evil; for a people afflicted by the hand of God is metaphorically compared by them to a sick man. They say that *healing* is bestowed,[1] when the Lord releases from punishment. But as this healing depends on the pardon of sins, *Mark* describes appropriately and justly its cause and source, *lest they should be converted, and their sins should be forgiven them.* For whence comes the mitigation of chastisements, but because God has been reconciled to us, and makes us the objects of his blessing? Sometimes, no doubt, after removing our guilt, he continues to punish us, either with the view of humbling us the more, or of making us more cautious for the future. And yet, not only does he show evidences of his favour by restoring us to life and health; but as punishments usually terminate when the guilt is removed, *healing* and *forgiveness* are properly introduced together. It must not, however, be concluded, that repentance is the cause of pardon, as if God received into his favour *converted* men, because they deserved it;[2] for *conversion* itself is a mark of God's free favour. Nothing more is expressed than such an order and connection, that God does not forgive the sins of any but those who are dissatisfied with themselves.

[1] " Ils disent qu'il guarit, et remet en santé ;"—" they say that he heals, and restores to health."
[2] " Il ne faut pas conclurre par cela que la repentance, ou conversion, soit cause de nous faire avoir remission et pardon de nos pechez ; comme si Dieu prenoit à merci ceux qui se convertissent, pource qu'ils en sont dignes, et le meritent ;"—" we must not therefore conclude, that repentance, or conversion, is the cause of making us have forgiveness and pardon of our sins ; as if God exercised mercy towards those who are converted, because they are worthy of it, and deserve it."

Matthew XIII. 16. *But blessed are your eyes.* Luke appears to represent this statement as having been spoken at another time; but this is easily explained, for in that passage he throws together a variety of our Lord's sayings, without attending to the order of dates. We shall, therefore, follow the text of Matthew, who explains more clearly the circumstances from which Christ took occasion to utter these words. Having formerly reminded them of the extraordinary favour which they had received, in being separated by our Lord from the common people, and familiarly admitted to the mysteries of his kingdom, he now magnifies that grace by another comparison, which is, that they excel ancient *Prophets* and holy *Kings*. This is a far loftier distinction than to be preferred to an unbelieving multitude. Christ does not mean any kind of *hearing*, or the mere *beholding* of the flesh, but pronounces their *eyes* to be *blessed*, because they perceive in him a glory which is worthy of the only-begotten Son of God, so as to acknowledge him as the Redeemer; because they perceive shining in him the lively image of God, by which they obtain salvation and perfect happiness; and because in them is fulfilled what had been spoken by the Prophets, that those who have been truly and perfectly *taught by the Lord* (Isa. liv. 13) do not need to *learn every man from his neighbour*, (Jer. xxxi. 34.)

This furnishes a reply to an objection that might be drawn from another saying of Christ, that *blessed are they who have not seen, and yet have believed*, (John xx. 29;) for there he describes that kind of *seeing* which Thomas desired in consequence of his gross apprehension.[1] But that *seeing*, of which Christ now speaks, has been enjoyed by believers in every age in common with the Apostles. We do not see Christ, and yet we see him; we do not hear Christ, and yet we hear him: for in the Gospel we behold him, as Paul says, *face to face, so as to be transformed into his image*, (2 Cor. iii. 18;) and the perfection of wisdom, righteousness, and life, which was formerly exhibited in him, shines there continually.

---

[1] "Selon son apprehension carnale et grossiere;"—"according to his carnal and gross apprehension."

Luke X. 24. *Many Prophets and Kings have desired to see.* The condition of the Church, at the present day, is justly pronounced to be preferable to that of the holy fathers, who lived under the Law ; because to them was exhibited, under shadows and figures only, what is now openly manifested in the shining face of Christ. *The vail of the temple being rent,* (Matth. xxvii. 51,) we enter by faith into the heavenly sanctuary, and are freely permitted to approach to God. Although the fathers were satisfied with their lot, and enjoyed a blessed peace in their own minds, yet this did not prevent their desires from extending farther. Thus, Abraham *saw the day of Christ afar off, and rejoiced,* (John viii. 56,) and yet longed to enjoy a nearer view, but did not obtain his wish. Simeon spoke the sentiments of all,[1] when he said, *Now thou sendest thy servant away in peace,* (Luke ii. 29.) And indeed it was impossible that, under the burden of that curse by which the human race is crushed, they should be otherwise than altogether inflamed with the desire of a promised deliverance.[2] Let us therefore learn, that they breathed after Christ, like hungry persons, and yet possessed a serene faith ; so that they did not murmur against God, but kept their minds in patient expectation till the full time of revelation.

Matthew.	Mark.	Luke.
XIII. 18. Hear therefore the parable of the sower. 19. When any one heareth the word of the kingdom, and understandeth not, that wicked one cometh, and taketh away what was sown in the heart. This is he who received seed near the road. 20. But	IV. 13. And he said to them, Know you not this parable? and how shall you know all parables? 14. The sower is he that soweth the word. 15. And there are some that (receive the seed) near the road, in whom the word is sown; and when they have heard,	VIII. 11. Now the parable is this : The seed is the word of God. 12. And they that (received the seed) near the road are those who hear : afterwards cometh the devil, and taketh the word

---

[1] " Simeon disoit selon l'affection de tous les Peres ;"—" Simeon spoke according to the feeling of all the Fathers."
[2] " Et de faict, il ne se pouvoit faire que ces bons personnages ne fussent tous ravis, et comme enflambez d'un grand desir de la delivrance promise."—" And indeed it was impossible that those good men should not be altogether transported, and as it were inflamed with a great desire of the promised deliverance."

MATTHEW.	MARK.	LUKE.
he that received the seed thrown into stony places, is he that heareth the word, and immediately receiveth it with joy: 21. But hath not root in himself, but is of short duration: when affliction or persecution ariseth on account of the word, immediately he is offended. 22. And he that received the seed among thorns is he that heareth the word, and the care of this life, and the deceitfulness of riches, choke the word, and it becometh unfruitful. 23. But he who receiveth seed into a good soil is he that heareth the word and understandeth it, and who afterwards yieldeth and produceth fruit,[1] some a hundred-fold, some sixty-fold, and some thirty-fold.	immediately Satan cometh, and taketh away the word which was sown in their hearts. 16. And in like manner there are others who receive the seed into stony places, who, when they have heard the word, immediately receive it with joy; 17. And have not root in themselves, but are of short duration: afterwards, when affliction or persecution ariseth on account of the word, immediately they are offended. 18. And there are others who receive the seed among thorns: these are they that hear the word, 19. And the anxieties of this life, and the deceitfulness of riches, and the desires of other things, entering in, choke the word, and it is rendered unfruitful. 20. There are others who have received the seed into a good soil, who hear the word, and receive it, and bear fruit, some thirty, some sixty, some a hundred.	out of their heart, that they may not believe and be saved. 13. For they that are on the rock are those who, when they have heard, receive the word with joy: but these have not roots, who for a time believe, and in the time of temptation fall away. 14. And what fell among thorns are those who have heard, and, going away, are choked by the anxieties, and riches, and pleasures of life, and do not yield fruit. 15. And what fell into a good soil are those who, with a good and upright heart, hearing the word, keep it, and yield fruit with patience.

According to Matthew and Luke, Christ explains the parable to his disciples simply, and unaccompanied by a reproof; but according to Mark, he indirectly blames them for being slow of apprehension, because those who were to be the teachers of all did not run before others.[2] The general truth conveyed is, that the doctrine of the Gospel, when it is scattered like seed,[3] is not everywhere fruitful; because

---

[1] " Celuy qui oit la Parole, et l'entend, à scavoir celuy qui porte et produit fruict ;"—" he who heareth the word, and understandeth it, that is he who beareth and produceth fruit."

[2] " Ne passent autrement les autres pour leur monstrer le chemin ;"— " did not go beyond others to show them the road."

[3] " Estant espandue çà et là comme le blé qu'on iette en terre ;"— " being scattered here and there, like the corn which is thrown into the earth."

it does not always meet with a fertile and well cultivated soil. He enumerates four kinds of hearers: the first of which do not receive the seed;[1] the second appear, indeed, to receive it,[2] but in such a manner that it does not take deep root; in the third, the corn is choked;[3] and so there remains a fourth part, which produces fruit. Not that one hearer only out of four, or ten out of forty, embrace the doctrine, and yield fruit; for Christ did not intend here to fix down an exact number, or to arrange the persons, of whom he speaks, in equal divisions; and, indeed, where the word is sown, the produce of faith is not always alike, but is sometimes more abundant, and at other times more scanty. He only intended to warn us, that, in many persons, the seed of life is lost on account of various defects, in consequence of which it is either destroyed immediately, or it withers, or it gradually degenerates. That we may derive the greater advantage from this warning, we ought to bear in mind, that he makes no mention of despisers who openly reject the word of God, but describes those only in whom there is some appearance of docility. But if the greater part of such men perish, what shall become of the rest of the world, by whom the doctrine of salvation is openly rejected? I now come down to each class.

Matthew XIII. 19. *When any one heareth the word of the kingdom, and understandeth it not.* He mentions, in the first place, the barren and uncultivated, who do not receive the seed within, because there is no preparation in their hearts. Such persons he compares to a stiff and dry soil, like what we find on a public road, which is trodden down, and becomes hard, like a pavement. I wish that we had not occasion to see so many of this class at the present day, who come forward to hear, but remain in a state of amazement,

---

[1] " Desquels les premiers ne retienent pas la semence en leurs coeurs pour germer;"—" the first of which do not retain the seed in their hearts so as to spring up."
[2] " Les seconds semblent bien l'avoir gardee iusques à venir à germer;"—" the second appear to have kept it till it came to spring up."
[3] " Aux troisiemes, le blé estant en herbe est estouffé;"—" in the third, the corn, while yet in the blade, is choked."

and acquire no relish for the word, and in the end differ little from blocks or stones. Need we wonder that they utterly vanish away?

That which was sown in their heart. This expression, which Christ employs, is not strictly accurate, and yet it is not without meaning; for the wickedness and depravity of men do not make the word to lose its own nature, or to cease to have the character of seed. This must be carefully observed, that we may not suppose the favours of God to cease to be what they are, though the good effect of them does not reach us. With respect to God, the word *is sown in the hearts*, but it is far from being true, that the hearts of all *receive with meekness* what is planted in them, as James (i. 21) exhorts us to *receive the word.* So then the Gospel is always a fruitful seed as to its power, but not as to its produce.[1]

Luke adds, that *the devil*[2] *taketh away the seed out of their heart, that they may not believe and be saved.* Hence we infer that, as hungry birds are wont to do at the time of sowing, this enemy of our salvation, as soon as the doctrine is delivered, watches and rushes forth to seize it, before it acquires moisture and springs up. It is no ordinary praise of the word, when it is pronounced to be the cause of our salvation.

20. *But he that received the seed thrown into stony places.* This class differs from the former; for temporary faith, being a sort of vegetation of the seed,[3] promises at first some fruit; but their hearts are not so properly and thoroughly subdued, as to have the softness necessary for their continued nourishment.[4] We see too many of this class in our own day, who eagerly embrace the Gospel, and shortly afterwards fall off; for they have not the lively affection that is necessary to give them firmness and perseverance. Let every one then examine

---

[1] "Mais non pas à ce qui s'accomplit és hommes;"—"but not as to what is accomplished in men."
[2] "Le mauvais;"—"the wicked one."
[3] "La foy temporelle, qui est comme le germe de la semence;"—"temporary faith, which is as it were the germ of the seed."
[4] "Mais les cœurs ne sont point tellement cultivez et preparez, qu'ils ayant une douceur pour nourrir et entretenir ce qui est commencé;"—"but the hearts are not so cultivated and prepared, as to have a softness for nourishing and supporting what is begun."

himself thoroughly, that the alacrity which gives out a bright flame may not quickly go out, as the saying is, like a fire of tow;[1] for if the word does not fully penetrate the whole heart, and strike its roots deep, faith will want the supply of moisture that is necessary for perseverance. Great commendation is due, no doubt, to that promptitude, which receives the word of God with joy, and without delay, as soon as it is published; but let us learn, that nothing has been done, till faith acquires true firmness, that it may not wither in the first blade.

21. *When affliction or persecution ariseth on account of the word.* By way of example, Christ says that such persons are made uneasy by the offence of the cross. And certainly, as the heat of the sun discovers the barrenness of the soil, so *persecution* and the cross lay open the vanity of those, who are slightly influenced by I know not what desire, but are not actually moved by earnest feelings of piety. Such persons, according to Matthew and Mark, are *temporary*,[2] not only because, having professed, for a time, that they are the disciples of Christ, they afterwards fall away through temptation, but because they imagine that they have true faith. According to Luke, Christ says that they *believe for a time;* because that honour which they render to the Gospel resembles faith.[3] At the same time we ought to learn, that they are not truly regenerated by the incorruptible seed, *which never fadeth*, as Peter tells us, (1 Pet. i. 4;) for he says that these words of Isaiah, *The word of God endureth for ever*, (Isa. xl. 8 ; 1 Pet. i. 25,) are fulfilled in the hearts of believers, in whom the truth of God, once fixed, never passes away, but retains its vigour to the end. Still, those persons who take delight in the word of God, and cherish some reverence for it, do in some manner

---

[1] " De peur que ceste ardeur et alaigreté qui est de grand monstre pour le commencement, ne s'en aille bien tost en fumee comme un feu d'estouppes, ainsi que porte le proverbe commun ;"—" lest that ardour and alacrity, which makes a great show at the beginning, may soon vanish into smoke, like a fire of tow, as the common proverb goes."

[2] " Temporels, c'est à dire, de petite duree ;"—" temporary, that is to say, of short duration."

[3] " Ressemble aucunement à la foy ;"—" somewhat resembles faith."

believe; for they are widely different from unbelievers, who give no credit to God when he speaks, or who reject his word. In a word, let us learn that none are partakers of true faith, except those who are sealed with the Spirit of adoption, and who sincerely call on God as their Father; and as that Spirit is never extinguished, so it is impossible that the faith, which he has once engraven on the hearts of the godly, shall pass away or be destroyed.

22. *And he who received the seed among thorns.* He places in the third class, those who would have been disposed to receive the seed within, if they had not permitted *other things* to corrupt and render it degenerate. Christ compares to *thorns* the pleasures of this life, or wicked desires, and covetousness, and the other anxieties of the flesh. Matthew mentions only *the care of this life,* along with covetousness, but the meaning is the same; for under that term he includes the allurements of pleasures, which Luke mentions, and every kind of desire. As corn, which otherwise might have been productive, no sooner rises into the stalk than it is choked by thorns and other matters injurious to its growth; so the sinful affections of the flesh prevail over the hearts of men, and overcome faith, and thus destroy the force of the heavenly doctrine, before it has reached maturity.

Now though sinful desires exert their power on the hearts of men, before the word of the Lord springs up into the blade, yet, at first, their influence is not perceived, and it is only when the corn has grown up, and given promise of fruit, that they gradually make their appearance. Each of us ought to endeavour to tear the *thorns* out of his heart, if we do not choose that the word of God should be *choked;* for there is not one of us whose heart is not filled with a vast quantity, and, as I may say, a thick forest, of *thorns.* And, indeed, we perceive how few there are that reach maturity; for there is scarcely one individual out of ten that labours, I do not say to root out, but even to cut down the *thorns.* Nay more, the very number of the *thorns,* which is so prodigious that it ought to shake off our sloth, is the reason why most people give themselves no trouble about them.

The deceitfulness of riches. Christ employs this phrase to denote *covetousness.* He expressly says, that riches are imposing or *deceitful,* in order that men may be more desirous to guard against falling into their snares. Let us remember that the affections of our flesh, the number and variety of which are incalculable, are so many injurious influences to corrupt *the seed* of life.

23. *But he that received the seed into a good soil.* None are compared by Christ to a *good and fertile soil,* but those in whom the word of God not only strikes its roots deep and solid, but overcomes every obstacle that would prevent it from yielding fruit. Is it objected that it is impossible to find any one who is pure and free from thorns? It is easy to reply, that Christ does not now speak of the perfection of faith, but only points out those in whom the word of God yields fruit. Though the produce may not be great, yet every one who does not fall off from the sincere worship of God is reckoned a *good and fertile soil.* We ought to labour, no doubt, to pull out the *thorns;* but as our utmost exertion will never succeed so well, but that there will always be some remaining behind, let each of us endeavour, at least, to deaden them, that they may not hinder the fruit of the word. This statement is confirmed by what immediately follows, when Christ informs us that all do not yield fruit in an equal degree.

Some a hundred-fold, and some sixty-fold, and some thirty-fold. Though the fertility of that soil, which yields a *thirty-fold* produce, is small, compared with that which yields a *hundred-fold,* yet we perceive that our Lord classes together all kinds of soil which do not entirely disappoint the labours and expectation of the husbandman.[1] Hence too we learn, that we have no right to despise those who occupy a lower degree of excellence; for the master of the house himself, though he gives to one the preference above another on account of more abundant produce, yet bestows the general designation, *good,* even on inferior soils. Those three gradations are absurdly

[1] "Esquelles le laboureur ne perd pas du tout sa peine;"—"in which the husbandman does not entirely lose his trouble."

tortured by *Jerome,* to denote virgins, widows, and married persons; as if that produce which the Lord demands from us belonged to celibacy alone, and as if the piety of married persons did not, in many cases, yield more abundantly every fruit of virtue. It must also be observed, in passing, that what Christ says about a *hundred-fold* produce is not hyperbolical; for such was at that time the fertility of some countries, as we learn from many historians, who give their report as eye-witnesses.

MATTHEW.

XIII. 24. He put forth to them another parable, saying, The kingdom of heaven is compared to a man sowing good seed in his field. 25. But while men were asleep, his enemy came, and sowed tares among the wheat, and went away. 26. And when the blade sprang up, and yielded fruit, then appeared also the tares. 27. And the servants of the household approaching, said to him, Lord, didst not thou sow good seed in thy field? Whence then hath it tares?[1] 28. And he said to them, An enemy[2] hath done this. And his servants said to him, Is it thy will then that we go away and gather them? 29. But he said, No; lest, while you are gathering the tares, you root out along with them the wheat also. 30. Allow both to grow together till the harvest; and at the time of harvest I will say to the reapers, Gather first the tares, and bind them in bundles to burn them; but collect the wheat into my barn.—(*A little after.*) 36. Then Jesus sent the multitude away, and came into the house, and his disciples approached him, saying, Explain to us the parable of the tares of the field. 37. But he answering, said to them, He that soweth the good seed is the Son of man. 38. And the field is the world. The good seed is the children of the kingdom; but the tares are the children of that wicked one. 39. And the enemy that soweth them is the devil; the harvest is the end of the world, and the reapers are the angels. 40. So then as the tares are gathered, and are burned in the fire, so shall it be at the end of this world. 41. The Son of man will send his angels, and will gather out of his kingdom all stumbling-blocks, and those who commit iniquity. 42. And they will cast them into a furnace of fire: there shall be lamentation and gnashing of teeth. 43. Then the righteous will shine as the sun in the kingdom of their Father. He that hath ears to hear, let him hear.

In order to reap the advantage of this parable, it is necessary to ascertain the object which Christ had in view. Some think that, to guard a mixed multitude against satisfying themselves with an outward profession of the Gospel,[3] he told

---

[1] "D'ou vient donc qu'il y a de l'yvroye?"—"Whence comes it then that there are tares?"

[2] "L'homme ennemi, (*ou, quelque ennemi;*)"—"the enemy, (or, some enemy.)"

[3] "Pour retirer le commun populaire d'une folle presomption, à cause

them, that in his own field bad seed is often mixed with the good, but that a day is coming, when the tares shall be separated from the wheat.[1] They accordingly connect this parable with the one immediately preceding, as if the design of both had been the same. For my own part, I take a different view. He speaks of a separation, in order to prevent the minds of the godly from giving way to uneasiness or despondency, when they perceive a confused mixture of the good along with the bad. Although Christ has cleansed the Church with his own blood, that it may be without spot or blemish, yet hitherto he suffers it to be polluted by many stains. I speak not of the remaining infirmities of the flesh, to which every believer is liable, even after that he has been renewed by the Holy Spirit. But as soon as Christ has gathered a small flock for himself, many hypocrites mingle with it, persons of immoral lives creep in, nay, many wicked men insinuate themselves; in consequence of which, numerous stains pollute that holy assembly, which Christ has separated for himself. Many persons, too, look upon it as exceedingly absurd, that ungodly, or profane, or unprincipled men should be cherished within the bosom of the Church. Add to this, that very many, under the pretence of zeal, are excessively displeased, when every thing is not conducted to their wish, and, because absolute purity is nowhere to be found, withdraw from the Church in a disorderly manner, or subvert and destroy it by unreasonable severity.

In my opinion, the design of the parable is simply this: So long as the pilgrimage of the Church in this world continues, bad men and hypocrites will mingle in it with those who are good and upright, that the children of God may be armed with patience, and, in the midst of offences which are fitted to disturb them, may preserve unbroken stedfastness of faith. It is an appropriate comparison, when the Lord calls the Church his *field*, for believers are the seed of it; and

---

qu'en apparence externe ils faisoyent quelque profession de l'Evangile;"
—" to withdraw the common people from a foolish presumption, because in outward appearance they made some profession of the Gospel."

[1] " Qu'on separera l'yvroye d'avec le bon blé;"—" when the tares shall be separated from the good corn."

though Christ afterwards adds that *the field is the world,* yet he undoubtedly intended to apply this designation, in a peculiar manner, to the Church, about which he had commenced the discourse. But as he was about to drive his plough through every country of the world, so as to cultivate fields, and scatter the seed of life, throughout the whole world, he has employed a *synecdoche,* to make *the world* denote what more strictly belonged only to a part of it.

We must now inquire what he means by *the wheat,* and what by *the tares.* These terms cannot be explained as referring to doctrine, as if the meaning had been that, when the Gospel *is sown,* it is immediately corrupted and adulterated by wicked inventions; for Christ would never have forbidden them to labour strenuously to purge out that kind of corruption. With respect to morals, those faults of men which cannot be corrected must be endured; but we are not at liberty to extend such a toleration to wicked errors, which corrupt the purity of faith.[1] Besides, Christ removes all doubt, by saying expressly, that *the tares are the children of the wicked one.* And yet it must also be remarked, that this cannot be understood simply of the persons of men, as if by creation God sowed good men and the devil sowed bad men. I advert to this, because the present passage has been abused by the Manicheans, for the purpose of lending support to their notion of two principles. But we know that whatever sin exists, either in the devil or in men, is nothing else than the corruption of the whole nature. As it is not by creation that God makes his elect, who have been tainted with original sin, to become a good seed, but by regenerating them through the grace of his Spirit; so wicked men are not created by the devil, but, having been created by God, are corrupted by the devil, and thrown into the Lord's field, in order to corrupt the pure seed.

37. *He that soweth the good seed.* He had formerly said

---

[1] "Mais c'est autre chose de la doctrine : car il ne faut iamais endurer les erreurs meschantes qui corrompent la pureté de la foy ;"—"but it is quite otherwise with doctrine; for we must never tolerate the wicked errors which corrupt the purity of faith."

that *the kingdom of heaven resembles a man sowing.* The mode of expression is unusual, but plainly means, that the same thing happens with the preaching of the Gospel as usually takes place in the sowing of fields; *the tares grow up along with the wheat.* One peculiarity, however, is pointed out by him, when he says that the sowing of tares in the field was effected by the trick of *an enemy.* This is intended to inform us that, when many wicked men are mingled with believers, this is no accidental or natural occurrence, as if they were the same seed, but that we must learn to charge the blame of this evil on the devil. Not that, by condemning him, men are acquitted of guilt; but, in the first place, that no blame whatever may be laid on God on account of this fault which arose from the agency of another; and, secondly, that we may not be surprised to find *tares* frequently growing in the Lord's field, since Satan is always on the watch to do mischief. Again, when Christ says, not that the ministers of the word sow, but that he alone sows, this is not without meaning; for though this cannot be supposed to be restricted to his person, yet as he makes use of our exertions, and employs us as his instruments, for cultivating his field, so that He alone acts by us and in us, he justly claims for himself what is, in some respects, common to his ministers. Let us, therefore, remember, that the Gospel is preached, not only by Christ's command, but by his authority and direction; in short, that we are only his hand, and that He alone is the Author of the work.

39. *The harvest is the end of the world.* This is, no doubt, a very distressing consideration, that the Church is burdened with the reprobate to the very *end of the world;* but Christ enjoins on us to exercise patience till that time, that we may not deceive ourselves with a vain hope. Pastors ought to labour strenuously to purify the Church; and all the godly, so far as their respective callings enable them, ought to lend assistance in this matter; but when all shall have devoted their united exertions to the general advantage, they will not succeed in such a manner as to purify the Church entirely from every defilement. Let us therefore hold, that

nothing was farther from the design of Christ than to encourage pollution by lending countenance to it. All that he intended was, to exhort those who believed in him not to lose courage, because they are under the necessity of retaining wicked men among them; and, next, to restrain and moderate the zeal of those who fancy that they are not at liberty to join in a society with any but pure angels.[1]

This passage has been most improperly abused by the Anabaptists, and by others like them,[2] to take from the Church the power of the sword. But it is easy to refute them; for since they approve of excommunication, which cuts off, at least for a time, the bad and reprobate, why may not godly magistrates, when necessity calls for it, use the sword against wicked men? They reply that, when the punishment is not capital,[3] there is room allowed for repentance; as if the thief on the cross (Luke xxiii. 42) did not find the means of salvation. I shall satisfy myself with replying, that Christ does not now speak of the office of pastors or of magistrates, but removes the offence which is apt to disturb weak minds, when they perceive that the Church is composed not only of the elect, but of the polluted dregs of society.

The reapers are the angels. This term must be viewed in reference to the present subject. In another passage, the Apostles are called *reapers,* as compared with the Prophets, because they have *entered into their labours,* (John iv. 38,) and it is enjoined on all the ministers of the word, *that they should bring forth fruit, and that their fruit should remain,* (John xv. 16.) Such also is the import of that statement, that *the fields are white,* and are in want of reapers, (John iv. 35;) and again, that *the harvest is abundant, but the labourers are few,* (Matth. ix. 37.) But here the comparison is applied in a different manner; for those who occupy a place

---

[1] "Qui ne pensent point qu'il soit bon de s'adioindre à la compagnie des fideles, sinon que tout y soit pur comme entre les Anges;"—" who do not think that it is proper to join themselves to the society of believers, unless every thing in it be as pure as among the Angels."
[2] "Et semblables reveurs;"—" and similar dreamers."
[3] "Quand la peine n'est pas à mort (comme est l'excommunication;)"—"when the punishment, as in the case of excommunication, is not to death."

in the Church are said to be planted in the Lord's field. Nor is this inconsistent with what is said elsewhere, that Christ, as soon as he comes forth with his Gospel, *hath a winnowing-fan in his hand, and will thoroughly cleanse his thrashing-floor,* (Matth. iii. 12.) These words describe the commencement of that cleansing, which, this passage declares, will not take place before the last day, because not till then will it be fully completed. Christ will put the last hand to the cleansing of the Church by means of *angels,* but he now begins to do the work by means of pious teachers. He assigns this office to *angels,* because they will not remain idle spectators before his tribunal,[1] but will hold themselves in readiness to execute his commands. It follows, that those who proceed, with undue haste, to root out whatever displeases them, prevent, as far as lies in their power, the sentence of Christ, deprive *angels* of their office, and rashly take that office on themselves.

41. *They shall gather out of his kingdom all stumbling-blocks.* The words that follow, *and those who commit iniquity,* are added for the sake of exposition; for it is not intended to point out two different things, but to state, that then will be the full and seasonable time, when all things shall be restored to regular order, and when the *wicked* shall be removed, who are now *stumbling-blocks.* They are so called, because not only are their own lives wicked, but they undermine the faith of many, retard others in the right course, draw some entirely aside, and drive others headlong. We ought to draw from this a useful admonition, not to become indolent and careless on account of our being surrounded by so many *stumbling-blocks,* but to be zealous and active in guarding against them. It reproves also the effeminacy of those who are so delicate, that the smallest possible *stumbling-blocks* make them turn back.[2] It is difficult, I admit, not to stumble frequently, and even sometimes to fall, when *stumbling-blocks* without number lie across our path. But our

---

[1] " Devant le siege iudicial de sa maiesté ;"—" before the judgment-seat of his majesty."
[2] " Ils tournent incontinent bride ;"—" they immediately wheel about."

minds ought to be fortified with confidence; for the Son of God, who commands his followers to walk in the midst of *stumbling-blocks*, will unquestionably give us strength to overcome them all. He pronounces likewise an awful punishment against any hypocrites and reprobate persons, who now appear to be the most distinguished citizens of the Church.

42. *And shall cast them into a furnace of fire.* This is a metaphorical expression; for, as the infinite glory which is laid up for the sons of God so far exceeds all our senses, that we cannot find words to express it, so the punishment which awaits the reprobate is incomprehensible, and is therefore shadowed out according to the measure of our capacity. From ignorance of this, the Sophists have tortured themselves, to no purpose, by fruitless disputes, as we have already hinted on a former occasion.[1] Some commentators, I am aware, carry their ingenious inquiries into every minute phrase; but as there is reason to fear that subtleties, which rest on no solid grounds, may lead us into idle fooleries, I choose to philosophise more sparingly, and to rest satisfied with the plain and natural meaning. If we put a question to those who are so delighted with matters of curiosity, how it comes about that, while Christ is *asleep*, and unacquainted with the affair, the devil sows tares among the good seed, they will have nothing to reply; but while I desire to exercise caution, I have endeavoured to leave out nothing that is useful and necessary to be known.

43. *Then will the righteous shine.* What a remarkable consolation! The sons of God, who now lie covered with dust, or are held in no estimation, or even are loaded with reproaches, *will then shine* in full brightness, as when the sky is serene, and every cloud has been dispelled. The adverb *then* ($\tau \acute{o} \tau \epsilon$) is emphatic; for it contains an implied contrast between their present state and the ultimate restoration, by the expectation of which Christ animates those who believe

---

[1] Harmony, vol. i. p. 200.

in him. The meaning therefore is, Though many wicked men now hold a high rank in the Church, yet that blessed day is assuredly to be expected, when the Son of God shall raise his followers on high, and remove every thing that now tends to dim or conceal their brightness. It is no doubt true, that the future glory is promised to none but those in whom the image of God already shines, and who are transformed into it by continued advances of glory. But as the life of the godly is now hidden, and as their salvation is invisible, because it consists in hope, Christ properly directs the attention of believers to heaven, where they will find the glory that is promised to them.

In order to make a deeper impression on his hearers, our Lord unquestionably refers here to a passage in Daniel, (xii. 3,) *And they that are wise shall shine as the brightness of the firmament.* "The Prophet," he seems to say, "when he predicts a future brightness, intimates also that there is a temporary obscurity: and so, if we admit the prediction, we ought to endure patiently that mixture which, for a time, classes the elect of God with the reprobate." By comparing this glory to *the sun,* he does not determine that it will be alike in all. As Christ now distributes his gifts variously[1] among believers, in like manner will he crown these gifts at the last day. But we must recollect what I have said, that the restoration, which is delayed till the last coming of Christ, is compared with the cloudy state of the world.[2]

The kingdom of the Father, as the inheritance of the godly, is contrasted with the earth, to remind them that here they are pilgrims, and therefore ought to look upwards towards heaven. In another passage, *the kingdom of God* is said to be *within us,* (Luke xvii. 21,) but we shall not obtain the full enjoyment of it till *God be all in all,* (1 Cor. xv. 28.)

---

[1] " Diversement, aux uns plus, aux autres moins ;"—" variously, to some more, to others less."

[2] " Avec l'estat present du monde, qui est comme tout obscurci de brouillars ;"—" with the present state of the world, which is entirely, so to speak, obscured by mists."

MATTHEW.	MARK.	LUKE.
XIII. 31. He delivered another parable to them, saying, The kingdom of heaven is like a grain of mustard, which a man took and sowed in his field: 32. Which indeed is the least of all seeds: but when it is grown up, it is the largest among herbs,[1] and becometh a tree, so that the fowls of heaven come and make their nests among its branches. 33. He spake another parable to them: The kingdom of heaven is like leaven, which a woman took and hid among three measures of meal, till the whole was leavened. 34. All these things Jesus spoke in parables to the multitudes, and without a parable he spoke nothing to them. 35. That it might be fulfilled which was spoken by the prophet, who saith, I will open my mouth in parables; I will utter things which have been hidden from the foundation of the world.	IV. 26. And he said, The kingdom of God is as if a man should cast seed into the ground, 27. And sleep, and rise by night and day, and the corn should spring and grow up, while he knoweth not how. 28. For the earth yieldeth fruit of itself, first the blade, then the ear, and then the full corn in the ear. 29. And when the fruit is matured, he immediately applieth the sickle, because the harvest is at hand. 30. And he said, To what shall we say that the kingdom of God is like? or with what comparison shall we compare it? 31. As a grain of mustard, which, when it is sown in the earth, is smaller than all the seeds which are in the earth; 32. And when it is sown, it springs up, and is larger than all herbs,[2] and putteth forth great branches, so that the fowls of heaven can make their nests under its shadow. 33. And by such parables he spake the word to them, as they were able to bear it: 34. But without a parable he did not speak to them, but he explained all things to his disciples when they were apart.	XIII. 18. Therefore he said, To what is the kingdom of God like? and to what shall I compare it? 19. It is like a grain of mustard, which a man took and cast into his garden, and it grew, and became a large tree, and the fowls of the air made their nests among its branches. 20. And again he said, To what shall I compare the kingdom of God? It is like leaven, which a woman took and hid in three measures of meal, till the whole was leavened. 22. And he went through the cities and villages, teaching and journeying towards Jerusalem.

By these parables Christ encourages his disciples not to be offended and turn back on account of the mean beginnings of the Gospel. We see how haughtily profane men despise the Gospel, and even turn it into ridicule, because the ministers by whom it is preached are men of slender reputation and of low rank; because it is not instantly re-

---

[1] "Il est plus grand que les autres herbes;"—"it is larger than the other herbs."
[2] "Que toute autre herbe;"—"than every other herb."

ceived with applause by the whole world; and because the few disciples whom it does obtain are, for the most part, men of no weight or consideration, and belong to the common people. This leads weak minds to despair of its success, which they are apt to estimate from the manner of its commencement. On the contrary, the Lord opens his reign with a feeble and despicable commencement, for the express purpose, that his power may be more fully illustrated by its unexpected progress.[1]

The kingdom of God is compared to *a grain of mustard, which is the smallest among the seeds,* but grows to such a height that it becomes a shrub, *in which the birds build their nests.* It is likewise compared to *leaven,* which, though it may be small in amount, spreads its influence in such a manner, as to impart its bitterness to a large quantity of meal.[2] If the aspect of Christ's kingdom be despicable in the eyes of the flesh, let us learn to raise our minds to the boundless and incalculable power of God, which at once created all things out of nothing, and every day raises up *things that are not,* (1 Cor. i. 28,) in a manner which exceeds the capacity of the human senses. Let us leave to proud men their disdainful laugh, till the Lord, at an unexpected hour, shall strike them with amazement. Meanwhile, let us not despond, but rise by faith against the pride of the world, till the Lord give us that astonishing display of his power,[3] of which he speaks in this passage.

The word *leaven* is sometimes taken in a bad sense, as when Christ warns them to *beware of the leaven of the Pharisees and of the Sadducees,* (Matth. xvi. 11;) and when Paul says, that *a little leaven leaveneth the whole lump,* (1 Cor. v. 6.) But here the term must be understood simply as applying to the present subject. As to the meaning of the

[1] " A fin que sa puissance soit tant mieux cognuë, quand on verra les avancemens qu'on n'avoit iamais attendus;"—"in order that his power may be so much the better known, when the progress, which had not been anticipated, shall be seen."
[2] " Qu'il fait aigrir et lever une grande quantité de paste;"—" that it embitters and causes to rise a large quantity of paste."
[3] " Iuques à ce que le Seigneur nous face sentir l'effect de cette vertu incomprehensible;"—" till the Lord make us feel the effect of that incomprehensible power."

phrase, *the kingdom of God,* and *the kingdom of heaven,* we have spoken on former occasions.

Mark IV. 26. *So is the kingdom of God.* Though this comparison has the same object with the two immediately preceding, yet Christ appears to direct his discourse purposely to the ministers of the word, that they may not grow indifferent about the discharge of their duty, because the fruit of their labour does not immediately appear. He holds out for their imitation the example of husbandmen, who *throw seed into the ground* with the expectation of reaping, and do not torment themselves with uneasiness and anxiety, but go to bed and rise again ; or, in other words, pursue their ordinary and daily toil, till the corn arrive at maturity in due season. In like manner, though the seed of the word be concealed and choked for a time, Christ enjoins pious teachers to be of good courage, and not to allow their alacrity to be slackened through distrust.

Matthew XIII. 34. *All these things Jesus spoke in parables.* Though Mark expressly says, that Christ *spoke the word to them as they were able to bear it,* yet I think it probable that he continued to employ *parables,* not so much for the purpose of instruction, as to keep the attention of his hearers awake till a more convenient time. For why did he explain them familiarly to his disciples when they were apart? Was it because they were more slow of apprehension than the great body of the people? No; but because he wished to convey to them privately a knowledge of his meaning, and to allow others to remain in a state of suspense, till a fitter opportunity should arrive. These were only a sort of introduction to the Gospel, the full brightness and publication of which was delayed till the proper time.

There is an apparent contradiction between this statement of Matthew and the prediction of Isaiah, which was quoted a little before. But this is easily removed; for, though he withdrew the light of doctrine from the reprobate, yet this did not prevent him from accommodating himself to their capacity, so as to render them inexcusable. He therefore adopted a method of teaching which was proper and suitable to hearers, whom he knew to be not yet sufficiently prepared to receive instruction.

35. *That it might be fulfilled.* Matthew does not mean, that the psalm, which he quotes, is a prediction which relates peculiarly to Christ, but that, as the majesty of the Spirit was displayed in the discourse of the Prophet, in the same manner was his power manifested in the discourse of Christ. The Prophet, when he is about to speak of God's covenant, by which he adopted the seed of Abraham, of the benefits which he continued to bestow upon his people, and of the whole government of the Church, introduces his subject in lofty terms, *I will open my mouth in parables,* (Ps. lxxviii. 2:) that is, "I will not speak of trifling matters, but will handle with becoming gravity subjects of the highest importance." When he adds, *I will utter dark sayings,* the meaning is the same; such repetitions being very frequent in the Psalms. The Hebrew word מְשָׁלִים (*Meshalim*) signifies *comparisons;* and it came afterwards to be applied to "weighty sentences," because *comparisons* generally impart beauty and energy to a discourse. The word חִידוֹת (*Chidoth*) sometimes denotes "riddles," and at other times, "short sayings."

Now though Matthew seems to allude to the word *parable,* he undoubtedly means, that Christ spoke figuratively, in order that his very style, being more brilliant than ordinary discourse, might carry more weight and dignity. In short, he says that what is contained in the psalm was *fulfilled;* because the use of allegories and figures tended to show, that Christ was treating of the hidden mysteries of God, and to prevent his doctrine from being despised. Hence, too, we infer, that there was no inconsistency in the various objects which Christ had in view, when he spoke to the people in a dark manner. Though he intended to conceal from the reprobate what he was saying, yet he laboured to make them feel, even in the midst of their amazement, that there was something heavenly and divine in his language.[1]

---

[1] "Car combien qu'il voulust parler en telle sorte que les reprouvez n'y entendissent rien, il a toutesfois tellement moderé son style, qu'en leur

Luke XIII. 22. *Journeying towards Jerusalem.* It is uncertain whether Luke speaks only of one journey, or means that, while Christ walked throughout Judea, and visited each part of it for the purpose of teaching, he was wont to *go up to Jerusalem* at the festivals. The former clause, certainly, appears to describe that course of life which Christ invariably pursued, from the time that he began to discharge the office which had been committed to him by the Father. To make the latter clause agree with this, the meaning will be, that, when the festivals were at hand, he attended, along with others,[1] the holy assemblies.

MATTHEW.

XIII. 44. Again, the kingdom of heaven is like a treasure hid in a field, which when found a man hideth,[2] and for the joy which he hath on account of it, goeth away, and selleth all that he hath, and buyeth that field. 45. Again, the kingdom of heaven is like a merchant, seeking beautiful pearls,[3] 46. Who, having found one valuable pearl, went away, and sold all that he possessed, and bought it. 47. Again, the kingdom of heaven is like a net cast into the sea, and collecting of every kind,[4] 48. Which, when it was full, they drew to shore, and sat down, and collected the good into vessels, but cast away the bad.[5] 49. So shall it be at the end of the world: the Angels will come, and will separate the bad from the midst of the righteous, 50. And will cast them into a furnace of fire: there shall be lamentation and gnashing of teeth. 51. Jesus saith to them, Have you understood all these things? They say to him, Yes, Lord. 52. But he said to them, Therefore every scribe instructed in reference to the kingdom of heaven[6] is like a householder, who bringeth forth out of his treasure things new and old.

The first two of these parables are intended to instruct stupidité ils ont senti que son parler avoit quelque vertu celeste et Divine;"—" for, though he intended to speak in such a manner, that the reprobate might understand nothing of it, yet he so regulated his style that, amidst their stupidity, they felt that his manner of speaking had some Divine and heavenly power."

[1] " Sa coustume estoit de se trouver ;"—" his custom was to be present."
[2] " Que quelqu'un a trouvé et caché ;"—" which some one hath found and hidden."
[3] " Qui cherche de bonnes perles ;"—" who seeks good pearls."
[4] " De toutes sortes de choses ;"—" of all sorts of things."
[5] " Lequel estant plein, ' les pescheurs' le tirent en haut sur la rive : et estant assis mettent le bon à part en leurs vaisseaux, et iettent hors ce qui ne vaut rien ;"—" which being full, ' the fishers' draw it upwards on the bank ; and sitting down, put the good aside in their vessels, and throw away what is worth nothing."
[6] " Quant au royaume des cieux ;"—" as to the kingdom of heaven."

believers to prefer *the kingdom of heaven* to the whole world, and therefore to deny themselves and all the desires of the flesh, that nothing may prevent them from obtaining so valuable a possession. We are greatly in need of such a warning; for we are so captivated by the allurements of the world, that eternal life fades from our view;[1] and in consequence of our carnality, the spiritual graces of God are far from being held by us in the estimation which they deserve. Justly, therefore, does Christ speak in such lofty terms of the excellence of eternal life, that we ought not to feel uneasiness at relinquishing, on account of it, whatever we reckon in other respects to be valuable.

First, he says, that *the kingdom of heaven is like a hidden treasure.* We commonly set a high value on what is visible, and therefore the new and spiritual life, which is held out to us in the Gospel, is little esteemed by us, because it is *hidden*, and lies in hope. There is the highest appropriateness in comparing it to *a treasure*, the value of which is in no degree diminished, though it may be buried in the earth, and withdrawn from the eyes of men. These words teach us, that we ought not to estimate the riches of the grace of God according to the views of our flesh, or according to their outward display, but in the same manner as a *treasure*, though it be *hidden*, is preferred to a vain appearance of wealth. The same instruction is conveyed by the other parable. *One pearl*, though it be small, is so highly valued, that a skilful *merchant* does not hesitate to *sell* houses and lands in order to purchase it. The excellence of the heavenly life is not perceived, indeed, by the sense of the flesh; and yet we do not esteem it according to its real worth, unless we are prepared to deny, on account of it, all that glitters in our eyes.

We now perceive the leading object of both parables. It is to inform us, that none are qualified for receiving the grace of the Gospel but those who disregard all other desires, and devote all their exertions, and all their faculties, to obtain it. It deserves our attention, also, that Christ

[1] " Que nous venons à oublier la vie eternelle ;"—" that we come to forget eternal life."

does not pronounce the *hidden treasure,* or the *pearl,* to be so highly valued by all. The *treasure* is ascertained to be valuable, after that it has been *found* and known; and it is the skilful *merchant* that forms such an opinion about the *pearl.*[1] These words denote the knowledge of faith. "The heavenly kingdom," Christ tells us, "is commonly held as of no account, because men are incapable of relishing it, and do not perceive the inestimable value of that treasure which the Lord offers to us in the Gospel."

But it is asked, is it necessary that we abandon every other possession, in order that we may enjoy eternal life? I answer briefly. The natural meaning of the words is, that the Gospel does not receive from us the respect which it deserves, unless we prefer it to all the riches, pleasures, honours, and advantages of the world, and to such an extent, that we are satisfied with the spiritual blessings which it promises, and throw aside every thing that would keep us from enjoying them; for those who aspire to heaven must be disengaged from every thing that would retard their progress. Christ exhorts those who believe in him to deny those things only which are injurious to godliness; and, at the same time, permits them to use and enjoy God's temporal favours, as if they did not use them.

46. *And bought it.* By the word *buy* Christ does not mean, that men bring any price, with which they may purchase for themselves the heavenly life; for we know on what condition the Lord invites believers in the book of Isaiah, (lv. 1,) *Come and buy wine and milk without money and without price.* But though the heavenly life, and every thing that belongs to it, is the free gift of God, yet we are said to *buy* it, when we cheerfully relinquish the desires of the flesh, that nothing may prevent us from obtaining it; as Paul says, that he *reckoned all things to be loss and dung, that he might gain Christ,* (Phil. iii. 8.)

47. *Again, the kingdom of heaven is like a net.* No new

[1] "C'est le bon *marchand* qui fait telle estime de la *perle*;"—"it is the good *merchant* who sets so high a value on the *pearl.*"

instruction is here given by Christ; but what he formerly taught is confirmed by another parable, that the Church of God, so long as it exists in the world, is a mixture of the good with the bad, and is never free from stains and pollutions. And yet the design of this parable is perhaps different. It may be that Christ intends not only to remove the offence which perplexes many weak minds, because they do not find in the world all the purity that might be desired, but likewise to employ the influence of fear and modesty, in restraining his disciples from delighting themselves with the empty title, or mere profession, of faith. For my own part, I cheerfully adopt both views. Christ informs us, that a mixture of the good and the bad must be patiently endured till *the end of the world;* because, till that time, a true and perfect restoration of the Church will not take place. Again, he warns us, that it is not enough, and—what is more—that it is of little consequence to us, to be gathered into the fold, unless we are his true and chosen sheep. To this effect is the saying of Paul, *The Lord knoweth who are his; and let every one that calleth on the name of the Lord depart from iniquity,* (2 Tim. ii. 19.)

The preaching of the Gospel is justly compared to a *net* sunk beneath the water, to inform us that the present state of the Church is confused. *Our God is the God of order, and not of confusion,* (1 Cor. xiv. 33,) and, therefore, recommends to us discipline; but he permits hypocrites to remain for a time among believers, till the last day, when he will bring his kingdom to a state of perfection. So far as lies in our power, let us endeavour to correct vices, and let us exercise severity in removing pollutions; but the Church will not be free from every spot and blemish, until Christ shall have *separated the sheep from the goats,* (Matth. xxv. 32.)

51. *Have you understood all these things?* We must keep in recollection what we have formerly seen, that all the parables of Christ were explained in private. And now the Lord, after having taught them in this kind and familiar manner, warns them at the same time, that his object, in taking so much pains to instruct them, was not merely that they might

be well informed,¹ but that they might communicate to others what they had received. In this way he whets and excites their minds more and more to desire instruction. He says that teachers *are like householders*, who are not only careful about their own food, but have a store laid up for the nourishment of others; and who do not live at ease as to the passing day, but make provision for a future and distant period. The meaning, therefore, is, that the teachers of the Church ought to be prepared by long study for giving to the people, as out of a storehouse,² a variety of instruction concerning the word of God, as the necessity of the case may require. Many of the ancient expositors understand by *things new and old* the Law and the Gospel; but this appears to me to be forced. I understand them simply to mean a varied and manifold distribution, wisely and properly adapted to the capacity of every individual.

LUKE.

VII. 36. And one of the Pharisees requested him to take food with him; and he entered into the house of the Pharisee, and sat down at table. 37. And, lo, a woman in the city, who was a sinner, when she knew that he sat at table in the house of the Pharisee, brought an alabaster box of ointment:³ 38. And sitting at his feet behind him, and weeping, she began to wash his feet with tears, and wiped them with the hairs of her head, and kissed his feet, and anointed them with ointment.⁴ 39. And the Pharisee, who had invited him, seeing it, said, speaking within himself, If this man were a Prophet, he would certainly know who and what sort of woman this is that toucheth him; for she is a sinner.⁵ 40. And Jesus answering, said to him, Simon, I have something to say to thee. And he said, Master, say on. 41. A certain creditor had two debtors: one owed five hundred pence, and another fifty. 42. And when they had nothing to pay, he forgave them both. Tell me then, which of them will love him more? 43. Simon answering said, I suppose that it will be he to whom he forgave more. And he said to him, Thou hast decided aright. 44. And

---

¹ "Qu'ils gardent ceste cognoissance pour eux-mesmes seulement;"—"that they may keep that knowledge for themselves only."

² "Comme nous voyons que le pere de famille tire de son cellier ou grenier toutes sortes de provisions;"—"as we see that the master of a family draws from his cellar or granary all kinds of provisions."

³ "Or voyci il y avoit une femme de la ville qui avoit esté de mauvaise vie, laquelle ayant cognu qu'il estoit assis à table en la maison du Pharisien, apporta une boiste d'ongnement;"—"but, lo, there was a woman of the city who was of wicked life, who, having learned that he sat at table in the house of the Pharisee, brought a box of ointment."

⁴ "Et les frottoit d'ongnement;"—"and rubbed them with ointment."

⁵ "Car elle est de mauvaise vie;"—"for she is of wicked life."

LUKE.

turning to the woman, he said to Simon, Seest thou this woman? I entered into thy house, thou gavest not water for my feet; but she hath moistened my feet with tears, and wiped them with the hairs of her head. 45. Thou gavest me not a kiss; but she, since the time that I entered, hath not ceased to kiss my feet. 47. For which reason I say to thee, Her many sins are forgiven, for she hath loved much; but he to whom less is forgiven loveth less. 48. And he said to her, Thy sins are forgiven thee. 49. And those who sat at table with him began to say within themselves, Who is this that even forgiveth sins? 50. And he said to the woman, Thy faith hath saved thee; go in peace.

36. *And one of the Pharisees requested him.* This narrative shows the captious disposition, not only to take, but to seek out, offences, which was manifested by those who did not know the office of Christ. A *Pharisee* invites Christ; from which we infer, that he was not one of those who furiously and violently opposed, nor of those who haughtily despised his doctrine. But whatever might be his mildness, he is presently offended when he sees Christ bestow a gracious reception on a woman who, in his opinion, ought not to have been permitted to approach or to converse with him; and, accordingly, disowns him as *a prophet,* because he does not acknowledge him to be the Mediator, whose peculiar office it was to bring miserable sinners into a state of reconciliation with God. It was something, no doubt, to bestow on Christ the honour due to a prophet; but he ought also to have inquired for what purpose he was sent, what he brought, and what commission he had received from the Father. Overlooking the grace of reconciliation, which was the main feature to be looked for in Christ, the Pharisee concluded that he was *not a prophet.* And, certainly, had it not been that through the grace of Christ this woman had obtained the forgiveness of her sins, and a new righteousness, she ought to have been rejected.

Simon's mistake lies only in this: Not considering that Christ came to save what was lost, he rashly concludes that Christ does not distinguish between the worthy and the unworthy. That we may not share in this dislike, let us learn, first, that Christ was given as a Deliverer to miserable and lost men,[1] and to restore them from death to life. Secondly, let every man examine himself and his life, and then we will not wonder that others are admitted along with us, for no one will dare to place himself above others. It is hypocrisy alone that leads men to be careless about themselves,[2] and haughtily to despise others.

37. *A woman who was a sinner.* The words stand literally as I have translated them, (ἥτις ἦν ἁμαρτωλός.) *Erasmus* has chosen to take the pluperfect tense, *who* HAD BEEN *a sinner*,[3] lest any one should suppose that at that time she still *was a sinner.* But by so doing, he departed from the natural meaning; for Luke intended to express the place which the woman held in society, and the opinion universally entertained respecting her. Though her sudden conversion had rendered her a different person in the sight of God from what she had previously been, yet among men the disgrace attaching to her former life had not yet been effaced. She was, therefore, in the general estimation of men *a sinner,* that is, a woman of wicked and infamous life; and this led *Simon* to conclude, though erroneously, that Christ had not the Spirit of discernment, since he was unacquainted with that infamy which was generally known.[4]

40. *And Jesus answering said.* By this reply Christ shows how egregiously Simon was mistaken. Exposing to public view his silent and concealed thought, he proves himself to possess something more excellent than what belonged to the *Prophets;* for he does not reply to his words, but refutes the sentiment which he kept hidden within his breast. Nor was it only on Simon's account that this was done, but in order to assure every one of us, that we have no reason to fear lest

---

[1] " Que Christ a esté donne pour liberateur au genre humain, miserable et perdu ;"—" that Christ was given as a deliverer to the human race, miserable and lost."

[2] " Qui fait que les hommes se me cognoissent ;"—" which makes men forget themselves."

[3] *Quæ fuerat peccatrix.*

[4] " Veu qu'il ne cognoist point l'infamie de la vie de ceste femme qui estoit notoire à un chacun ;"—" since he does not know the infamy of the life of this woman, which was notorious to every one."

any sinner be rejected by him, who not only gives them kind and friendly invitations, but is prepared with equal liberality, and—as we might say—with outstretched arms, to receive them all.

41. *A certain creditor had two debtors.* The scope of this parable is to demonstrate, that Simon is wrong in condemning the woman who is acquitted by the heavenly judge. He proves that she is righteous, not because she pleased God, but because *her sins were forgiven;* for otherwise her case would not correspond to the parable, in which Christ expressly states, that the creditor *freely forgave the debtors who were not able to pay.* We cannot avoid wondering, therefore, that the greater part of commentators have fallen into so gross a blunder as to imagine that this woman, by her *tears,* and her *anointing,* and her *kissing his feet,* deserved the pardon of her sins. The argument which Christ employs was taken, not from the cause, but from the effect; for, until a favour has been received, it cannot awaken gratitude,[1] and the cause of reciprocal love is here declared to be a free forgiveness. In a word, Christ argues from the fruits or effects that follow it, that this woman has been reconciled to God.

44. *And turning to the woman.* The Lord appears to compare Simon with the woman, in such a manner as to make him chargeable with nothing more than light offences. But this is spoken only in the way of concession. " Suppose now, Simon," he says, " that the guilt from which God discharges thee was light,[2] and that this woman has been guilty of many and very heinous offences. Yet you see how she proves by the effect that she has obtained pardon. For what mean those profuse tears, those frequent kisses of the feet, that precious ointment? What mean they but to acknowledge, that she had been weighed down by an enormous burden of condem-

[1] " Veu que le remerciment presuppose tousiours qu'on ait avant receu quelque bien ;"—" since gratitude always presupposes that some favour has been received."
[2] " Mettons le cas, Simon, que le fardeau des pechez, desquels Dieu t'a deschargé fust petit ;"—" let us put the case, Simon, that the burden of the sins, from which God has discharged thee, was small."

nation? And now she regards the mercy of God with a fervour of love proportioned to her conviction that her necessity had been great."

From the words of Christ, therefore, we are not at liberty to infer, that Simon had been a debtor to a small amount, or that he was absolved from guilt.[1] It is more probable that, as he was a blind hypocrite, he was still plunged in the filth of his sins. But Christ insists on this single point, that, however wicked the woman may have been, she gave undoubted proofs of her righteousness, by leaving no kind of duty undone to testify her gratitude, and by acknowledging, in every possible way, her vast obligations to God. At the same time, Christ reminds Simon, that he has no right to flatter himself, as if he were free from all blame; for that he too needed mercy; and that if even he does not obtain the favour of God without pardon, he ought to look upon this woman's gifts, whatever might have been her former sins, as evidences of repentance and gratitude.

We must attend to the points of contrast, in which the woman is preferred to Simon. SHE *moistened his feet with tears, and wiped them with the hairs of her head;* while *he* did not even order *water* to be given, according to custom. SHE *did not cease to kiss his feet,* while *he* did not deign to receive Christ with the kiss of hospitality.[2] *She* poured precious *ointment on his feet,* while *he* did not even *anoint his head with oil.* But why did our Lord, who was a model of frugality and economy, permit the expense of the *ointment?* It was because, in this way, the wretched sinner testified that she owed all to him. He had no desire of such luxuries, was not gratified by the sweet odour, and did not approve of gaudy dress. But he looked only at her extraordinary zeal to testify her repentance, which is also held out to us by Luke as an example; for her sorrow, which is the commencement of repentance, was proved by her tears. By placing herself *at*

---

[1] "Et s'il avoit esté absous de la condamnation qu'il avoit encouruë;"—"and if he had been absolved from the condemnation which he had incurred."

[2] "En lieu que l'autre n'a pas mesme daigné le baiser par une façon commune de civilité;"—"whereas the other did not even deign to kiss him, according to an ordinary custom of civility."

Christ's feet behind him, and there lying on the ground, she discovered her modesty and humility. By the *ointment,* she declared that she offered, as a sacrifice to Christ, herself and all that she possessed. Every one of these things it is our duty to imitate; but the pouring of the *ointment* was an extraordinary act, which it would be improper to consider as a rule.[1]

47. *Her many sins are forgiven.* Some interpret the verb differently, *may her many sins be forgiven,* and bring out the following meaning:—" As this woman evinces by remarkable actions, that she is full of ardent love to Christ, it would be improper for the Church to act harshly and severely towards her; but, on the contrary, she ought to be treated with gentleness, whatever may have been the aggravations of her offences." But as ἀφέωνται is used, in accordance with the Athic dialect, for ἀφεῖνται, we must dispense with that subtlety of exposition which is disapproved by the context; for a little after, Christ uses the same words in his address to the woman, where the imperative mood would not apply. Here, too, is added a corresponding clause, that *he to whom less is forgiven loveth less.*

The verb, which is in the present tense, must, no doubt, be resolved into a preterite.[2] From the eager desire which she had manifested to discharge all the duties of piety, Christ infers that, although this woman might have been guilty of many sins, the mercy of God was so abundant towards her, that she ought no longer to be regarded as a sinner. Again, *loving* is not here said to be the cause of pardon,[3] but a subsequent manifestation, as I have formerly mentioned; for the

[1] " A esté un acte special et extraordinaire, duquel si on vouloit faire une reigle generale, ce seroit un abus;"—" was a special and extraordinary act, of which, if we wished to make a general rule, it would be a mistake."

[2] " Combien qu'il faut resoudre le verbe du temps present en un temps passé: comme quand il dit, *Ses pechez luy sont pardonnez :* il faut entendre, *Ont esté pardonnez;*"—" though the verb must be resolved from the present tense into a past tense: as when he says, *Her sins are forgiven,* we must understand it to mean, *Have been forgiven.*"

[3] " Il n'est pas dit ici que la dilection ou amour des hommes envers Dieu soit la cause de la remission des pechez;"—" it is not here said that the *loving,* or the love of men towards God, is the cause of the forgiveness of sins."

meaning of the words is this:—" They who perceive the display of deep piety in the woman form an erroneous judgment, if they do not conclude that God is already reconciled to her;" so that the free pardon of sins comes first in order. Christ does not inquire at what price men may purchase the favour of God, but argues that God has already forgiven this wretched sinner, and that, therefore, a mortal man ought not to treat her with severity.

48. *Thy sins are forgiven.* It may be asked, why does Christ now promise to her the pardon which she had obtained, and of which she had been assured? Some reply that these words were uttered, not so much on her own account, as for the sake of others. For my own part, I have no doubt that it was chiefly on her own account; and this appears more clearly from the words that follow. Nor ought we to wonder, that the voice of Christ again pronounces an absolution of the woman, who had already tasted his grace, and who was even convinced that he was her only refuge of salvation. Thus, at the present day, faith is previously necessary, when we pray that the Lord would forgive our sins; and yet this is not a useless or superfluous prayer, but the object of it is, that the heavenly Judge may more and more seal his mercy on our hearts, and in this manner may give us peace. Though this woman had brought with her a confident reliance on that grace which she had obtained, yet this promise was not superfluous, but contributed greatly to the confirmation of her faith.

49. *And those who sat at table with him began to say within themselves.* Hence we again learn, that ignorance of Christ's office constantly leads men to conceive new grounds of offence. The root of the evil is, that no one examines his own wretched condition, which undoubtedly would arouse every man to seek a remedy. There is no reason to wonder that hypocrites, who slumber amidst their vices,[1] should murmur at it as a thing new and unexpected, when Christ forgives sins.

[1] " Qui se plaisent et flattent en leurs vices ;"—" who please and flatter themselves amidst their vices."

50. *Thy faith hath saved thee.* To repress those murmurings,[1] and, at the same time, to confirm the woman, Christ commends her faith. Let others grumble as they may, but do thou adhere stedfastly to that faith which has brought thee an undoubted salvation.[2] At the same time, Christ claims for himself the authority which had been given to him by the Father; for, as he possesses the power of healing, to him faith is properly directed. And this intimates that the woman was not led by rashness or mistake to come to him, but that, through the guidance of the Spirit, she had preserved the straight road of faith. Hence it follows, that we cannot believe in any other than the Son of God, without considering that person to have the disposal of life and death. If the true reason for believing in Christ be, that God hath given him authority to forgive sins, whenever faith is rendered to another, that honour which is due to Christ must of necessity be taken from him. This saying refutes also the error of those who imagine that the forgiveness of sins is purchased by charity; for Christ lays down a quite different method, which is, that we embrace by faith the offered mercy. The last clause, *Go in peace,* denotes that inestimable fruit of faith which is so frequently commended in Scripture. It brings *peace* and joy to the consciences, and prevents them from being driven hither and thither by uneasiness and alarm.

LUKE.

X. 38. And it happened, while they were travelling, that he entered into a certain village; and a certain woman, called Martha, received him into her house. 39. And she had a sister called Mary, who also, sitting at the feet of Jesus, heard his word. 40. And Martha was cumbered about much serving; who stood, and said, Lord, hast thou no care that my sister hath left me to serve alone? bid her therefore assist me. 41. And Jesus answering said to her, Martha, Martha, thou art anxious and distressed about many things. 42. But one thing is necessary: Mary hath chosen the good part, which shall not be taken from her.

38. *And it happened that he entered into a certain village.*

[1] "Pour reprimer les murmures de ces gens;"—"to repress the murmurings of those people."
[2] "Qui t'a apporté certitude de salut;"—"which has brought thee certainty of salvation."

This narrative shows, that Christ, wherever he came, did not devote himself to his private concerns, or consult his own ease or comfort; but that the single object which he kept in view was, to do good to others, and to discharge the office which had been committed to him by the Father. Luke relates that, having been hospitably received by Martha, as soon as he entered the house, he began to teach and exhort. As this passage has been basely distorted into the commendation of what is called a Contemplative life, we must inquire into its true meaning, from which it will appear, that nothing was farther from the design of Christ, than to encourage his disciples to indulge in indolence, or in useless speculations. It is, no doubt, an old error,[1] that those who withdraw from business, and devote themselves entirely to a contemplative, lead an Angelical life. For the absurdities which the *Sorbonnists*[2] utter on this subject they appear to have been indebted to Aristotle, who places the highest good, and ultimate end, of human life in contemplation, which, according to him, is the enjoyment of virtue. When some men were driven by ambition to withdraw from the ordinary intercourse of life, or when peevish men gave themselves up to solitude and indolence, the resolution to adopt

---

[1] "Il est vray que ceste erreur n'est pas d'auiourd'huy, mais est bien ancien;"—" it is true that this error is not of to-day, but is very old."

[2] Some readers may happen to ask, Who were the *Sorbonnists*, or, as they are often called, *the Doctors of the Sorbonne?* In reply, I take the liberty of extracting from a volume, which I gave to the world a few years ago, a few remarks on this subject.—" The College of the *Sorbonne*, in Paris, takes its name from *Robert de Sorbonne*, who founded it in the middle of the thirteenth century. Its reputation for theological learning, philosophy, classical literature, and all that formerly constituted a liberal education, was deservedly high. In the Doctors of the Sorbonne the Reformation found powerful adversaries. The very name of this University, to which the greatest scholars in Europe were accustomed to pay deference, would be regarded by the multitude with blind veneration. If such men as Calvin, Beza, Melancthon, and Luther, were prepared by talents and acquirements of the first order to brave the terrors of that name, they must have frequently lamented its influence on many of their hearers. Yet our author meets undaunted this formidable array, and enters the field with the full assurance of victory. Despising, as we naturally do, the weak superstitions and absurd tenets held by the Church of Rome, we are apt to underrate our obligations to the early champions of the Reformed faith, who encountered with success those veteran warriors, and *contended earnestly* (Jude, ver. 3) *for the faith which was once delivered to the saints.*"—(*Biblical Cabinet*, vol. xxx. p. 140.)—*Ed.*

that course was followed by such pride, that they imagined themselves to be like the angels, because they did nothing; for they entertained as great a contempt for active life, as if it had kept them back from heaven. On the contrary, we know that men were created for the express purpose of being employed in labour of various kinds, and that no sacrifice is more pleasing to God, than when every man applies diligently to his own calling, and endeavours to live in such a manner as to contribute to the general advantage.[1]

How absurdly they have perverted the words of Christ to support their own contrivance, will appear manifest when we have ascertained the natural meaning. Luke says that *Mary sat at the feet of Jesus.* Does he mean that she did nothing else throughout her whole life? On the contrary, the Lord enjoins his followers to make such a distribution of their time, that he who desires to make proficiency in the school of Christ shall not always be an idle hearer, but shall put in practice what he has learned; for there is a time to hear, and a time to act.[2] It is, therefore, a foolish attempt of the monks to take hold of this passage, as if Christ were drawing a comparison between a contemplative and an active life, while Christ simply informs us for what end, and in what manner, he wishes to be received.

Though the hospitality of Martha deserved commendation, and is commended, yet there were two faults in it which are pointed out by Christ. The first is, that Martha carried her activity beyond proper bounds; for Christ would rather have chosen to be entertained in a frugal manner, and at moderate expense, than that the holy woman should have submitted to so much toil. The second fault was, that Martha, by distracting her attention, and undertaking more labour than was necessary, deprived herself of the advantage of Christ's visit. The excess is pointed out by Luke, when he speaks of *much serving;* for Christ was satisfied with

[1] " Met peine de vivre en sorte qu'il apporte quelque profit à la societé commune des hommes ;"—" endeavours to live so as to yield some advantage to the general society of men."
[2] " Car il y a temps d'ouir, et temps de faire, et de mettre la main à la besongne ;"—" for there is a time to hear, and a time to act, and to put the hand to the work."

little. It was just as if one were to give a magnificent reception to a prophet, and yet not to care about hearing him, but, on the contrary, to make so great and unnecessary preparations as to bury all the instruction. But the true way of receiving prophets is, to accept the advantage which God presents and offers to us through their agency.

We now see that the kind attention of Martha, though it deserved praise, was not without its blemishes. There was this additional evil, that Martha was so delighted with her own bustling operations, as to despise her sister's pious eagerness to receive instruction.[1] This example warns us, that, in doing what is right, we must take care not to think more highly of ourselves than of others.

42. *But one thing is necessary.* Some give a very meagre interpretation of these words, as if they meant that one sort of dish is enough.[2] Others make ingenious inquiries, but beside the purpose, about Unity.[3] But Christ had quite another design, which was, that whatever believers may undertake to do, and in whatever employments they may engage, there is one object to which every thing ought to be referred. In a word, we do but wander to no purpose, if we do not direct all our actions to a fixed object. The hospitality of Martha was faulty in this respect, that she neglected the main business, and devoted herself entirely to household affairs. And yet Christ does not mean that every thing else, with the exception of this *one thing*, is of no importance, but that we must pay a proper attention to order, lest what is *accessory*—as the phrase is—become our chief concern.

Mary hath chosen the good part. There is no comparison here, as unskilful and mistaken interpreters dream. Christ

---

[1] "En la conduite du banquet, et bruit de mesnage;"—"in the preparation of the entertainment, and the noise of household affairs."

[2] "Comme si Christ entendoit qu'il y a assez d'un mets, ou d'une sorte de viande;"—"as if Christ meant that one dish, or one sort of food, is enough."

[3] "De Monade."—"Les autres plus subtilement, mais mal à propos, traittans ici de l'unité: comme si par ce mot de Un, Iesus Christ eust voulu exclurre tout nombre;"—"others more ingeniously, but inappropriately, treating here of *unity:* as if, by the word *One,* Jesus Christ intended to exclude all diversity of employment."

only declares, that Mary is engaged in a holy and profitable employment, in which she ought not to be disturbed. "You would have a good right," he says, "to blame your sister, if she indulged in ease, or gave herself up to trifling occupations, or aimed at something unsuitable to her station, and left to you the whole charge of the household affairs. But now, when she is properly and usefully employed in hearing, it would be an act of injustice to withdraw her from it; for an opportunity so favourable is not always in her power." There are some, indeed, who give a different interpretation to the latter clause, *which shall not be taken away from her*, as if Christ intended to say, that *Mary hath chosen the good part*, because the fruit of heavenly doctrine can never perish. For my own part, I have no objection to that opinion, but have followed the view which appeared to me to be more in accordance with Christ's design.[1]

LUKE.

XII. 13. And one out of the multitude said to him, Master, bid my brother divide the inheritance with me. 14. And he said to him, Man, who made me a judge or a divider over you? 15. And he said to them, Take heed and beware of covetousness; for the life of any man does not consist in the abundance of those things which he possesseth.[2] 16. And he spoke a parable to them, saying, The field of a certain rich man yielded an abundant produce. 17. And he thought within himself, saying, What shall I do? for I have no place in which I can collect my fruits. 18. And he said, I will do this: I will pull down my barns, and will build larger ones, and there I will collect all my fruits and my goods. 19. And I will say to my soul, Soul, thou hast many goods laid up for many years: take thine ease, eat, drink, and enjoy thyself.[3] 20. But God said to him, Fool, this night they shall demand thy soul from thee;[4] and as to the

---

[1] CALVIN appears to interpret the words, *which shall not be taken from her*, not as a doctrinal statement, but as a command, or, at least, as marking out the line of conduct which ought to be pursued by *Martha* and others towards *Mary*. *The good part*, or, as he explains it, "the holy and profitable employment," *shall not be taken from her*. "She ought not to be disturbed," and "it would be an act of injustice to withdraw her from it."—*Ed.*

[2] "Car encore que 'les biens' abondent à quelqu'un, si n'a-il pas vie par les biens;"—"for though a man may abound in wealth, yet he has not life by his wealth."

[3] "Et fay grand'chere;"—"and make great cheer."

[4] "En ceste nuict ton ame te sera ostee, ou, on te redemandera ton ame;"—"this night thy soul shall be taken from thee, or, thy soul shall be asked again from thee."

LUKE.

things which thou hast provided, to whom shall they go? 21. So is he that layeth up for himself,[1] and is not rich toward God.

13. *Bid my brother divide.* Our Lord, when requested to undertake the office of *dividing an inheritance,* refuses to do so. Now as this tended to promote brotherly harmony, and as Christ's office was, not only to reconcile men to God, but to bring them into a state of agreement with one another, what hindered him from settling the dispute between the two brothers?[2] There appear to have been chiefly two reasons why he declined the office of *a judge.* First, as the Jews imagined that the Messiah would have an earthly kingdom,[3] he wished to guard against doing any thing that might countenance this error. If they had seen him divide *inheritances,* the report of that proceeding would immediately have been circulated. Many would have been led to expect a carnal redemption, which they too ardently desired; and wicked men would have loudly declared, that he was effecting a revolution in the state, and overturning the Roman Empire. Nothing could be more appropriate, therefore, than this reply, by which all would be informed, that the kingdom of Christ is spiritual. Let us learn from this to regulate our conduct by prudence, and to undertake nothing which may admit of an unfavourable construction.

Secondly, our Lord intended to draw a distinction between the political kingdoms of this world and the government of his Church; for he had been appointed by the Father to be a Teacher, who should *divide asunder, by the sword of the word, the thoughts and feelings, and penetrate into the souls of men,* (Heb. iv. 12,) but was not a magistrate to *divide inheritances.* This condemns the robbery of the Pope

[1] "Ainsi est celuy qui thesaurize (*ou, a fait grand amas de biens*) pour soy;"—"so is he that hoards up (*or, has formed a great heap of goods*) for himself."

[2] "On pourroit demander qui a empesché qu'il ne se soit entremis d'oster toute occasion de debat entre deux freres?"—"It might be asked, what hindered him from undertaking to remove all ground of quarrel between two brothers?"

[3] "Que le Messias regneroit à la façon des princes terriens;"—"that the Messiah would reign in the manner of earthly princes."

and his clergy, who, while they give themselves out to be pastors of the Church, have dared to usurp an earthly and secular jurisdiction, which is inconsistent with their office; for what is in itself lawful may be improper in certain persons.

There was also, in my opinion, a third reason of great weight. Christ saw that this man was neglecting doctrine, and was looking only to his private concerns. This is too common a disease. Many who profess the Gospel do not scruple to make use of it as a false pretence for advancing their private interests, and to plead the authority of Christ as an apology for their gains. From the exhortation,[1] which is immediately added, we may readily draw this inference; for if that man had not availed himself of the Gospel as a pretext for his own emolument, Christ would not have taken occasion to give this warning against *covetousness*. The context, therefore, makes it sufficiently evident, that this was a pretended disciple, whose mind was entirely occupied with lands or money.

It is highly absurd in the Anabaptists to infer from this reply, that no Christian man has a right to *divide inheritances*, to take a part in legal decisions, or to discharge any public office. Christ does not argue from the nature of the thing itself, but from his own calling. Having been appointed by the Father for a different purpose, he declares that he is not a *judge*, because he has received no such command. Let us hold by this rule, that every one keep within the limits of the calling which God has given him.

15. *Take heed and beware of covetousness.* Christ first guards his followers against *covetousness*, and next, in order to cure their minds entirely of this disease, he declares, that *our life consisteth not in abundance.* These words point out the inward fountain and source, from which flows the mad

---

[1] " En considerant la circonstance de l'exhortation qui est ici adioustee, il est aisé a iuger que cestuy-ci estoit mené d'une telle affection perverse ;" —" by considering the circumstance of the exhortation which is here added, it may easily be inferred that this man was under the influence of such a wicked disposition."

eagerness for gain. It is because the general belief is, that a man is happy in proportion as he possesses much, and that the happiness of life is produced by riches. Hence arise those immoderate desires, which, like a fiery furnace, send forth their flames, and yet cease not to burn within. If we were convinced that riches, and any kind of *abundance*, are evils of the present life, which the Lord bestows upon us with his own hand, and the use of which is accompanied by his blessing, this single consideration would have a powerful influence in restraining all wicked desires; and this is what believers have come to learn from their own experience.[1] For whence comes it, that they moderate their wishes, and depend on God alone, but because they do not look upon their life as necessarily connected with *abundance*, or dependent upon it, but rely on the providence of God, who alone upholds us by his power, and supplies us with whatever is necessary?

16. *And he spoke a parable to them.* This parable presents to us, as in a mirror, a lively portrait of this sentiment, that men *do not live by their abundance.* Since the life even of the richest men is taken away in a moment, what avails it that they have accumulated great wealth? All acknowledge it to be true, so that Christ says nothing here but what is perfectly common, and what every man has constantly in his mouth. But where is the man that honestly believes it? Do not all, on the contrary, regulate their life, and arrange their schemes and employments in such a manner as to withdraw to the greatest distance from God, making their life to rest on a present abundance of good things? It is therefore necessary that all should immediately arouse themselves, lest, by imagining their happiness to consist in riches, they entangle themselves in the snares of *covetousness.*

This parable shows us, first, that the present life is short and transitory. Secondly, it points out to us, that riches are of no avail for prolonging life. We must add a third, which is not expressed, but may easily be inferred from the other

[1] " Ce que les fideles experimentent ton les iours en eux-mesmes estre vray;"—" which believers every day experience in themselves to be true."

two; that it is a most excellent remedy for believers, to ask from the Lord their daily bread, and to rely on his providence alone, whether they are rich or poor.

17. *What shall I do?* Wicked men are driven to perplexity in their deliberations, because they do not know how any thing is to be lawfully used;[1] and, next, because they are intoxicated with a foolish confidence which makes them forget themselves. Thus we find that this *rich man* lengthens out his expectation of life in proportion to his large income, and drives far away from him the remembrance of death. And yet this pride is accompanied by distrust; for those men, when they have had their fill, are still agitated by insatiable desire, like this *rich man,* who enlarges his *barns,* as if his belly, which had been filled with his former *barns,* had not got enough. At the same time, Christ does not expressly condemn this man for acting the part of a careful householder in storing up his produce, but because his ravenous desire, like a deep whirlpool, swallows up and devours many *barns ;* from which it follows that he does not comprehend the proper use of an abundant produce.

19. *Take thine ease, eat, drink, enjoy thyself.* When he exhorts himself to *eat and drink,* he no longer remembers that he is a man, but swells into pride by relying on his abundance. We daily perceive striking instances of this disdainful conduct[2] in irreligious men, who hold up the mass of their riches, as if it were nothing less than a brazen rampart against death. When he says, *Eat, my soul, and enjoy thyself,* there is an emphatic meaning in this Hebrew idiom;[3] for he addresses himself in such a manner as to imply, that he has all that is necessary for gratifying all his senses and all his desires.

[1] " Pource qu'ils ne scavent point quel est le droit et legitime usage des creatures de Dieu ;"—" because they know not what is the proper and lawful use of the creatures of God."
[2] " D'une telle mecognoissance et fierté ;"—" of such ingratitude and pride.'
[3] " En ceste locution Hebraique il y a une vehemence et proprie plus que les mots n'emportent de prime face ;"—" in that Hebrew form of expression there is greater force and propriety than the words at first sight bear."

20. *Fool, this night they will demand thy soul from thee.* The word *soul* carries an allusion. Formerly, the *rich man* addressed his *soul* as the seat of all the affections: but now, he speaks of the life itself, or the vital spirit. The words, *they will demand,* (ἀπαιτοῦσιν,) though in the plural number, are used indefinitely, and mean nothing more than that the *life* of the *rich man,* which he imagined to be in his own power, was at the disposal of another. I advert to this, because some take occasion from them to make unfounded speculations about angels. The design of Christ is simply to show that the life of men, which they imagine to be strongly protected by the fortress of their riches, is every moment[1] taken away. The *rich man* is thus convicted of folly, in not knowing that his life depended on another.

21. *So is he that layeth up for himself.* As the two clauses are evidently contrasted, the one must be taken into account for the exposition of the other. Let us ascertain, therefore, what is meant by being *rich in God,* or, "towards God," or, "with respect to God." Those who are tolerably acquainted with the Scriptures know that the preposition εἰς not unfrequently takes the sense of ἐν. But whether it be understood in the one sense or in the other, is of little consequence; for the meaning comes to this, that they are *rich according to God,* who do not trust to earthly things, but depend solely on his providence. It matters not whether they are in abundance or in want, provided that both classes present their sincere prayers to the Lord for their daily bread. The corresponding phrase, *layeth up for himself,* conveys the idea that this man paid no attention to the blessing of God, but anxiously heaped up an immense store, so that his confidence was shut up in his *barns.*[2] Hence we may easily conclude that the parable was intended to show, that vain are the deliberations and foolish attempts of those who, trusting to the abundance

---

[1] "Que d'heure en heure la vie est ostee aux hommes;"—"that from hour to hour the life of man is taken away."

[2] "En sorte que la fiance de l'homme est en ses greniers, ou en ses coffres;"—"so that the confidence of the man is in his granaries, or in his chests."

of their wealth, do not rely on God alone, and are not satisfied with their own share, or prepared for whatever may befall them;[1] and, finally, that such persons will suffer the penalty of their own folly.

LUKE.

XIII. 1. And at that time some were present, who told him of the Galileans, whose blood Pilate had mingled with their sacrifices. 2. And Jesus answering said to them, Do you imagine that these Galileans were sinners beyond all the Galileans, because they suffered such things? 3. I tell you, no; but unless you repent, you will all perish in like manner. 4. Or those eighteen, on whom the tower in Siloah fell and slew them, do you imagine that they were debtors beyond all men that dwell in Jerusalem?[2] 5. I tell you, no; but unless you repent, you shall all perish in like manner. 6. And he spake this parable: A certain man had a fig-tree planted in his vineyard, and came seeking fruit on it, and did not find it. 7. And he said to the vine-dresser, Lo, there are three years that I come seeking fruit on this fig-tree, and find none: cut it down; why does it even occupy the ground?[3] 8. But he answering, said to him, Lord, let it alone this year also, till I shall dig about it, and dung it: 9. And if it bear fruit:[4] but if not, afterwards thou shalt cut it down.

2. *Do you imagine? &c.* This passage is highly useful, were it for no other reason than that this disease is almost natural to us, to be too rigorous and severe in judging of others, and too much disposed to flatter our own faults. The consequence is, that we not only censure with excessive severity the offences of our brethren; but whenever they meet with any calamity, we condemn them as wicked and reprobate persons. On the other hand, every man that is not sorely pressed by the hand of God slumbers at ease in the midst of his sins, as if God were favourable and reconciled to him. This involves a double fault; for when God chastises any one before our eyes, he warns us of his judgments, that each of us may examine himself, and consider what he deserves. If he spares us for a time, we are so far from having a right to take such

---

[1] "Estans prests à recevoir ce qu'il plaira à Dieu leur envoyer;"—"being prepared to receive what God may be pleased to send to them."

[2] "Eussent offensé plus que tous les habitans de Ierusalem;"—"had offended more than all the inhabitants of Jerusalem."

[3] "A quel propos aussi empesche-t-il la terre?"—"for what end does it even cumber the ground?"

[4] "Que s'il fait fruict, 'bien:' sinon tu le couperas ci-apres;"—"and if it bears fruit, 'well:' if not, thou shalt cut it down afterwards."

kindness and forbearance as an opportunity for slumber, that we ought to regard it as an invitation to repentance.

To correct the false and cruel judgment which we are accustomed to pass on wretched sufferers, and, at the same time, to shake off the indulgence which every man cherishes towards himself, he shows, first, that those who are treated with severity are not the most wicked of all men; because God administers his judgments in such a manner, that some are instantly seized and punished, and others are permitted to remain long in the enjoyment of ease and luxury, Secondly, he declares that all the calamities which happen in the world are so many demonstrations of the wrath of God; and hence we learn what an awful destruction awaits us,[1] if we do not avert it.

The immediate occasion for this exhortation was, that *some told him that Pilate had mingled* human *blood with sacrifices*, in order that so shocking an event might bring *sacrifices* into abhorrence. As it is probable that this outrage was committed on the Samaritans, who had departed from the pure service of the Law, the Jews would easily and readily be disposed to condemn the Samaritans, and by so doing to applaud themselves. But our Lord applies it to a different purpose. As that whole nation was hated and detested by them on account of ungodliness, he puts the question, " Do you imagine that those wretched persons, who have been put to death by Pilate, were worse than others? You are perfectly aware, that that country is full of ungodly men, and that many who deserved the same punishment are still alive. He is a blind and wicked judge who decides as to the sins of all men by the punishments which they now endure. It is not always the most wicked man who is first dragged to punishment; but when God selects a few out of a large number to be punished, he holds out in their person a threatening that he will take vengeance on the remainder, in order that all may be alarmed."

Having spoken of the Samaritans, he now approaches more

---

[1] " Dont nous avons à penser quelle punition et damnation nous sentirons ;"—" by which we are led to consider what punishment and condemnation we shall receive."

closely to the Jews themselves. *Eighteen men* had at that time been killed by the fall of a *tower* in Jerusalem. He declares that those men were not more wicked than others, but that their death was held out to all as a ground of alarm; for if in them God gave a display of his judgment, no more would others, though they might be spared for a time, escape his hand. Christ does not, however, forbid believers to consider attentively the judgments of God, but enjoins them to observe this order, to begin with their own sins. They will thus obtain the highest advantage; for they will avert God's chastisements by voluntary repentance. To the same purpose is the warning which Paul gives, *Let no man deceive you with vain words; for on account of these things the wrath of God cometh against the rebellious,* (Eph. v. 6.)

6. *He spoke also this parable.* The substance of it is, that many are endured for a time who deserve to be cut off; but that they gain nothing by the delay, if they persist in their obstinacy. The wicked flattery, by which hypocrites are hardened, and become more obstinate, arises from this cause, that they do not think of their sins till they are compelled; and, therefore, so long as God winks at these, and delays his chastisements, they imagine that he is well satisfied with them. Thus they indulge themselves more freely, as if, to use the words of Isaiah, (xxviii. 15,) they *had made a covenant with death, and were in friendship with the grave.* And this is the reason why Paul denounces them in such earnestness of language for *treasuring up to themselves the wrath of God against the last day,* (Rom. ii. 5.) It is well known that trees are sometimes preserved, not because their owners find them to be useful and productive, but because the careful and industrious husbandman makes every possible trial and experiment before he determines to remove them out of the field or vineyard. This teaches us that, when the Lord does not immediately take vengeance on the reprobate, but delays to punish them, there are the best reasons for his forbearance. Such considerations serve to restrain human rashness, that no man may dare to murmur against the supreme Judge of all, if He does not always execute his judgments in one uniform man-

ner. A comparison is here drawn between the *owner* and the *vine-dresser:* not that God's ministers go beyond him in gentleness and forbearance, but because the Lord not only prolongs the life of sinners, but likewise cultivates them in a variety of ways, that they may yield better fruit.

LUKE.

XIII. 10. And he was teaching in one of the synagogues on the Sabbath. 11. And, lo, a woman who had a spirit of infirmity during eighteen years, and was bent down, and was altogether unable to lift up her head.[1] 12. Whom when Jesus saw, he called her to him, and said to her, Woman, thou art delivered from thine infirmity. 13. And he laid his hands on her, and immediately she stood upright, and glorified God. 14. And the ruler of the synagogue answering, being offended because Christ had performed a cure on the Sabbath, said to the multitude, There are six days on which we ought to work: on them therefore come, and you shall be cured, and not on the Sabbath-day. 15. And the Lord answering said to her, Doth not each of you, on the Sabbath, loose his ox or his ass from the stall, and lead him away to watering? 16. And must not this daughter of Abraham, whom Satan hath bound, lo, eighteen years, be loosed from this bond on the Sabbath-day? 17. And while he was saying these things, all his adversaries were ashamed, and all the people rejoiced on account of all the glorious actions which were done by him.

I have resolved to place in immediate connection some events which are detailed by Luke alone, without a direct reference to dates; for on that point, as we have formerly mentioned, the Evangelists did not care much about exactness. We shall afterwards find a more suitable time for returning to the *Harmony of the Three Evangelists.*

11. *And, lo, a woman.* Here is related a miracle performed on a woman who was cured, and the offence which the malignity of the Jews led them to take up, because our Lord had cured her on a *Sabbath*-day. Luke says that the *woman* was held by a *spirit of infirmity,* so that her body was bent by the contraction of her nerves. As the nature of the disease is no farther described, it is probable that it was not one of an ordinary kind, or which was understood by physicians; and, therefore, he calls it a spirit of *infirmity.* We know that diseases of an unusual and extraordinary kind are, for the most

---

[1] "Laquelle estoit courbe, et ne pouvoit aucunement se dresser;"—"who was bent down, and was quite unable to stand upright."

part, inflicted on men through the agency of the devil; and this gave the more striking display of the divine power of Christ, which triumphed over Satan. Not that Satan rules over men according to his pleasure, but only so far as God grants to him permission to injure them. Besides, as the Lord, from whom alone all our blessings flow, makes his glory to shine with peculiar brightness in those blessings which are more remarkable, and of rare occurrence; so, on the other hand, it is his will that the power and tyranny of Satan should be chiefly regarded in extraordinary chastisements, though his agency is likewise employed in those more gentle applications of the rod, which we experience from day to day.

12. *Woman, thou art delivered.* In this miracle, as well as in others, Christ exhibited a proof both of his power and of his grace; for in this manner he testified that he had come for the purpose of granting relief to the wretched. His power is expressed in these words, *Woman, thou art delivered;* for he authoritatively declares that deliverance was at his own disposal, and employs, at the same time, the outward sign, the use of which we have explained on a former occasion.

13. *And glorified God.* As to the people *glorifying God*, it is mentioned in order to inform us, that this was distinctly perceived to be a heavenly blessing. It was not some doubtful work which allowed room for argument on either side, but one which afforded ample and undoubted grounds for praising God. This discovers more strongly the malignity of the *ruler of the synagogue.*

14. *There are six days.* This reprover does not venture to pass censure openly on Christ, but points the venom of his dislike to another quarter, and indirectly condemns Christ in the person of the multitude. What an astonishing display of furious malice! *Six days*, he tells them, were set apart for labour; but how incorrectly and foolishly does he define that *work*, which is not permitted but on *six days!* Why does he not likewise forbid them to enter the synagogue, lest they should violate the Sabbath? Why does he

not order them to refrain from all the exercises of godliness? But granting that men are restrained from following their own employments *on the Sabbath-day,* how unreasonable is it that the grace of God should be limited in that manner!

On them, therefore, come and you shall be cured. He bids them come on the other days to seek a *cure,* as if the power of God lay asleep *on Sabbath,* and were not rather exerted chiefly on that day for the salvation of his people. What purpose is to be served by the holy assemblies, except to give an opportunity to believers for entreating the Divine assistance? That ungodly *hypocrite* talks as if the lawful observation of *the Sabbath* interrupted the course of God's favours, hindered men from calling upon him, and took away from them all feeling of his kindness.

15. *Doth not every one of you? &c.* Such a combination of malice and stupidity might easily have been exposed in many ways, but Christ satisfied himself with this single argument. If it be lawful *on the Sabbath* to perform the offices of humanity to cattle, it is ridiculous to imagine that the due observance of it will prevent assistance from being granted to the children of God. The words of Christ present a twofold comparison : that of the cattle with the *daughter of Abraham,* and that of the halter by which the *ass* or the *ox* is tied to *its stall* with the chains of Satan, by which he holds men bound to their destruction. "You," says he, "who are so scrupulous about observing the Sabbath, venture to *loose oxen and asses, and lead them away to watering.* And why may not I be permitted to perform a similar office of kindness to the elect people of God; especially when the necessity is more urgent, when some one is to be delivered from the *snares of Satan?*"

Now though the wicked reprover was struck dumb with shame, yet we perceive that Christ never performed any work, however illustrious, which wicked men did not seize as an occasion for slander. Nor need we wonder that Satan laboured, with incessant zeal and exertions, to subvert the glory of Christ; for he is constantly employed in spreading his clouds, in order to darken the holy actions of believers.

It deserves our attention, that Christ gives the designation, *daughter of Abraham,* to one whose body had been *enslaved by Satan during eighteen years.* She was so called, not only in reference to her lineage, as all the Jews without exception gloried in this title, but because she was one of the true and actual members of the Church. Here we perceive also what Paul tells us, that some are *delivered to Satan for the destruction of the flesh, that the spirit may be saved in the day of the Lord Jesus,* (1 Cor. v. 5.) And the length of time points out to us that, though the Lord does not immediately relieve our distresses, yet we ought not to despair.

LUKE.

XIII. 31. The same day some of the Pharisees came, saying to him, Depart, and go hence: for Herod intends to kill thee. 32. And he said to them, Go, tell that fox, Lo, I cast out devils, and I perform cures to-day and to-morrow, and the third day I am completed.[1] 33. But yet I must walk to-day and to-morrow, and the following day ; for it is not a usual occurrence that a prophet perish anywhere else than in Jerusalem.[2]

It is difficult to ascertain the precise time when this happened, farther than that Christ was at that time residing in Galilee, as during the whole period of his public calling he remained longer there than in any other place. Certain persons, wishing to be considered as his friends, advise him that, if he wishes to be in safety, he should go beyond the boundaries of Herod's jurisdiction. In what manner those who gave that advice were affected towards him we have no means of knowing ; but I am strongly inclined to conjecture, that they attempted to drive him to some other place, because they saw that the greater part of the people in that place were attached to Christ, so that the Gospel was generally received. We must observe who those advisers were. Luke says that they were *some of the Pharisees.* Now we know that that sect was not so favourable to Christ as to make it probable that those men were anxious about his life. What then ? Their design was, to awaken in him such fears as would

---

[1] " Et au troisieme iour ie pren fin ;"—" and on the third day I conclude."

[2] " Car il n'advient point qu'aucun Prophete meure hors de Ierusalem ;" —" for it does not happen that any Prophet dies out of Jerusalem."

drive him to some place of concealment; for they expected that, in a short time, his authority would decline, and that his whole doctrine would vanish away. But we must also direct our attention to the first originator and contriver of this scheme, Satan; for, as he endeavoured at that time to interrupt the progress of the Gospel, by terrifying the Son of God, so he constantly invents and hatches up new grounds of alarm, to strike the ministers of Christ with dismay, and to constrain them to turn aside.

32. *Go, tell that fox.* It is certain, that the person here spoken of is Herod Antipas. Though he had throughout the character of a *fox*, and was as remarkable for servility as for cunning, I do not think that the term, *fox*, is intended to refer generally to the cunning of his whole life, but rather to the insidious methods by which he laboured to undermine the doctrine of the Gospel, when he did not venture to attack it openly. Christ tells him that, with all his craftiness, he will gain nothing by his schemes. "Whatever artifices he may devise," says Christ, " *to-day and to-morrow* I will discharge the office which God has enjoined upon me; and when I shall have reached the end of my course, I shall then be offered in sacrifice." That we may perceive more clearly the meaning of the words, Christ acknowledges, in the former part of his message, that on *the third day*—that is, within a very short time—he must die; and in this way shows, that he could not be deterred from his duty by any fear of death, to which he advanced boldly, with fixed purpose of mind.

33. *It does not usually happen, &c.* He next adds, that it is an idle bugbear, which is held out by false and hypocritical advisers; because there is no danger of death *anywhere else than at Jerusalem.* In this second clause he sharply attacks the Pharisees. "Is it you, who—I foresee—will be my executioners, that advise me to beware of *Herod?*" The reproof extends, indeed, much farther; for he says, not only that preparations had been made for his own death in *Jerusalem,* but that it might be said to have been, for a long period, a den of robbers, in which almost all the *prophets* had been

murdered. Many had, no doubt, been slain in other places, and particularly at the time when that cruel fury,[1] Jezebel, (1 Kings xix. 2,) raged against them; but because in no other place had the *prophets*, at any time, been fiercely tormented, Christ justly brings this reproach against the ungodly inhabitants of the holy city.

It usually happened that the prophets were slain there; because not only was it the source of all the ungodliness which spread over the whole of Judea, but it was also the field on which God trained his *prophets*.[2] We know that the more brightly the light of doctrine shines, so as to press more closely on wicked men, they are driven to a greater pitch of madness. What a dreadful example was it, that a place which had been chosen to be the sanctuary of divine worship, and the residence of the Law and of heavenly wisdom, should be polluted not by one or another murder, but by a regular butchery of the *prophets!* It undoubtedly shows how obstinate is the rebellion of the world in rejecting sound doctrine.

The exclamation which immediately follows in Luke, (xiii. 34,) appears to be connected in such a manner, as if Christ had taken occasion from the present occurrence to inveigh, at this time, against *Jerusalem*. But for my own part, I rather think, that Luke, having said that *Jerusalem* had been formerly stained by the blood of the *prophets*, nay, had been, through an uninterrupted succession of many ages, the slaughter-place, where the prophets were cruelly and wickedly put to death, immediately inserts, according to his custom, a statement which harmonized with that discourse. We have seen, on former occasions, that it is by no means unusual with him to introduce into one place a collection of Christ's sayings, which were uttered at various times.

[1] " Cette cruelle diablesse ;"—" that cruel female devil."
[2] " Auquel Dieu a voulu que ses Prophetes ayent soustenu de grans combats et rudes alarmes ;"—" on which God determined that his Prophets should sustain powerful combats and fierce alarms."

LUKE.

XI. 37. And while he was speaking, a certain Pharisee requested him to dine with him; and he entered and sat down at table. 38. And when the Pharisee saw it, he wondered that he had not first washed before dinner. 39. And the Lord said to him, Now you Pharisees cleanse the outside of the cup and of the plate; and what is within you is full of cruelty and wickedness. 40. Fools, did not he who made what is without make also what is within? 41. But out of what you have[1] give alms; and, lo, all things are clean to you.

This narrative agrees in some respects, but not entirely, with the doctrine laid down by Matthew, (xv. 1—20,) that Christ, in order to correct the superstition of the people, and particularly of the scribes, intentionally disregarded outward ceremonies of human invention, which the Jews were too solicitous to observe. God had prescribed in his Law certain kinds of *washings*, that by means of them he might train his people usefully to the consideration of true purity. The Jews, not satisfied with this moderate portion, had added many other washings, and more especially, that no person should partake of food till he had been washed with the water of purification, as Mark relates more minutely, (vii. 3, 4,) and as is also evident from John, (ii. 6.) This fault was accompanied by wicked confidence; for they cared little about the spiritual worship of God, and thought that they had perfectly discharged their duty, when the figure was substituted in the place of God. Christ is fully aware that his neglect of this ceremony will give offence, but he declines to observe it, in order to show that God sets very little value on outward cleanness, but demands the spiritual righteousness of the heart.

39. *Now you Pharisees.* Christ does not here charge the *Pharisees*, as in Matthew, (xv. 1—20,) and Mark, (vii. 2—13,) with serving God in an improper manner by human inventions, and breaking the law of God for the sake of their traditions; but merely glances at their hypocrisy, in having no desire of purity except before the eyes of men, as if they had not to deal with God. Now this reproof applies to all

---

[1] " Des choses presentes, *ou, de ce que vous avez;*"—" of present things, or, of what you have."

hypocrites, even to those who believe that righteousness consists in ceremonies appointed by God. Christ includes more than if he had said, that it is *in vain to serve God by the commandments of men*, (Mark vii. 7;) for he condemns generally the error of worshipping God by ceremonies, and not spiritually, by faith and a pure affection of the heart.

On this point the prophets had always contended earnestly with the Jews; but, as the minds of men are strongly inclined to hypocrisy, they proudly and obstinately adhered to the conviction, that God is pleased with external worship, even when it is not accompanied by faith. But in the time of Christ, they had sunk to such depth of folly, that they made religion to consist entirely in absolute trifles. Accordingly, he directs his accusation against the *Pharisees*, for being extremely careful to *wash cups*, and cherishing *within their hearts the most abominable filth of cruelty and wickedness*. He charges them with folly on this ground, that God, who created *that which is within the man*, his soul, as truly as the body, cannot be satisfied with a mere external appearance. The chief reason why men are deceived is, that they do not consider that they have to deal with God, or, they transform Him according to the vanity of their senses, as if there were no difference between Him and a mortal man.

41. *But out of what you have, give alms.* Christ, according to his custom, withdraws the Pharisees from ceremonies to charity, declaring that it is not water, but liberality,[1] that cleanses both men and food. By these words he does not disparage the grace of God, or reject the ceremonies of the Law as vain and useless; but addresses his discourse to those who feel confident that God will be amused by mere signs. "It is the lawful use alone," he says, "that sanctifies food. But food is rightly and properly used by those who supply from their abundance the necessities of the poor. It would therefore be better *to give alms out of what you have*, than to be careful about washing hands and cups, and to neglect the poor."

[1] "Mais que c'est une prompte affection de faire bien à ceux qui sont en necessité;"—"but that it is an active disposition to do good to those who are in want."

The inference which the Papists draw from these words, that *alms* are satisfactions, by which we are cleansed from our sins, is too absurd to require a lengthened refutation. Christ does not here inform us by what price we must purchase the forgiveness of sins, but says that those persons eat their bread with cleanness, who bestow a part of it on the poor. I understand the words, τὰ ἐνόντα, to mean " the present supply,"[1] and not, as Erasmus and the old translator render them, " what remains over."[2]

The reproofs which immediately follow may be reserved, with greater propriety, for another occasion. I do not think it probable that Christ, while sitting at table, indulged in this continuous strain of invective against *scribes and Pharisees*, but that Luke has introduced here what was spoken at another time; for the Evangelists, as we have frequently mentioned, paid little attention to the order of dates.

LUKE.

XIV. 1. And it happened that he entered into the house of a certain ruler of the Pharisees on a Sabbath, to take food, and they watched him. 2. And, lo, a certain man who had a dropsy was before him, 3. And Jesus answering said to the lawyers[3] and Pharisees, saying, Is it lawful to cure on the Sabbath? 4. But they were silent; and he took and cured him, and sent him away. 5. And he answering to them said, Which of you shall have an ass or an ox that shall fall into a pit, and will not immediately pull him out on the Sabbath-day? 6. And they could not answer him to these things.

This narrative contains nothing more than a miracle which Christ performed, in order to correct the superstitious observance of the Sabbath. For he did not intend, as some imagine, absolutely to abolish the Sabbath, but only to point

---

[1] " *Les presentes choses*, comme aussi ie l'ay traduit au texte ;"—" the *present things*, as also I have translated it in the text."

[2] It seems quite as natural to suppose, with other interpreters, that τὰ ἐνόντα answers to τὸ ἔσωθεν in the 39th and 40th verses. Πλὴν (κατὰ) τὰ ἐνόντα δότε ἐλεημοσύνην will thus be equivalent to πλὴν (κατὰ) τὸ ἔσωθεν (τοῦ ποτηρίου) δότε ἐλεημοσύνην, *but as to what is within* the cup *give alms out of it.* The next clause commences with καὶ, followed by an ellipsis of (κατὰ) τὸ ἔξωθεν (τοῦ ποτηρίου) μὴ μεριμνήσητε, *and give yourselves no concern about what is outside of the cup;* for, *lo, all things are clean to you.*—*Ed.*

[3] " Aux Docteurs de la Loy ;"—" to the Doctors of the Law."

out, that neither the works of God, nor the duties of charity, violate the holy rest which is enjoined by the law. Whether or not those very persons had purposely brought the dropsical man to that place cannot be known with certainty. He unquestionably could not be present at the table by accident, nor break into a private dwelling without the permission and consent of the owner. It is therefore probable, that he was placed there with the concealed design of tempting Christ, which, on their part, was as foolish an action as it was wicked; for they had already known by experience what Christ was accustomed to do, whenever a similar occasion presented itself.

3. *Is it lawful to cure on Sabbath?* The meaning of this question is, ought the *curing* of a man to be reckoned among the works which violate the Sabbath? If they had said that the observance of the Sabbath is violated in this way, the reply was obvious, that it is a work of God. Now the law of the Sabbath goes no farther, than that men shall rest from their own works. Christ first puts the question to them, and he does so for the purpose of guarding against offence. It would not have been necessary for him to pacify them, if they had not been instigated by hardened malice. Not that he always laid himself under this restriction; for in many cases he did what had been enjoined on him by the Father, without attending to the offence that might arise from it. But he intended to show by this example, that he did not inconsiderately perform miracles on Sabbath, because he was prepared to assign a reason for what he did. They, on the other hand, make it evident by their silence, that their desire of finding fault is stronger than their zeal for the law; and therefore Christ treats with utter indifference their opinion about his action, because it was evident that they intentionally sought out an occasion of offence.

5. *Which of you shall have an ox or an ass?* Though they did not deserve that Christ should take pains to remove the offence, yet he shows that he did nothing inconsistent with the observance of the Sabbath. And this he undoubtedly

does, not so much with the view of instructing them, as of protecting himself against their slanders; for he knew that they were too much blinded by virulent hatred to yield submissively to argument, but wished to triumph over their malice, by compelling them through shame to be silent. If we are at liberty to relieve brute animals on Sabbath, it would be unreasonable that we should not perform a similar office of kindness to man, who is formed after the image of God.

LUKE.

XIV. 7. And he spoke a parable to those who were invited, observing how they chose the first seats, saying to them: 8. When thou shalt be invited by any one to a marriage, do not sit at table in the first seat, lest perhaps a more honourable person than thyself be invited by him, 9. And he who invited thee and him come and say to thee, Give place to this man, and thou begin then with shame to occupy the lowest place. 10. But on the contrary, when thou shalt be invited, go, and sit at table in the lowest place, that when he who hath invited thee shall come, he may say to thee, Friend, go up higher: then shalt thou have honour in presence of those who sit at table with thee. 11. For every one that exalteth himself shall be humbled, and he that humbleth himself shall be exalted. 12. And he said to him by whom he had been invited, When thou makest a dinner or supper, invite not thy friends, nor thy brethren, nor thy relatives, nor rich neighbours, lest they also in their turn invite thee, and a recompense be made thee. 13. But when thou makest a banquet, invite the poor, the maimed, the lame, the blind. 14. And thou shalt be blessed, because they cannot recompense thee; for thou shalt be recompensed at the resurrection of the righteous.

7. *And he spoke a parable to those who were invited.* We know to what an extent ambition prevailed among the Pharisees and all the scribes. While they desired to exercise a haughty dominion over all other men, the superiority among themselves was likewise an object of emulation. It is constantly the case with men who are desirous of empty applause, that they cherish envy towards each other, every one endeavouring to draw to himself what others imagine to be due to them. Thus the Pharisees and scribes, while they were all equally disposed, in presence of the people, to glory in the title of a holy order, are now disputing among themselves about the degree of honour, because every one claims for himself the highest place.

This ambition of theirs Christ exposes to ridicule by an appropriate parable. If any one sitting at another man's table were to occupy the highest place, and were afterwards compelled to give way to a *more honourable* person, it would not be without shame and dishonour that he was ordered by the master of the feast to take a different place. But the same thing must happen to all who proudly give themselves out as superior to others; for God will bring upon them disgrace and contempt. It must be observed, that Christ is not now speaking of outward and civil modesty; for we often see that the haughtiest men excel in this respect, and *civilly,* as the phrase is, profess great modesty. But by a comparison taken from men, he describes what we ought to be inwardly before God. " Were it to happen that a guest should foolishly take possession of the highest place, and should, on that account, be put down to the lowest, he would be so completely overpowered with shame as to wish that he had never gone higher. Lest the same thing should happen to you, that God would punish your arrogance with the deepest disgrace, resolve, of your own accord, to be humble and modest."

11. *For every one that exalteth himself shall be humbled.* This clause makes it evident that ambition was the subject of which Christ was speaking; for he does not state what usually happens in the ordinary life of men, but declares that God will be their Judge, who *resisteth the proud,* and humbleth their haughtiness, *but giveth grace to the humble,* (James iv. 6; 1 Peter v. 5; Ps. cxxxviii. 6.) Scripture is full of similar testimonies, that God is an enemy to all who desire to exalt themselves, as all who claim for themselves any merit must of necessity make war with Him. It is a manifestation of pride to boast of the gifts of God, as if there were any excellence in ourselves, that would exalt us on the ground of our own merit. Humility, on the other hand, must be not only an unfeigned abasement, but a real annihilation of ourselves, proceeding from a thorough knowledge of our own weakness, the entire absence of lofty pretensions, and a conviction that whatever excellence we possess comes from the grace of God alone.

12. *When thou makest a dinner.* Those who think that this

is an absolute condemnation of entertainments given by relatives and friends to each other, take away a part of civility from among men. It were not only unfeeling, but barbarous, to exclude relatives from the hospitable table, and to class them only with strangers. Christ did not intend to dissuade us from every thing courteous, but merely to show, that acts of civility, which are customary among men, are no proof whatever of charity. To perform any act, in the hope of a reward, to rich men, from whom we expect a similar return, is not generosity, but a system of commercial exchange; and, in like manner, kind offices, rendered from mercenary views, are of no account in the sight of God, and do not deserve to be ascribed to charity. If I entertain at supper my relatives or rich friends, the act of civility ought not in itself to be condemned, but, as a proof of charity, it will have no value whatever; for we frequently see that persons who are extremely selfish grudge no expense or luxury in treating their friends. What then? You may spread a table for the rich, but, at the same time, you must not neglect the poor; you may feast with your friends and relatives, but you must not shut out strangers, if they shall happen to be poor, and if you shall have the means of relieving their wants. In a word, the meaning of the passage is, that those who are kind to relatives and friends, but are niggardly towards the poor, are entitled to no commendation; because they do not exercise charity, but consult only their own gain or ambition.

Christ addresses, in a particular manner, the person who had invited him; because he perceived that he was too much addicted to pomp and luxury, and was so desirous to obtain the applause and favour of the rich, that he cared very little about the poor. Accordingly, in the person of one man, this reproof is directed against all those who spend their wealth in ambitious display, or who bargain for mutual compensation, but leave nothing over for the poor, as if they were afraid that whatever is gratuitously bestowed would be lost.

14. *And thou shalt be blessed.* Christ pronounces those to be *blessed* who exercise liberality without any expectation of earthly reward; for they manifestly look to God. Those

who constantly keep in view their own advantage, or who are driven by the gale of popularity, have no right to expect a reward from God.

MATTHEW.

XXII. 1. And Jesus answering, spoke again by parables, and said, 2. The kingdom of heaven is like a human king who made a marriage for his son, 3. And sent out his servants to call those who were invited to the marriage, and they refused to come. 4. Again he sent out other servants, saying, Tell those who are invited, Lo, I have prepared my dinner, my oxen and fatlings are killed, and all things are ready: come to the marriage. 5. But they treated it with indifference, and went away, one to his farm, and another to his merchandise: 6. And the rest took his servants, and abused and killed them. 7. But when the king heard it, he was angry, and sent his soldiers, and slew these murderers, and burnt up their city. 8. Then he said to his servants, The marriage is indeed ready, but those who were invited were not worthy. 9. Go then to the highways, and whomsoever you shall find invite to the marriage. 10. And his servants went out to the roads, and collected all that they found, both bad and good, so that the marriage-apartment was filled with guests. 11. And the king, having come in to see the guests, when he saw there a man not wearing the wedding-garment, 12. Said to him, Friend, how camest thou hither, not having the wedding-garment? And he was speechless. 13. Then said the king to his attendants, Bind him hand and foot, and cast him into outer darkness: weeping and gnashing of teeth will be there. 14. For many are called, but few are chosen.

LUKE.

XIV. 15. And when one of those who sat at table with him heard these things, he said to him, Blessed is he that eateth[1] bread in the kingdom of God. 16. But he said to him, A certain man had prepared a great supper, and had invited many. 17. And he sent his servant at the hour of supper to say to those who were invited, Come; for all things are now ready. 18. And they all began together[2] to excuse themselves. 19. The first said to him, I have purchased an estate, and I must go and see it: I beseech thee hold me excused. 20. And another said, I have married a wife, and therefore I cannot come. 21. And the servant returned, and brought back these things to his master. Then the master of the house, being angry, said to his servant, Go out quickly into the streets and lanes of the city, and bring in hither the poor, and the maimed, and the lame, and the blind. 22. And the servant said, Sir, it is done as thou hast commanded, and still there is room. 23. And the master said to the servant, Go out to the roads and hedges, and compel them to come in, that my house may be filled. 24. For I say to you, That none of those men who were invited shall taste of my supper.

Matthew XXII. 1. *And Jesus answering.* Though *Matthew* relates this parable among other discourses which were de-

---

[1] "Bien-hereux sera celuy qui mangera;"—"blessed shall he be who shall eat."
[2] "D'un accord;"—"with one accord."

livered by Christ about the time of the last Passover, yet as he does not specify any particular time, and as *Luke* expressly affirms that Christ delivered this discourse *while he sat at table in the house of a Pharisee,* I have thought it better to follow this order. The design which Matthew had in view was, to point out the reasons why the scribes were excited to the highest pitch of fury; and therefore he properly placed it in the midst of those discourses which were hateful to them, and interwove it with those discourses, without attending to the order of time. But we must attend to *Luke's* narrative, who says that, *when one of those who sat at table with him said, Blessed is he that eateth bread in the kingdom of God,* Christ took occasion from it to upbraid the Jews with ingratitude. It is by no means probable, that the guest and friend of a Pharisee broke out into this exclamation from any sincere feeling of piety. Still, I do not look upon it as having been spoken in derision; but, as persons who have a moderate knowledge of the faith, and are not openly wicked, are in the habit of indulging, amidst their cups, in idle talk about eternal life, I think that this man threw out a remark about future blessedness, in order to draw out some observation in return from Christ. And his words make it manifest, that he had nothing in view beyond what was gross and earthly; for he did not employ the phrase, *eat bread,* as a metaphor for *enjoy eternal life,* but appears to have dreamed of I know not what state, filled with prosperity and abundance of all things. The meaning is, *Blessed shall they be who shall eat the bread of God,*[1] after that he has collected his children into *his kingdom.*

2. *The kingdom of heaven is like a human king.* As it was long ago said by a Spartan, that the Athenians knew what was right, but did not choose to practise it; so Christ now brings it as a reproach against the Jews, that they gave utterance to beautiful expressions about *the kingdom of God,* but, when God kindly and gently invited them, they rejected his grace with disdain. There is no room to doubt that the discourse

---

[1] " Qui seront nourris de Dieu;"—"who shall be fed by God."

is expressly levelled against the Jews, as will more plainly appear a little afterwards.

Matthew and *Luke* differ in this respect, that *Matthew* details many circumstances, while *Luke* states the matter summarily, and in a general manner. Thus, *Matthew* says that *a king made a marriage for his son:* *Luke* only mentions *a great supper.* The former speaks of *many servants*, while the latter refers to no more than *one servant;* the former describes *many* messages, the latter mentions *one* only; the former says that some of the servants were *abused* or slain, the latter speaks only of their being treated with contempt. Lastly, the former relates that a man was cast out, who *had gone in to the marriage without a wedding-garment*, of which Luke makes no mention. But we have formerly pointed out a similar distinction, that *Matthew*, in explaining the same thing, is more copious, and enters into fuller details. There is a remarkable agreement between them on the main points of the parable.

God bestowed on the Jews distinguished honour, by providing for them, as it were, a hospitable table; but they despised the honour which had been conferred upon them. The marriage of the king's son is explained by many commentators to mean, that *Christ is the end of the Law,* (Rom. x. 4,) and that God had no other design in his covenant, than to make him the Governor of his people, and to unite the Church to him by the sacred bond of a spiritual marriage. I have no objection to that view. But when he says, that the *servants were sent to call those who were invited*, these words are intended to point out a double favour which the Jews had received from God; first, in being preferred to other nations; and, secondly, in having their adoption made known to them by the prophets. The allusion is to a practice customary among men, that those who intended to *make a marriage* drew up a list of the persons whom they intended to have as guests, and afterwards sent invitations to them by their servants. In like manner, God elected the Jews in preference to others, as if they had been his familiar friends, and afterwards *called them* by the prophets to partake of the promised redemption, which was, as it were, to feast *at a marriage.* It is true that those who were first invited did not live till the coming of Christ; but we know that all received an offer of the same salvation, of which they were deprived by their ingratitude and malice; for from the commencement, God's invitation was impiously despised by that people.[1]

4. *Again he sent other servants.* He speaks as if it had been the same persons who were invited, for it was one body of the people. The meaning is, that when the happy and joyful day of redemption drew near, they were warned to be ready; for they had been long ago informed as to the time. But now Christ told them that, at the very hour, fresh messengers were sent to entreat them to come with haste; for the first invitation which he mentions includes all the former prophecies, down to the publication of the Gospel. For a long period, they exercised cruelty on the prophets; but their fury grew as the time advanced, and at length spent all its force on Christ and the apostles. For this reason, he charges the ancient people with nothing more than contempt and pride, but says, that the servants who had been last sent, and who arrived at the hour of supper, were *abused* or *slain.* That people arrived at the highest pitch of their crimes, when their haughty rejection of his grace was followed by the madness of cruelty. And yet he does not charge all of them equally with crime; for even at the latest call, which was given by the Gospel, the grace of God was in part ridiculed by careless despisers, and in part was furiously rejected by hypocrites. And thus it usually happens, that ungodly men break out into fiercer rage against God, in proportion to the earnestness with which he invites them to salvation.

We must now consider that part of doctrine which is conveyed both by Matthew and by Luke. *One went to his field, and another to his merchandise;* or, as Luke expresses it, one

---

[1] "Ce peuple-là a vileinement et meschamment mesprisé l'honneur auquel Dieu le convioit;"—"that people basely and wickedly despised the honour to which God invited them."

pleaded that *he had married a wife;* another that he had *purchased a field;* and another that he had *bought five yoke of oxen.* By these words Christ pronounces the Jews to have been so entirely devoted to the world and to earthly things, that no man found leisure to approach to God; for the cares of this world, when we become entangled by them, are so many impediments in our way to keep us back from the kingdom of God. It is truly base and shameful, that men who were created for a heavenly life, should be under the influence of such brutish stupidity, as to be entirely carried away after transitory things. But this disease is universally prevalent; so that hardly one person in a hundred can be found, who prefers the kingdom of God to fading riches, or to any other kind of advantages. Though all are not infected with the same disease, every man is led away by his desires; in consequence of which, all are wandering in various directions.

Besides, it deserves our attention, that ungodly men hold out fair pretences for rejecting the grace of God; as if their indolence might be excused, because they are entirely occupied with the affairs of the present life, and care little about a heavenly inheritance. But we see how Christ takes from us all such excuses, that no man may imagine it to be of any advantage for him to plead that he is detained by engagements of an earthly nature. On the contrary, men commit a double fault, when they allow themselves to be retarded by those things which are in themselves lawful, and which ought rather to have aided their progress. For why does God allow us the conveniences of the present life, but in order to draw us to himself? And yet so far is it from being true, that all have earnest desires towards heaven, in proportion as they are assisted by acts of the Divine kindness, that even holy marriage, and fields, and other riches, are so many snares to bind every man more closely to the earth.

7. *But when the king heard it.* This punishment is mentioned by *Matthew* alone; for Luke makes no mention of

any outrage committed on the servants. Both concur in stating, that those who did not come at the appointed time were shut out, and deprived of the honour of being present at the banquet. But this doctrine applies equally to us; for the same destruction which Christ denounces against the Jews awaits all the ungodly, who violently oppose the ministers of the Gospel. Those who are so entirely occupied with earthly cares, as to set no value on the divine invitation, will at length perish miserably in famine and want; and therefore, whenever God calls us, let us be prepared and ready to follow.

9. *Go therefore to the highways.* Having shown that they are unworthy of the grace of God who disdainfully reject it when offered to them, he now says that their place is supplied by others, by the mean and despised common people. And here is described the calling of the Gentiles, which is to excite the Jews to jealousy, as we have it in the Song of Moses; *They have provoked me by those who are not gods, and I will provoke them by that which is not a people, and by a foolish nation will I enrage them,* (Deut. xxxii. 21.) Having been first elected, they imagined that the grace of God was bound to them, as if God could not want them; and how haughtily they despised all others is well known. Thus by way of admission, he compares the Gentiles to *the poor, the blind,* and *the lame.* He says that they are called from the *cross-roads,* and from the *streets,* as strangers and unknown persons; but yet declares that they will occupy that place which friends and domestics had treated with indifference. What the prophets had obscurely foretold about creating a new church is now plainly expressed. This dishonour was the completion of the divine vengeance on the Jews, when God *cut them off, and ingrafted wild branches into the stock of the olive-tree,* (Rom. xi. 17;) when he threw them off, and received the polluted and filthy Gentiles into his house. But if at that time *he spared not the natural branches,* (Rom. xi. 21,) the same punishment will this day be inflicted on us, if we do not answer to his call. The supper which had been prepared for us will not be lost, but God will invite other guests.

Luke XIV. 23. *Compel them to come in.* This expression means, that the master of the house would give orders to make use, as it were, of violence for compelling the attendance of the poor, and to leave out none of the lowest dregs of the people. By these words Christ declares that he would rake together all the offscourings of the world, rather than he would ever admit such ungrateful persons to his table. The allusion appears to be to the manner in which the Gospel invites us; for the grace of God is not merely offered to us, but doctrine is accompanied by exhortations fitted to arouse our minds. This is a display of the astonishing goodness of God, who, after freely inviting us, and perceiving that we give ourselves up to sleep, addresses our slothfulness by earnest entreaties, and not only arouses us by exhortations, but even *compels* us by threatenings to draw near to him. At the same time, I do not disapprove of the use which Augustine frequently made of this passage against the Donatists, to prove that godly princes may lawfully issue edicts, for *compelling* obstinate and rebellious persons to worship the true God, and to maintain the unity of the faith; for, though faith is voluntary, yet we see that such methods are useful for subduing the obstinacy of those who will not yield until they are compelled.

Matthew XXII. 11. *And the king, having come in to see the guests.* Here Christ does not reproach the Jews with having wickedly despised the grace and calling of God; but gives early warning to those who would be placed in their room, not to pollute with their filth the holy marriage, when God shall bestow upon them admission to his table. Hitherto he has taught that the Jews, on account of their ungodly and disdainful conduct, would be deprived of the peculiar honour and privilege which they had enjoyed; and that from among the irreligious and abhorred Gentiles would men be called to occupy their place. But now he threatens that, out of this very number, those who bring reproach upon the Church will be expelled; for God invites all indiscriminately by the Gospel, and thus many unholy and abominable persons creep in, who, though for a time they are admitted along with others, yet, when God reviews the guests, will be thrown out and dragged to punishment. The general truth conveyed is, that not all who have once entered the Church will become partakers of everlasting life, but only those who are found to wear the dress which befits the heavenly palace.

As to the *wedding-garment*, is it faith, or is it a holy life? This is a useless controversy; for faith cannot be separated from good works, nor do good works proceed from any other source than from faith. But Christ intended only to state, that the Lord calls us on the express condition of our being renewed by the Spirit after his image; and that, in order to our remaining permanently in his house, we must *put off the old man with his pollutions,* (Col. iii. 9; Eph. iv. 22,) and lead a new life, that the *garment* may correspond to so honourable a calling. But a question arises, how comes it that a beggar is punished so severely for not bringing a *wedding-garment;* as if it were unusual to see the wretched people, who beg their bread on the public roads, wearing tattered and ugly clothes? I reply, the question is not as to the manner in which the *garment* is to be procured; for whomsoever the Lord invites he at the same time supplies with clothing, and in all of us is fulfilled what Ezekiel says, (xvi. 6–14,) that God finds nothing in us but wretchedness, and nakedness, and abominable filth, but adorns us with magnificent attire. We know also, that there is no other way in which we are formed anew after the image of God, but by *putting on Christ,* (Rom. xiii. 14; Gal. iii. 27.) It is not, therefore, the declaration of Christ, that the sentence of *casting them into outer darkness* will be executed on wretched men who did not bring a costly *garment* taken from their own wardrobe, but on those who shall be found in their pollution, when God shall come to make a scrutiny of his guests.

14. *For many are called, but few are chosen.* The object of the parable is pointed out by the conclusion, that *few are chosen,* though *many are called;* from which we infer, that we ought not to attempt an ingenious explanation of every minute clause. But lately, Christ did not threaten that the greater part would be thrown out, but mentioned one man

only; and now we learn from him, that out of a large number few will be retained. And certainly, though in the present day a more numerous body of men is collected into the Church by the Gospel than was formerly collected by the Law, it is but a small portion of them whose faith is evinced by newness of life. Let us not flatter ourselves with the empty title of faith, but let every man seriously examine himself, that at the final review he may be pronounced to be one of the lawful guests; for, as Paul reminds us, that *the vessels* in the Lord's house are not all of the same kind, so *let every one that calleth on the name of the Lord depart from iniquity,* (2 Tim. ii. 19, 20.) I enter no farther, at present, into the question about the eternal election of God; for the words of Christ mean nothing more than this, that the external profession of faith is not a sufficient proof that God will acknowledge as his people all who appear to have accepted of his invitation.[1]

Luke.

XVI. 1. And he said also to his disciples, There was a certain rich man who had a steward, and he was accused to him that he was wasting his estate. 2. And he called him, and said to him, What is this that I hear of thee? render an account of thy stewardship, for thou shalt no longer have it in thy power to be steward. 3. And the steward said within himself, What shall I do, since my master taketh from me my stewardship? I cannot dig, and am ashamed to beg. 4. I know what I shall do, that, when I shall be dismissed from the stewardship, they may receive me[2] into their houses. 5. Having therefore sent for each of his master's debtors, he said to the first, How much owest thou to my master? 6. And he said, A hundred baths of oil. And he said to him, Take thy bill, and sit down quickly, and write fifty.[3] 7. Then he said to another, And how much owest thou? Who said, A hundred measures of barley. He saith to him, Take thy bill, and write eighty. 8. And the master commended the unjust steward, because he had acted prudently; for the children of this world are more prudent in their generation than the children of light. 9. And I say to you, Make to yourselves friends of the unjust mammon, that, when you shall fail, they may receive you into eternal habitations. 10. He that is faithful in that which is least is faithful also in much; and he that is unjust in that which is least is unjust also in much. 11. If therefore you have not been faithful in the unjust mammon, who shall

---

[1] "Tous ceux qui semblent s'estre rangez sous son enseigne;"—"all those who appear to have ranked themselves under his banner."
[2] "Que 'quelques uns' me recoyvent;"—"that 'some persons' may receive me."
[3] "Et en escri cinquante;"—"and write fifty of them."

entrust to you what is true?[1] 12. And if you have not been faithful in what belongs to another, who will give you what is your own?—(*A little after*.) 14. And the Pharisees, who were covetous, heard all these things, and they ridiculed him. 15. And he said to them, It is you that justify yourselves in the sight of men: but God knoweth your hearts; for that which is highly esteemed among men is abomination in the sight of God.

The leading object of this parable is, to show that we ought to deal kindly and generously with our neighbours; that, when we come to the judgment-seat of God, we may reap the fruit of our liberality. Though the parable appears to be harsh and far-fetched, yet the conclusion makes it evident, that the design of Christ was nothing else than what I have stated. And hence we see, that to inquire with great exactness into every minute part of a parable is an absurd mode of philosophizing. Christ does not advise us to purchase by large donations the forgiveness of fraud, and of extortion, and of wasteful expenditure, and of the other crimes associated with unfaithful administration. But as all the blessings which God confers upon us are committed by Him to our administration, our Lord now lays down a method of procedure, which will protect us against being treated with rigour, when we come to render our account.

They who imagine that alms are a sufficient compensation for sensuality and debauchery, do not sufficiently consider, that the first injunction given us is, to live in sobriety and temperance; and that the next is, that the streams which flow to us come from a pure fountain. It is certain that no man is so frugal, as not sometimes to waste the property which has been entrusted to him; and that even those who practise the most rigid economy are not entirely free from the charge of unfaithful *stewardship*. Add to this, that there are so many ways of abusing the gifts of God, that some incur guilt in one way, and some in another. I do not even deny, that the very consciousness of our own faulty *stewardship* ought to be felt by us as an additional excitement to kind actions.

[1] " Du vray ' thresor' qui s'en fiera en vous?"—" who shall entrust to you the true (treasure?)"

But we ought to have quite another object in view, than to escape the judgment of God by paying a price for our redemption; and that object is, first, that seasonable and well-judged liberality may have the effect of restraining and moderating unnecessary expenses; and, secondly, that our kindness to our brethren may draw down upon us the mercy of God. It is very far from being the intention of Christ to point out to his disciples a way of escape, when the heavenly Judge shall require them to give their account; but he warns them to lose no time in guarding against the punishment which will await their cruelty, if they are found to have swallowed up the gifts of God, and to have paid no attention to acts of beneficence.[1] We must always attend to this maxim, that *with what measure a man measures, it shall be recompensed to him again,* (Matth. vii. 2.)

8. *And the master commended the unjust steward.* Here it is obvious that if we were to attempt to find a meaning for every minute circumstance, we would act absurdly. To make donations out of what belongs to another man, is an action which is very far from deserving applause; and who would patiently endure that an unprincipled villain should rob him of his property, and give it away according to his own fancy? It were indeed the grossest stupidity, if that man who beheld a portion of his substance taken away, should *commend* the person who stole the remainder of it and bestowed it on others. But Christ only meant what he adds a little afterwards, that ungodly and worldly men are more industrious and skilful in conducting the affairs of this fading life, than the children of God are anxious to obtain the heavenly and eternal life, or careful to make it the subject of their study and meditation.

By this comparison he charges us with highly criminal indifference, in not providing for the future, with at least as

[1] " S'il est trouvé qu'ils n'ayent en aucun soin d'exercer charité envers leurs prochains, et n'ayent pensé qu'à despendre en tout exces et à leur plaisir, les biens de Dieu ;"—" if it is found that they have given themselves no concern about exercising charity to their neighbours, and have thought only of spending in every excess, and at their own pleasure, the gifts of God."

much earnestness as ungodly men display by attending to their own interests in this world. How disgraceful is it that *the children of light*, whom God enlightens by his Spirit and word, should slumber and neglect the hope of eternal blessedness held out to them, while worldly men are so eagerly bent on their own accommodations, and so provident and sagacious! Hence we infer, that our Lord does not intend to compare the wisdom of the Spirit to the wisdom of the flesh, (which could not have been done without pouring contempt on God himself,) but only to arouse believers to consider more attentively what belongs to the future life, and not to shut their eyes against the light of the Gospel, when they perceive that even the blind, amidst their darkness, see more clearly. And, indeed, *the children of light* ought to be more powerfully excited, when they behold *the children of this world* making provision against a distant period, for a life which is fading, and which passes in a moment.

9. *Make to yourselves friends.* As in the words which were last considered Christ did not enjoin us to offer sacrifices to God out of the fruits of extortion, so now he does not mean that we ought to search for defenders or advocates, who will throw around us the shield of their protection; but teaches us that by acts of charity we obtain favour with God, who has promised, that *to the merciful he will show himself merciful*, (Psal. xviii. 25.) It is highly foolish and absurd to infer from this passage, that the prayers or approbation of the dead are of service to us: for, on that supposition, all that is bestowed on unworthy persons would be thrown away; but the depravity of men does not prevent the Lord from placing on his records all that we have expended on the poor. The Lord looks not to the persons, but to the work itself, so that our liberality, though it may happen to be exercised towards ungrateful men, will be of avail to us in the sight of God. But then he appears to intimate that eternal life depends on our merits. I reply: it is sufficiently plain from the context that he speaks after the manner of men. One who possesses extensive influence or wealth, if he procure friends during his prosperity, has persons who will support him when he is

visited by adversity. In like manner, our kindness to the poor will be a seasonable relief to us; for whatever any man may have generously bestowed on his neighbours the Lord acknowledges as if it had been done to himself.

When you fail. By this word he expresses the time of death, and reminds us that the time of our administration will be short, lest the confident expectation of a longer continuance of life should make us take a firmer grasp. The greater part are sunk in slumber through their wealth; many squander what they have on superfluities; while the niggardliness of others keeps it back, and deprives both themselves and others of the benefit. Whence comes all this, but because they are led astray by an unfounded expectation of long life, and give themselves up to every kind of indulgence?

Of the mammon of unrighteousness. By giving this name to riches, he intends to render them an object of our suspicion, because for the most part they involve their possessors in *unrighteousness.* Though in themselves they are not evil, yet as it rarely happens that they are obtained without deceit, or violence, or some other unlawful expedient, or that the enjoyment of them is unaccompanied by pride, or luxury, or some other wicked disposition, Christ justly represents them as worthy of our suspicion; just as on another occasion he called them *thorns,* (Matth. xiii. 7, 22.) It would appear that a contrast, though not expressed, is intended to be supplied, to this effect; that riches, which otherwise, in consequence of wicked abuse, polluted their possessors, and are almost in every case allurements of sin, ought to be directed to a contrary object, to be the means of procuring favour for us. Let us also remember what I have formerly stated, that God does not demand sacrifice to be made from booty unjustly acquired, as if he were the partner of thieves, and that it is rather a warning given to believers to keep themselves free from *unrighteousness.*

10. *He who is faithful in that which is least.* Those maxims are proverbs taken from ordinary practice and experience, and it is quite enough if they are generally true. It will sometimes happen, no doubt, that a deceiver, who had disregarded a

small gain, shall display his wickedness in a matter of importance. Nay, many persons, by affecting honesty in trifling matters, are only in pursuit of an enormous gain;[1] as that author[2] says: "Fraud establishes confidence in itself in small matters, that, when a fit opportunity shall arrive, it may deceive with vast advantage." And yet the statement of Christ is not inaccurate; for in proverbs, as I have mentioned, we attend only to what usually happens.

Christ, therefore, exhorts his disciples to act faithfully in small matters, in order to prepare themselves for the exercise of fidelity in matters of the highest importance. He next applies this doctrine to the proper *stewardship* of spiritual graces, which the world, indeed, does not estimate according to their value, but which far surpass, beyond all question, the fading riches of this world. Those persons, he tells us, who act improperly and unfaithfully in things of small value, such as the transitory riches of the world, do not deserve that God should entrust to them the inestimable treasure of the Gospel, and of similar gifts. There is, therefore, in these words an implied threatening, that there is reason to fear lest, on account of our abuse of an earthly *stewardship*, we fail to obtain heavenly gifts. In this sense, *what is true* is contrasted with *riches*, as what is solid and lasting is contrasted with what is shadowy and fading.[3]

12. *And if you have not been faithful in what belongs to another.* By the expression, *what belongs to another*, he means what is not within man; for God does not bestow riches upon us on condition that we shall be attached to them, but makes us *stewards* of them in such a manner, that they may not bind us with their chains. And, indeed, it is impossible that our minds should be free and disengaged for dwelling

---

[1] "Et mesmes plusieurs sont contens d'user de simplicité et fidelité en de petites choses, à fin d'attraper puis apres un grand profit tout d'un coup;"—"and many are even willing to practise honesty and fidelity in small matters, in order afterwards to seize all at once on a large profit."

[2] Livy.

[3] "D'une chose caduque, et qui n'est qu'une ombre;"—"with a fading thing, and which is only a shadow."

in heaven, if we did not look upon every thing that is in the world as *belonging to another.*

Who shall entrust to you what is your own? Spiritual riches, on the other hand, which relate to a future life, are pronounced by him to be *our own,* because the enjoyment of them is everlasting. But now he employs a different comparison. There is no reason, he tells us, to expect that we shall make a proper and moderate use of *our own* property, if we have acted improperly or unfaithfully in *what belonged to another.* Men usually care less about abusing, and allow themselves greater liberty in squandering, *their own* property, because they are not afraid that any person will find fault with them; but when a thing has been entrusted to them either in charge or in loan, and of which they must afterwards render an account, they are more cautious and more timid.

We thus ascertain Christ's meaning to be, that they who are bad *stewards* of earthly blessings would not be faithful guardians of spiritual gifts. He next introduces a sentence: *You cannot serve God and mammon;* which I have explained at Matth. vi. 24. There the reader will find an explanation of the word *Mammon.*[1]

14. *And the Pharisees, who were covetous, heard all these things.* They who imagine that Christ was *ridiculed by the Pharisees,* because he chose to employ a plain and familiar style, and made no use of swelling words,[2] do not sufficiently comprehend what Luke means. Haughty and disdainful men, I do acknowledge, view the doctrine of the Gospel with

---

[1] " Et là aussi on trouvera la signification de ce mot Mammona, lequel est ici mis, et que nous avons traduit *Richesses.*"—" And *there* will also be found the meaning of the word *Mammon,* which is used here, and which we have translated *Riches.*"—In an earlier portion of this Commentary, to which our author refers, (Harmony, vol. i. p. 337,) no direct or formal explanation of the word *Mammon* is to be found; but a careful reader of the expository remarks on Matthew vi. 24 will easily perceive that CALVIN understands *riches* to be one of the *two masters* spoken of in that passage. An indirect definition of the term is afforded by his French version of the text, both in Matth. vi. 24, and in Luke xvi. 13 : " Vous ne pouvez servir à Dieu et aux richesses ;"—" *you cannot serve God and riches.*"

[2] " En affectant des termes exquis, et bien remplissans la bouche ;"— " by affecting nicely chosen words, and that fill the mouth well."

contempt; but Luke expressly declares the reason why Christ was the object of their derision to have been, that they *were covetous.* Entertaining a firm and deep-seated conviction that the rich are happy, and that there is nothing better for men than to increase their wealth by every possible method, and earnestly to guard whatever they have acquired, they reject as foolish paradoxes[1] all the sayings of Christ which had a contrary tendency. And, certainly, any one that speaks of despising riches, or bestowing alms on the poor, is regarded by the *covetous* as a madman. Horace's words on this subject are well known :[2] " The people hiss at me, but I am well satisfied with myself."[3] But if, even when they are condemned by universal opinion, they continue to flatter themselves, how much more will they ridicule as a fable that philosophy of Christ which is far removed from the ordinary belief?

Some other pretence, I have no doubt, was held out by the Pharisees for ridiculing and evading a doctrine which opposed their vice. But we must attend to the motive by which they were actuated; for it is a disease which almost always prevails in the world, that the greater part of men affect to despise whatever does not fall in with their corrupt morals. Hence the ridicule, and jest, and merriment, with which the word of God is frequently assailed; for every man fights in defence of his own vices, and all imagine that their witticisms will serve for a cloud to screen their criminality.

15. *It is you that justify yourselves before men.* We see that Christ does not give way to their disdainful conduct, but constantly maintains the authority of his doctrine in opposition to their mockery; and it is the duty of all the ministers of the Gospel to pursue the same course, by meeting ungodly despisers with the dreadful judgment of God.

[1] " Comme choses absurdes, et contre l'opinion commune ;"—" as absurd statements, and opposed to the common belief."
[2] " Horace, Poëte Latin, dit parlant en la personne d'un avaricieux ;"— " Horace, a Latin Poet, says, speaking in the person of a covetous man."
[3] " Populus me sibilat, at mihi plaudo."—*Sat.* I. i. 66.

He declares that the hypocrisy, with which they deceive the eyes of men, will be of no avail to them at the judgment-seat of God. They were unwilling to have it thought that their mockery was intended as a defence of their *covetousness.* But Christ affirms that this venom breaks out from a concealed ulcer; just as if one were to tell the mitred prelates of our own day, that their hostility to the Gospel arises from the severity with which it attacks their hidden vices.

But God knoweth your hearts. He says that they reckon it enough if they appear to be good in the eyes of men, and if they can boast of a pretended sanctity; but that *God, who knoweth the hearts,* is well acquainted with the vices which they conceal from the view of the world. And here we must attend to the distinction between the judgments of God and the judgments of men; for men bestow approbation on outward appearances, but at the judgment-seat of God nothing is approved but an upright heart. There is added a striking observation:

What is highly esteemed by men is abomination in the sight of God. Not that God rejects those virtues, the approbation of which He hath engraved on the hearts of men; but that God detests whatever men are disposed, of their own accord, to applaud. Hence it is evident in what light we ought to view all pretended acts of worship which the world contrives according to its own fancy. How much soever they may please their inventors, Christ pronounces that they are not only vain and worthless, but are even destestable.

Luke.

XVI. 19. There was a certain rich man, who was clothed in purple and fine linen,[1] and feasted sumptuously every day: 20. And there was a certain beggar, named Lazarus, who lay at his gate, full of sores, 21. And desiring to be fed from the crumbs which fell from the rich man's table: and even the dogs came and licked his sores. 22. And it happened that the beggar died, and was carried by the angels into Abraham's bosom: the rich man also died, and was buried; 23. And, lifting up his eyes in hell, when he was in torments, he seeth Abraham afar off, and Lazarus in his bosom. 24. And he, crying out, said, Father Abraham, have compassion on me, and send Lazarus to dip the tip of his finger in

---

[1] "De pourpre et de soye;"—"in purple and silk."

LUKE.

water, and cool my tongue; for I am tormented in this flame. 25. And Abraham said, Son, remember that thou in thy lifetime receivedst thy good things, and Lazarus likewise evil things: but now he enjoys comfort, and thou art tormented. 26. And besides all these things, a vast gulf lieth between us and you; so that they who wish to pass hence to you cannot, nor can they pass to us thence. 27. And he said, I beseech thee, therefore, father, to send him to my father's house: 28. For I have five brothers, that he may testify to them, lest they also come into this place of torment. 29. Abraham saith to him, They have Moses and the prophets: let them hear them. 30. But he said, Nay, father Abraham; but if one went to them from the dead, they will repent. 31. And he said to him, If they hear not Moses and the prophets, neither will they be persuaded though one rose from the dead.

Though Luke introduces some things between them, there can be no doubt that this example was intended by Christ to confirm the discourse which we have last examined. He points out what condition awaits those[1] who neglect the care of the poor, and indulge in all manner of gluttony; who give themselves up to drunkenness and other pleasures, and allow their neighbours to pine with hunger; nay, who cruelly kill with famine those whom they ought to have relieved, when the means of doing so were in their power. Some look upon it as a simple parable; but, as the name *Lazarus* occurs in it, I rather consider it to be the narrative of an actual fact. But that is of little consequence, provided that the reader comprehends the doctrine which it contains.

19. *There was a certain rich man.* He is, first of all, described as *clothed in purple and fine linen*, and enjoying every day splendour and luxury. This denotes a life spent amidst delicacies, and superfluity, and pomp. Not that all elegance and ornaments of dress are in themselves displeasing to God, or that all the care bestowed on preparing victuals ought to be condemned; but because it seldom happens that such things are kept in moderation. He who has a liking for fine dress will constantly increase his luxury by fresh additions; and it is scarcely possible that he who indulges in sumptuous and well garnished tables shall avoid

---

[1] "Quelle sera hors de ce monde la condition de ceux;"—"what will be out of this world the condition of those."

falling into intemperance. But the chief accusation brought against this man is his cruelty in suffering *Lazarus,* poor and *full of sores, to lie* out of doors *at his gate.*

These two clauses Christ has exhibited in contrast. The *rich man,* devoted to the pleasures of the table and to display, swallowed up, like an unsatiable gulf, his enormous wealth, but remained unmoved by the poverty and distresses of *Lazarus,* and knowingly and willingly suffered him to pine away with hunger, cold, and the offensive smell of his *sores.* In this manner Ezekiel (xvi. 49) accuses *Sodom* of not stretching out her hand to the poor amidst *fulness of bread* and wine. The *fine linen,* which is a peculiarly delicate fabric, is well-known to have been used by the inhabitants of eastern countries for elegance and splendour; a fashion which the Popish priests have imitated in what they call their *surplices.*

21. *And even the dogs came.* It was quite enough to prove the hardened cruelty of the *rich man,* that the sight of wretchedness like this did not move him to compassion. Had there been a drop of humanity in him, he ought at least to have ordered a supply from his kitchen for the unhappy man. But the crowning exhibition of his wicked, and savage, and worse than brutal disposition was, that he did not learn pity even from *the dogs.* There can be no doubt that those *dogs* were guided by the secret purpose of God, to condemn that man by their example. Christ certainly produces them here as witnesses to convict him of unfeeling and detestable cruelty. What could be more monstrous than to see *the dogs* taking charge of a man, to whom his neighbour is paying no attention; and, what is more, to see the very crumbs of bread refused to a man perishing of hunger, while *the dogs* are giving him the service of their tongues for the purpose of healing his *sores?* When strangers, or even brute animals, supply our place, by performing an office which ought rather to have been discharged by ourselves, let us conclude that they are so many witnesses and judges appointed by God, to make our criminality the more manifest.

22. *And it happened that the beggar died.* Christ here points out the vast change which death effected in the condition of the two men. Death was no doubt common to both; but to be after death *carried by angels into Abraham's bosom* was a happiness more desirable than all the kingdoms of the world. On the other hand, to be sentenced to everlasting torments is a dreadful thing, for avoiding which a hundred lives, if it were possible, ought to be employed. In the person of *Lazarus* there is held out to us a striking proof that we ought not to pronounce men to be accursed by God, because they drag out, in incessant pain, a life which is full of distresses. In him the grace of God was so entirely hidden, and buried by the deformity and shame of the cross, that to the eye of the flesh nothing presented itself except the curse; and yet we see that in a body which was loathsome and full of rottenness there was lodged a soul unspeakably precious, which is *carried by angels* to a blessed life. It was no loss to him that he was forsaken, and despised, and destitute of every human comfort, when heavenly spirits deign to accompany him on his removal from the prison of the flesh.

And the rich man also died, and was buried. In *the rich man* we see, as in a bright mirror, how undesirable is that temporal happiness which ends in everlasting destruction. It deserves our attention, that Christ expressly mentions the *burial of the rich man,* but says nothing of what was done to *Lazarus.* Not that his dead body was exposed to wild beasts, or lay in the open air, but because it was thrown carelessly, and without the slightest attention, into a ditch; for it may naturally be inferred from the corresponding clause, that no more attention was paid to him when he was dead than when he was alive. *The rich man,* on the other hand, buried magnificently according to his wealth, still retains some remnant of his former pride.[1] In this respect, we see ungodly men striving, as it were, against nature, by affecting a pompous and splendid funeral for the sake of preserving their superiority after death; but their souls *in hell* attest the folly and mockery of this ambition.

---

[1] " De l'orgueil de sa vie passee;"—" of the pride of his past life."

And Lazarus was carried by angels. When he says that *Lazarus was carried,* it is a figure of speech by which a part is taken for the whole; for the soul being the nobler part of man, properly takes the name of the whole man.[1] This office is, not without reason, assigned by Christ to angels, who, we are aware, have been appointed to be *ministering spirits* (Heb. i. 14) to believers, that they may devote their care and labour to their salvation.

Into Abraham's bosom. To detail the variety of speculations about *Abraham's bosom,* in which many commentators of Scripture have indulged, is unnecessary, and, in my opinion, would serve no good purpose. It is quite enough that we receive what readers well acquainted with Scripture will acknowledge to be the natural meaning. As Abraham is called *the father* of believers, because to him was committed the covenant of eternal life, that he might first preserve it faithfully for his own children, and afterwards transmit it to all nations, and as all who are heirs of the same promise are called *his children;* so those who receive along with him the fruit of the same faith are said, after death, to be collected into his *bosom.* The metaphor is taken from a father,[2] in whose *bosom,* as it were, the children meet, when they all return home in the evening from the labours of the day. The children of God are scattered during their pilgrimage in this world; but as, in their present course, they follow the faith of their *father Abraham,* so they are received at death into that blessed rest, in which he awaits their arrival. It is not necessary to suppose that reference is made here to any one place; but the assemblage of which I have spoken is described, for the purpose of assuring believers, that they have not been fruitlessly employed in fighting for the faith under the banner of *Abraham,* for they enjoy the same habitation in heaven.

It will perhaps be asked, Is the same condition reserved after death for the godly of our own day, or did Christ, when

---

[1] "A bon droict on dit simplement, L'homme, encore que cela ne convient qu'à l'ame;"—"we properly say simply *Man,* though it applies only to the soul."

[2] "D'un pere terrien;"—"from an earthly father."

he rose, open his *bosom* to admit *Abraham* himself, as well as all the godly? I reply briefly: As the grace of God is more clearly revealed to us in the Gospel, and as Christ himself, *the Sun of Righteousness*, (Mal. iv. 2,) has brought to us that salvation, which the fathers were formerly permitted to behold at a distance and under dark shadows, so there cannot be a doubt that believers, when they die, make a nearer approach to the enjoyment of the heavenly life. Still, it must be understood, that the glory of immortality is delayed till the last day of redemption. So far as relates to the word *bosom*, that quiet harbour at which believers arrive after the navigation of the present life, may be called either *Abraham's bosom* or *Christ's bosom;* but, as we have advanced farther than the fathers did under the Law, this distinction will be more properly expressed by saying, that the members of Christ are associated with their Head; and thus there will be an end of the metaphor about *Abraham's bosom*, as the brightness of the sun, when he is risen, makes all the stars to disappear. From the mode of expression which Christ has here employed, we may, in the meantime, draw the inference, that the fathers under the Law embraced by faith, while they lived, that inheritance of the heavenly life into which they were admitted at death.

23. *And, lifting up his eyes in hell.* Though Christ is relating a history, yet he describes spiritual things under figures, which he knew to be adapted to our senses. Souls have neither *fingers* nor *eyes*, and are not liable to thirst, nor do they hold such conversations among themselves as are here described to have taken place between *Abraham* and *the rich man;* but our Lord has here drawn a picture, which represents the condition of the life to come according to the measure of our capacity. The general truth conveyed is, that believing souls, when they have left their bodies, lead a joyful and blessed life out of this world, and that for the reprobate there are prepared dreadful torments, which can no more be conceived by our minds than the boundless glory of the heavens. As it is only in a small measure—only so far as we are enlightened by the Spirit of God—that we taste

by hope the glory promised to us, which far exceeds all our senses, let it be reckoned enough that the inconceivable vengeance of God, which awaits the ungodly, is communicated to us in an obscure manner, so far as is necessary to strike terror into our minds.

On these subjects the words of Christ give us slender information, and in a manner which is fitted to restrain curiosity. The wicked are described as fearfully tormented by the misery which they feel; as desiring some relief, but cut off from hope, and thus experiencing a double torment; and as having their anguish increased by being compelled to remember their crimes, and to compare the present blessedness of believers with their own miserable and lost condition. In connection with this a conversation is related, as if persons who have no intercourse with each other were supposed to talk together. When *the rich man* says, *Father Abraham*, this expresses an additional torment, that he perceives, when it is too late, that he is cut off from the number of the children of *Abraham*.

25. *Son, remember.* The word *son* appears to be used ironically, as a sharp and piercing reproof to *the rich man*, who falsely boasted in his lifetime that he was one of the *sons* of Abraham. It seems as if pain inflicted by a hot iron wounded his mind, when his hypocrisy and false confidence are placed before his eyes. When it is said that he is tormented in hell, because *he had received his good things in his lifetime,* we must not understand the meaning to be, that eternal destruction awaits all who have enjoyed prosperity in the world. On the contrary, as Augustine has judiciously observed, poor Lazarus was carried into the bosom of rich Abraham, to inform us, that riches do not shut against any man the gate of the kingdom of heaven, but that it is open alike to all who have either made a sober use of riches, or patiently endured the want of them. All that is meant is, that *the rich man*, who yielded to the allurements of the present life, abandoned himself entirely to earthly enjoyments, and despised God and His kingdom, now suffers the punishment of his own neglect.

Receivedst THY *good things.* The pronoun *thy* is emphatic, as if Abraham had said : Thou wast created for an immortal life, and the Law of God raised thee on high to the contemplation of the heavenly life ; but thou, forgetting so exalted a condition, didst choose to resemble a sow or a dog, and thou therefore receivest a reward which befits brutal pleasures. *But now he enjoys comfort.* When it is said of Lazarus, on the other hand, that *he enjoys comfort,* because he had suffered many distresses in the world, it would be idle to apply this to all whose condition is wretched ; because their afflictions, in many cases, are so far from having been of service to them, that they ought rather to bring upon them severer punishment. But *Lazarus* is commended for patient endurance of the cross, which always springs from faith and a genuine fear of God; for he who obstinately resists his sufferings, and whose ferocity remains unsubdued, has no claim to be rewarded for patience, by receiving from God *comfort* in exchange for the cross.

To sum up the whole, they who have patiently endured the burden of the cross laid upon them, and have not been rebellious against the yoke and chastisements of God, but, amidst uninterrupted sufferings, have cherished the hope of a better life, have a rest laid up for them in heaven, when the period of their warfare shall be terminated. On the contrary, wicked despisers of God, who are wholly engrossed in the pleasures of the flesh, and who, by a sort of mental intoxication, drown every feeling of piety, will experience, immediately after death, such torments as will efface their empty enjoyments. It must also be recollected, that this *comfort,* which the sons of God enjoy, lies in this, that they perceive a crown of glory prepared for them, and rest in the joyful expectation of it ; as, on the other hand, the wicked are tormented by the apprehension of the future judgment, which they see coming upon them.

26. *A vast gulf lieth.* These words describe the permanency of the future state, and denote, that the boundaries which separate the reprobate from the elect can never be broken through. And thus we are reminded to return early

to the path, while there is yet time, lest we rush headlong into that abyss, from which it will be impossible to rise. The words must not be strictly interpreted, when it is said, that no one is permitted to pass who would wish to descend from heaven to hell; for it is certain, that none of the righteous entertain any such desire.

27. *I beseech thee, father.* To bring the narrative into more full accordance with our modes of thinking, he describes *the rich man* as wishing that his brothers, who were still alive, should be warned by *Lazarus.* Here the Papists exercise their ingenuity very foolishly, by attempting to prove that the dead feel solicitude about the living. Any thing more ridiculous than this sophistry cannot be conceived; for with equal plausibility I might undertake to prove, that believing souls are not satisfied with the place assigned to them, and are actuated by a desire of removing from it to hell, were it not that they are prevented by *a vast gulf.* If no man holds such extravagant views, the Papists are not entitled to congratulate themselves on the other supposition. It is not my intention, however, to debate the point, or to defend either one side or another; but I thought it right to advert, in passing, to the futility of the arguments on which they rest their belief that the dead intercede with God on our behalf. I now return to the plain and natural meaning of this passage.

29. *They have Moses and the prophets.* In the persons of *the rich man* and *Abraham* Christ reminds us, that we have received an undoubted rule of life, and that therefore we have no right to expect that the dead will rise to instruct and persuade us. *Moses and the prophets* were appointed to instruct, while they lived, the men of their own age; but it was with the design, that the same advantage should be derived by posterity from their writings. As it is the will of God that we should receive instructions, in this manner, about a holy life, there is no reason why the dead should assure us of the rewards and punishments of the future state; nor is there any excuse for the indifference of those who shelter themselves under the pretext, that they do not know

what is going on beyond this world. Among irreligious men, we are aware, is frequently heard this wicked saying, or rather this grunting of hogs, that it is foolish in men to distress themselves with fears about a matter of uncertainty, since no one has ever returned to bring us tidings about hell.

With the view of counteracting every enchantment of Satan of this description, Christ draws their attention to the Law and the Prophets, agreeably to that passage in the writings of Moses : *It is not in heaven, that thou shouldest say, Who shall go up for us to heaven, and bring it unto us, that we may hear it, and do it? Neither is it beyond the sea, that thou shouldest say, Who shall go over the sea for us, and bring it unto us, that we may hear it, and do it? But the word is very nigh unto thee, even in thy mouth, and in thy heart, that thou shouldest do it,* (Deut. xxx. 12–14.) They who ridicule as fabulous what Scripture testifies as to the future judgment, will one day feel how shocking is the wickedness of giving the lie to the holy oracles of God. From such lethargy Christ arouses his followers, that they may not be deceived by the hope of escaping punishment, and thus fail to improve the time allowed for repentance.

Abraham's reply amounts to this : By *Moses and the prophets* God had sufficiently made known to his people the doctrine of salvation, and nothing remains for us but that it obtain the assent of all. So thoroughly infected is the mind of man with a depraved curiosity, that the greater part of men are always gaping after new revelations. Now as nothing is more displeasing to God than when men are so eager to go beyond due bounds, he forbids them to inquire at magicians and soothsayers respecting the truth, and to consult pretended oracles after the manner of the Gentiles; and in order to restrain that itching curiosity, he promises, at the same time, that he will give *prophets,* from whom the people may learn whatever is necessary to be known for salvation, (Deut. xviii. 9, 15.) But if *the prophets* were sent for the express purpose, that God might keep his people under the guidance of his word, he who is not satisfied with this method of instruction is not actuated by a desire to learn, but tickled by ungodly wantonness; and therefore God complains that He is insulted, when He alone is not heard *from the living to the dead,* (Isa. viii. 19.)

The division of the word of God, which Abraham makes, into the Law and the Prophets, refers to the time of the Old Testament. Now that the more ample explanation of the Gospel has been added, there is still less excuse for our wickedness, if our dislike of that doctrine hurries us in every possible direction, and, in a word, if we do not permit ourselves to be regulated by the word of God. Hence too we infer how solid is the faith of Papists about purgatory and such fooleries, when it rests on nothing but phantoms.[1]

30. *Nay, father Abraham.* This is a personification, as we have said, which expresses rather the feelings of the living than the anxiety of the dead. The doctrine of the *Law* is little esteemed by the world, the *Prophets* are neglected, and no man submits to hear God speaking in his own manner. Some would desire that angels should descend from heaven; others, that the dead should come out of their graves; others, that new miracles should be performed every day to sanction what they hear; and others, that voices should be heard from the sky.[2] But if God were pleased to comply with all their foolish wishes, it would be of no advantage to them; for God has included in his word all that is necessary to be known, and the authority of this word has been attested and proved by authentic seals. Besides, faith does not depend on miracles, or any extraordinary sign, but is the peculiar gift of the Spirit, and is produced by means of the word. Lastly, it is the prerogative of God to draw us to himself, and he is pleased to work effectually through his own word. There is not the slightest reason, therefore, to expect that those means, which withdraw us from obedience to the word, will be of any service to us. I freely acknowledge, that there is nothing to which the flesh is more strongly inclined than to

---

[1] " Veu qu'elle n'est appuyee et fondee qu'en des apparitions et vaines imaginations d'aucuns cerveaux esventez;"—" since it rests and is founded only on apparitions and vain imaginations of certain giddy brains."

[2] " Les autres, que Dieu parlast à eux du ciel en personne;"—" others, that God would speak to them from heaven in person."

listen to vain revelations; and we see how eagerly those men, to whom the whole of Scripture is an object of dislike, throw themselves into the snares of Satan. Hence have arisen necromancy and other delusions, which the world not only receives with avidity, but runs after with furious rage. But all that is here affirmed by Christ is, that even the dead could not reform,[1] or bring to a sound mind, those who are deaf and obstinate against the instructions of the law.

Luke.

XVII. 7. But which of you that hath a servant ploughing or feeding, when he hath returned from the field, will immediately say to him, Come,[2] and sit down at table? 8. And doth not rather say to him, Prepare supper for me, and gird thyself, and serve me, till I have eaten and drunk, and, after that, eat and drink thou.[3] 9. Doth he thank that servant,[4] because he did the things which were commanded him? I suppose not. 10. So likewise, when you shall have done those things which were commanded you, do you say, We are unprofitable servants: we have done what we were bound to do.

The object of this parable is to show that God claims all that belongs to us as his property, and possesses an entire control over our persons and services; and, therefore, that all the zeal that may be manifested by us in discharging our duty does not lay him under obligation to us by any sort of merit; for, as we are his property, so he on his part can owe us nothing.[5] He adduces the comparison of *a servant*, who, after having spent the day in severe toil, returns home in the evening, and continues his labours till his master is pleased to relieve him.[6] Christ speaks not of such servants as we have in the present day, who work for hire, but of the slaves that lived in ancient times, whose condition in society was such, that they gained nothing for themselves, but all that belong-

[1] "Ne s'amenderont point, mesmes quand les morts viendroyent parler à eux, et les advertir;"—"will not reform, even though the dead should come to talk to them and warn them."
[2] "Avance-toy incontinent;"—"come forward immediately."
[3] "Et apres cela tu mangeras et boiras;"—"and after that thou shalt eat and drink."
[4] "Sçait-il gré à ce serviteur-là?"—"does he feel obliged to that servant?"
[5] "Il ne peut pas estre nostre deteur;"—"he cannot be our debtor."
[6] "Iusqu'à ce qu'il se soit acquitté au bon plaisir du maistre; et qu'on luy dise, C'est assez;"—"till he is discharged at the good pleasure of the master; and till he is told, It is enough."

ed to them—their toil, and application, and industry, even to their very blood—was the property of their masters. Christ now shows that a bond of servitude not less rigorous binds and obliges us to serve God; from which he infers, that we have no means of laying Him under obligations to us.

It is an argument drawn from the less to the greater; for if a mortal man is permitted to hold such power over another man, as to enjoin upon him uninterrupted services by night and by day, and yet contract no sort of mutual obligation, as if he were that man's debtor, how much more shall God have a right to demand the services of our whole life, to the utmost extent that our ability allows, and yet be in no degree indebted to us? We see then that all are held guilty of wicked arrogance, who imagine that they deserve any thing from God, or that he is bound to them in any way. And yet no crime is more generally practised than this kind of arrogance; for there is no man that would not willingly call God to account, and hence the notion of merits has prevailed in almost every age.

But we must attend more closely to the statement made by Christ, that we render nothing to God beyond what he has a right to claim, but are so strongly bound to his service, that we owe him every thing that lies in our power. It consists of two clauses. First, our life, even to the very end of our course, belongs entirely to God; so that, if a person were to spend a part of it in obedience to God, he would have no right to bargain that he should rest for the remainder of the time; as a considerable number of men, after serving as soldiers for ten years, would gladly apply for a discharge. Then follows the second clause, on which we have already touched, that God is not bound to pay us hire for any of our services. Let each of us remember, that he has been created by God for the purpose of labouring, and of being vigorously employed in his work; and that not only for a limited time, but till death itself, and, what is more, that he shall not only *live, but die, to God,* (Rom. xiv. 8.)

With respect to merit, we must remove the difficulty by which many are perplexed; for Scripture so frequently promises a reward to our works, that they think it allows them some merit. The reply is easy. A reward is promised, not as a debt, but from the mere good-pleasure of God. It is a great mistake to suppose that there is a mutual relation between Reward and Merit; for it is by his own undeserved favour, and not by the value of our works, that God is induced to reward them. By the engagements of the Law,[1] I readily acknowledge, God is bound to men, if they were to discharge fully all that is required from them; but still, as this is a voluntary obligation, it remains a fixed principle, that man can demand nothing from God, as if he had merited any thing. And thus the arrogance of the flesh falls to the ground; for, granting that any man fulfilled the Law, he cannot plead that he has any claims on God, having done no more than he was bound to do. When he says that *we are unprofitable servants*, his meaning is, that God receives from us nothing beyond what is justly due, but only collects the lawful revenues of his dominion.

There are two principles, therefore, that must be maintained: first, that God naturally owes us nothing, and that all the services which we render to him are not worth a single straw; secondly, that, according to the engagements of the Law, a reward is attached to works, not on account of their value, but because God is graciously pleased to become our debtor.[2] It would evince intolerable ingratitude, if on such a ground any person should indulge in proud vaunting. The kindness and liberality which God exercises towards us are so far from giving us a right to swell with foolish confidence, that we are only laid under deeper obligations to Him. Whenever we meet with the word *reward*, or whenever it occurs to our recollection, let us look upon this as the crowning act of the goodness of God to us, that, though we are completely in his debt, he condescends to enter into a bargain with us. So much the more detestable is the invention of the Sophists, who have had the effrontery to forge a kind

---

[1] " Selon les conventions contenus en la Loy;"—" according to the engagements contained in the Law."
[2] " Mais en telle sorte que Dieu se rend volontairement deteur, sans qu'il y soit tenu;"—" but in such a manner that God voluntarily becomes our debtor, though he is under no obligation to do so."

of merit, which professes to be founded on a just claim.[1] The word *merit*, taken by itself, was sufficiently profane and inconsistent with the standard of piety; but to intoxicate men with diabolical pride, as if they could merit any thing by a just claim, is far worse.

10. *We have done what we were bound to do.* That is, "we have brought nothing of our own, but have only done what we were bound by the law to do." Christ speaks here of an entire observance of the law, which is nowhere to be found; for the most perfect of all men is still at a great distance from that righteousness which the law demands. The present question is not, Are we justified by works? but, Is the observance of the law meritorious of any reward from God? This latter question is answered in the negative; for God holds us for his slaves, and therefore reckons all that can proceed from us to be his just right. Nay, though it were true, that a reward is due to the observance of the law in respect of merit, it will not therefore follow that any man is justified by the merits of works; for we all fail: and not only is our obedience imperfect, but there is not a single part of it that corresponds exactly to the judgment of God.

LUKE.

XVIII. 1. And he spake also a parable to them, that they ought always to pray, and not to grow weary: 2. Saying, There was a judge in a city, who neither feared God, nor regarded man. 3. And there was a widow in that city, who came to him, saying, Do me justice on my adversary. 4. And he refused for some time,[2] but afterwards said within himself, Though I neither fear God, nor regard man, 5. Yet because this widow is troublesome to me,[3] I will do her justice, lest by coming perpetually she

---

[1] "Et d'autant plus est detestable la sophisterie des Theologiens Scholastiques, ou Sorbonnistes, lesquels ont osé forger leur merite, qu'ils appellent De condigno;"—"And so much the more detestable is the sophistry of the Scholastic Theologians, or Sorbonnists, (*see* p. 142, n. 2, *of this volume,*) who have dared to forge their merit, which they call *De condigno.*" The reader will find not only the general doctrine of *merit,* but this particular aspect of it, fully treated by our Author in his *Institutes of the Christian Religion,* Book III. ch. xv.

[2] "Et par un temps il n'en voulut rien faire;"—"and for a time he would do nothing in it."

[3] "Pourtant que ceste vefue me donne fascherie;"—"because this widow gives me annoyance."

LUKE.

weary me out.[1] 6. And the Lord said, Hear what the unjust judge saith. 7. And will not God avenge his elect, who cry to him night and day, even though he forbear with respect to them?[2] 8. I tell you that he will speedily avenge them. But when the Son of man shall come, will he find faith on the earth?[3]

We know that perseverance in prayer is a rare and difficult attainment; and it is a manifestation of our unbelief that, when our first prayers are not successful, we immediately throw away not only hope, but all the ardour of prayer. But it is an undoubted evidence of our faith, if we are disappointed of our wish, and yet do not lose courage. Most properly, therefore, does Christ recommend to his disciples to persevere in praying.

The *parable* which he employs, though apparently harsh, was admirably fitted to instruct his disciples, that they ought to be importunate in their prayers to God the Father, till they at length draw from him what He would otherwise appear to be unwilling to give. Not that by our prayers we gain a victory over God, and bend him slowly and reluctantly to compassion, but because the actual facts do not all at once make it evident that he graciously listens to our prayers. In the *parable* Christ describes to us a *widow*, who obtained what she wanted from an unjust and cruel *judge*, because she did not cease to make earnest demands. The leading truth conveyed is, that God does not all at once grant assistance to his people, because he chooses to be, as it were, wearied out by prayers; and that, however wretched and despicable may be the condition of those who pray to him, yet if they do not desist from the uninterrupted exercise of prayer, he will at length regard them and relieve their necessities.

The parties between whom the comparison is drawn are, indeed, by no means equal; for there is a wide difference

---

[1] "Et me rompe la teste."

[2] "Combien qu'il il differe de se courroucer pour eux; *ou, et aura-il patience quant à eux?*"—"Though he delay to be offended on their account; *or, and will he have patience in reference to them?*"

[3] "Pensez-vous qu'il trouve foy en terre?"—"Do you think that he will find faith on the earth?"

between a wicked and cruel man and God, who is naturally inclined to mercy. But Christ intended to assure believers that they have no reason to fear lest their persevering entreaties to the Father of mercy should be refused, since by importunate supplication they prevail on men who are given to cruelty. The wicked and iron-hearted *judge* could not avoid yielding at length, though reluctantly, to the earnest solicitations of the widow: how then shall the prayers of believers, when perseveringly maintained, be without effect? If exhaustion and weakness are felt by us when we give way after a slight exertion, or if the ardour of prayer languishes because God appears to lend a deaf ear, let us rest assured of our ultimate success, though it may not be immediately apparent. Entertaining this conviction, let us contend against our impatience, so that the long delay may not induce us to discontinue our prayers.

7. *And shall not God avenge his elect?* That *judge*, whom Christ has described to us as altogether desperate, as not only hardened against the contemplation of God, but so entirely devoid of shame, that he had no anxiety about his reputation, at length opened his eyes to the distresses of the *widow*. We have no reason to doubt that believers will derive, at least, equal advantage from their prayers, provided they do not cease to plead earnestly with God. Yet it must be observed that, while Christ applies the parable to his subject, he does not make God to resemble a wicked and cruel *judge*, but points out a very different reason why those who believe in him are kept long in suspense, and why he does not actually and at once stretch out his hand to them: it is because he *forbears*. If at any time God winks at the injuries done to us longer than we would wish, let us know that this is done with a fatherly intention—to train us to patience. A temporary overlooking of crimes is very different from allowing them to remain for ever unpunished. The promise which he makes, that *God will speedily avenge them*, must be referred to his providence; for our hasty tempers and carnal apprehension lead us to conclude that he does not come quickly enough to grant relief. But if we could penetrate

into his design, we would learn that his assistance is always ready and seasonable, as the case demands, and is not delayed for a single moment, but comes at the exact time.

But it is asked, How does Christ instruct his disciples to seek vengeance, while he exhorts them on another occasion, *pray for those who injure and persecute you?* (Matth. v. 44.) I reply: what Christ says here about vengeance does not at all interfere with his former doctrine. God declares that he will avenge believers, not for the purpose of giving a loose rein to their carnal affections, but in order to convince them that their salvation is dear and precious in his sight, and in this manner to induce them to rely on his protection. If, laying aside hatred, pure and free from every wicked desire of revenge, and influenced by proper and well-regulated dispositions, they implore divine assistance, it will be a lawful and holy wish, and God himself will listen to it. But as nothing is more difficult than to divest ourselves of sinful affections, if we would offer pure and sincere prayers, we must ask the Lord to guide and direct our hearts by his Spirit. Then shall we lawfully call on God to be our avenger, and he will answer our prayers.

8. *When the Son of man shall come.* By these words Christ informs us that there will be no reason to wonder if men shall afterwards sink under their calamities: it will be because they neglect the true remedy. He intended to obviate an offence which we are daily apt to take, when we see all things in shameful confusion. Treachery, cruelty, imposture, deceit, and violence, abound on every hand; there is no regard to justice, and no shame; the poor groan under their oppressors; the innocent are abused or insulted; while God appears to be asleep in heaven. This is the reason why the flesh imagines that the government of fortune is blind. But Christ here reminds us that men are justly deprived of heavenly aid, on which they have neither knowledge nor inclination to place reliance. They who do nothing but murmur against the Lord in their hearts, and who allow no place for his providence, cannot reasonably expect that the Lord will assist them.

Shall he find faith on the earth? Christ expressly foretells that, from his ascension to heaven till his return, unbelievers will abound; meaning by these words that, if the Redeemer does not so speedily appear, the blame of the delay will attach to men, because there will be almost none to look for him. Would that we did not behold so manifest a fulfilment of this prediction! But experience proves that though the world is oppressed and overwhelmed by a huge mass of calamities, there are few indeed in whom the least spark of *faith* can be discerned. Others understand the word *faith* to denote uprightness, but the former meaning is more agreeable to the context.

LUKE.

XVIII. 9. And he spoke also this parable to some who trusted in themselves that they were righteous, and despised others: 10. Two men went up into the temple to pray; the one a Pharisee, and the other a publican. 11. The Pharisee standing[1] prayed these things within himself: God, I thank thee that I am not as other men, extortioners, unjust, adulterous, or even as this publican. 12. I fast twice in the week, I give tithes of all that I possess. 13. And the publican standing at a distance, did not even wish to raise his eyes towards heaven, but smote upon his breast, saying, Lord, be reconciled to me a sinner. 14. I say to you, this man went down into his house justified rather than the other; for every one that exalteth himself shall be humbled, and he that humbleth himself shall be exalted.

Christ now gives directions about another virtue, which is necessary to acceptable prayer. Believers must not come into the presence of God but with humility and abasement. No disease is more dangerous than arrogance; and yet all have it so deeply fixed in the marrow of their bones, that it can scarcely be removed or extirpated by any remedy. It is no doubt strange that men should be so mad as to venture to raise their crests against God, and to plead their own merits before him. Though men are carried away by their ambition, yet when we come into the presence of God, all presumption ought to be laid aside; and yet every man thinks that he has sufficiently humbled himself, if he only presents a hypocritical prayer for forgiveness. Hence we

---

[1] " Le Pharisien se tenant là ;"—" the Pharisee standing there."

infer that this warning which our Lord gives was far from being unnecessary.

There are two faults at which Christ glances, and which he intended to condemn,—wicked confidence in ourselves, and the pride of despising brethren, the one of which springs out of the other. It is impossible that he who deceives himself with vain confidence should not lift himself up above his brethren. Nor is it wonderful that it should be so; for how should that man not despise his equals, who vaunts against God himself? Every man that is puffed up with self-confidence carries on open war with God, to whom we cannot be reconciled in any other way than by denial of ourselves; that is, by laying aside all confidence in our own virtue and righteousness, and relying on his mercy alone.

10. *Two men went up.* Christ makes a comparison between the two men, both of whom, by *going up to pray,* seem to manifest the same ardour of piety, while yet they are exceedingly unlike. *The Pharisee,* possessing outward sanctity, approaches to God with a commendation which he pronounces on his whole life, and as if he had an undoubted right to offer the sacrifice of praise. *The publican,* on the other hand, as if he had been some outcast, and knew that he was unworthy to approach, presents himself with trembling and with humble confession. Christ affirms that *the Pharisee* was rejected, and that the prayers of *the publican* were acceptable to God. The reasons why the Pharisee was rejected are stated to be these two: *he trusted in himself that he was righteous, and despised others.*

11. *God, I thank thee.* And yet he is not blamed for boasting of the strength of his free-will, but for trusting that God was reconciled to him by the merits of his works. For this thanksgiving, which is presented exclusively in his own name, does not at all imply that he boasted of his own virtue, as if he had obtained righteousness from himself, or merited any thing by his own industry. On the contrary, he ascribes it to the grace of God that he is righteous. Now though his

thanksgiving to God implies an acknowledgment, that all the good works which he possessed were purely the gift of God, yet as he places reliance on works, and prefers himself to others, himself and his prayer are alike rejected. Hence we infer that men are not truly and properly humbled, though they are convinced that they can do nothing, unless they likewise distrust the merits of works, and learn to place their salvation in the undeserved goodness of God, so as to rest upon it all their confidence.

This is a remarkable passage; for some think it enough if they take from man the glory of good works, so far as they are the gifts of the Holy Spirit; and accordingly they admit that we are justified freely, because God finds in us no righteousness but what he bestowed. But Christ goes farther, not only ascribing to the grace of the Spirit the power of acting aright, but stripping us of all confidence in works; for the Pharisee is not blamed on the ground of claiming for himself what belongs to God, but because he trusts to his works, that God will be reconciled to him, because he deserves it. Let us therefore know that, though a man may ascribe to God the praise of works, yet if he imagines the righteousness of those works to be the cause of his salvation, or rests upon it, he is condemned for wicked arrogance. And observe, that he is not charged with the vainglorious ambition of those who indulge in boasting before men, while they are inwardly conscious of their own wickedness, but is charged with concealed hypocrisy; for he is not said to have been the herald of his own praises, but to have prayed silently within himself. Though he did not proclaim aloud the honour of his own righteousness, his internal pride was abominable in the sight of God. His boasting consists of two parts: first, he acquits himself of that guilt in which all men are involved; and, secondly, he brings forward his virtues. He asserts that he is *not as other men,* because he is not chargeable with crimes which everywhere prevail in the world.

12. *I fast twice in the week, I give tithes of all that I possess.* This is equivalent to saying that he performed more than the

law required; just as the Popish monks talk loftily of their works of *supererogation,* as if they found no great difficulty in fulfilling the law of God. It must be admitted that each of us, according to the measure of the virtues which God has bestowed upon him, is the more strongly bound to thank the Author of them; and that it is an exercise of holy meditation for each of us to ponder on the benefits which he has received, so as not to bury in ingratitude the kindness of God. But there are two things here that must be observed: we must not swell with confidence, as if we had satisfied God; and, next, we must not look down with disdainful contempt upon our brethren. In both respects the Pharisee erred; for, by falsely claiming righteousness for himself, he left nothing to the mercy of God; and, next, he despised all others in comparison of himself. And, indeed, that thanksgiving would not have been disapproved by Christ, if it had not laboured under these two defects;[1] but as the proud hypocrite, by winking at his sins, met the justice of God with a pretence of complete and perfect righteousness, his wicked and detestable hardihood could not but make him fall. For the only hope of the godly, so long as they labour under the weakness of the flesh, is, after acknowledging what is good in them,[2] to betake themselves to the mercy of God alone, and to rest their salvation on prayer for forgiveness.[3]

But it may be asked, how did this man, who was blinded by wicked pride, maintain such sanctity of life; for such integrity proceeds only from the Spirit of God, who, we are certain, does not reign in hypocrites? I reply: he trusted only to outward appearance, as if the hidden and inward uncleanness of the heart would not be taken into the account. Though he was full of wicked desires within, yet as he looks only at the appearance, he boldly maintains his innocence.

---

[1] " Si ces deux vices n'y estoyent, qui gastent tout;"—" if those two faults had not been in it, which spoil the whole."

[2] " Apres avoir recognu le bien qui est en eux par la grace de Dieu;" —" after having acknowledged the good that is in them by the grace of God."

[3] " Et mettre leur salut en la confession de leurs pechez, et remission d'iceux;"—" and to place their salvation in the confession of their sins, and forgiveness of them."

Our Lord does not, indeed, accuse him of vanity, in falsely claiming for himself what he does not possess; but it ought to be believed that no man is pure from extortion, injustice, uncleanness, and other vices, unless he is governed by the Spirit of God.

The word *Sabbath* (σάββατον) denotes in this passage, as in many others, *a week.* But God never enjoined in the Law that his servants should *fast every week;* so that this *fasting* and the tithes were voluntary exercises beyond the prescriptions of the Law.[1]

13. *The publican standing at a distance.* Here Christ did not intend to lay down a general rule, as if it were necessary, whenever we pray, to cast down our eyes to the ground. He merely describes the tokens of humility, which alone he recommends to his disciples. Now humility lies in not refusing to acknowledge our sins, but condemning ourselves, and thus anticipating the judgment of God; and, with the view of being reconciled to God, in making an honest confession of guilt. Such, too, is the cause of that shame which always accompanies repentance; for Christ insists chiefly on this point, that *the publican* sincerely acknowledged himself to be miserable and lost, and fled to the mercy of God. Though he is a sinner, he trusts to a free pardon, and hopes that God will be gracious to him. In a word, in order to obtain favour, he owns that he does not deserve it. And, certainly, since it is the forgiveness of sins that alone reconciles God to us,[2] we must begin with this, if we desire that he would accept our prayers. He who acknowledges that he is guilty and convicted, and then proceeds to implore pardon, disavows all confidence in works; and Christ's object was to show that God will not be gracious to any but those who betake themselves with trembling to his mercy alone.[3]

---

[1] "Estoyent des exercises volontaires, et inventez à plaisir;"—"were voluntary exercises, and invented at pleasure."

[2] "Qui nous rende agreables à Dieu;"—"which renders us acceptable to God."

[3] "Qui tremblans à cause d'un vray sentiment de leur pechez, recourront à sa seule misericorde;"—"who, trembling on account of a true conviction of their sins, shall have recourse to his mercy alone."

14. *This man went down justified.* The comparison is not exact; for Christ does not merely assign to *the publican* a certain degree of superiority, as if *righteousness* had belonged alike to both, but means that *the publican* was accepted by God, while *the Pharisee* was totally rejected. And this passage shows plainly what is the strict meaning of the word *justified:* it means, to stand before God as if we were righteous. For it is not said that *the publican* was justified, because he suddenly acquired some new quality, but that he obtained grace, because his guilt was blotted out, and his sins were washed away. Hence it follows, that *righteousness* consists in the forgiveness of sins. As the virtues of *the Pharisee* were defiled and polluted by unfounded confidence, so that his integrity, which deserved commendation before the world, was of no value in the sight of God; so *the publican*, relying on no merits of works, obtained righteousness solely by imploring pardon,[1] because he had no other ground of hope than the pure mercy of God.

But it may be thought absurd, that all should be reduced to the same level, since the purity of saints is widely different from that of *the publican.* I reply: whatever proficiency any man may have made in the worship of God and in true holiness, yet if he consider how far he is still deficient, there is no other form of prayer which he can properly use than to begin with the acknowledgment of guilt; for though some are more, and others less, yet all are universally guilty. We cannot doubt, therefore, that Christ now lays down a rule for all to this effect, that God will not be pacified towards us, unless we distrust works, and pray that we may be freely reconciled. And, indeed, the Papists are compelled to acknowledge this in part, but immediately afterwards they debase this doctrine by a wicked invention. They admit that all need the remedy of forgiveness, because no man is perfect; but they first intoxicate wretched men with reliance on what they call *imperfect righteousness*, and next add satisfactions, in order to blot out their guilt. But our faith needs no other

---

[1] " Seulement en confessant sa faute, et demandant pardon;"—" solely by confessing his fault, and asking pardon."

support than this, that God has accepted us, not because we deserved it, but because he does not impute our sins.

LUKE.

XVII. 11. And it happened, while he was going to Jerusalem, that he passed through the midst of Samaria and of Galilee. 12. And as he was entering into a certain village, there met him ten men, lepers, who stood at a distance; 13. And, lifting up their voice, said, Jesus, Master, take pity on us. 14. When he saw them, he said, Go, show yourselves to the priests. And it happened that, while they were going, they were cleansed. 15. And one of them, when he saw that he was cleansed, turned back, glorifying God with a loud voice, 16. And fell on his face[1] at his feet, thanking him: and he was a Samaritan. 17. And Jesus answering said, Were not ten cleansed? But where are the nine? 18. None are found that have returned to give glory to God except this stranger. 19. And he saith to him, Arise, go, thy faith hath saved thee.[2] 20. And being interrogated by the Pharisees, when the kingdom of God would come, he replied to them and said, The kingdom of God will not come with observation:[3] 21. For they shall not say, Lo, he is here! or, Lo, he is there! for, lo, the kingdom of God is within you.

As, on a former occasion, Matthew and the other two Evangelists (Matth. viii. 1; Mark i. 40; Luke v. 12) related that *a leper* had been *cleansed* by Christ, so Luke mentions that the same miracle of healing was performed on *ten lepers*. The object of this narrative, however, is different; for it describes the base and incredible ingratitude of the Jewish nation, to prevent us from wondering that so many of Christ's favours had been suppressed, and so many of his wonderful works buried, among them. One circumstance, too, is added, which greatly heightens the infamy of their crime. Our Lord had *cured nine Jews:* yet not one of them returned thanks, but, with the view of obliterating the remembrance of their disease, they privately stole away. One man only—a Samaritan—acknowledged his obligation to Christ. There is, therefore, on the one hand, a display of Christ's divine power; and, on the other hand, a reproof of the impiety of the Jews, in consequence of which so remarkable a miracle as this received scarcely any attention.

[1] " Et se ietta en terre sur sa face ;"—" and threw himself on the ground on his face."
[2] "Ta foy t'a guairi, *ou, sauvé;*"—"thy faith hath healed, *or, saved* thee."
[3] " Le regne de Dieu ne viendra point à veuë d'œil, *ou, avec apparence ;*"—"the kingdom of God will not come visibly, *or, manifestly.*"

13. *Jesus, Master.*[1] It is evident that all of them possessed some measure of faith, not only because they implore Christ's assistance, but because they honour him with the title of *Master.* That they made use of that expression sincerely, and not in hypocrisy, may be inferred from their ready obedience; for, although they perceive that the filthy scab still remains in their flesh, yet as soon as they are commanded to *show themselves to the priests,* they do not refuse to obey. Add to this that, but for the influence of faith, they would never have set out to *show themselves to the priests;* for it would have been absurd to present themselves to the judges of leprosy, for the purpose of attesting that they had been cleansed, if the promise of Christ had been regarded by them as of no more value than a mere inspection of the disease. They bear a visible leprosy in their flesh; and yet, trusting to Christ's word alone, they have no scruple about declaring that they are clean. It cannot therefore be denied, that some seed of faith had been implanted in their hearts. Now though it is certain that they were not regenerated by the Spirit of adoption, yet there is no absurdity in supposing that they had some beginnings of piety. There is the greater reason to fear that sparks of faith, which make their appearance in us, may be extinguished; for, although lively faith, which has its roots deeply fixed by the Spirit of regeneration, never dies, yet we have seen formerly that many conceive a temporary faith, which immediately disappears. Above all, it is too common a disease that, when we are urged by strong necessity, and when the Lord himself prompts us by a secret movement of the Spirit, we seek God, but, when we have obtained our wishes, ungrateful forgetfulness swallows up that feeling of piety. Thus poverty and hunger beget faith, but abundance kills it.

14. *Show yourselves to the priests.* This reply was equivalent to saying, "You are clean;" for we know that the discernment of leprosy belonged *to the priests,* who were enjoined in the law to distinguish between the clean and the unclean,

---

[1] "*Iesus,* nostre *Maistre;*"—"*Jesus,* our *Master.*"

(Lev. xiv. 2.) Thus Christ preserves their right entire, and appeals to them as witnesses for approving of the miracle which he had wrought; and we have accordingly said, that pious and devout sentiments concerning Christ must have been entertained by those men who were instantly led, by his bare word, to entertain the hope of a cure.

On this passage the Papists absurdly build their *auricular* confession. The lepers, I admit, were sent by Christ to the priests; but it was not for the purpose of vomiting out their sins into their ears. On the contrary, they were sent to offer a sacrifice, as the Law had enjoined. They were not sent to cleanse themselves, as the Papists imagine that cleanness is produced by confession, but to *show to the priests* that they were already clean. It is an additional proof of the folly of the Papists, that they do not consider what a foul stain of infamy they throw on their confession; for, according to their reasoning, it will be quite enough if, out of the whole troop of those who have gone *to the priests,* a tenth part only shall return to Christ, and all the rest shall wickedly revolt. They cannot plead this passage in behalf of their confession, without giving us liberty to throw back upon them this advantage which it yields, that none return from the priests *to give glory to God.* But, not to dwell on these fooleries, we have ascertained the reason why *the priests* were mentioned.

It happened that, while they were going, they were cleansed. Here was displayed the divine power of Christ and of his words, and there was also a proof of the high estimation in which God holds the obedience of faith; for the great suddenness of the cure arose from the confident hope which induced them to undertake the journey, without hesitation, at the command of Christ. But if that transitory faith—which wanted a living root, and produced nothing more than the blade—was honoured by God with a remarkable effect, how much more valuable is the reward that awaits our faith, if it is sincerely and permanently fixed on God? Though the *nine lepers* derived no advantage to salvation from the cure of the flesh, but only obtained a temporary gift by means of a fleeting and transitory faith, yet this figure points out to us the great efficacy which will attend true faith.

15. *And one of them, &c.* It is uncertain if he returned when they were half-way, and Luke's words appear to imply this; but I think it more probable, that it was not till he had heard the decision of the priests that he returned to give thanks. He must have obtained permission from the priests to return to the ordinary intercourse of life; and he had no right to neglect the command of Christ, and to defraud the temple of God of a sacrifice. Some will perhaps be better pleased with a different conjecture, that as soon as he saw that he was cleansed, and before he applied to the priests for a testimony, he was seized with a devout and holy zeal, and returned to the Author of the cure, so as to commence his sacrifice with thanksgiving. The words of Christ contain an expostulation with the whole nation; for it is by way of reproach that he draws a comparison between one stranger and many Jews, because it was customary with them to swallow up God's favours without any feeling of piety. And this was the reason why Christ gained hardly any reputation among them by miracles so numerous and so splendid. Let us learn that this complaint is brought generally against all of us, if we do not at least repay the divine favours by the duty of gratitude.

19. *Thy faith hath saved thee.* The word *save* is restricted by some commentators to the cleanness of the flesh.[1] But if this be the case, since Christ commends the lively faith of this Samaritan, it may be asked, how were the other nine *saved?* for all of them without exception obtained the same cure.[2] We must therefore arrive at the conclusion, that Christ has here pronounced a different estimate of the gift of God from that which is usually pronounced by ungodly men;

---

[1] "Le mot dont a ici usé l'Evangeliste est celuy mesme que quasi par tout on tourne, *Sauver*."—"The word which the Evangelist has here employed (σέσωκε) is the same word which is almost always rendered *save*."
[2] "Une mesme guairison corporelle;"—"the same bodily cure."

namely, that it was a token or pledge of God's fatherly love. The *nine lepers were cured;* but as they wickedly efface the remembrance of the grace of God, the cure itself is debased and contaminated by their ingratitude, so that they do not derive from it the advantage which they ought. It is faith alone that sanctifies the gifts of God to us, so that they become pure, and, united to the lawful use of them, contribute to our salvation. Lastly, by this word Christ has informed us in what manner we lawfully enjoy divine favours. Hence we infer, that he included the eternal salvation of the soul along with the temporal gift. The *Samaritan* was *saved* by his *faith.* How? Certainly not because he was cured of leprosy, (for this was likewise obtained by the rest,) but because he was admitted into the number of the children of God, and received from His hand a pledge of fatherly kindness.

20. *And being interrogated by the Pharisees.* This question was undoubtedly put in mockery; for, since Christ was continually speaking of the kingdom of God as at hand, while no change was taking place in the outward condition of the Jews, wicked and malicious persons looked upon this as a plausible excuse for harassing him. As if all that Christ said about the kingdom of God were idle talk and mere trifling, they put a sarcastic question to him, "When shall that kingdom come?" If any one shall consider this question to have been put on account of the grossness of their own views, rather than for the sake of jeering, I have no objection.

The kingdom of God will not come with observation. My opinion is, that Christ now disregards those dogs, and accommodates this reply to the disciples; just as on many other occasions, when he was provoked by wicked men, and seized the opportunity of giving instruction. In this manner God disappoints their malice, while the truth, which is maintained in opposition to their sophistry, is the more fully displayed.

The word *observation* is here employed by Christ to denote

extraordinary splendour;[1] and he declares, that the kingdom of God will not make its appearance at a distance, or attended by pompous display. He means, that they are greatly mistaken who seek with the eyes of the flesh *the kingdom of God*, which is in no respect carnal or earthly, for it is nothing else than the inward and spiritual renewal of the soul. From the nature of the kingdom itself he shows that they are altogether in the wrong, who look around *here* or *there*, in order to observe visible marks. "That restoration of the Church," he tells us, "which God has promised, must be looked for *within;* for, by quickening his elect into a heavenly newness of life, he establishes his kingdom *within them.*" And thus he indirectly reproves the stupidity of the Pharisees, because they aimed at nothing but what was earthly and fading. It must be observed, however, that Christ speaks only of the beginnings of the kingdom of God; for we now begin to be formed anew by the Spirit after the image of God, in order that our entire renovation, and that of the whole world, may afterwards follow in due time.

MATTHEW.	MARK.
XIII. 53. And it happened, when Jesus had concluded these discourses,[2] that he departed thence. 54. And when he was come into his own country, he taught them in their synagogue, so that they were amazed, and said, Whence hath this man this wisdom and these miracles? 55. Is not this the carpenter's son? Is not his mother called Mary, and his brothers James, and Joses, and Simon, and Judas?	VI. 1. And he departed thence, and came into his own country, and his disciples followed him. 2. And when it was Sabbath, he began to teach in the synagogue, and many hearing were amazed, saying,Whence hath this man these things?[3] And what is the wisdom that hath been given to him, so that such miracles are done by his hands? 3. Is not this the carpenter, the son of Mary, the brother of James, and Joses, and Judas, and Simon? Are not his sisters also here with us? And they

[1] "Là où nous avons traduit, *à veuë d'œil,* le Grec a mot à mot *avec observation;* c'est à dire, avec quelque grande apparence, en sorte qu'un chacun y puisse prendre garde."—"Where we have rendered, *visibly,* the Greek literally runs, *with observation;* that is to say, with some great display, so that every person may take notice of it."

[2] "Quand Iesus eut achevé ces similitudes-ci;"—"when Jesus had concluded these parables."

[3] "D'ou vienent ces choses à cestuy-ci?'—"Whence comes these things to this man?"

MATTHEW.	MARK.
56. And his sisters, do not they all live amongst us? Whence then hath this man all these things? 57. And they were offended at him. But Jesus said to them, A prophet is not destitute of honour, except in his own country and in his own house. 58. And he did not perform many miracles there on account of their unbelief.	were offended at him. 4. And Jesus said to them, A prophet is not devoid of honour,[1] except in his own country, and among his relatives, and in his own family. 5. And he could not perform any miracle there, except that he cured a few sick persons by laying his hands on them. 6. And he wondered at their unbelief, and walked about through the surrounding villages teaching.

Matthew xiii. 53. *When Jesus had concluded.* Matthew does not mean, that immediately after delivering these discourses, he came into his own country; for it is evident from *Mark*, that some interval of time elapsed. But the meaning is, that after having taught for some time in Judea, he returned again to the Galileans, but did not receive from them kind treatment. A narrative which Luke gives (iv. 22) is nearly similar, but is not the same. Nor ought we to wonder that Christ's countrymen, when they perceived that his family was mean and despised, and that he had been poorly educated, were at first so much offended as to murmur at his doctrine, and afterwards persevered in the same malice to such an extent, that they did not cease to slander him, when he chose to discharge the office of a prophet amongst them. This second rejection of Christ shows that the space of time which had intervened had not effected a reformation on the inhabitants of Nazareth, but that the same contempt was constantly thrown as an obstacle in the way, to prevent them from hearing Christ.[2]

54. *So that they were amazed.* They are struck with *amazement* at the novelty of the occurrence, that Christ, who had not learned letters, but had been employed from youth to manhood in a mechanical occupation, is so eminent a teacher, and is filled with divine wisdom. In this miracle they ought to have perceived the hand of God; but their

---

[1] " Un prophete n'est deshonoré ;"—" a prophet is not dishonoured."
[2] " A fin de n'approcher de luy, et de ne recevoir sa doctrine ;"—" that they might not approach to him, and might not receive his doctrine."

ingratitude made them cover themselves with darkness.[1] They are compelled to admire him, whether they will or not; and yet they treat him with contempt. And what is this but to reject a prophet whom God has taught, because he has not been educated by men? They cut their throat by means of their own acknowledgment, when they render so honourable a testimony to the doctrine of Christ, which after all has no influence on them, because it does not take its origin, in the usual way, from the earth. Why do they not rather lift their eyes to heaven, and learn that what exceeds human reason must have come from God?

Besides, the miracles, which were added to the doctrine, ought to have affected them the more powerfully, or at least to have aroused them from their excessive carelessness and stupidity to glorify God; for certainly, when God adopts unwonted methods of procedure, so much the more clearly does he display the power of his hand. And yet this was the very reason why the inhabitants of Nazareth maliciously drew a veil over their eyes. We see, then, that it is not mere ignorance that hinders men, but that, of their own accord, they search after grounds of offence, to prevent them from following the path to which God invites. We ought rather to argue in the opposite way, that, when human means fail, the power of God is clearly revealed to us, and ought to receive undivided praise.

55. *Is not this the carpenter's son?* It was, we are aware, by the wonderful purpose of God, that Christ remained in private life till he was thirty years of age. Most improperly and unjustly, therefore, were the inhabitants of Nazareth offended on this account; for they ought rather to have received him with reverence, as one who had suddenly come down from heaven. They see God working in Christ, and intentionally turn away their eyes from this sight, to behold Joseph, and Mary, and all his relatives; thus interposing a

---

[1] " Mais par leur ingratitude ils se sont eblouis l'entendement, à fin de ne faire leur profit de ce qu'ils voyoyent devant leurs yeux;"—" but by their ingratitude their understanding was dazzled, so that they did not derive advantage from what they saw before their eyes."

veil to shut out the clearest light. The word *brothers*, we have formerly mentioned, is employed, agreeably to the Hebrew idiom, to denote any relatives whatever; and, accordingly, *Helvidius* displayed excessive ignorance in concluding that Mary must have had many sons, because Christ's *brothers* are sometimes mentioned.[1]

57. *A prophet is not devoid of honour.* I have explained this statement at considerable length, where it occurs in the Gospel of John,[2] (iv. 44.) It may, no doubt, be a general proverb, that those who are distinguished by eminent gifts are nowhere held in less estimation than *in their own country;* and this manifests the ingratitude of men, who, in proportion to the greater familiarity with which God exhibits himself to them, are the more bold to reject him in the influences of his Spirit. I readily agree, however, with Chrysostom, who thinks that this proverb was applied in a peculiar manner to the Jews. But what was usually spoken against the whole nation, Christ now asserts with special reference to his Galilean countrymen; for nowhere did he receive less honour than on his native soil. There were good grounds for the charge which he brings against them, that, instead of being the first to accept the grace offered to them, as they ought to have been, they drive him to a distance from them; for it is truly extraordinary that a prophet of God, whom others warmly receive as a newly-arrived stranger, should be despised in the place where he was born.

58. *And he did not perform many miracles in that place.* Mark states it more emphatically, that *he could not perform any miracle.* But they are perfectly agreed as to the substance of what is said, that it was the impiety of Christ's countrymen that closed the door against the performance of

---

[1] *Jerome* replied to *Helvidius* in a work entitled, *Contra Helvidium de Beatæ Mariæ Virginitate.* CALVIN has formerly alluded to the controversy between these two authors, (Harmony, vol. i. p. 107.)—*Ed.*

[2] Our Author's Preface to his Commentary on John's Gospel is dated 1st January 1553; while the Preface to the Harmony is dated 1st August 1555. This accounts for the former being always referred to as an earlier work.—*Ed.*

a greater number of miracles among them. He had already given them some taste of his power; but they willingly stupify themselves, so as to have no relish for it. Accordingly, *Augustine* justly compares faith to the open mouth of a vessel, while he speaks of faith as resembling a stopper, by which the vessel is closed, so as not to receive the liquor[1] which God pours into it. And undoubtedly this is the case; for when the Lord perceives that his power is not accepted by us, he at length withdraws it; and yet we complain that we are deprived of his aid, which our unbelief rejects and drives far from us.

When *Mark* declares that Christ *could not perform any miracles*, he represents the aggravated guilt of those by whom his goodness was prevented; for certainly unbelievers, as far as lies in their power, bind up the hands of God by their obstinacy; not that God is overcome, as if he were an inferior, but because they do not permit him to display his power. We must observe, however, what *Mark* adds, that *some sick people*, notwithstanding, *were cured*; for hence we infer, that the goodness of Christ strove with their malice, and triumphed over every obstacle.[2] We have experience of the same thing daily with respect to God; for, though he justly and reluctantly restrains his power, because the entrance to us is shut against him, yet we see that he opens up a path for himself where none exists, and ceases not to bestow favours upon us. What an amazing contest, that while we are endeavouring by every possible method to hinder the grace of God from coming to us, it rises victorious, and displays its efficacy in spite of all our exertions!

MATTHEW.	MARK.	LUKE.
XIV. 1. At that time, Herod the tetrarch heard of the fame of Jesus,	VI. 14. And king Herod heard of him, (for his name had become celebrated,) and said, John, who baptized, hath risen from the	IX. 7. Now Herod the tetrarch heard of all that was done by him, and was perplexed, because it was said by some that Christ had

---

[1] "La bonne liqueur;"—"the good liquor."

[2] "En sorte que quelques empeschemens qu'ils ayent seen y mettre, encore est—elle venue au dessus, et s'est monstree en quelque maniere."—"So that, whatever obstacles they might be able to throw in the way, still it rose above them, and was in some measure displayed."

MATTHEW.	MARK.	LUKE.
2. And said to his servants, This is John the Baptist: he is raised from the dead, and therefore miracles work in him.	dead, and therefore miracles are performed by him. 15. Others said, It is Elijah; and others said, It is a prophet, or as one of the prophets. 16. But when Herod heard that, he said, It is John whom I beheaded, he hath risen from the dead.	risen from the dead; 8. And by some, that Elijah had appeared; and by others, that one of the ancient prophets had risen again. 9. And Herod said, John have I beheaded, but who is this of whom I hear such things? And he desired to see him.

The reason why the Evangelists relate this occurrence is, to inform us that the name of Christ was universally celebrated, and, therefore, the Jews could not be excused on the plea of ignorance. Many might otherwise have been perplexed by this question, "How came it that, while Christ dwelt on the earth, Judea remained in a profound sleep, as if he had withdrawn into some corner, and had displayed to none his divine power?" The Evangelists accordingly state, that the report concerning him was everywhere spread abroad, and penetrated even into the court of Herod.

2. *And said to his servants.* From the words of Luke it may be inferred, that Herod did not of his own accord adopt this conjecture, but that it was suggested to him by a report which was current among the people. And, indeed, I have no doubt that the hatred which they bore to the tyrant, and their detestation of so shocking a murder, gave rise, as is commonly the case, to those rumours. It was a superstition deeply rooted, as we have formerly mentioned, in the minds of men, that the dead return to life in a different person. Nearly akin to this is the opinion which they now adopt, that Herod, when he cruelly put to death the holy man, was far from obtaining what he expected; because he had suddenly risen from the dead by the miraculous power of God, and would oppose and attack his enemies with greater severity than ever.

Mark and *Luke*, however, show that men spoke variously on this subject: some thought that he was *Elijah*, and others that he was *one of the prophets*, or that he was so eminently endued with the gifts of the Spirit, that he might be compared to *the prophets.* The reason why they thought that he might be *Elijah*, rather than any other prophet, has been already stated. Malachi having predicted (iv. 5, 6) that *Elijah would come* to gather the scattered Church, they misunderstood that prediction as relating to the person of *Elijah,* instead of being a simple comparison to the following effect: " That the coming of Messiah may not be unknown, and that the people may not remain ignorant of the grace of redemption, there will be an *Elijah* to go before, like him who of old raised up that which was fallen, and the worship of God which had been overthrown. *He will go before,* by a remarkable power of the Spirit, to proclaim *the great and dreadful day of the Lord.*" The Jews, with their usual grossness of interpretation, had applied this to *Elijah the Tishbite,* (1 Kings xvii. 1,) as if he were to appear again and discharge the office of a prophet. Others again conjecture, either that some one of the ancient prophets had risen, or that he was some great man, who approached to them in excellence.

It was astonishing that, amidst the diversity of views which were suggested, the true interpretation did not occur to any one; more especially as the state of matters at that very time directed them to Christ. God had promised to them a Redeemer, who would relieve them when they were distressed and in despair. The extremity of affliction into which they had been plunged was a loud call for divine assistance. The Redeemer is at hand, who had been so clearly pointed out by the preaching of John, and who himself testifies respecting his office. They are compelled to acknowledge that some divine power belongs to him, and yet they fall into their own fancies, and change him into the persons of other men. It is thus that the world is wont, in base ingratitude, to obliterate the remembrance of the favours which God has bestowed.

With respect to Herod himself, as I hinted a little ago, the conjecture that John had risen did not at first occur to himself; but as bad consciences are wont to tremble and hesitate, and turn with every wind, he readily believed what he dreaded. With such blind terrors God frequently alarms wicked men; so that, after all the pains they take to harden themselves, and to escape agitation, their internal executioner gives them no rest, but chastises them with severity.

And therefore miracles work in him. We naturally wonder what reasoning could have led them to this conclusion. John had performed no miracle during the whole course of his preaching. There appears to be no probability, therefore, in the conjecture, that it was John whom they saw performing extraordinary miracles. But they imagine that miracles are now performed by him for the first time, in order to prove his resurrection, and to show that the holy prophet of God had been wickedly put to death by Herod, and now came forward with a visible and divine protection, that no man might afterwards venture to assail him. They think that *miracles work* (ἐνεργοῦσιν) *in him;* that is, are powerfully displayed, so as to give him greater authority, and make it evident that the Lord is with him.

MATTHEW.	MARK.
XIV. 3. For Herod had seized John, and bound him, and put him in prison, on account of Herodias, the wife of his brother Philip. 4. For John said to him, It is not lawful for thee to have her. 5. And though he wished to put him to death, he feared the multitude, because they accounted him a prophet. 6. But when Herod's birth-day was kept, the daughter of Herodias danced before the company, and pleased Herod. 7. And therefore he promised with an oath, that he would give her whatever she would ask. 8. But she, after having been instructed by her mother, said, Give me here in a dish the head of John the Baptist. 9. And the king was sorry: yet on account of the oath, and of those who sat with him at table, he command-	VI. 17. For Herod himself had sent, and seized John, and bound him in prison, on account of Herodias, the wife of his brother Philip, because he had married her. 18. For John said to Herod, It is not lawful for thee to have thy brother's wife. 19. And Herodias lay in wait for him, and wished to kill him, and could not. 20. For Herod dreaded John, knowing that he was a just and holy man, and observed him, and, having heard him, did many things, and heard him gladly. 21. And when a convenient day came, when Herod on his birth-day made a supper to the nobles, and captains, and distinguished men of Galilee; 22. And when the daughter of Herodias entered, and danced, and pleased Herod and those who sat at table with him, the king said to the girl, Ask any thing from me,[1] and I will give it to thee. 23. And he swore to her, Whatever thou shalt ask of me I will give to thee, even to the half of my kingdom. 24. But she went out and said to her mother, What shall I ask? And she said, The head of John the Baptist. 25. And she went in immediately with haste to the king, and asked, saying, I wish that thou wouldst give to me immediately in a dish the head of John

[1] "Demande-moy ce que tu voudras;"—"ask of me what thou wilt."

MATTHEW.	MARK.
ed that it should be given. 10. And he sent and beheaded John in the prison. 11. And his head was brought in a dish and given to the girl, and she carried it to her mother. 12. And his disciples came and carried away the body, and buried it, and went and told Jesus.	the Baptist. 26. And the king being sorry on account of the oath, and of those who sat at table with him, would not refuse her.[1] 27. And he immediately sent a spearman,[2] and commanded that his head should be brought: and he went, and beheaded him in the prison. 28. And he brought his head in a dish, and gave it to the girl, and the girl gave it to her mother. 29. And when his disciples heard of this, they came and carried off his body, and laid it in a tomb.

This narrative is at present omitted by Luke, because he had explained it on a former occasion; and for my own part, as I am unwilling to annoy my readers by writing the same thing twice, I shall handle this passage with greater brevity.[3] The Evangelists relate that John was seized, because he had openly condemned *Herod* for carrying off *Herodias*, and for his incestuous marriage with her. Josephus assigns a different reason, namely, that Herod, dreading on his own account a change of affairs, regarded John with suspicion, (Ant. xviii. v. 2;) and it is possible that this may have been the pretext on which the tyrant excused his crime, or that such a report may have been in circulation; for it frequently happens that various motives are assigned for unjust violence and cruelty. The true state of the fact, however, is pointed out by the Evangelists: Herod was offended at the holy man, because he had been reproved by him.

Josephus is mistaken in supposing that Herodias was carried off, not from his brother Philip, but from Herod, King of Chalcis, his uncle, (Ant. xviii. v. 4.) For not only was the crime still recent when the Evangelists wrote, but it was committed before the eyes of all. What is elsewhere stated by Josephus, (Ant. xviii. iv. 6,) that Philip was a person of amiable dispositions, emboldened Herod, I have no doubt, to

---

[1] "Le roy estant fort marri, ne la voulut point 'toutesfois' esconduire ou reietter;"—"The king being very angry, did not wish, however, to deny or refuse her."

[2] "Ainsi envoya incontinent le bourreau;"—"so he immediately sent the executioner."

[3] The allusion is to his exposition of Luke iii. 19, 20, which will be found in *Harmony*, vol. i. p. 222.—*Ed.*

expect that an outrage committed on a mild, gentle, and peaceable man, would pass with impunity. Another probable conjecture may be mentioned. There is greater reason to suppose that Herodias was married to her uncle Philip than to her grand-uncle, her grandfather's brother, who must have been at that time in the decrepitude of old age. Now Herod Antipas (who is here mentioned) and Philip were not brothers by the same mother; for Herod was the son of Marthaca, third wife of Herod the Great, and Philip was the son of Cleopatra.[1]

To return to the Evangelists, they tell us that John was thrown into prison, because he had reproved Herod's crime with greater freedom than the ferocity of the tyrant would endure. The atrocious character of the deed was in itself sufficiently detestable and infamous; for not only did he keep in his own house another man's wife, whom he had torn away from lawful wedlock, but the person on whom he had committed this outrage was his own brother. When, in addition to this, he is freely reproved by John, Herod has some reason to fear that sedition will suddenly break out. His lust did not allow him to correct his fault; but having imprisoned the prophet of God, he promises to himself repose and liberty.[2]

Ignorance of history has led many persons into a fruitless debate; "Have I a right to marry the woman who was formerly married to my brother?" Though the modesty of nature recoils from such a marriage,[3] yet John condemns the rape still more than the incest; for it was by violence or by stratagem[4] that Herod had deprived his brother of his lawful wife: and otherwise it would have been less lawful for him

---

[1] The apparent discrepancy between Josephus and the sacred historians is removed, as was formerly suggested, (*Harmony*, vol. i. p. 223, n. 1,) by a hypothesis which appears to be generally admitted, that the name of the person in question was *Herod-Philip.*—Ed.

[2] "Il se fait accroire qu'il sera en repos, et qu'il pourra continuer sa meschanceté sans aucune crainte;"—"he makes himself believe that he will be at ease, and that he will have it in his power to continue his wickedness without any dread."

[3] "Combien que l'honnesté naturelle condamne un tel marriage;"—"though natural decency condemns such a marriage."

[4] "Ou par force et violence, ou par quelque ruse et moyen subtil;"—"either by force and violence, or by some trick and cunning method."

to marry his niece than to marry his brother's widow. There cannot be a doubt, that a crime so flagrant was universally blamed. But others loaded Herod with their curses in his absence. John alone comes into his presence, and reproves him boldly to his face, if by any means he may be brought to repentance. Hence we learn with what unshaken fortitude the servants of God ought to be armed when they have to do with princes; for in almost every court hypocrisy and servile flattery are prevalent; and the ears of princes, having been accustomed to this smooth language, do not tolerate any voice which reproves their vices with any severity. But as a prophet of God ought not to overlook so shocking a crime, John steps forward, though a disagreeable and unwelcome adviser, and, rather than fail in his duty, scruples not to incur the frown of the tyrant, even though he knew Herod to be so strongly held by the snares of the prostitute, that he could scarcely be moved from his purpose.

5. *And though he wished to put him to death.* There is some appearance of contradiction between the words of *Matthew* and *Mark:* for the former says that Herod was desirous to commit this shocking murder, but was restrained by the fear of the people; while the latter charges Herodias alone with this cruelty. But the difficulty is soon removed. At first Herod would have been unwilling, if a stronger necessity had not compelled him reluctantly to do so, to put to death the holy man; because he regarded him with reverence, and, indeed, was prevented by religious scruples from practising such atrocious cruelty against a prophet of God; and that he afterwards shook off this fear of God, in consequence of the incessant urgency of Herodias; but that afterwards, when infuriated by that demon he longed for the death of the holy man, he was withheld by a new restraint, because he dreaded on his own account a popular commotion. And here we must attend to the words of Mark, *Herodias lay in wait for him;*[1] which imply, that as Herod was not of himself sufficiently disposed to commit the murder, she either attempted

---

[1] " *Herodias cherchoit occasion ;*"—" *Herodias sought an opportunity.*"

to gain him over by indirect wiles, or laboured to find some secret method of putting the holy man to death. I am more disposed to adopt the former view, that she employed stratagems for influencing the mind of her husband, but did not succeed, so long as Herod was prevented by remorse of conscience from pronouncing sentence of death on the holy man. Next followed another fear, that the business of his death should excite the people to some insurrection. But Mark glances only at what prevented Herod from yielding immediately to the entreaties of the prostitute; for Herodias would have wished that, as soon as John was thrown into prison, he should be privately executed.

Herod, on the contrary, reverenced the holy man, so far as even to comply willingly with his advices: *Herod feared John.* Now the *fear* which is here mentioned, was not a *dread* arising from a mistaken opinion, as we *dread* those who have obtained some authority over us, though we reckon them to be unworthy of the honour. But this *fear* was a voluntary respect; for Herod was convinced that he was a holy man and a faithful servant of God, and therefore did not dare to despise him.[1] And this deserves our attention; for though John knew by experience that it was, in many respects, advantageous for him to have some share in the good wishes of the tetrarch,[2] yet he was not afraid to offend him, when he could find no other way of securing that favour, than by wickedly conniving at a known and disgraceful crime. He might indeed have protested that he did not at all consult his private interests, and that he had no other object in view than the public advantage; for it is certain that he requested nothing from motives of ambition,[3] but that Herod yielded to his holy counsels, which had a reference to the lawful administration of the kingdom. But as

[1] " Estoit aucunement contreint en soy mesme de luy porter l'honneur, et ne l'osoit pas mespriser ;"—" was somewhat constrained in himself to bear respect towards him, and did not dare to despise him."

[2] " Qu'il eust quelque entree en la Cour, et que le Roy l'eust aucunement agreable ;"—" that he should have some access to the Court, and that the King should be somewhat favourable to him."

[3] " Qu'il n'a rien demandé au Roy pour se faire valoir, ou pour monstrer son credit ;"—" that he asked nothing from the King to put himself forward, or to display his influence."

he perceives that he has no right to accept this kind of compensation,[1] which would procure for him some kind offices by betraying the truth, he chooses rather to turn a friend into an enemy than to encourage, by flattery or silence, an evil which he is laid under the necessity of reproving with severity.

John has thus, by his example, furnished an undoubted rule for pious teachers, not to wink at the faults of princes, so as to purchase their favour at this price, how advantageous soever that favour might appear to be to the public interests.[2] In Herod, on the other hand, the Spirit of God exhibits, as in a mirror, how frequently it happens that those who do not sincerely worship God are nevertheless willing, in some measure, to obey His commands, provided that He will grant them some indulgence or abatement. But whenever they are hard pressed, they throw off the yoke, and break out not only into obstinacy, but into rage. There is no reason, therefore, why they who comply with many sound advices should be well satisfied with themselves, till they have learned to yield and surrender themselves unreservedly to God.

6. *And when Herod's birth-day was kept.* The Evangelists now begin to relate the stratagem by which Herodias at length succeeded in a design which she had long meditated, the taking away of John's life. The opportunity was afforded to her by an annual festival, when Herod was celebrating his birth-day. It is scarcely possible that such magnificent preparations should not draw luxury, pride, unbridled merriment, and other crimes, and likewise many other evils, along with them. Not that there is any thing wrong in the mere act of preparing an expensive banquet; but such is the tendency of the human mind to licentiousness, that when the reins are loosened, they quickly go astray.

---

[1] "Que ceste façon de compensation n'est point honneste, ne selon Dieu;"—"that this kind of compensation is not honourable, nor according to God."

[2] "Encore qu'ils ne la cherchent point pour leur regard particulier, mais seulement pour avoir occasion de profiter plus en d'autres endroits;"—"even though they do not seek it for their private interest, but solely in order to have an opportunity of doing more good in other respects."

The ancient custom of observing a birth-day every year as an occasion of joy cannot in itself be disapproved; for that day, as often as it returns, reminds each of us to give thanks to God, who brought us into this world, and has permitted us, in his kindness, to spend many years in it; next, to bring to our recollection how improperly and uselessly the time which God granted to us has been permitted to pass away; and, lastly, that we ought to commit ourselves to the protection of the same God for the remainder of our life.

But nothing is so pure that the world shall not taint it with its own vices. A *birth-day*, which ought to have been held sacred, is profaned by the greater part of men with disgraceful abuses; and there is scarcely a single entertainment at all costly that is free from wicked debauchery. First, men drink more freely; next, the door is opened to filthy and immodest conversation; and, lastly, no moderation is observed. This was the reason why the patriarch Job was in the habit of offering sacrifices, while his sons were feasting alternately in each other's houses, (Job i. 5.) It was because he thought that, when the guests invite one another to mirth, they are far from maintaining due moderation, and sin in a variety of ways.

Thus it happened that Herod, intending to give a rich entertainment to his guests, permitted his wife's daughter to dance. Hence, too, it appears what sort of discipline existed at his court; for, though most people at that time thought themselves at liberty to dance, yet for a marriageable young woman to dance was a shameful display of the impudence of the strumpet. But the unchaste Herodias had moulded her daughter Salome to her own manners in such a manner that she might not bring disgrace upon her.[1] And what was the consequence? The wicked murder of a holy prophet. The heat of wine had such an influence on Herod, that, forgetting gravity and prudence, he promised to a dancing girl, that he would give her *even to the half of his kingdom.* A shameful example truly, that a drunken king not only

[1] " Si elle eust mieux fallu que sa mere;"—" if she were more highly esteemed than her mother."

permits himself to behold with approbation a spectacle[1] which was disgraceful to his family, but holds out such a reward! Let us therefore learn to be careful in anticipating and resisting the devil, lest he entangle us in such snares.

Mark VI. 24. *And she went out, and said to her mother.* We need not wonder that Herodias attached so much importance to John's death.[2] The conjecture thrown out by some—that she was actuated by revenge—is not at all probable. It was rather the dread of being cast off that inflamed and tormented her; as it usually happens that, when adulterers are visited with feelings of uneasiness, they become ashamed of their own lust. But she hoped that this crime would bind Herod more closely to her than ever, if the disgrace of a pretended marriage were washed out by the blood of the prophet. That her power might be more secure for the future, she longed for the death of that man whom she imagined to be her only opponent; and this shows us the wretched anxiety by which a bad conscience is always tormented. John was detained in prison, and the haughty and cruel woman might have issued orders that no man should converse with or approach him; and yet she has no rest, but is oppressed with anxiety and alarm, till the prophet be removed out of the way. This likewise serves to show the power of the word of God, that the voice of the holy man, even when shut up in prison, wounds and tortures in the keenest manner the mind of the king's wife.[3]

26. *And the king being sorry.* His heart, as we have said, was no longer influenced by religious sentiments; but, foreseeing the detestation that will be excited by such a crime,

---

[1] "Non seulement prend plaisir à un fol passe-temps;"—"not only takes pleasure in a foolish pastime."

[2] "De ce qu' Herodias a estimé un grand avantage pour elle de faire mourir Iean;"—"that Herodias reckoned it a great advantage to her to put John to death."

[3] "Ne laisse pas d'espouvanter asprement, et navrer au vif le cœur de ceste femme;"—"fails not vehemently to alarm and cut to the quick the heart of the woman."

he dreads both the loss of character and positive harm, and consequently repents of his levity. And yet he has not the courage to give a refusal to a dancing girl, lest he should incur the reproach of unsteadiness; as if it were more dishonourable to retract a rash and foolish promise than to persist in a heinous crime. With the wonted vanity of kings, he does not choose that what he has once uttered shall be recalled, and orders that the prophet shall be instantly slain. We infer that Herod was at that time supping in the castle of Macherus, where, Josephus tells us, John was imprisoned, (Ant. xviii. 5. 2.)

On account of the oath, and of those who sat at table with him. It deserves our attention that the Evangelists state this to be the reason of his grief; and hence we infer that, though he had sworn a hundred times, yet if there had been no witness, he would not have held by his oath. No inward feelings of religion constrained Herod to do this, but the mere love of power drove him headlong; for he reckoned that he would sink in the estimation of those who were present, if he did not fulfil his engagement. Thus it frequently happens that ungodly men fail to perform their duty, because they do not look to God, but are only intent on this object, that they may not incur the reproaches of men.[1] But though Herod had kept before his eyes the sacredness of an oath alone, and not the dread of the opinion of men, he committed a more heinous offence in fulfilling a foolish promise than if he had violated his oath. First, he was deeply in fault for such haste in swearing; for the design of an oath is to confirm a promise in a doubtful matter. Next, when it appeared that he could not be relieved from his engagement without involving himself in an aggravated crime, he had no right to implicate the sacred name of God in such wickedness; for what could be more at variance with the nature of God than to lend his countenance to a shocking murder? If a private loss is at stake, let him who has made a rash oath suffer the punishment of his folly; but,

---

[1] "Et ne se soucient seulement que d'eviter le blasme et la moquerie des hommes;"—" and are only anxious to avoid the censure and ridicule of men."

when a man has taken the name of God in vain, let him beware of doubling his guilt by employing this as a pretence for committing some enormous crime. Hence it follows, that monastic vows, which are attended by open impiety, do not bind the conscience any more than the enchantments of magicians; for it is not the will of God that his sacred name shall give support to what is sinful. But this passage teaches us, that we ought to beware of making promises without consideration; and next, that lightness must not be followed by obstinacy.

28. *And gave it to the girl.* It was an additional aggravation of this detestable crime, that the head of the holy man was made, after his death, a matter of sport. But in this way the Lord sometimes gives up his people to the pride of wicked men, till he at length makes it evident that their blood is *precious in his sight*, (Ps. cxvi. 15.) *Herodias* is delighted with the thought of having gained her wicked purpose, and cruelly triumphs over her reprover; but when afterwards, stripped of her wealth, and not only deprived of the title of queen, but driven from her native country, and destitute of all means of support, she dragged out a wretched life in poverty and banishment, she presented a spectacle gratifying to angels and to all good people. When we perceive that the guests are compelled to pollute their eyes by beholding this detestable exhibition, let us learn from it, that those who sit at the tables of kings are often involved in many crimes; for, granting that the table is not stained by murder, every thing partakes so largely of all sorts of wickedness, that they who approach to it must be at least given up to debauchery.

29. *His disciples came.* One thing only remained to complete the woman's cruelty. It was, to leave the corpse of the holy man unburied; for there is reason to believe that, when *his disciples* performed this duty, the attendants of the tyrant had thrown out the corpse. Though the honour of burial is of no importance to the dead, yet it is the will of the Lord that we should observe this ceremony as a token of the last resurrection; and therefore God was pleased with

the carefulness which was manifested by the disciples, when they came to commit to the tomb the body of their master. Moreover, it was an attestation of their piety; for in this way they declared that the doctrine of their master continued to have a firm hold of their hearts after his death. This confession was therefore worthy of praise, more especially as it was not without danger; for they could not do honour to a man who had been put to death by the executioner without exciting against themselves the rage of the tyrant.

MATTHEW.	MARK.	LUKE.
XIV. 13. When Jesus heard this, he departed thence in a ship to a desert place apart; and when the multitudes heard it, they followed him on foot out of the cities. 14. And Jesus, when leaving (the ship,) saw a great multitude, and was moved with compassion towards them, and healed such of them as were diseased. 15. And when the evening was drawing on, his disciples came to him, saying, It is a desert place, and the time is now past: send the multitudes away, that they may go into the villages, and purchase victuals for themselves. 16. And Jesus said to them, It is not necessary that they	VI. 30. And the Apostles assembled to Jesus, and related to him all things, both what they had done and what they had taught.[1] 31. And he said to them, Come you apart into a desert place, and rest for a little. For there were many who were coming and going, so that there was not even leisure to take food.[2] 32. And he went into a desert place by ship apart. 33. And the multitudes saw them departing, and many recognized him, and ran hither on foot out of all the cities, and went before them, and came together to him. 34. And Jesus, as he was leaving (the ship,) saw a great multitude, and was moved with compassion towards them, because they were as sheep not having a shepherd, and he began to teach them many things. 35. And when a great part of the day was already past, his disciples came to him, saying, It is a desert place, and the day is now far advanced. 36. Send	IX. 10. And the Apostles, having returned,[3] related to him all that they had done. And he took them, and withdrew apart into a desert place, near a city which is called Bethsaida. 11. And when the multitudes knew it, they followed him; and he received them, and spoke to them about the kingdom of God, and healed those who needed healing. 12. And the day began to decline; and the twelve approached and said to him, Send away the multitudes, that they may go into the neighbouring towns and villages, and procure food; for we are here in a desert place. 13. And he said to them, Give you to them

[1] "Tout ce qu'ils avoyent fait et enseigné;"—"all that they had done and taught."
[2] "Tellement qu'ils n'avoyent pas mesmes loisir de manger;"—"so that they had not even leisure to eat."
[3] "Quand les Apostres furent retournez;"—"when the Apostles were returned."

MATTHEW.	MARK.	LUKE.
should go away: give you to them something to eat. 17. And they say to him, We have nothing here but five loaves and two fishes. 18. And he said, Bring them hither to me. 19. And he commanded the multitudes to sit down on the grass, and, taking the five loaves and the two fishes, and raising his eyes to heaven, he blessed.[1] And when he had broken the loaves, he gave them to the disciples, and the disciples to the multitudes. 20. And they all ate, and were satisfied, and carried away what remained of the fragments [2] twelve baskets full. 21. And they who had eaten were nearly five thousand men, besides women and children.	them away, that they may go into the surrounding towns and villages, and purchase bread for themselves; for they have nothing to eat. 37. And he answering said to them, Give you to them something to eat. And they said to him, Shall we go and purchase bread for two hundred pence, and give them something to eat? 38. And he said to them, How many loaves have you? Go and see. And when they knew, they say, Five, and two fishes. 39. And he commanded them to make them all sit down, arranging the guests on the green grass. 40. And they sat down, arranged in hundreds and fifties. 41. And when he had taken the five loaves and the two fishes, raising his eyes to heaven, he blessed,[3] and brake the loaves, and gave to the disciples to set before them, and divided the two fishes among them all. 42. And they all ate, and were satisfied. 43. And they carried away twelve baskets full of the fragments and of the fishes. 44. Now they who had eaten were about five thousand men.	something to eat. And they said, We have no more than five loaves and two fishes; unless we go and buy food for all this people. 14. Now they were about five thousand men. And he saith to his disciples, Make them sit down, fifty in each division. 15. And they did so, and made them all sit down. 16. And, taking the five loaves and the two fishes, he raised his eyes to heaven, and blessed them, and broke them,[4] and gave them to the disciples to set before the multitude. 17. And they all ate, and were satisfied; and there was carried away what was left of the fragments, twelve baskets.

Matthew XIV. 13. *When Jesus heard it.* *John*, who relates the same narrative, does not mention the reason why Jesus crossed over to the opposite bank, (vi. 5.) *Mark* and *Luke* differ somewhat from *Matthew;* for they describe the occasion of the journey to have been to give some repose to his disciples, after that they had returned from their embassy. But there is no contradiction here; for it is possible that he intended to withdraw his disciples into a desert

---

[1] "Rendit graces;"—"gave thanks."
[2] "Puis recueillerent le residu des pieces des pains;"—"then gathered what was left of the pieces of bread."
[3] "Rendit graces;"—"gave thanks."
[4] "Les benit, et les rompit."

place, in order that he might be more at leisure to train them for higher labours, and that, about the same time, an additional reason arose out of the death of John. Minds which were still feeble might have been terrified by the death of John, learning from the melancholy end of that eminent prophet what condition awaited them all. Certainly, as it was formerly related that, when John was imprisoned, Christ removed from Herod's territory, in order to avoid his fury for the time, so we may now infer that Christ, in order to keep his trembling disciples at a distance from the flame, *withdrew into a desert place.*

How long the Apostles were employed in their first embassy it is not in our power to determine; for the Evangelists, as we have formerly remarked, either did not attend to dates, or did not observe them with great exactness. I think it highly probable that their commission to proclaim the kingdom of Christ was not confined to a single occasion, but that, as opportunities were offered, they either repeated their visit to some places, or went to others after a lapse of time. The words, *they came together to him,* I look upon as meaning that ever afterwards they were his constant attendants; as if the Evangelist had said, that they did not leave their Master so as to be individually and constantly employed in the ordinary office of teaching, but that, having discharged a temporary commission, they went back to school to make greater advances in learning.

They followed him on foot out of the cities. Though Christ, who foresaw all things before they happened, was in no respect ignorant of what would take place, yet he wished, as a man, to forewarn his disciples, that the fact might testify the anxiety which he had about them. The vast crowd that had assembled shows how widely his fame was spread in every direction: and this left the Jews without excuse in depriving themselves, by their own carelessness, of the salvation which was offered to them; for even out of this great multitude, which was inflamed by a sudden zeal to follow Christ, it is evident from what is stated by John, (vi. 66; xii. 37,) that not more than a very small number yielded a true and steady adherence to his doctrine.

14. *He was moved with compassion towards them.* The other two Evangelists, and particularly Mark, state more clearly the reason why this *compassion* (συμπάθεια) was awakened in the mind of Christ. It was because he saw famishing souls, whom the warmth of zeal had carried away from their homes and led into *a desert place.* This scarcity of teaching indicated a wretched state of disorder; and accordingly Mark says that *Jesus was moved with compassion towards them, because they were as sheep not having a shepherd.* Not that, as to his Divine nature, he looked upon them all as sheep, but that, as man, he judged according to the present aspect of the case. It was no small manifestation of piety that they left their own homes, and flocked in crowds to the Prophet of God, though he purposely concealed himself from them. Besides, it ought to be remarked, that Christ was mindful of the character which he sustained; for he had been commanded to discharge the duties of a public teacher, and was therefore bound to look upon all the Jews, for the time being, as belonging to the flock of God and to the Church, till they withdrew from it.

So strongly was Christ moved by this feeling of *compassion*, that though, in common with his disciples, he was fatigued and almost worn out by uninterrupted toil, he did not spare himself. He had endeavoured to obtain some relaxation, and that on his own account as well as for the sake of his disciples; but when urgent duty calls him to additional labour, he willingly lays aside that private consideration,[1] and devotes himself to teaching the multitudes. Although he has now laid aside those feelings which belonged to him as a mortal man, yet there is no reason to doubt that he looks down from heaven on poor sheep that have no shepherd, provided they ask relief of their wants. Mark says, that *he began to teach them* MANY *things;* that is, he spent a long time in preaching, that they might reap some lasting advantage. Luke says, that he *spoke to them concerning the kingdom of God,* which amounts to the same thing.

---

[1] "Mettant arriere ceste consideration particuliere de donner repos au corps;"—"setting aside that private consideration of giving rest to the body."

Matthew makes no mention of any thing but miracles, because they were of great importance in establishing Christ's reputation; but it may naturally be concluded that he did not leave out doctrine, which was a matter of the highest importance.

15. *When the evening was drawing on.* The disciples had now lost their object, and they see that Christ is again absorbed in teaching, while the multitudes are so eager to receive instruction that they do not think of retiring. They therefore advise that, for the sake of attending to their bodily wants, Christ should *send them away into the neighbouring villages.* He had purposely delayed till now the miracle which he intended to perform; first, that his disciples might consider it more attentively, and might thus derive from it greater advantage; and next, that the very circumstance of the time might convince them that, though he does not prevent, and even does not immediately supply, the wants of his people, yet he never ceases to care for them, but has always at hand the assistance which he affords at the very time when it is required.

16. *Give you to them something to eat.* As a fuller exposition of this miracle will be found at the sixth chapter of John's Gospel, instead of troubling my readers with a repetition of what I have said, I would rather send them to that exposition; but rather than pass over this passage entirely, I shall offer a brief recapitulation. Hitherto Christ had bestowed his whole attention on feeding souls, but now he includes within his duties as a shepherd the care even of their bodies. And in this way he confirms his own saying, that to those who *seek the kingdom of God, and his righteousness, all other things will be added,* (Matth. vi. 33.) We have no right, indeed, to expect that Christ will always follow this method of supplying the hungry and thirsty with food; but it is certain that he will never permit his own people to want the necessaries of life, but will stretch out his hand from heaven, whenever he shall see it to be necessary to relieve their necessities. Those who wish to have Christ for their pro-

vider, must first learn not to long for refined luxuries, but to be satisfied with barley-bread.

Christ commanded that the people should sit down *in companies;* and he did so, first, that by this arrangement of the ranks the miracle might be more manifest; secondly, that the number of the men might be more easily ascertained, and that, while they looked at each other, they might in their turn bear testimony to this heavenly favour. Thirdly, perceiving that his disciples were anxious, he intended to make trial of their obedience by giving them an injunction which at first sight appeared to be absurd; for, as no provisions were at hand, there was reason to wonder why Christ was making arrangements that resembled a feast. To the same purpose is what follows, that *he gave them the loaves,* in order that in their hands the astonishing increase might take place, and that they might thus be the ministers of Christ's divine power; for as if it had been of small importance that they should be eye-witnesses, Christ determined that his power should be handled by them.[1] *Two hundred pence,* according to the computation of Budæus, are worth about thirty-four French *livres;*[2] and so when the disciples speak of what is *sufficient for them, that every one of them may take a little,* they calculate at the rate of a farthing for each individual. Forming so high an estimate of the sum of money that would be required to purchase bread barely sufficient for procuring a morsel to the people, they are entitled to no small praise for their obedience, when they implicitly comply with the command of Christ, and leave the result to his disposal.

[1] " Car Christ ne se contentant point de leur faire voir de leurs propres yeux sa vertu, a voulu mesme qu'elle passast par leurs mains, et qu'ils la touchassent ;"—" for Christ, not satisfied with making them see his power with their own eyes, determined even that it should pass through their hands, and that they should touch it."

[2] The value of a *livre* was so much affected both by time and by place, that it is not easy to determine with exactness how it was rated by Budæus or Calvin. Most probably, the reference is to *la livre Parisis*, which was three times the value of a *franc*, or about two shillings and sixpence sterling; and thirty-four of these would amount to *four pounds, five shillings, sterling.* Now reckoning the Roman *denarius*, or the eighth part of an ounce of silver, to be worth sevenpence halfpenny of our own money, *une livre Parisis* must have been equal to four *denarii*, and therefore *two hundred denarii* must have been worth—not *thirty-four* but *fifty livres Parisis*, or *six pounds, five shillings, sterling.—Ed.*

19. *He blessed.* In this passage, as in many others, *blessing* denotes thanksgiving. Now Christ has taught us, by his example, that we cannot partake of our food with holiness and purity, unless we express our gratitude to God, from whose hand it comes to us. Accordingly, Paul tells us, that every kind of food which God bestows upon us *is sanctified by the word of God and prayer,* (1 Tim. iv. 5;) by which he means, that brutal men, who do not regard by faith the blessing of God, and do not offer to him thanksgiving, corrupt and pollute by the filth of their unbelief all that is by nature pure; and, on the other hand, that they are corrupted and defiled by the food which they swallow, because to unbelievers nothing is clean. Christ has therefore laid down for his followers the proper manner of taking food, that they may not profane their own persons and the gifts of God by wicked sacrilege.

Raising his eyes towards heaven. This expresses warm and earnest supplication. Not that such an attitude is at all times necessary when we pray, but because the Son of God did not choose to disregard the outward forms which are fitted to aid human weakness. It ought also to be taken into account, that *to raise the eyes* upwards is an excitement well fitted to arouse us from sloth, when our minds are too strongly fixed on the earth.

20. *And carried away what was left.* The *fragments* that remained after satisfying so vast a multitude of men were more than twelve times larger in quantity than what was at first put into their hands, and this contributed not a little to the splendour of the miracle. In this way all came to know that the power of Christ had not only created out of nothing the food that was necessary for immediate use, but that, if it should be required, there was also provision for future wants; and, in a word, Christ intended that, after the miracle had been wrought, a striking proof of it should still remain, which, after being refreshed by food, they might contemplate at leisure.

Now though Christ does not every day multiply our bread, or feed men without the labour of their hands or the cultivation of their fields, the advantage of this narrative extends even to us. If we do not perceive that it is the blessing of God which multiplies the corn, that we may have a sufficiency of food, the only obstacle is, our own indolence and ingratitude. That, after we have been supported by the annual produce, there remains seed for the following year, and that this could not have happened but for an increase from heaven, each of us would easily perceive, were he not hindered by that very depravity which blinds the eyes both of the mind and of the flesh, so as not to see a manifest work of God. Christ intended to declare that, as all things have been delivered into his hands by the Father, so the food which we eat proceeds from his grace.

MATTHEW.

XIV. 22. And immediately Jesus constrained his disciples to embark, and to go before him to the opposite bank, till he had sent away the multitudes. 23. And when he had sent away the multitudes, he went up into a mountain alone to pray; and when the evening came, he was there alone. 24. But the ship was now in the midst of the sea, tossed with waves; for the wind was contrary. 25. And about the fourth watch of the night Jesus came to them, walking on the sea. 26. And when the disciples saw him walking on the sea, they were terrified, saying, It is an apparition, and cried out for fear. 27. But immediately Jesus spoke to them, saying, Take courage; it is I, be not afraid. 28. And Peter replying to him said, Lord, if it be thou, bid me come to thee on the water. 29. And he said, Come. And when Peter had come down out of the ship, he walked on the water, to go to Jesus. 30. But when he perceived the wind to be boisterous, he was afraid; and when he began to sink, he cried, saying, Lord, save me. 31. And immediately Jesus stretched out his hand and caught him, and said to him, O man of little faith, why didst thou doubt? 32. And when they had entered into the ship, the wind ceased. 33. Then

MARK.

VI. 45. And immediately he constrained his disciples to embark, and to go before him, across the lake, to Bethsaida, while he sent away the multitude. 46. And when he had sent them away, he went into the mountain[1] to pray. 47. And when the evening came, the ship was in the midst of the sea, and he was alone on the land. 48. And he saw that they had difficulty in rowing, (for the wind was contrary to them;) and about the fourth watch of the night he came to them, walking on the sea, and intended to pass by them. 49. But when they saw him walking on the sea, they thought that it was an apparition, and cried out; 50. For they all saw him, and were alarmed. And immediately he spoke to them, and said to them, Take courage; it is I, be not afraid. 51. And he went up to them into the ship, and the wind ceased; and they were greatly astonished within themselves beyond measure,

---

[1] "En la montagne."

MATTHEW.	MARK.
they that were in the ship approached and worshipped him, saying, Truly thou art the Son of God.	and wondered. 52. For they had not understood about the loaves; for their heart was blinded.¹

Matthew XIV. 22. *And immediately Jesus constrained his disciples.* They must have been *constrained;* for they would never, of their own accord, have left him, and gone to the other side. Now in this they testify their great veneration for him, when, contrary to their own opinions, they yield to his command and obey it. And, indeed, it had an appearance of absurdity, that he should remain alone *in a desert place,* when night was approaching. But so much the greater commendation is due to the submissiveness of those who set a higher value on the authority of their heavenly teacher than on all that could be pleaded on the other side. And, indeed, we do not truly and perfectly obey God, unless we implicitly follow whatever he commands, though our feelings may be opposed to it. There is always the best reason, no doubt, for every thing that God does; but he often conceals it from us for a time, in order to instruct us not to be wise in ourselves, but to depend entirely on the expression of his will. And thus Christ *constrained his disciples* to cross over, in order to train them to that rule of obedience which I have mentioned; though there cannot be a doubt that he intended to prepare the way for the miracle which will immediately come under our consideration.

23. *He went up into a mountain alone.* It is probable that the Son of God, who was fully aware of the tempest that was coming on, did not neglect the safety of his disciples in his prayers; and yet we naturally wonder that he did not rather prevent the danger than employ himself in prayer. But in discharging all the parts of his office as Mediator, he showed himself to be God and man, and exhibited proofs of

---

¹ "Car ils n'avoyent point entendu le faict des pains, d'autant que leur cœur estoit aveuglé, *ou, estourdi;*"—"for they had not understood what happened as to the loaves, because their heart was blinded, *or, bewildered.*"

both natures, as opportunities occurred. Though he had all things at his disposal, he showed himself to be a man by praying; and this he did not hypocritically, but manifested sincere and human affection towards us. In this manner his divine majesty was for a time concealed, but was afterwards displayed at the proper time.

In *going up into the mountain* he consulted his convenience, that he might have more leisure for praying when removed from all noise. We know how easily the slightest interruptions destroy the ardour of prayer, or at least make it languish and cool. Though Christ was in no danger of this fault, yet he intended to warn us by his example, that we ought to be exceedingly careful to avail ourselves of every assistance for setting our minds free from all the snares of the world, that we may look direct towards heaven. Now in this respect solitude has a powerful influence, by disposing those who engage in prayer, when God is their only witness, to be more on their guard, to pour their heart into his bosom, to be more diligent in self-examination; and, in a word—remembering that they have to do with God—to rise above themselves. At the same time, it must be observed, that he did not lay down a fixed rule, as if we were never permitted to pray except in retirement; for Paul enjoins us to *pray everywhere, lifting up clean hands*, (1 Tim. ii. 8;) and Christ himself sometimes prayed in presence of others, and even instructed his disciples to assemble together for offering social prayer. But that permission to pray in all places does not hinder them from engaging in secret prayer at proper seasons.

24. *The ship was now in the midst of the sea.* The reader will find this narrative expounded by me at the sixth chapter of John's Gospel, and therefore I shall treat it more briefly here. When Christ permitted his disciples to be tossed about in a perilous condition, for a time, by an opposing storm, it was to fix their attention more powerfully on the assistance which he brought to them. For the adverse wind arose about midnight, or at least a little before it, and Christ appears *about the fourth watch*, that is, three hours before

sunrise. Their arms were not more fatigued by rowing than their faith was shaken by grievous terrors. But when they were urged by strong necessity to desire the presence of their Master, it showed very extraordinary stupidity to be alarmed at his appearance as if he had been a ghost.

For this reason Mark tells us, that *their heart was blinded*, and that *they understood not about the loaves;* for that miracle had given abundant evidence that Christ possessed divine power to assist his followers, and that he was careful to assist them, when necessity required. Justly, therefore, are they now charged with stupidity in not immediately recollecting that heavenly power, having beheld, on the preceding day, so astonishing a proof of it, which ought to have been still before their eyes. It is, no doubt, true, that their blameworthy slowness of apprehension was the reason why they were astonished; for they had not profited, as they ought to have done, by other and preceding miracles. But the principal charge brought against them is *blindness*, in allowing so recent an exhibition to fade from their memory, or rather in not directing their mind to the contemplation of Christ's divinity, of which the multiplication of the loaves was a sufficiently bright mirror.

Two things are expressed by the words of Mark; first, that they did not properly consider the glory of Christ, which was exhibited in the multiplication of the loaves; and, secondly, a reason is assigned, that *their heart was blinded*. This appears to have been added, not only as an aggravation of their fault, but as a warning to us respecting the corruption of our understanding, that we may seek from the Lord new eyes. It certainly was a proof—as I have lately mentioned—of brutal ignorance, that they did not perceive the power of God, when they might almost feel it with their hands; but as the whole human race labours under the same disease, Mark purposely mentions *blindness*, in order to inform us that it is no new thing if men have their eyes closed against the manifest works of God, till they are enlightened from above; as Moses also said, *The Lord hath not yet given thee a heart to understand*, (Deut. xxix. 4.) Now though the word *heart* more frequently denotes the will or the seat of the affections, yet here, as in that passage which I have now quoted from Moses, it is put for the understanding.

27. *But immediately Jesus spake to them.* As Christ is not known to be a Deliverer till he actually makes his appearance, he speaks, and desires his disciples to recognize him. That confidence, to which he exhorts them, is represented by him as founded on his presence; plainly implying that, since they perceive him to be present with them, there are abundant grounds of hope. But as terror had already overpowered their minds, he corrects that terror, lest it should hinder or abate their confidence : not that they could all at once lay aside fear and experience unmingled joy, but because it was necessary that the fear which had seized them should be allayed, that it might not destroy their confidence. Although to the reprobate the voice of the Son of God is deadly, and his presence appalling, yet the effect which they produce on believers is here described to us as widely different. They cause inward peace and strong confidence to hold the sway over our hearts, that we may not yield to carnal fears. But the reason why we are disturbed by unfounded and sudden alarms is, that our ingratitude and wickedness prevent us from employing as shields the innumerable gifts of God, which, if they were turned to proper account, would give us all necessary support. Now though Christ appeared at the proper time for rendering assistance, yet the storm did not immediately cease, till the disciples were more fully aroused both to desire and to expect his grace. And this deserves our attention, as conveying the instruction, that there are good reasons why the Lord frequently delays to bestow that deliverance which he has ready at hand.

28. *And Peter answering.* The condition which he lays down shows that his faith was not yet fully settled. *If it is thou,* says he, *bid me come to thee on the water.* But he had heard Christ speak. Why then does he still argue with himself under doubt and perplexity? While his faith is so small and weak, a wish not well considered bursts into a flame. He ought rather to have judged of himself accord-

ing to his capacity, and to have supplicated from Christ an increase of faith, that by its guidance and direction he might walk over seas and mountains. But now, without the wings of faith, he desires to fly at will; and though the voice of Christ has not its due weight in his heart, he desires that the waters should be firm under his feet. And yet there is no room to doubt that this longing sprung from a good principle; but as it degenerates into a faulty excess, it cannot be applauded as good.

Hence too it happens that Peter immediately begins to smart for his rashness. Let believers, therefore, instructed by his example, beware of excessive haste. Wherever the Lord calls, we ought to run with alacrity; but whoever proceeds farther, will learn from the mournful result what it is to overleap the bounds which the Lord has prescribed. Yet it may be asked, Why does Christ comply with Peter's wish? for by so doing he seems to approve of it. But the answer is obvious. In many cases God promotes our interests better by refusing our requests; but at times he yields to us, that by experience we may be the more fully convinced of our own folly. In this manner, it happens every day that, by granting to those who believe in him more than is actually needed, he trains them to modesty and sober-mindedness for the future. Besides, this was of advantage to Peter and to the other disciples, and it is of advantage to us at the present day. The power of Christ shone more brightly in the person of Peter, when he admitted him as a companion, than if he had walked alone on the waters. But Peter knows, and the rest see plainly, that, when he does not rest with a firm faith, and rely on the Lord, the secret power of God, which formerly made the water solid, begins to disappear; and yet Christ dealt gently with him by not permitting him to sink entirely under the waters.[1] Both of these things happen to us; for as Peter was no sooner seized with fear than he began to sink, so the fleeting and transitory thoughts of the flesh immediately cause us to sink in the midst of our

---

[1] "Ne permettant qu'il enfondre du tout en l'eau, et se noye;"—"not allowing him to sink entirely in the water, and be drowned."

course of employments.¹ Meanwhile, the Lord indulges our weakness, and stretches out his hand, that the waters may not swallow us up altogether. It must also be observed that Peter, when he perceives the unhappy and painful consequences of his rashness, betakes himself to the mercy of Christ. And we too, though enduring just punishment, ought to betake ourselves to him, that he may have compassion on us, and bestow the aid of which we are unworthy.

31. *O man of little faith.* While our Lord kindly preserves Peter, he does not connive at Peter's fault. Such is the object of the chastisement administered, when Peter is blamed for the weakness of his faith. But a question arises, Does every kind of fear give evidence of a weakness of faith? for Christ's words seem to imply that, where faith reigns, there is no room for doubt.² I reply: Christ reproves here that kind of doubt which was directly opposed to faith. A man may sometimes doubt without any fault on his part; and that is, when the word of the Lord does not speak with certainty on the matter. But the case was quite different with Peter, who had received an express command from Christ, and had already experienced his power, and yet leaves that twofold support, and falls into foolish and wicked fear.

33. *They that were in the ship.* I understand these words to refer not only to the disciples, but to the sailors and other passengers. So then those who had not yet declared that he was their Master, instantly acknowledge that he is the Son of God, and by this term render to him the honour of the Messiah. Though at that time this lofty *mystery* was not generally known, how *God was* to be *manifested in the flesh,* (1 Tim. iii. 16,) yet as they had learned from the pro-

---

¹ "Ainsi les vaines et folles pensees de la chair font qu'à tous coups nous defaillons au milieu des affaires, comme si nous estions plongez en l'eau iusques par dessus la teste;"—"so the vain and foolish thoughts of the flesh cause us to stumble at every step in the midst of business, as if we were plunged in the water over the head."
² "Que Doute et Crainte ne peuvent avoir lieu ou la foy regne;"— "that Doubt and Fear cannot have place where faith reigns."

phets, that he who was to be the Redeemer would be called the Son of God, those who under this designation proclaim the glory of Christ, declare their belief that he is the Christ.[1]

MATTHEW.	MARK.
XIV. 34. And when they had passed over, they came into the country of Gennesareth. 35. And when the men of that place had recognized him, they sent messengers into all the surrounding country, and brought to him all that were diseased, 36. And besought him that they might touch only the fringe of his robe ; and as many as touched were made whole.	VI. 53. And when they had passed over, they came into the country of Gennesareth, and landed. 54. And when they had left the ship, they immediately knew him.[2] 55. And, running through all that country round about, they began to carry to him in beds those that were sick, wheresoever they heard that he was. 56. And to what place soever he went, into villages, or into cities, or into towns, they laid the diseased in the streets, and besought him that they might touch only the fringe of his robe ; and as many as touched him were healed.

Matthew XIV. 34. *They came into the country of Gennesareth.* The Evangelists give that designation to the country which borrowed its name from the lake, though it is uncertain if it was not rather the name of the country that was bestowed on the lake ; but that is a matter of little consequence. Our chief business is, to attend to the object which the Evangelists have in view. It is, to show that the glory of Christ was attested not by one or by another miracle, but that this part of Judea was filled with innumerable proofs of it, the report of which might easily be carried to Jerusalem and to other towns in every direction. Hence we infer, that singularly base and wicked must have been the ingratitude of that nation which wickedly shut its eyes from perceiving, and even endeavoured, as far as lay in its power, to extinguish the brightness of the divine glory which was exhibited before them. Our present business is, to perceive, amidst so large an assemblage of miracles, the reason why Christ came, which was, that he might offer himself as a physician to heal

---

[1] " Declarent qu'ils croyent qu'il est le Christ et le Messias ;"—" declare that they believe that he is the Christ and the Messiah."
[2] " (Les gens) le cognurent incontinent ;"—" (the people) immediately knew him."

all the diseases of all men.[1] For we must bear in mind what Matthew had formerly quoted from the Prophet Isaiah, (liii. 4,) that in healing bodies he shadowed out something greater, namely, that he restores our souls to health, and that it is his peculiar office to remove spiritual diseases.[2] He is not now an inhabitant of the earth; but it is certain that, now that he is in heaven, he is authorized to bestow those favours of which he then exhibited a visible proof. Now as we labour under every kind of diseases till he heal us, let each of us not only present himself to him, but endeavour to bring others who need the same remedy.

36. *That they might touch the fringe.* There is reason to believe that they were under the influence of some superstition, when they limited the grace of Christ to a touch of his robe; at least, they defrauded him of a part of his honour, since they did not expect any efficacy[3] to be derived from his bare word. But that he may not *quench the smoking flax,* (Isa. xlii. 3,) he accommodates himself to their ignorance. Yet there is nothing here that lends countenance to the views of those who seek the grace of God in wood, or nails, or robes; while Scripture expressly declares, that we have no right to form any conception respecting Christ but what is spiritual and consistent with his heavenly glory. The weakness of those who, not knowing that Christ is God, desired to make a nearer approach to him, was endured for a time. Now that he fills heaven and earth with the sweet savour of his grace, we must embrace—not with hands or eyes, but by faith—the salvation which he offers to us from heaven.

---

[1] "En guairissant toutes sortes de maladies en toutes personnes;"—"by healing all kinds of diseases in all persons."
[2] See Harmony, vol. i. p. 251.
[3] "Veu qu'ils n'esperoyent point de sentir aucun secours de sa vertu;"—"since they did not hope to experience any relief from his power."

MATTHEW.	MARK.
XV. 1. Then scribes and Pharisees, who had come from Jerusalem, approach to Jesus, saying, 2. Why do thy disciples transgress the tradition of the elders? for they wash not their hands when they eat bread. 3. But he answering said to them, Why do you also transgress the commandment of God on account of[1] your tradition? 4. For God commanded, saying, Honour thy father and mother; and, He that curseth father or mother, dying let him die. 5. But you say, Whosoever shall say to his father or mother, Whatever is a gift from me shall profit thee; and shall not honour his father or his mother. 6. Therefore you have annulled the commandment of God on account of your tradition. 7. Hypocrites, Isaiah hath justly prophesied concerning you, saying, 8. This people draw nigh to me with their mouth, and honour me with the lips; but their heart is far distant from me. 9. But in vain do they worship me, teaching doctrines, commandments of men.	VII. 1. And the Pharisees, and some of the scribes, who had come from Jerusalem, assemble to him. 2. And when they saw some of his disciples eat bread with common, that is to say, with unwashen hands, they found fault. 3. For the Pharisees, and all the Jews, do not take food without frequently washing their hands, holding the traditions of the elders; 4. And returning from market, they eat not till they have washed; and many other things are there which they have undertaken to keep, namely, the washings of cups, and pots, and brazen vessels, and beds. 5. Then the Pharisees and scribes ask him, saying, Why do not thy disciples walk according to the tradition of the elders, but eat bread with unwashen hands? 6. And he answering said to them, Well hath Isaiah prophesied concerning you hypocrites, as it is written, This people honour me with the lips, but their heart is far from me. 7. But in vain do they worship me, teaching doctrines, commandments of men. 8. For, laying aside the commandment of God, you keep a tradition of men, the washings of pots and cups, and many other things similar to these you do. 9. And he said to them, Well do you reject the commandment of God, that you may keep your own tradition. 10. For Moses said, Honour thy father and mother; and, He that curseth father or mother, dying let him die. 11. But you say, If a man shall say to his father or mother, Every Corban (that is, gift) that cometh from me shall profit thee. 12. And you do not permit him to do any thing more to his father or his mother. 13. Annulling the word of God by your tradition, which you have delivered; and many things similar to this you do.

Matthew XV. 1. *Then scribes and Pharisees.* As the fault that is here corrected is not only common but highly dangerous, the passage is particularly worthy of our attention. We see the extraordinary insolence that is displayed by men as to the form and manner of worshipping God; for they are perpetually contriving new modes of worship, and when any one wishes to be thought wiser than others, he displays

---

[1] " Propter ;"—" par vostre ordonnance ;"—" by your statute."

his ingenuity on this subject. I speak not of foreigners, but of the very domestics of the Church, on whom God has conferred the peculiar honour of declaring with their lips the rule of godliness. God has laid down the manner in which he wishes that we should worship him, and has included in his law the perfection of holiness. Yet a vast number of men, as if it were a light and trivial matter to obey God and to keep what he enjoins, collect for themselves, on every hand, many additions. Those who occupy places of authority bring forward their inventions for this purpose, as if they were in possession of something more perfect than the word of the Lord. This is followed by the slow growth of tyranny; for, when men have once assumed to themselves the right to issue commands, they demand a rigid adherence to their laws, and do not allow the smallest iota to be left out, either through contempt or through forgetfulness. The world cannot endure lawful authority, and most violently rebels against enduring the Lord's yoke, and yet easily and willingly becomes entangled in the snares of vain traditions; nay, such bondage appears to be, in the case of many, an object of desire. Meanwhile, the worship of God is corrupted, of which the first and leading principle is obedience. The authority of men is preferred to the command of God. Sternly, and therefore tyrannically, are the common people compelled to give their whole attention to trifles. This passage teaches us, first, that all modes of worship invented by men are displeasing to God, because he chooses that he alone shall be heard, in order to train and instruct us in true godliness according to his own pleasure; secondly, that those who are not satisfied with the only law of God, and weary themselves by attending to the traditions of men, are uselessly employed; thirdly, that an outrage is committed against God, when the inventions of men are so highly extolled, that the majesty of his law is almost lowered, or at least the reverence for it is abated.

Scribes who had come from Jerusalem. With what design those *scribes* came to Jesus is not stated; but I think it probable that their attention was excited by his fame, and that they came with the desire of receiving instruction, provided that they should approve of him as a competent teacher;[1] though it is possible that they were sent to spy. However that may be, as they had brought their haughty disdain along with them, they are easily provoked by the slightest offence to bite or snarl at Christ. Hence we see with what difficulty those who are influenced by ambition and the lust of power are brought to submit to sound doctrine. Those especially whose attachment to ceremonies has been strengthened by long practice cannot endure any novelty, but loudly condemn every thing to which they have not been accustomed. In short, any thing more haughty or more disdainful than this class of men cannot be imagined.

Both Evangelists mention that they were *scribes and Pharisees;* but Matthew puts the *scribes* first, and Mark puts them second. They convey the same meaning, that the *scribes* belonged to various sects, but that the *Pharisees* were the leaders, because they occupied an honourable station, and at that time held the government. That the Pharisees should be the first to take offence at disregard of the laws of which they were authors ought not to excite surprise; for, as we have said, though they boasted that they were expounders of the law, and though their name was derived from that circumstance,[2] they had corrupted by their inventions the purity of the word of God. All the traditions that then existed among the Jews had come out of their workshop;[3] and this was the reason why they displayed more than ordinary zeal and bitterness in defending them.

2. *Why do thy disciples transgress?* When we speak of human traditions, this question has no reference to political laws, the use and object of which are widely different from enjoining the manner in which we ought to worship God. But as there are various kinds of human traditions, we must make some distinction among them. Some are manifestly

---

[1] " En cas qu'ils l'eussent trouvé bon maistre à leur gré ;"—" provided that they should find him to be a good master to their liking."

[2] See Harmony, vol. i. p. 281.

[3] " Elles avoyent esté forgees en leur boutique;"—" they had been manufactured in their workshop."

wicked, for they inculcate acts of worship which are wicked and diametrically opposed to the word of God. Others of them mingle profane trifles with the worship of God, and corrupt its purity. Others, which are more plausible, and are not chargeable with any remarkable fault, are condemned on this ground, that they are imagined to be necessary to the worship of God; and thus there is a departure from sincere obedience to God alone, and a snare is laid for the conscience.

To this last description the present passage unquestionably relates; for the *washing of hands,* on which the Pharisees insisted, could not in itself be charged with wicked superstition; otherwise Christ would not have permitted the water-pots to be used at the marriage, (John ii. 6,) if it had not been an allowable ceremony; but the fault lay in this, that they did not think that God could be properly worshipped in any other way. It was not without a specious pretext that the practice of *washings* was first introduced. We know how rigidly the Law of God demands outward cleanness; not that the Lord intended that this should occupy the whole attention of his servants, but that they might be more careful to guard against every spiritual defilement. But in *washings* the Law preserved some moderation. Next came teachers, who thought that they would not be reckoned sufficiently acute, if they did not make some appendage to the word of God;[1] and hence arose *washings* of which no mention was made in the Law. The legislators themselves did not give out that they delivered any thing new,[2] but only that they administered cautions, which would be of service to assist in keeping the Law of God. But this was immediately followed by great abuse, when ceremonies introduced by men began to be regarded as a part of divine worship; and again, when in matters that were free and voluntary uniformity was absolutely

---

[1] " Sinon qu'ils adioustassent à la parole de Dieu quelques repetasseries de leur invention;"—"if they did not add to the word of God some patches of their own invention."

[2] " Les premiers autheurs de ces loix ne disoyent pas qu'ils voulussent commander rien de nouveau;"—"the first authors of these laws did not say that they intended to issue any new command."

enjoined. For it was always the will of God, as we have already said, that he should be worshipped according to the rule laid down in his word, and therefore no addition to his Law can be endured. Now as he permits believers to have outward ceremonies, by means of which they may perform the exercises of godliness, so he does not suffer them to mix up those ceremonies with his own word, as if religion consisted in them.[1]

For they wash not their hands. The ground of offence is explained more fully by Mark; but the substance of his explanation is, that many things were practised by *the scribes,* which they had voluntarily undertaken to keep. They were secondary laws invented by the curiosity of men, as if the plain command of God were not enough. God commanded that those who had contracted any defilement should wash themselves, (Lev. xi. 25, 28;) and this extended to cups, and pots, and raiment, and other articles of household furniture, (Lev. xi. 32,) that they might not touch any thing that was polluted or unclean. But to invent other ablutions was idle and useless.[2] They were not destitute of plausibility, as Paul tells us that the inventions of men have *an appearance of wisdom,* (Col. ii. 23;) but if they had rested in the Law of God alone, that modesty would have been more agreeable to Him than solicitude about small matters.

They were desirous to warn a person not to take food while he was unclean, through want of consideration; but the Lord reckoned it enough to wash away those defilements of which they were aware. Besides, no end or limit could be set to such cautions; for they could scarcely move a finger without contracting some new spot or stain. But a far worse abuse lay in this, that the consciences of men were tormented with scruples which led them to regard

---

[1] "Qu'elles soyent meslees avec sa Parole, et mises en mesme rang, comme si quelque partie du service de Dieu gisoit en icelles;"—"that they should be mixed with his Word, and put in the same rank, as if any part of the worship of God lay in them."

[2] "C'a esté un amusement de gens oisifs, et qui ne sçavoyent que faire;"—"it was an amusement of persons that were idle, and did not know what to do."

every person as chargeable with pollution, who did not on every occasion wash his body with water. In persons who belonged to a private rank they would perhaps have overlooked the neglect of this ceremony; but as they had expected from Christ and his disciples something uncommon and extraordinary, they reckoned it unbecoming that ceremonies, which were *traditions of the elders,* and the practice of which was held sacred by *the scribes,* should not be observed by the disciples of a master who undertook to reform the existing state of things.

It is a great mistake to compare the sprinkling of the water of purification, or, as the Papists call it, *blessed water,* with the Jewish *washing;* for, by repeating so frequently the one baptism,[1] Papists do all that is in their power to efface it. Besides, this absurd sprinkling is used for exorcising.[2] But if it were lawful in itself, and were not accompanied by so many abuses, still we must always condemn the urgency with which they demand it as if it were indispensable.

3. *Why do you also transgress?* There are here two answers that are given by Christ, the former of which is addressed, as we say, to the person; while the latter decides as to the fact and the question in hand. *Mark* inverts that order; for he first represents Christ as speaking on the whole subject, and afterwards adds the reproof which is directed against hypocrites. We shall follow the narrative of Matthew. When the Lord, in his turn, puts the question to the scribes *why* they break the Law of God on account of their traditions, he does not as yet pronounce a direct acquittal of his disciples from the crime charged against them; but only points out how improper and unwarrantable is this readiness to take offence. They are displeased when *the commandments*

---

[1] "Le Baptesme, qui suffit une fois receu;"—"Baptism, which is enough when once received."

[2] "En apres, ceste badinerie d'eau beniste est appliquee à faire exorcismes et coniurations, et ils croyent fermement qu'elle a vertu d'effacer les pechez;"—"Besides, this foolery of *blessed water* is applied to exorcising and conjuring, and they firmly believe that it has power to blot out sins."

of men are not observed with exactness; and how much more criminal is it to spend the whole time in observing them, to the disregard of the law of God? It is manifest, therefore, that their wrath is kindled rather by ambition than by a proper kind of zeal, when they thus prefer men to God.

When he says that they *transgress the commandments of God,* the meaning of the expression is easily learned from the context. They did not openly or professedly set aside the law of God, so as to look upon any thing as lawful which the law had forbidden; but there was an indirect *transgression* of it, for they permitted duties which God had enjoined to be neglected with impunity. A plain and familiar instance is adduced by Christ. The *commandment of God* is, that children shall honour their parents, (Exod. xx. 12.) Now as the sacred offerings yielded emolument to the priests, the observance of them was so rigidly enforced, that men were taught to regard it as a more heinous sin not to make a free-will offering than to defraud a parent of what was justly due to him. In short, what the Law of God declared to be voluntary was, in the estimation of the scribes, of higher value than one of the most important of the commandments of God. Whenever we are so eager to keep the laws of men as to bestow less care and attention on keeping the law of God itself, we are held as *transgressing* it. Shortly afterwards he says, that they had *annulled the commandment of God on account of the traditions of men;* for the scribes led the people to entertain so strong an attachment to their own injunctions, that they did not allow them leisure to attend to the word of God. Again, as they reckoned those persons to have discharged their duty well who obeyed these injunctions to the letter, hence arose a liberty to commit sin; for whenever holiness is made to consist in any thing else than in observing the Law of God, men are led to believe that the law may be violated without danger.

Let any man now consider whether this wickedness does not at present abound more among the Papists than it formerly did among the Jews. It is not indeed denied by the Pope, or by the whole of his filthy clergy, that we ought to obey God; but when we come to the point, we find that they consider the act of eating a morsel of flesh as nothing less than a capital crime, while theft or fornication is regarded as a venial fault, and thus, on account of their traditions, they overturn the Law of God; for it is utterly insufferable that the enactments of men shall withdraw any part of that obedience which is due to God alone. Besides, the honour which God commands to be yielded to parents extends to all the duties of filial piety.[1] The latter clause which Christ adds, that *he who curseth father or mother* deserves to be put to death, is intended to inform us, that it is no light or unimportant precept to *honour* parents, since the violation of it is so severely punished. And this is no small aggravation of the guilt of the scribes, that so severe a threatening does not terrify them from granting an extension of liberty to those who despised their parents.

5. *But you say, &c.* The mode of expression is defective, and is more fully exhibited by Mark, who adds, *you suffer them not to do anything more to their father or to their mother.* The meaning is, that the scribes were altogether wrong in acquitting those persons who fail to perform their duties to their parents, provided that this deficiency be supplied, on their part, by a voluntary sacrifice, which might have been omitted without offending God. For we must not understand Christ's words to bear that the scribes had forbidden men to render all proper obedience;[2] but they were so eager to pursue their own gain, that children were allowed, in the meantime, to neglect their duties to their parents.

7. *Well hath Isaiah prophesied concerning you.* Our Lord now proceeds farther ; for he decides on the question in hand, which he divides into two clauses. The first is, that they relied on outward ceremonies alone, and set no value on true holiness, which consists in sincere uprightness of heart ; and the second is, that they worshipped God in a wrong

---

[1] "Comprend tous devoirs d'obeissance, secours, et soulagement;"— "includes every duty of obedience, assistance, and relief."

[2] "De faire aucune assistance au pere et à la mere;"—"to grant any relief to their father or mother."

way, according to their own fancy. Now though his reproof of pretended and hypocritical holiness appears hitherto to be restricted to persons, yet it includes the substance of this doctrine, from which the full conclusion was, first, that the worship of God is spiritual, and does not consist in the sprinkling of water, or in any other ceremony; and, secondly, that there is no reasonable worship of God but what is directed by the rule of his word. Although Isaiah (xxix. 13) did not prophesy for futurity alone, but had regard to the men of his own age, yet Christ says that this prediction relates to the Pharisees and scribes, because they resemble those ancient hypocrites with whom the prophet had to contend. Christ does not quote that passage exactly as it stands; but the prophet expressly mentions two offences by which the Jews provoked against themselves the divine vengeance. *With their lips* only, and by an outward profession, they made a pretence of godliness; and, next, they turned aside to modes of worship invented by men. First, then, it is wicked hypocrisy, when the honour which men render to God is only in outward appearance; for to *approach to God with the mouth, and to honour him with the lips,* would not be in itself evil, provided that the heart went before. The substance of what our Lord states on this subject is, that, since the worship of God is spiritual, and as nothing pleases him that is not accompanied by the inward sincerity of the heart, they who make holiness to consist in outward display are hypocrites.

9. *But in vain do they worship me.* The words of the prophet run literally thus: *their fear toward me has been taught by the precept of men.* But Christ has faithfully and accurately given the meaning, that *in vain is God worshipped,* when the will of men is substituted in the room of doctrine. By these words, all kinds of *will-worship,* (ἐθελοθρησκεία,) as Paul calls it, (Coloss. ii. 23,) are plainly condemned. For, as we have said, since God chooses to be worshipped in no other way than according to his own appointment, he cannot endure new modes of worship to be devised. As soon as men allow themselves to wander beyond the limits of the

Word of God, the more labour and anxiety they display in worshipping him, the heavier is the condemnation which they draw down upon themselves; for by such inventions religion is dishonoured.

Teaching doctrines, commandments of men. In these words there is what is called *apposition;*[1] for Christ declares them to be mistaken who bring forward, in the room of *doctrine,* *the commandments of men,* or who seek to obtain from them the rule for worshipping God. Let it therefore be held as a settled principle, that, since *obedience* is more highly esteemed by God than *sacrifices,* (1 Sam. xv. 22, 23,) all kinds of worship invented by men are of no estimation in his sight; nay more, that, as the prophet declares, they are accursed and detestable.

MATTHEW.	MARK.	LUKE.
XV. 10. And having called the multitudes to him, he said to them, Hear and understand. 11. What entereth into the mouth polluteth not the man, but what goeth out of the mouth polluteth the man. 12. Then his disciples approaching said to him, Knowest thou that the Pharisees were offended when they heard that saying? 13. But he answering said, Every plant which my heavenly Father hath not planted shall be rooted up. 14. Let them alone: they are blind leaders of the blind. And if a blind man shall lead a blind man, both will fall into the ditch. 15. And Peter answering said to him, Explain to us that parable. 16. And Jesus said, Are you also still void of understanding? 17. Do	VII. 14. And when he had called to him the whole multitude, he said to them, Listen to me, all of you, and understand. 15. There is nothing from without a man which, entering into him, can pollute him; but those things which come out of a man are the things which pollute a man. 16. If any man have ears to hear, let him hear. 17. And when he had entered into the house, and withdrawn from the multitude, his disciples asked him concerning the parable. 18. And he saith to them, Are you also void of understanding? Do you not yet understand that whatsoever entereth into a man from without cannot pollute him? 19. Be-	VI. 39. And he spoke a parable to them,[2] Can a blind man lead a blind man? Will not both fall into the ditch?

[1] " C'est une figure et façon de parler que les Latins nomment Apposition;"—" it is a figure and mode of speech which the Latins call Apposition."—The Latin Grammarians employ the word *Appositio* to denote a figure, by which two words, denoting the same thing, are put in the same case, such as, *Urbs Roma, Fluvius Sequana.* In the same sense the Greek word ἐπεξήγησις was often used.—*Ed.*

[2] "Pareillement il leur disoit une similitude;"—" in like manner he spoke to them a parable."

MATTHEW.	MARK.	LUKE.
you not yet understand that whatever entereth into the mouth passeth into the belly, and is thrown into the sink? 18. But those things which proceed out of the mouth come from the heart itself, and they pollute the man. 19. For out of the heart proceed wicked thoughts, murders, adulteries, fornications, thefts, false testimonies, calumnies. 20. These are the things which pollute the man. But to take food with unwashed hands polluteth not the man.	cause it entereth not into his heart, but into the belly, and goeth out into the sink, purifying all the food? 20. And he said, It is what goeth out of a man that polluteth him. 21. For from within, out of the heart of man proceed wicked thoughts, adulteries, fornications, murders, 22. Thefts, evil desires, frauds, deceit, wantonness, an evil eye, calumnies, pride, foolishness: 23. All these evil things proceed from within, and pollute the man.	

Matthew XV. 10. *And having called the multitudes to him.* Here Christ turns[1] to those who are ready to receive instruction, and explains more fully the truth at which he had formerly glanced, that *the kingdom of God does not consist in meat and drink*, as Paul also teaches us, (Rom. xiv. 17;) for, since outward things are by nature pure, the use of them is free and pure, and uncleanness is not contracted from the good creatures of God. It is therefore a general statement, that pollution does not come from without into a man, but that the fountain is concealed within him. Now when he says that all the evil actions which any man performs come *out of the mouth of man*, he employs a *synecdoche;*[2] for he says so by way of allusion to the subject in hand, and conveys this instruction, that we do not draw uncleanness into our mouth along with *meat and drink*, but that every kind of defilement proceeds from ourselves.

Knowest thou that the Pharisees were offended? As the scribes

[1] "Christ laissant là ces orgueilleux, se retourne vers les dociles;"—"Christ, leaving there these proud men, turns towards the teachable."

[2] "Au reste, quand il dit que les maux qu'un chacun fait *procedent de la bouche*, c'est autant comme s'il disoit qu'ils procedent de la personne mesme; et c'est une figure et maniere de parler qu'on appelle *Synecdoche*, quand on prend une partie pour le tout;"—"besides, when he says that the evils which any man does *proceed out of the mouth*, it is as much as if he said that they proceed from the person himself; and it is a figure and way of speaking that is called *Synecdoche*, when a part is taken for the whole."

were presumptuous and rebellious, Christ did not take great pains to pacify them, but satisfied himself with repelling their hypocrisy and pride. The offence which they had formerly taken up was doubled, when they perceived that—not through oversight, but seemingly on purpose—Christ despised their *washings* as trifles. Now when Christ did not hesitate to inflame still more, by keen provocation, wicked and malicious persons, let us learn from his example, that we ought not to be exceedingly solicitous to please every one by what we say and do. His disciples, however—as is usually the case with ignorant and unlearned people—no sooner perceive the result to be unfavourable, than they conclude that Christ's reply had been unseasonable and improper.[1] For the object of their advice was, to persuade Christ to soothe the rage of the Pharisees by softening the harsh expression which he had employed.[2]

It almost always happens with weak persons, that they form an unfavourable judgment about a doctrine, as soon as they find that it is regarded with doubt or meets with opposition. And certainly it were to be wished, that it should give no offence, but receive the calm approbation of all; but, as the minds of many are blinded, and even their hearts are kindled into rage, by Satan, and as many souls are held under the benumbing influence of brutal stupidity, it is impossible that all should relish the true doctrine of salvation. Above all, we ought not to be surprised to behold the rage of those who inwardly nourish the venom of malice and obstinacy. Yet we ought to take care that, so far as may be in our power, our manner of teaching shall give no offence; but it would be the height of madness to think of exercising greater moderation than we have been taught to do by our heavenly Master. We see how his discourse was made an occasion of offence by wicked and obstinate men; and we see at the

---

[1] "Voyans que le propos n'avoit pas esté bien prins, il leur semble avis que Christ a respondu peu autrement qu'il ne faloit;"—"perceiving that the discourse was not well taken, they conclude that Christ had replied somewhat differently from what he ought to have done."

[2] "En redressant ce qu'il avoit dit un peu trop asprement, comme il leur sembloit;"—"by correcting what he had said a little too harshly, as they imagined."

same time, how that kind of offence which arose from malignity was treated by him with contempt.

13. *Every plant.* As the indifferent success of the doctrine had wounded their weak minds, Christ intended to remedy this evil. Now the remedy which he proposes is, that good men ought not to be distressed, or entertain less reverence for the doctrine, though to many it be an occasion of death. It is a mistaken view of this passage which some have adopted, that all the inventions of men, and every thing that has not proceeded from the mouth of God, must be *rooted up* and perish; for it was rather to men that Christ referred, and the meaning is, that there is no reason to wonder if the doctrine of salvation shall prove deadly to the reprobate, because they are always carried headlong to the destruction to which they are doomed.

By the persons that have been *planted* by the hand of God we are to understand those who, by his free adoption, have been ingrafted into the tree of life, as Isaiah also, when speaking of the Church renewed by the grace of God, calls it a branch planted by the Lord, (Isa. lx. 21.) Now as salvation depends solely on the election of God, the reprobate must perish, in whatever way this may be effected; not that they are innocent, and free from all blame, when God destroys them, but because, by their own malice, they turn to their destruction all that is offered to them, however salutary it may be. To those who willingly perish the Gospel thus becomes, as Paul assures us, *the savour of death unto death,* (2 Cor. ii. 16;) for, though it is offered to all for salvation, it does not yield this fruit in any but the elect. It belongs to a faithful and honest teacher to regulate every thing which he brings forward by a regard to the advantage of all; but whenever the result is different, let us take comfort from Christ's reply. It is beautifully expressed by the parable, that the cause of perdition does not lie in the doctrine, but that the reprobate who have no root in God, when the doctrine is presented to them, throw out their hidden venom, and thus accelerate that death to which they were already doomed.

Which my heavenly Father hath not planted. Hypocrites, who appear for a time to have been *planted* like good trees, are particularly described by Christ; for Epicureans, who are noted for open and shameful contempt of God, cannot properly be said to resemble trees, but the description must be intended to apply to those who have acquired celebrity by some vain appearance of godliness. Such were *the scribes,* who towered in the Church of God like the cedars in Lebanon, and whose revolt might on that account appear the more strange. Christ might have said that it is right that those should perish who disdainfully reject salvation; but he rises higher, and asserts that no man will remain stedfast, unless his salvation be secured by the election of God. By these words he expressly declares, that the first origin of our salvation flows from that grace by which God elected us to be his children before we were created.

14. *Let them alone.* He sets them aside as unworthy of notice, and concludes that the offence which they take ought not to give us much uneasiness. Hence has arisen the distinction, of which we hear so much, about avoiding offences, that we ought to beware of offending the weak, but if any obstinate and malicious person take offence, we ought not to be uneasy; for, if we determined to satisfy all obstinate people, we must bury Christ, who is *the stone of offence,* (1 Pet. ii. 8.) Weak persons, who are offended through ignorance, and afterwards return to just views, must be distinguished from haughty and disdainful men who are themselves the authors of offences. It is of importance to attend to this distinction, in order that no one who is weak may be distressed through our fault. But when wicked men dash themselves through their obstinacy, let us walk on unmoved in the midst of offences; for he who spares not weak brethren tramples, as it were, under foot those to whom we are commanded to stretch out the hand. It would be idle to attend to others, whom we cannot avoid offending, if we wish to keep the right path; and when, under the pretext of taking offence, they happen to fall off and revolt from Christ, we

must *let them alone,* that they may not drag us along with them.[1]

They are blind leaders of the blind. Christ means that all who allow themselves to be driven hither and thither at the disposal of those men will miserably perish; for, when they stumble on a plain road, it is evident that they are wilfully blind. Why then should any one allow himself to be directed by them, except that he might fall into the same ditch? Now Christ, who has risen upon us as *the Sun of righteousness,* (Mal. iv. 2,) and not only points out the road to us by the torch of his Gospel, but desires that we should keep it before us, justly calls on his disciples to shake off that slothfulness, and not to wander, as it were, in the dark, for the sake of gratifying the blind.[2] Hence also we infer that all who, under the pretence of simplicity or modesty, give themselves up to be deceived or ensnared by errors, are without excuse.

Luke VI. 39. *And he spake to them a parable.* Luke relates this saying without mentioning any occurrence, but states generally, that Christ made use of this *parable;* as in recording many of Christ's discourses he says nothing as to the occasion on which they were delivered. It is no doubt possible that Christ may have spoken this parable more than once; but, as no place more appropriate was to be found, I have not hesitated to insert here what Luke relates without fixing the time.

Matthew XV. 15. *And Peter answering said.* As the disciples betray excessive ignorance, Christ justly reproves and upbraids them for being *still void of understanding,* and yet does not fail to act as their teacher. What Matthew ascribes in a peculiar manner to Peter is related by Mark, in the same sense, as a question put by them all; and this is evident

---

[1] " De peur qu'ils nous tirent en perdition avec eux;"—"lest they draw us to perdition along with them."
[2] " A bon droict retire ses disciples de ceste nonchalance et stupidité de suyvre les aveugles, et pour leur faire plaisir d'aller tastonnant en tenebres comme eux;"—" properly withdraws his disciples from that indifference and stupidity in following the blind, and—for the sake of gratifying them—in groping in the dark like them."

from Christ's reply, in which he reproves the ignorance, not of Peter only, but of all of them alike. The general meaning is, that men are not polluted by food, but that they have within themselves the pollution of sins, which afterwards shows itself in the outward actions. Is it objected that intemperance in eating is defilement? The solution is easy. Christ speaks only of the proper and lawful use of those things which God has put in our power. To eat and drink are things in their own nature free and indifferent: if any corruption be added, it proceeds from the man himself, and therefore must be regarded not as external, but internal.[1]

19. *For out of the heart proceed wicked thoughts.* Hence we infer that the word *mouth*, as I have mentioned, was used by Christ in a former verse by way of allusion to the context; for now he makes no mention of *the mouth*, but merely says that *out of the heart* of man proceeds all that is sinful and that corrupts by its pollution. Mark differs from Matthew in this respect, that he gives a larger catalogue of sins, such as *lusts*, or *irregular desires*. The Greek word (πλεονεξίαι) is by some rendered *covetousness;* but I have preferred to take it in a general acceptation. Next come *fraud* and intemperance, and those which immediately follow. Though the mode of expression be figurative, it is enough to understand Christ's meaning to be, that all sins proceed from the wicked and corrupt affections of the heart. To say that *an evil eye* proceeds from the heart is not strictly accurate, but it involves nothing that is absurd or ambiguous; for it means, that an unholy heart pollutes the eyes by making them the ministers, or organs, of wicked desires. And yet Christ does not speak as if every thing that is evil in man were confined to open sins; but, in order to show more clearly that the heart of man is the abode of all evils,[2] he says that the proofs and results appear in the sins themselves.

[1] "Et pourtant le vice est tousiours interieur, et ne vient point d'ailleurs;"—"and therefore sin is always internal, and does not come from without."
[2] "Que le cœur de l'homme est le siege et la source de tous maux;"—"that the heart of man is the seat and the source of all evils."

And pollute the man. Instead of the verb *pollute,* the Greek term is κοινοῖ, *make common;* as Mark, a little before, (vii. 2,) used the phrase, κοιναῖς χερσί, *with* COMMON *hands,* for *with* UNCLEAN *hands.*[1] It is a Hebrew phrase;[2] for, since God had set apart the Jews on the condition that they should separate themselves from all the pollutions of the Gentiles, everything that was inconsistent with this holiness was called *common,* that is, *profane.*

MATTHEW.	MARK.
XV. 21. And Jesus departing thence withdrew into the territories of Tyre and Sidon. 22. And, lo, a woman of Canaan, who had come from those territories, cried saying, Have compassion on me, O Lord, thou son of David; my daughter is grievously afflicted by a devil. 23. But he made no reply to her, and his disciples approaching implored him, saying, Send her away; for she crieth after us. 24. But he answering said, I am not sent but to the lost sheep of the house of Israel. 25. And she came and worshipped him, saying, Lord, help me. 26. But he answering said, It is not seemly to take the children's bread, and throw it to the dogs. 27. But she said, Certainly, O Lord; yet the dogs eat of the crumbs that fall from the table of their masters. 28. Then Jesus answering said to her, O woman, great is thy faith; be it to thee as thou desirest. And her daughter was cured from that time.[3]	VII. 24. And he arose and departed thence into the borders of Tyre and Sidon; and, entering into a house, he wished that no man should know it, but he could not be concealed. 25. For a woman, whose daughter had an unclean spirit, no sooner heard of him than she came and fell at his feet, 26. (For the woman was a Greek, a Syrophenician by birth,) and implored him to cast the devil out of her daughter. 27. And Jesus said to her, Allow the children to be first satisfied; for it is not seemly to take the children's bread, and throw it to the dogs. 28. But she replied and said to him, Certainly, O Lord; for even the dogs[4] under the table eat of the children's crumbs. 29. And he said to her, On account of that saying go away, the devil is gone out of thy daughter. 30. And when she had gone to her own house, she found that the devil had gone out, and her daughter lying on the bed.

In this miracle we are informed in what manner the grace of Christ began to flow to the Gentiles; for, though the full

---

[1] "*Les mains communes* pour *souillees* et *non lavees;*"—"*common hands* for *polluted* and *not washed.*"
[2] "C'est une façon de parler propre aux Hebrieux;"—"it is a mode of speaking peculiar to the Hebrews."
[3] "Et dès ce mesme instant sa fille fut guairie;"—"and from that very instant her daughter was cured."
[4] "Car les chiens mangent, *ou, mais aussi* les chiens mangent;"—"for the dogs eat, *or, but even* the dogs eat."

time was not yet come when Christ would make himself known to the whole world, yet he intended to give some early manifestations of the common mercy which was at length offered indiscriminately to Jews and Gentiles after his resurrection. A remarkable picture of faith is presented to us in the woman of Canaan, for the purpose of instructing us by means of comparison, that the Jews were justly deprived of the promised redemption, since their impiety was so shameful.

The *woman*, whom Matthew describes as *of Canaan*, is said by Mark to have been *a Greek*, and *a Syrophenician by birth*. But there is no contradiction here; for we know that it was the prevailing custom among the Jews to call all foreign nations *Greeks*, and hence that contrast between *Greeks* and *Jews*, which occurs so frequently in the writings of Paul. As she was a native of *the territories of Tyre and Sidon*, we need not wonder that she is called a *Syrophenician;* for that country was called *Syria*, and formed part of *Phenicia.* The Jews disdainfully gave the name of *Canaanites* to all the inhabitants of that district; and it is probable that the majority of them were descended from the tribes of *Canaan*, who, when banished from their native country, fled to a sort of retreat in the neighbourhood. Both agree in this point, that the woman was a native of a heathen nation, that she had not been instructed in the doctrine of the law, and that she came of her own accord to Christ, humbly to entreat his aid.

Mark VII. 24. *He wished that no man should know it.* We must attend to this circumstance, which is mentioned by Mark, that when Christ came to that place, he did not erect his banner, but endeavoured to remain concealed for a time, in that obscure situation, like a private individual. Mark speaks according to the ordinary perception of the flesh; for, although Christ by his divine Spirit foresaw what would happen, yet so far as he was the minister and ambassador of the Father, he kept himself, as his human nature might have led us to expect, within the limits of that calling which God had given him; and in that respect it is said that what he wished, *as man*, he was unable to accomplish. Meanwhile, this occurrence, as I have said, tends powerfully to condemn the Jews, who—though they boasted that they were the heirs of the covenant of the Lord, his peculiar people, and a royal priesthood—were blind and deaf when Christ, with a loud voice and with the addition of miracles, offered to them the promised redemption; while this woman, who had no relationship with the children of Abraham, and to whom, at first sight, the covenant did not at all belong, came of her own accord to Christ, without having heard his voice or seen his miracles.

Matthew XV. 22. *Have compassion on me, O Lord.* Though this woman was an alien, and did not belong to the Lord's flock, yet she had acquired some taste of piety;[1] for, without some knowledge of the promises, she would not have called Christ the *Son of David*. The Jews indeed had almost entirely departed, or at least had greatly turned aside, from the pure and sound doctrine of the Gospel; but a report of the promised redemption was extensively prevalent. As the restoration of the Church depended on the reign of David, whenever they spoke of the Messiah, it was customary for them to employ the name, *Son of David;* and indeed this confession was heard from the lips of all. But when the true faith had died out amongst them, it was an amazing and incredible display of the goodness of God that the sweet savour of the promises reached the neighbouring nations. Though this woman had not been regularly educated by any teacher, yet her faith in Christ was not a notion adopted by her at random, but was formed out of the law and the prophets. It was therefore not less absurd than wicked in that dog, Servetus, to abuse this example for the purpose of proving that faith may exist without promises. I do not deny that, in this sense, there may sometimes be a sort of implicit faith, that is, a faith which is not accompanied by a full and distinct knowledge of sound doctrine; provided we also hold that faith always springs from the word of God, and takes

[1] "Quelque goust de pieté et vraye religion;"—"some taste of piety and true religion."

its origin from true principles, and therefore is always found in connection with some light of knowledge.

23. *But he made no reply to her.* In various ways the Evangelists bestow commendation on the faith of this woman. Here they bring before us her unshaken constancy; for the silence of Christ was a sort of refusal, and there is reason to wonder that she was not cast down by this trial, but her continuance in prayer was a proof of her perseverance. This appears, however, to be inconsistent with the nature of *faith* and of *calling upon God,* as it is described by Paul, who assures us that no man can pray aright till he has heard the word of God. *How shall they call on him in whom they have not believed? and how shall they believe in him of whom they have not heard?* (Rom. x. 14.) Who then will say that this woman had faith, who takes courage from her own feelings, though Christ is silent? But as Christ has two ways of speaking and of being silent, it must be observed, that though he withheld at that time the words of his mouth, yet he spoke within to the mind of the woman, and so this secret inspiration was a substitute for the outward preaching. Besides, her prayer arose out of the *hearing of faith,* (Rom. x. 17;) and, therefore, though Christ does not immediately reply, she continually hears the sound of that doctrine[1] which she had already learned, that Christ came as a Redeemer. In this way the Lord often acts towards those who believe in him; he speaks to them, and yet is silent. Relying on the testimonies of Scripture, where they hear him speaking, they firmly believe that he will be gracious to them; and yet he does not immediately reply to their wishes and prayers, but, on the contrary, seems as if he did not hear. We see then that the design of Christ's silence was not to extinguish the woman's faith, but rather to whet her zeal and inflame her ardour. But if a small seed of doctrine in *a woman of Canaan* yielded such abundant fruit, it ill becomes us to be dejected, if at any

[1] "Toutesfois ceste doctrine ne laisse pas tousiours de retentir en son cœur;"—"yet that doctrine does not fail to resound continually in her heart."

time he delays and does not immediately grant a favourable answer.

Send her away. The disciples present no request in favour of the woman, but as they are annoyed by her importunity, they desire that, in some way or other, she may be dismissed. It is a childish contrivance, which the Papists have endeavoured to support by means of this passage, that departed saints are allowed to plead for us; for, granting that this woman solicited the disciples to give her some favour or assistance—which, however, cannot be proved from the passage—still there is a wide difference between the dead and the living.[1] It must also be observed, that the disciples feel displeasure in listening to her, and that, if they really intended to aid her by their advocacy, they obtain nothing.

24. *I am not sent.* He informs the Apostles that his reason for refusing the *woman of Canaan* arises out of his desire to devote himself entirely to the Jews, to whom alone he was appointed to be a minister of the grace of God. He argues from the call and the command of the Father, that he must not yield any assistance to strangers; not that the power of Christ was always confined within so narrow limits, but because present circumstances rendered it necessary that he should begin with the Jews, and at that time devote himself to them in a peculiar manner. For, as I have said[2] in expounding Matthew x. 5, *the middle wall of partition* (Eph. ii. 14) was not thrown down till after Christ's resurrection, that he might proclaim peace to the nations which were aliens from the kingdom of God; and therefore he prohibited the Apostles, at that time, from scattering anywhere but in Judea the first seed of doctrine. Justly, therefore, does he affirm that, on this occasion, he was sent to the Jews only, till the Gentiles also followed in the proper order.

---

[1] "Neantmoins ce qui a lieu envers les vivans, il ne s'ensuit pas qu'on le doyve pratiquer envers ceux qui sont hors de ce monde;"—"yet it does not follow that what takes place among the living must be practised among those who are out of this world."

[2] See Harmony, vol. i. p. 440.

To the lost sheep of the house of Israel. He bestows the designation of *sheep of the house of Israel* not on the elect only, but on all who were descended from the holy fathers; for the Lord had included all in the covenant, and was promised indiscriminately to all as a Redeemer, as he also revealed and offered himself to all without exception. It is worthy of observation, that he declares himself to have been *sent to* LOST *sheep*, as he assures us in another passage that he *came to save that which was lost*, (Matth. xviii. 11.) Now as we enjoy this favour, at the present day, in common with the Jews, we learn what our condition is till he appear as our Saviour.

25. *And she came and worshipped him.* We might be apt to think that this woman contends with some measure of obstinacy, as if she would extort something from Christ in spite of him; but there is no reason to doubt that she was animated by the conviction which she entertained as to the kindness of the Messiah. When Christ expressly declared that it did not belong to his office, she was not intimidated by that refusal, and did not desist from her purpose. The reason was, that she adhered firmly to that previous sentiment of faith which I have mentioned, and admitted nothing that was opposed to her hope. And this is the sure test of faith, that we do not suffer that general commencement of our salvation, which is founded on the word of God, to be in any way torn from us.

26. *It is not seemly.* Christ's reply is harsher than ever, and one would think that he intended by it to cut off all hope; for not only does he declare that all the grace which he has received from the Father belongs to the Jews, and must be bestowed on them, otherwise they will be defrauded of their just rights; but he disdainfully compares the woman herself to a *dog*, thus implying that she is unworthy of being a partaker of his grace. To make the meaning plain to us, it must be understood that the appellation of *the children's bread* is here given, not to the gifts of God of whatever description, but only to those which were bestowed in a

peculiar manner on Abraham and his posterity. For since the beginning of the world, the goodness of God was everywhere diffused—nay, filled heaven and earth—so that all mortal men felt that God was their Father. But as the children of Abraham had been more highly honoured than the rest of mankind, *the children's bread* is a name given to everything that relates peculiarly to the adoption by which the Jews alone were elected to be *children*. The light of the sun, the breath of life, and the productions of the soil, were enjoyed by the Gentiles equally with the Jews; but the blessing which was to be expected in Christ dwelt exclusively in the family of Abraham. To lay open without distinction that which God had conferred as a peculiar privilege on a single nation, was nothing short of setting aside the covenant of God; for in this way the Jews, who ought to have the preference, were placed on a level with the Gentiles.

And to throw it to the dogs. By using the word *throw*, Christ intimates that what is taken from the Church of God and given to heathens is not well bestowed. But this must be restricted to that time when it was in Judea only that men called on God; for, since the Gentiles were admitted to partake of the same salvation—which took place when Christ diffused everywhere the light of his Gospel—the distinction was removed, and those who were formerly *dogs* are now reckoned among the children. The pride of the flesh must fall down, when we learn that by nature we are *dogs*. At first, no doubt, human nature, in which the image of God brightly shone, occupied so high a station that this opprobrious epithet did not apply to all nations, and even to kings, on whom God confers the honour of bearing his name.[1] But the treachery and revolt of Adam made it proper that the Lord should send to the stable, along with *dogs*, those who through the guilt of our first parent became bastards; more especially when a comparison is made between the Jews, who were exempted from the common lot, and the Gentiles, who were banished from the kingdom of God.

Christ's meaning is more fully unfolded by Mark, who

[1] This is probably an allusion to Psalm lxxxii. 6, *I have said, Ye are gods; and all of you are* CHILDREN OF THE MOST HIGH.—*Ed.*

gives these words, *Allow the children first to be satisfied.* He tells the *woman of Canaan* that she acts presumptuously in proceeding—as it were, in the midst of the supper—to seize on what was on the table.¹ His chief design was, to make trial of the woman's faith; but he also pointed out the dreadful vengeance that would overtake the Jews, who rejected an inestimable benefit which was freely offered to them, and which they refused to those who sought it with warmth and earnestness.

27. *Certainly, Lord.* The woman's reply showed that she was not hurried along by a blind or thoughtless impulse to offer a flat contradiction² to what Christ had said. As God preferred the Jews to other nations, she does not dispute with them the honour of adoption, and declares, that she has no objection whatever that Christ should *satisfy* them according to the order which God had prescribed. She only asks that some *crumbs*—falling, as it were, accidentally—should come within the reach of *the dogs.* And at no time, certainly, did God shut up his grace among the Jews in such a manner as not to bestow a small taste of them on the Gentiles. No terms could have been employed that would have described more appropriately, or more justly, that dispensation of the grace of God which was at that time in full operation.

28. *Great is thy faith.* He first applauds the woman's *faith,* and next declares, that on account of her *faith* he grants her prayer. The greatness of her *faith* appeared chiefly in this respect, that by the aid of nothing more than a feeble spark of doctrine, she not only recognized the actual office of Christ, and ascribed to him heavenly power, but pursued her course steadily through formidable opposition; suffered herself to be annihilated, provided that she held by her conviction that she would not fail to obtain Christ's assistance;

---

¹ "De vouloir ainsi mettre la main sur la table des enfans, au milieu de souper;"—" in wishing thus to put her hand to the *children's* table in the midst of the supper."

² " Pour se rebequer et heurter directement;"—" to give a saucy and open contradiction."

and, in a word, so tempered her confidence with humility, that, while she advanced no unfounded claim, neither did she shut against her the fountain of the grace of Christ, by a sense of her own unworthiness. This commendation, bestowed on a woman who had been a heathen,[1] condemns the ingratitude of that nation which boasted that it was consecrated to God.

But how can the woman be said to *believe* aright, who not only receives no promise from Christ, but is driven back by his declaration to the contrary? On that point I have already spoken. Though he appears to give a harsh refusal to her prayers, yet, convinced that God would grant the salvation which he had promised through the Messiah, she ceases not to entertain favourable hopes; and therefore she concludes, that the door is shut against her, not for the purpose of excluding her altogether, but that, by a more strenuous effort of faith, she may force her way, as it were, through the chinks. *Be it unto thee as thou desirest.* This latter clause contains a useful doctrine, that faith will obtain anything from the Lord; for so highly does he value it, that he is always prepared to comply with our wishes, so far as it may be for our advantage.

MATTHEW.	MARK.
XV. 29. And Jesus departing thence, came near the sea of Galilee, and he went up into the mountain, and sat down there. 30. And great multitudes came to him, bringing with them the lame, the blind, the dumb, the maimed, and many others, and laid them at the feet of Jesus; and he cured them: 31. So that the multitudes wondered, when they perceived the dumb to speak, the maimed to be whole, the lame to walk, the blind to see; and they glorified the God of Israel. 32. And Jesus,	VII. 31. And again, departing from the territories of Tyre and Sidon, he came to the sea of Galilee, through the midst of the territories of Decapolis. 32. And they bring to him one who was deaf, and had an impediment in his speech, and implore him to lay his hand on him. 33. And when he had taken him aside from the multitude, he put his fingers into his ears, and spat, and touched his tongue; 34. And looking up to heaven, he sighed, and said to him, Ephphatha, that is, Be opened. 35. And immediately his ears were opened, and the string of his tongue was loosed, and he spoke distinctly. 36. Then he enjoined them not to tell it to any person; but the more he enjoined them, so much the more they published it: 37. And

[1] " Ceste femme, profane de nation;"—" that woman, a heathen as to her nation."

MATTHEW.	MARK.
having called his disciples to him, said, I have compassion on the multitude, because they have now remained with me three days, and have nothing to eat; and I do not choose to send them away fasting, lest they faint by the way. 33. His disciples say to him, Whence shall we obtain so many loaves in a solitary place as to satisfy so great a multitude? 34. And Jesus saith to them, How many loaves have you? And they say, Seven, and a few small fishes. 35. And he commanded the multitudes to sit down on the ground. 36. And he took those seven loaves and the fishes, and after that he had given thanks, he broke and gave to his disciples, and the disciples to the multitude. 37. And they all ate, and were satisfied; and they took up of the fragments that were left seven baskets full. 38. And they who had eaten were four thousand men, besides women and children. 39. And having sent away the multitudes, he embarked, and came to the borders of Magdala.	were amazed beyond measure, saying, He hath done all things well; he maketh both the deaf to hear and the dumb to speak. VIII. 1. In those days, when there was a very great multitude, and they had nothing to eat, Jesus called his disciples to him, and said to them, 2. I am moved with compassion towards the multitude, because they have now remained with me three days, and have nothing to eat. 3. And if I shall send them home fasting, they will faint by the way; for some of them have come from a distance. 4. And his disciples answered him, Whence shall any man be able to satisfy those persons with bread in this solitary place? 5. And he asked them, How many loaves have you? And they said, Seven. 6. And he commanded the multitude to sit down on the ground; and took the seven loaves, and, when he had given thanks, brake, and gave to his disciples to set before them, and they set them before the multitude. 7. And they had a few small fishes; and when he had blessed, he ordered these likewise to be set before them. 8. And they ate, and were satisfied; and of the fragments that remained they carried away seven baskets full. 9. And they that had eaten were about four thousand; and he sent them away. 10. And immediately embarking, he came with his disciples to the coasts of Dalmanutha.

Matthew XV. 29. *And Jesus departing thence.* Though it is unquestionably the same journey of Christ, on his return from the neighbourhood of Sidon, that is related by Matthew and by Mark, yet in some points they do not quite agree. It is of little moment that the one says *he came to the borders of Magdala,* and the other, that *he came to the coasts of Dalmanutha;* for the cities were adjacent, being situated on the lake of Gennesareth, and we need not wonder that the district which lay between them received both names.[1]

---

[1] "Est nommé maintenant de l'une, maintenant de l'autre ville;"— "was named sometimes from the one, and sometimes from the other town."

Decapolis was so called from its containing (δέκα πόλεις) *ten cities;* and as it was contiguous to Phenicia and to that part of Galilee which lay towards the sea, Christ must have passed through it, when he returned from Phenicia into Galilee of Judea. There is a greater appearance of contradiction in another part of the narrative, where *Matthew* says that our Lord cured *many* who laboured under various diseases, while *Mark* takes no notice of any but of one *deaf* man. But this difficulty need not detain us; for *Mark* selected for description a miracle which was performed during the journey, and the report of which was no sooner circulated than it aroused the inhabitants of every part of that country to bring *many* persons to Christ to be cured. Now we know that the Evangelists are not anxious to relate all that Christ did, and are so far from dwelling largely on miracles, that they only glance at a few by way of example. Besides, *Mark* was satisfied with producing one instance, in which the power of Christ is as brightly displayed as in others of the same sort which followed shortly afterwards.

Mark VII. 32. *And they bring to him one who was deaf.* The reason why *they implored him to lay his hands upon him* may be learned from passages which we have already considered; for the *laying on of hands* was a solemn symbol of consecration,[1] and by means of it, the gifts of the Holy Spirit were also bestowed. And there is no doubt that this ceremony was frequently used by Christ; so that those men requested nothing but what they knew that he had been formerly in the habit of doing. On the present occasion, Christ employs other symbols; for he puts his *spittle* on the *tongue* of the *dumb* man, *and puts his fingers into his ears.* The *laying on of hands* would of itself have been sufficiently efficacious, and even, without moving a finger, he might have accomplished it by a single act of his will; but it is evident that he made abundant use of outward signs, when they were found to be advantageous. Thus, by touching the *tongue* with *spittle,* he intended to point out that the faculty

---

[1] "Pour dedier et consacrer les personnes;"—" for dedicating and consecrating persons."

of speech was communicated by himself alone; and by *putting his finger into the ears,* he showed that it belonged to his office to pierce the ears of the deaf. There is no necessity for having recourse to allegories; and we find that those who have amused themselves with ingenious discussions on this subject, are so far from bringing forward any thing of real value, that they tend rather to hold up the Scriptures to ridicule. Readers of sobriety and judgment will be satisfied with this single instruction, that we obtain from Christ, in answer to our prayers, both speech and hearing; for he pours his energy into our tongues, and pierces our ears with his fingers.

33. *And when he had taken him aside from the multitude.* This was done, partly to afford to those who were ignorant, and not yet sufficiently qualified for becoming witnesses, an opportunity of perceiving at a distance the glory of his Divine nature, and partly that he might have a better opportunity of pouring out earnest prayer. When he *looked up to heaven and sighed,* it was an expression of strong feeling; and this enables us to perceive the vehemence of his love towards men, for whose miseries he feels so much compassion. Nor can it be doubted, that by conveying the spittle from his own mouth to the mouth of another, and by *putting his fingers into his ears,* he intended to manifest and express the same feeling of kindness. Yet that he has supreme power to remove all our defects, and restore us to health, is proclaimed by him when he simply orders the tongue and ears *to be opened;* for it was not without a good reason that Mark inserted that Chaldaic word, (ἐφφαθά,) *Ephphatha, be opened,* but to testify the divine power of Christ. Among other fooleries with which baptism has been debased by foolish men, the ceremony used by our Lord is turned into a piece of buffoonery; and this instance shows us that there is no end to licentiousness, when men wantonly change at their own pleasure the mysteries of God.

36. *Then he enjoined them not to tell it to any person.* Many commentators torture these *injunctions* to an opposite mean-

ing, as if Christ had purposely excited them to spread abroad the fame of the miracle; but I prefer a more natural interpretation which I have formerly stated,[1] that Christ only intended to delay the publication of it till a more proper and convenient time. I have no doubt, therefore, that their zeal was unseasonable, when, though *enjoined* to be silent, they were in haste to speak. We need not wonder that men unaccustomed to the doctrine of Christ are carried away by immoderate zeal, when it is not called for. Yet what they unwisely attempted to do, was made by Christ to promote his own glory; for not only was the miracle made known, but the whole of that district, in despising the Author of heavenly gifts, was rendered inexcusable.

37. *He hath done all things well.* Matthew, after collecting many miracles, concludes by saying that *the multitudes wondered, and glorified the God of Israel;* that is, because God, taking unusual methods of illustrating his power, had called up the remembrance of his covenant. But the words of Mark contain perhaps an implied contrast; for the reports concerning Christ were various, and the word *multitude* or *crowd* (ὄχλος) may be intended to mean that it was only wicked and malicious persons who slandered his actions, since all that he did was so far from exposing him to calumny that it deserved the highest praise. But we know, and it is what nature teaches us, that nothing is more unjust than to make the bestowal of favours an occasion of envy and ill-will.

Matthew XV. 32. *I have compassion on the multitude.* Here a miracle is related not unlike another which we have lately explained. The only difference is, that on the former occasion Christ satisfied *five thousand men* with *five loaves and two fishes*, while, on the present occasion, *four thousand men* are fed with *seven loaves and a few small fishes;* and that *twelve baskets* were then filled with fragments, while out of a greater abundance a smaller portion is left. Let us learn from this, that the power of God is not restricted to means

---

[1] Harmony, vol. i. p. 374.

or outward assistance, and that it is all one with Him whether there be much or little, as Jonathan[1] said when speaking of his own moderate army and the vast multitude of enemies: *there is no restraint to the Lord to save by many or by few*, (1 Sam. xiv. 6.) As the blessing of God can make one loaf suffice as well as twenty for satisfying a great multitude, so, if that be wanting, a hundred loaves will not be a sufficient meal for ten men; for when *the staff of bread is broken*, (Lev. xxvi. 26,) though the flour should come in full weight from the mill, and the bread from the oven, it will serve no purpose to stuff the belly. The *three days' fasting*, of which Christ speaks, must not be understood to mean that they had eaten nothing for three days; but that in desert places they had few conveniences, and must have wanted their ordinary food. Besides, in those warm countries, hunger is less keen than in our thick and cold atmosphere; and, therefore, we need not wonder that they should abstain longer from food.

33. *Whence shall we obtain so many loaves in a solitary place?* The disciples manifest excessive stupidity in not remembering, at least, that earlier proof of the power and grace of Christ, which they might have applied to the case in hand. As if they had never seen any thing of the same sort, they forget to apply to him for relief. There is not a day on which a similar indifference does not steal upon us; and we ought to be the more careful not to allow our minds to be drawn away from the contemplation of divine benefits, that the experience of the past may lead us to expect for the future the same assistance which God has already on one or more occasions bestowed upon us.

Matthew.	Mark.	Luke.
XVI. 1. And the Pharisees, together with the Sadducees, came, and tempting	VIII. 11. And the Pharisees came, and began	XII. 54. And he said also to the multitudes, When you see

---

[1] Instead of *Jonathan*, the French copy mentions *Asa*, whose words are similar, and were uttered on a similar occasion: *Lord, it is nothing with thee to help, whether with many, or with them that have no power*, (2 Chr. xiv. 11.)—*Ed.*

MATTHEW.	MARK.	LUKE.
desired that he would show them a sign from heaven. 2. But he answering said to them, About the commencement of the evening you say, It will be fine weather; for the sky is red. 3. And in the morning, There will be a storm to-day; for the sky is red and lowring. Hypocrites, you can judge aright of the face of the sky; but can you not judge of the signs of the times? 4. A wicked and adulterous nation demandeth a sign, and no sign shall be given to it but the sign of the prophet Jonah. And he left them, and departed.	to dispute with him, requesting from him a sign from heaven, tempting him. 12. And he groaned in his spirit, and said, Why doth this generation ask a sign? Verily, I say to you, That no sign shall be given to this generation. 13. And he left them, and returned to the ship, and departed across the lake.	a cloud rising out of the west, you immediately say, A shower is coming; and so it is. 55. And when you perceive the south wind blowing, you say that there will be hot weather; and so it is. 56. Hypocrites, you know how to judge of the appearance of the sky and of the earth, and how comes it that you do not understand this time? 57. And why even of yourselves do you not judge what is right?

Matthew XVI. 1. *And the Pharisees came.* Mark says that they *began to dispute,* from which we may conjecture that, when they had been vanquished in argument, this was their last resource; as obstinate men, whenever they are reduced to extremities, to avoid being compelled to yield to the truth, are accustomed to introduce something which is foreign to the subject. Though the nature of the dispute is not expressed, yet I think it probable that they debated about the calling of Christ, why he ventured to make any innovation, and why he made such lofty pretensions, as if by his coming he had fully restored the kingdom of God. Having nothing farther to object against his doctrine, they demand that he *shall give them a sign from heaven.* But it is certain that a hundred *signs* would have no greater effect than the testimonies of Scripture. Besides, many miracles already performed had placed before their eyes the power of Christ, and had almost enabled them to touch it with their hands. *Signs,* by which Christ made himself familiarly known, are despised by them; and how much less will they derive advantage from a distant and obscure *sign?* Thus the Papists of our own day, as if the doctrine of the Gospel had not yet been proved, demand that it be ascertained by means of new miracles.

The Pharisees, together with the Sadducees. It deserves our attention that, though *the Sadducees* and *the Pharisees* looked upon each other as enemies, and not only cherished bitter hatred, but were continually engaged in hostilities, yet they enter into a mutual league against Christ. In like manner, though ungodly men quarrel among themselves, their internal broils never prevent them from conspiring against God, and entering into a compact for joining their hands in persecuting the truth.

Tempting. By this word the Evangelists mean that it was not with honest intentions, nor from a desire of instruction, but by cunning and deceit, that they demanded what they thought that Christ would refuse, or at least what they imagined was not in his power. Regarding him as utterly mean and despicable, they had no other design than to expose his weakness, and to destroy all the applause which he had hitherto obtained among the people. In this manner unbelievers are said to *tempt* God, when they murmur at being denied what their fancy prompted them to ask, and charge God with want of power.

2. *About the commencement of the evening.* By these words Christ reminds them that his power had been sufficiently manifested, so that they must have recognised *the time of their visitation,* (Luke xix. 44,) had they not of their own accord shut their eyes, and refused to admit the clearest light. The comparison which he employs is beautiful and highly appropriate; for, though the aspect of the sky is changeable, so that sometimes a storm unexpectedly arises, and sometimes fair weather springs up when it was not expected, yet the instructions of nature are sufficient to enable men to predict from *signs* whether the day will be fair or cloudy. Christ therefore asks why they do not recognize the kingdom of God, when it is made known by *sign*s not less manifest; for this proved clearly that they were excessively occupied with earthly and transitory advantages, and cared little

about any thing that related to the heavenly and spiritual life, and were blinded not so much by mistake as by voluntary malice.

3. *Hypocrites, you can judge.* He calls them *hypocrites,* because they pretend to ask that which, if it were exhibited to them, they are resolved not to observe. The same reproof applies nearly to the whole world; for men direct their ingenuity, and apply their senses, to immediate advantage; and therefore there is scarcely any man who is not sufficiently well qualified in this respect, or at least who is not tolerably acquainted with the means of gaining his object. How comes it then that we feel no concern about the *signs* by which God invites us to himself? Is it not because every man gives himself up to willing indifference, and extinguishes the light which is offered to him? The calling of Christ, and the immediate exhibition of eternal salvation, were exhibited to the scribes both by the Law and the Prophets, and by his own doctrine, to which miracles were added.

There are many persons of the same description in the present day, who plead that on intricate subjects they have a good right to suspend their judgment, because they must wait till the matter is fully ascertained. They go farther, and believe that it is a mark of prudence purposely to avoid all inquiry into the truth; as if it were not an instance of shameful sloth that, while they are so eagerly solicitous about the objects of the flesh and of the earth, they neglect the eternal salvation of their souls, and at the same time contrive vain excuses for gross and stupid ignorance.

A very absurd inference is drawn by some ignorant persons from this passage, that we are not at liberty to predict from the aspect of the sky whether we shall have fair or stormy weather. It is rather an argument which Christ founds on the regular course of nature, that those men deserve to perish for their ingratitude, who, while they are sufficiently acute in matters of the present life, yet knowingly and wilfully quench the heavenly light by their stupidity.

Mark VIII. 12. *And groaning in his spirit.* By these words Mark informs us that it occasioned grief and bitter vexation to our Lord, when he saw those ungrateful men obstinately resist God. And certainly all who are desirous to promote the glory of God, and who feel concern about the salvation of men, ought to have such feelings that nothing would inflict on their hearts a deeper wound than to see unbelievers purposely blocking up against themselves the way of believing, and employing all their ingenuity in obscuring by their clouds the brightness of the word and works of God. The words, *in his spirit*, appear to me to be added emphatically, to inform us that this groan proceeded from the deepest affection of his heart, and that no sophist might allege that Christ resorted to outward attitudes to express a grief which he did not inwardly feel; for that holy soul, which was guided by the zeal of the Spirit, must have been moved by deep sadness at the sight of such wicked obstinacy.

Luke XII. 57. *And why even of yourselves, &c. ?* Here Christ opens up the source of the evil, and, as it were, applies the lancet to the ulcer. He tells them that they do not descend into their consciences, and there examine with themselves, as in the presence of God, what is right. The reason why hypocrites are so much disposed to make objections is, that they throw their swelling words into the air without any concern, and never exercise calm thought, or place themselves at the tribunal of God, that the truth, when once ascertained, may be fully embraced. When Luke says that this wa *spoken to the multitudes*, he does not contradict the narrative of Matthew and Mark; for it is probable that Christ adapted his style generally to the followers and disciples of the scribes, and to other despisers of God who resembled them, of whom he perceived that there were too many; as the present complaint or expostulation was applicable to the whole of that rabble.

Matthew XVI. 4. *A wicked and adulterous nation.* This passage was explained[1] under Matthew xii. 38. The general

---

[1] See page 93 of this volume.

meaning is, that the Jews are never satisfied with any *signs*, but are continually tickled by a wicked desire to tempt God. He does not call them *an adulterous nation* merely because they demand some kind of sign, (for the Lord sometimes permitted his people to do this,) but because they deliberately provoke God; and therefore he threatens that, after he has risen from the dead, he will be a prophet like Jonah. So Matthew at least says—for Mark does not mention Jonah—but the meaning is the same; for, strictly speaking, this was intended to serve as a *sign* to them, that Christ, when he had risen from the dead, would in every place cause the voice of his Gospel to be distinctly heard.

MATTHEW.	MARK.	LUKE.
XVI. 5. And his disciples, when they had come to the opposite bank, through neglect had not taken bread.[1] 6. And Jesus said to them, Take heed and beware of the leaven of the Pharisees and of the Sadducees. 7. But they considered within themselves, saying, We have not taken bread.[2] 8. And when Jesus knew this, he said to them, Why do you think within yourselves, O you of little faith, that you have not taken bread? 9. Do you not yet understand, and do you not remember those five loaves, when there were five thousand men, and how many baskets you carried away? 10. Nor those seven loaves, when there were four thousand men, and how many baskets you carried away? 11. How comes it that you do not understand that it was not about bread that I told	VIII. 14. And they had neglected to take bread, and had not more than one loaf with them in the ship. 15. And he charged them, saying, Take heed and beware of the leaven of the Pharisees, and of the leaven of Herod. 16. And they reasoned within themselves, saying, We have not bread.[2] 17. And Jesus, perceiving this, said to them, Why do you reason that you have no bread? Do you not yet consider or understand? Have you your heart yet blinded? 18. Having eyes, do you not see? and having ears, do you not hear? and do you not remember? 19. When I broke the five loaves among five thousand men, how many baskets full of fragments did you carry away? They say to him, Twelve. 20. And when	XII. 1. And when an innumerable multitude had assembled,[3] so that they trod one upon another, he began to say to his disciples, Above all, beware[4] of the leaven of the Pharisees, which is hypocrisy.

---

[1] "Et quand les disciples furent venus outre, ils avoyent oublié à prendre les pains;"—"and when the disciples were come across, they had forgotten to take bread."

[2] "[C'est pource que] nous n'avons point prins de pains;"—"[it is because] we have not taken bread."

[3] "Cependant une multitude s'estant assemblee à milliers;"—"meanwhile, a multitude having assembled by thousands."

[4] "En premier lieu, donnez-vous garde;"—"in the first place, beware."

MATTHEW.	MARK.	LUKE.
you to beware of the leaven of the Pharisees and of the Sadducees? 12. Then they understood that he did not bid them beware of the leaven of bread, but of the doctrine of the Pharisees and of the Sadducees.	[I broke] the seven among four thousand, how many baskets of the remains of the fragments did you carry away? And they said, Seven. 21. And he said to them, How is it that you do not understand?	

Matthew XVI. 5. *And when his disciples came.* Here Christ takes occasion from the circumstance that had just occurred[1] to exhort his disciples to beware of every abuse that makes an inroad on sincere piety. The Pharisees had come a little before; the Sadducees joined them; and apart from them stood Herod, a very wicked man, and an opponent and corrupter of sound doctrine. In the midst of these dangers it was very necessary to warn his disciples to be on their guard; for, since the human mind has a natural inclination towards vanity and errors, when we are surrounded by wicked inventions, spurious doctrines, and other plagues of the same sort, nothing is more easy than to depart from the true and simple purity of the word of God; and if we once become entangled in these things, it will never be possible for the true religion to hold an entire sway over us. But to make the matter more clear, let us examine closely the words of Christ.

6. *Beware of the leaven of the Pharisees.* Along with *the Pharisees* Matthew mentions *the Sadducees.* Instead of the latter, Mark speaks of *Herod.* Luke takes no notice of any but *the Pharisees,* (though it is not absolutely certain that it is the same discourse of Christ which Luke relates,) and explains *the leaven* to be *hypocrisy.* In short, he glances briefly at this sentence, as if there were no ambiguity in the words. Now the metaphor of *leaven,* which is here applied to false doctrine, might have been employed, at another time, to denote the hypocrisy of life and conduct, or the same

---

[1] "Ici Christ prenant occasion des propos precedens;"—"here Christ taking occasion from the former discourse."

words might even have been repeated a second time. But there is no absurdity in saying, that those circumstances which are more copiously detailed by the other two Evangelists, in the order in which they took place, are slightly noticed by Luke in a manner somewhat different, and out of their proper place or order, but without any real contradiction. If we choose to adopt this conjecture, *hypocrisy* will denote here something different from a pretended and false appearance of wisdom. It will denote the very source and occasion of empty display, which, though it holds out an imposing aspect to the eyes of men, is of no estimation in the sight of God. For, as Jeremiah (v. 3) tells us that *the eyes of the Lord behold the truth,* so they that believe in his word are instructed to maintain true godliness in such a manner as to cleave to righteousness with an honest and perfect heart; as in these words, *And now, O Israel, what doth the Lord require from thee, but that thou shouldst cleave to him with all thy heart, and with all thy soul?* (Deut. x. 12.) On the other hand, the traditions of men, while they set aside spiritual worship, wear a temporary disguise, as if God could be imposed upon by such deceptions; for to whatever extent outward ceremonies may be carried, they are, in the sight of God, nothing more than childish trifles, unless so far as they assist us in the exercise of true piety.

We now perceive the reason why *hypocrisy* was viewed by Luke as equivalent to doctrines invented by men, and why he included under this name the *leavens* of men, which only puff up, and in the sight of God contain nothing solid, and which even draw aside the minds of men from the right study of piety to empty and insignificant ceremonies. But it will be better to abide by the narrative of Matthew, which is more copious. The disciples, after having been reproved by our Lord, came at length to understand that he had charged them to be on their guard against certain doctrine. It was plainly, therefore, the intention of Christ to fortify them against prevailing abuses, by which they were attacked on all sides. The *Pharisees* and *Sadducees* were expressly named, because those two sects maintained at that time a tyrannical sway in the Church, and held opinions so utterly subversive of the doctrine of the Law and the Prophets, that almost nothing remained pure and entire.

But *Herod* did not in any way profess to teach; and a question arises, why does Mark class him with false teachers? *Beware of the leaven of the Pharisees, and* OF THE LEAVEN OF HEROD. I reply: he was half a Jew, was mean and treacherous, and availed himself of every contrivance that was within his reach to draw the people to his side; for it is customary with all apostates to contrive some mixture, for the purpose of establishing a new religion by which the former may be abolished. It was because he was labouring craftily to subvert the principles of true and ancient piety, and thus to give currency to a religion that would be exceedingly adapted to his tyranny, or rather because he was endeavouring to introduce some new form of Judaism, that our Lord most properly charged them to *beware of his leaven.* From the temple of God the scribes disseminated their errors, and the court of *Herod* was another workshop of Satan, in which errors of a different kind were manufactured.

Thus in our own day we find that not only from Popish temples, and from the dens of sophists and monks, does Antichrist vomit out her impostures, but that there is a Theology of the Court, which lends its aid to prop up the throne of Antichrist, so that no stratagem is left untried. But as Christ opposed the evils which then prevailed, and as he aroused the minds of his followers to guard against those which were the most dangerous, let us learn from his example to make a prudent inquiry what are the abuses that may now do us injury. Sooner shall water mix with fire than any man shall succeed in reconciling the inventions of the Pope with the Gospel. Whoever desires to become honestly a disciple of Christ, must be careful to keep his mind pure from those *leavens;* and if he has already imbibed them, he must labour to purify himself till none of their polluting effects remain. There are restless men, on the other hand, who have endeavoured in various ways to corrupt sound doctrine, and, in guarding also against such impostures, believers must maintain a strict watch, that they may keep a perpetual Passover *with the unleavened bread of sincerity and truth,* (1 Cor. v. 8.)

And as on every hand there now rages an impiety like that of Lucian,[1] a most pernicious leaven, or rather a worse than deadly poison, let them exercise this very needful caution, and apply to it all their senses.

8. *Why do you think within yourselves, &c. ?* The disciples again show how little they had profited by the instructions of their Master, and by his wonderful works. What he had said about being on their guard against *the leaven* is rashly interpreted by them as if Christ intended only to withdraw them from outward intercourse. As it was customary among the Jews not to take food in company with irreligious men, the disciples imagine that the Pharisees were classed with such persons. This ignorance might perhaps have been endured; but they are forgetful of a favour which they lately received, and do not consider that Christ has the remedy in his power to hinder them from being compelled to pollute themselves by meat and drink, and therefore he reproves them sharply, as they deserved. And certainly it was shameful ingratitude that, after having seen bread created out of nothing, and in such abundance as to satisfy many thousands of men, and after having seen this done twice, they are now anxious about bread, as if their Master did not always possess the same power. From these words we infer that all who have once or twice experienced the power of God, and distrust it for the future, are convicted of unbelief; for it is faith that cherishes in our hearts the remembrance of the

---

[1] "L'impieté des Lucianistes et des Atheistes;"—"the impiety of the Lucianists and Atheists." *Lucian,* a celebrated Greek writer, of the second century of the Christian era, author of *Dialogues of the Dead,* is here alluded to as the type of scoffers and *Atheists.* His subject naturally led him to treat with sportive humour the solemnities of death and the future judgment; and the wit and elegance of his pen, had it been guided by ordinary caution, would have been readily—far too readily—sustained as an apology for the tone of his work. But in defiance of the ordinary feelings of mankind, he attacked so fearlessly the most sacred truths, and offended the ear of modesty by such indecent allusions, that his character as a man has been stamped with infamy. Modern times have scarcely produced so daring an infidel, with the exception perhaps of *Voltaire,* who took no pains to conceal his intense hatred of Christianity and of good men. Had he appeared earlier, his name might perhaps have been substituted for that of *Lucian,* as the representative of his class.—*Ed.*

gifts of God, and faith must have been laid asleep, if we allow them to be forgotten.

12. *Then they understood.* The word *leaven* is very evidently used by Christ as contrasted with the pure and uncorrupted word of God. In a former passage, (Matth. xiii. 33,) Christ had used the word in a good sense, when he said that the Gospel resembled *leaven*;[1] but for the most part this word is employed in Scripture to denote some foreign substance, by which the native purity of any thing is impaired. In this passage, the naked truth of God, and the inventions which men contrive out of their own brain, are unquestionably the two things that are contrasted. The sophist must not hope to escape by saying that this ought not to be understood as applicable to every kind of doctrine; for it will be impossible to find any doctrine but what has come from God that deserves the name of pure and *unleavened.* Hence it follows that *leaven* is the name given to every foreign admixture; as Paul also tells us that faith is rendered spurious, as soon as we are *drawn aside from the simplicity of Christ,* (2 Cor. xi. 3.)

It must now be apparent who are the persons of whose doctrine our Lord charges us to beware. The ordinary government of the Church was at that time in the hands of the scribes and priests, among whom the Pharisees held the highest rank. As Christ expressly charges his followers to beware of *their* doctrine, it follows that all who mingle their own inventions with the word of God, or who advance any thing that does not belong to it, must be rejected, how honourable soever may be their rank, or whatever proud titles they may wear. Accursed and rebellious, therefore, is the obedience of those who voluntarily submit to the inventions and laws of the Pope.

---

[1] See page 127 of this volume.

MARK.

VIII. 22. And he cometh to Bethsaida, and they bring to him a blind man, and implore him to touch him. 23. Then taking the blind man by the hand, he led him out of the village. And when he had spat on his eyes, and laid his hands upon him, he asked him if he saw any thing. 24. And he looking up said, I see men; for I perceive them walking as if they were trees. 25. Then he again laid his hands upon his eyes, and desired him to look; and he was restored, so that he saw them all clearly. 26. And he sent him away to his own house, saying, Neither enter into the village, nor tell it to any one in the village.

This miracle, which is omitted by the other two Evangelists, appears to have been related by Mark chiefly on account of this circumstance, that Christ *restored* sight to *the blind man*, not in an instant, as he was generally accustomed to do, but in a gradual manner. He did so most probably for the purpose of proving, in the case of this man, that he had full liberty as to his method of proceeding, and was not restricted to a fixed rule, so as not to resort to a variety of methods in exercising his power. On this account, he does not all at once enlighten the eyes of *the blind man*, and fit them for performing their office, but communicates to them at first a dark and confused perception, and afterwards, by laying on his hands a second time, enables them to see perfectly. And so the grace of Christ, which had formerly been poured out suddenly on others, flowed by drops, as it were, on this man.

Mark VIII. 24. *I see men.* Our Lord had put the question to *the blind man* for the sake of his disciples, to inform them that the man had received something, but that hitherto nothing more than a slight commencement of the cure had been effected. The reply is, that he *sees men*, because he perceives some persons *walking* who are upright *like trees*. By these words he acknowledges that his sight is not yet so clear as to distinguish *men* from *trees*, but that he has already obtained some power of seeing, because he conjectures from the motion that those whom he perceives to be in an erect posture are men; and it is in this respect that he says they are *like trees*. We see then that he speaks only by conjecture when he says that he *sees men*.

26. *And he sent him away to his house.* Christ does not suffer him to return to *Bethsaida,* where there were many that had beheld the miracle. This is conjectured by some to have been done, because Christ intended to punish the inhabitants of that place by depriving them of the enjoyment of his favour. Whatever might be the reason, it is certain that no miracle was performed by him in order to remain perpetually buried, but that he intended to have it concealed along with many others, till, after having expiated by his death the sins of the world,[1] he should ascend to the glory of the Father.

MATTHEW.	MARK.	LUKE.
XVI. 13. And when Jesus came to the coasts of Cesarea Philippi, he asked his disciples, saying, Who do men say that I the Son of man am? 14. And they said, Some [say,] John the Baptist; and others, Elijah; and others, Jeremiah, or one of the prophets. 15. He saith to them, But who do you say that I am? 16. And Simon Peter answering said, Thou art the Christ, the Son of the living God. 17. And Jesus answering said to him, Blessed art thou, Simon Bar-Jona;[2] for flesh and blood hath not revealed it to thee, but my Father who is in heaven. 18. But I say to thee, That thou art Peter, and on this rock will I build my church; and the gates of hell shall not prevail against it. 19. And I will give to thee the keys of the kingdom of heaven; and whatsoever thou shalt bind on earth shall be bound in heaven; and whatsoever thou shalt loose on earth shall be loosed in heaven.	VIII. 27. And Jesus departed, and his disciples, into the villages of Cesarea, which is called Philippi; and by the way he asked his disciples, saying to them, Who do men say that I am? 28. And they replied, John the Baptist; and some, Elijah; and others, One of the prophets. 29. And he saith to them, But who do you say that I am? And Peter answering saith to him, Thou art the Christ.	IX. 18. And it happened, when he was alone praying, his disciples also were with him, and he asked them, saying, Who do the multitudes say that I am? 19. And they answering said, John the Baptist; and others, Elijah; and others, that one of the ancient prophets hath risen. 20. And he said to them, And who do you say that I am? Simon Peter answering said, The Christ of God.

Matthew XVI. 13. *And when Jesus came to the coasts of Cesarea Philippi.* Mark says that this conversation took place during the journey. Luke says that it took

---

[1] " Iusques à ce qu'ayant par sa mort accompli la satisfaction des pechez du monde ;"—" till having by his death rendered full satisfaction for the sins of the world."
[2] " Simon, fils de Iona ;"—" Simon, son of Jonah."

place while he was praying, and while there were none in company with him but his disciples. Matthew is not so exact in mentioning the time. All the three unquestionably relate the same narrative; and it is possible that Christ may have stopped at a certain place during that journey to pray, and that afterwards he may have put the question to his disciples. There were two towns called *Cesarea*, of which the former was more celebrated, and had been anciently called *The Tower of Strato;* while the latter, which is mentioned here, was situated at the foot of Mount Lebanon, not far from the river Jordan. It is for the sake of distinguishing between these two towns that *Philippi* is added to the name; for, though it is conjectured by some to have been built on the same spot where the town of Dan formerly stood, yet, as it had lately been rebuilt by *Philip* the Tetrarch, it was called *Philippi*.[1]

Who do men say that I am? This might be supposed to mean, What was the current rumour about the Redeemer, who became *the Son of man?* But the question is quite different, What do men think about Jesus the Son of Mary? He calls himself, according to custom, *the Son of man,* as much as to say, Now that clothed in flesh I inhabit the earth like other men, what is the opinion entertained respecting me? The design of Christ was, to confirm his disciples fully in the true faith, that they might not be tossed about amidst various reports, as we shall presently see.

14. *Some* [*say,*] *John the Baptist.* This inquiry does not relate to the open enemies of Christ, nor to ungodly scoffers, but to the sounder and better part of the people, who might be called the choice and flower of the Church. Those only are mentioned by the disciples who spoke of Christ with respect; and yet, though they aimed at the truth, not one of them reaches that point, but all go astray in their vain fancies. Hence we perceive how great is the weakness of the human mind; for not only is it unable of itself to understand what is right or true, but even out of true principles

[1] " On la nommoit Cesaree de Philippe ;"—" it was named Cesarea of Philip."

it coins errors. Besides, though Christ is the only standard of harmony and peace, by which God gathers the whole world to himself, the greater part of men seize on this subject as the occasion of prolonged strife. Among the Jews, certainly, the unity of faith related solely to Christ; and yet they who formerly appeared to have some sort of agreement among themselves now split into a variety of sects.

We see too how one error quickly produces another; for a preconceived opinion, which had taken a firm hold of the minds of the common people, that souls passed from one body to another, made them more ready to adopt this groundless fancy. But though, at the time of Christ's coming, the Jews were divided in this manner, such a diversity of opinions ought not to have hindered the godly from desiring to attain the pure knowledge of him. For if any man, under such a pretence, had given himself up to sloth, and neglected to seek Christ, we would have been forced to declare that there was no excuse for him. Much less then will any man escape the judgment of God who is led by the variety of sects to entertain a dislike of Christ, or who, disgusted by the false opinions of men, does not deign to attach himself to Christ.

15. *But who do you say that I am?* Here Christ distinguishes his disciples from the rest of the crowd, to make it more fully evident that, whatever differences may exist among others, we at least ought not to be led aside from the unity of faith. They who shall honestly submit to Christ, and shall not attempt to mix with the Gospel any inventions of their own brain, will never want the true light. But here the greatest vigilance is necessary, that, though the whole world may be carried away by its own inventions, believers may continually adhere to Christ. As Satan could not rob the Jews of the conviction which they derived from the Law and the Prophets, that Christ would come, he changed him into various shapes, and, as it were, cut him in pieces. His next scheme was, to bring forward many pretended Christs, that they might lose sight of the true Redeemer. By similar contrivances, he continued ever afterwards either

to tear Christ in pieces, or to exhibit him under a false character. Among the confused and discordant voices of the world, let this voice of Christ perpetually sound in our ears, which calls us away from unsettled and wavering men, that we may not follow the multitude, and that our faith may not be tossed about amongst the billows of contending opinions.

16. *Thou art the Christ.* The confession is short, but it embraces all that is contained in our salvation; for the designation *Christ,* or *Anointed,* includes both an everlasting Kingdom and an everlasting Priesthood, to reconcile us to God, and, by expiating our sins through his sacrifice, to obtain for us a perfect righteousness, and, having received us under his protection, to uphold and supply and enrich us with every description of blessings. Mark says only, *Thou art the Christ.* Luke says, *Thou art the Christ of God.* But the meaning is the same; for the *Christs* (χριστοί) *of God* was the appellation anciently bestowed on kings, who had been anointed by the divine command.[1] And this phrase had been previously employed by Luke, (ii. 26,) when he said that Simeon had been informed by a revelation from heaven that *he would not see death before he had seen the Lord's Christ.* For the redemption, which God manifested by the hand of his Son, was clearly divine; and therefore it was necessary that he who was to be the Redeemer should come from heaven, bearing the impress of the *anointing* of God. Matthew expresses it still more clearly, *Thou art the Son of the living God;* for, though Peter did not yet understand distinctly in what way Christ was the begotten of God, he was so fully persuaded of the dignity of Christ, that he believed him to come from God, not like other men, but by the inhabitation of the true and living Godhead in his flesh. When the attribute *living* is ascribed to God, it is for the purpose of distinguishing between Him and dead idols, who *are nothing,* (1 Cor. viii. 4.)

[1] See Harmony, vol. i. p. 92, n. 2; p. 142, n. 2.

17. *Blessed art thou, Simon Bar-Jona.* As *this is life eternal, to know the only true God, and him whom he hath sent, Jesus Christ,* (John xvii. 3,) Christ justly pronounces him to be *blessed* who has honestly made such a confession. This was not spoken in a peculiar manner to Peter alone, but our Lord's purpose was, to show in what the only happiness of the whole world consists. That every one may approach him with greater courage, we must first learn that all are by nature miserable and accursed, till they find a remedy in Christ. Next, we must add, that whoever has obtained Christ wants nothing that is necessary to perfect happiness, since we have no right to desire any thing better than the eternal glory of God, of which Christ puts us in possession.

Flesh and blood hath not revealed it to thee. In the person of one man Christ reminds all that we must ask faith from the Father, and acknowledge it to the praise of his grace; for the special illumination of God is here contrasted with *flesh and blood.* Hence we infer, that the minds of men are destitute of that sagacity which is necessary for perceiving the mysteries of heavenly wisdom which are hidden in Christ; and even that all the senses of men are deficient in this respect, till God opens our eyes to perceive his glory in Christ. Let no man, therefore, in proud reliance on his own abilities, attempt to reach it, but let us humbly suffer ourselves to be inwardly taught by *the Father of Lights,* (James i. 17,) that his Spirit alone may enlighten our darkness. And let those who have received faith, acknowledging the blindness which was natural to them, learn to render to God the glory that is due to Him.

18. *And I say to thee.* By these words Christ declares how highly he is delighted with the confession of Peter, since he bestows upon it so large a reward. For, though he had already given to his disciple, Simon, the name of *Peter,* (Matth. x. 2; John i. 42,) and had, out of his undeserved goodness, appointed him to be an apostle, yet these gifts, though freely bestowed,[1] are here ascribed to faith as if they

---

[1] "Ces dons qui estoyent procedez de sa pure liberalité;"—"those gifts which had proceeded altogether from his liberality."

had been a reward, which we not unfrequently find in Scripture. Peter receives a twofold honour, the former part of which relates to his personal advantage, and the latter to his office as an Apostle.

Thou art Peter. By these words our Lord assures him that it was not without a good reason that he had formerly given him this name, because, as a *living stone* (1 Pet. ii. 5) in the temple of God, he retains his stedfastness. This extends, no doubt, to all believers, each of whom is a temple of God, (1 Cor. vi. 19,) and who, united to each other by faith, make together one temple, (Eph. ii. 21.) But it denotes also the distinguished excellence of Peter above the rest, as each in his own order receives more or less, *according to the measure of the gift of Christ,* (Eph. iv. 7.)

And on this rock. Hence it is evident how the name *Peter* comes to be applied both to Simon individually, and to other believers. It is because they are founded on the faith of Christ, and joined together, by a holy consent, into a spiritual building, *that God may dwell in the midst of them,* (Ezek. xliii. 7.) For Christ, by announcing that this would be the common foundation of the whole Church, intended to associate with Peter all the godly that would ever exist in the world. "You are now," said he, "a very small number of men, and therefore the confession which you have now made is not at present supposed to have much weight; but ere long a time will arrive when that confession shall assume a lofty character, and shall be much more widely spread." And this was eminently fitted to excite his disciples to perseverance, that though their faith was little known and little esteemed, yet they had been chosen by the Lord as the first-fruits, that out of this mean commencement there might arise a new Church, which would prove victorious against all the machinations of hell.

Shall not prevail against it. The pronoun *it* ($αὐτῆς$) may refer either to *faith* or to *the Church;* but the latter meaning is more appropriate. Against all the power of Satan the firmness of the Church will prove to be invincible, because the truth of God, on which the faith of the Church rests, will ever remain unshaken. And to this statement corresponds that saying of John, *This is the victory which overcometh the world, your faith,* (1 John v. 4.) It is a promise which eminently deserves our observation, that all who are united to Christ, and acknowledge him to be Christ and Mediator, will remain to the end safe from all danger; for what is said of the body of the Church belongs to each of its members, since they are one in Christ. Yet this passage also instructs us, that so long as the Church shall continue to be a pilgrim on the earth, she will never enjoy rest, but will be exposed to many attacks; for, when it is declared that Satan will not conquer, this implies that he will be her constant enemy. While, therefore, we rely on this promise of Christ, feel ourselves at liberty to boast against Satan, and already triumph by faith over all his forces; let us learn, on the other hand, that this promise is, as it were, the sound of a trumpet, calling us to be always ready and prepared for battle. By the word *gates* ($\pi\acute{\upsilon}\lambda\alpha\iota$) is unquestionably meant every kind of power and of weapons of war.

19. *And I will give thee the keys.* Here Christ begins now to speak of the public office, that is, of the Apostleship, which he dignifies with a twofold title. First, he says that the ministers of the Gospel are porters, so to speak, of the kingdom of heaven, because they carry its *keys ;* and, secondly, he adds, that they are invested with a power of *binding and loosing,* which is ratified in heaven.[1] The comparison of *the keys* is very properly applied to the office of teaching; as when Christ says (Luke xi. 52) that the scribes and Pharisees, in like manner, have *the key* of the kingdom of heaven, because they are expounders of the law. We know that there is no other way in which the gate of life is opened to us than by the word of God; and hence it follows that the key is placed, as it were, in the hands of the ministers of the word.

Those who think that the word *keys* is here used in the plural number, because the Apostles received a commission not only to *open* but also to *shut,* have some probability on

[1] " Laquelle est receuë et advouee és cieux ;"—" which is received and acknowledged in heaven."

their side; but if any person choose to take a more simple view of the meaning, let him enjoy his own opinion.[1] Here a question arises, Why does the Lord promise that he will give to Peter what he appeared to have formerly given him by making him an Apostle? But this question has been already answered,[2] when I said that *the twelve* were at first (Matth. x. 5) nothing more than temporary preachers,[3] and so, when they returned to Christ, they had executed their commission; but after that Christ had risen from the dead, they then began to be appointed to be ordinary teachers of the Church. It is in this sense that the honour is now bestowed for the future.

Whatsoever thou shalt bind on earth. The second metaphor, or comparison, is intended directly to point out the forgiveness of sins; for Christ, in delivering us, by his Gospel, from the condemnation of eternal death, *looses* the cords of the curse by which we are held bound. The doctrine of the Gospel is, therefore, declared to be appointed for loosing our bonds, that, being loosed on earth by the voice and testimony of men, we may be actually *loosed* in heaven. But as there are many who not only are guilty of wickedly rejecting the deliverance that is offered to them, but by their obstinacy bring down on themselves a heavier judgment, the power and authority to *bind* is likewise granted to the ministers of the Gospel. It must be observed, however, that this does not belong to the nature of the Gospel, but is accidental; as Paul also informs us, when, speaking of the *vengeance* which he tells us that he has it in his power to execute against all unbelievers and rebels, he immediately adds, *When your obedience shall have been fulfilled,* (2 Cor. x. 6.) For were it not that the reprobate, through their own fault, turn life into death, the Gospel would be to all *the power of God to salvation,* (Rom. i. 16;) but as many persons no sooner hear it than their impiety openly breaks out, and provokes against

---

[1] " Ie n'y contredi point ;"—" I do not contradict him in it."
[2] Harmony, vol. i. p. 437.
[3] " Ambassadeurs ou prescheurs temporels ;"—" temporary messengers or preachers."

them more and more the wrath of God, to such persons its *savour* must be *deadly*, (2 Cor. ii. 16.)

The substance of this statement is, that Christ intended to assure his followers of the salvation promised to them in the Gospel, that they might expect it as firmly as if he were himself to descend from heaven to bear testimony concerning it; and, on the other hand, to strike despisers with terror, that they might not expect their mockery of the ministers of the word to remain unpunished. Both are exceedingly necessary; for the inestimable *treasure* of life is exhibited to us *in earthen vessels*, (2 Cor. iv. 7,) and had not the authority of the doctrine been established in this manner, the faith of it would have been, almost every moment, ready to give way.[1] The reason why the ungodly become so daring and presumptuous is, that they imagine they have to deal with men. Christ therefore declares that, by the preaching of the Gospel, is revealed on the earth what will be the heavenly judgment of God, and that the certainty of life or death is not to be obtained from any other source.

This is a great honour, that we are God's messengers to assure the world of its salvation. It is the highest honour conferred on the Gospel, that it is declared to be the *embassy* of mutual *reconciliation* between God and men, (2 Cor. v. 20.) In a word, it is a wonderful consolation to devout minds to know that the message of salvation brought to them by a poor mortal man is ratified before God. Meanwhile, let the ungodly ridicule, as they may think fit, the doctrine which is preached to them by the command of God, they will one day learn with what truth and seriousness God threatened them by the mouth of men. Finally, let pious teachers, resting on this assurance, encourage themselves and others to defend with boldness the life-giving grace of God, and yet let them not the less boldly thunder against the hardened despisers of their doctrine.

Hitherto I have given a plain exposition of the native meaning of the words, so that nothing farther could have been desired, had it not been that the Roman Antichrist,

[1] "D'heure en heure elle seroit revoquee en doute;"—"from hour to hour it would be called in question."

wishing to cloak his tyranny, has wickedly and dishonestly dared to pervert the whole of this passage. The light of the true interpretation which I have stated would be of itself sufficient, one would think, for dispelling his darkness; but that pious readers may feel no uneasiness, I shall briefly refute his disgusting calumnies. First, he alleges that Peter is declared to be the foundation of the Church. But who does not see that what he applies to the person of a man is said in reference to Peter's faith in Christ? There is no difference of meaning, I acknowledge, between the two Greek words Πέτρος (*Peter*) and πέτρα, (*petra, a stone* or *rock,*)[1] except that the former belongs to the Attic, and the latter to the ordinary dialect. But we are not to suppose that Matthew had not a good reason for employing this diversity of expression. On the contrary, the gender of the noun was intentionally changed, to show that he was now speaking of something different.[2] A distinction of the same sort, I have no doubt, was pointed out by Christ in his own language;[3] and therefore Augustine judiciously reminds the reader that it is not πέτρα (*petra, a stone* or *rock*) that is derived from Πέτρος, (*Peter,*) but Πέτρος (*Peter*) that is derived from πέτρα, (*petra, a stone* or *rock*.)

But not to be tedious, as we must acknowledge the truth and certainty of the declaration of Paul, that the Church can have no other *foundation* than Christ alone, (1 Cor. iii. 11; Eph. ii. 20,) it can be nothing less than blasphemy and

---

[1] "Ie confesse bien qu'en la langue Grecque il n'y a pas grande différence entre le mot qui signifie une pierre, et celuy qui signifie un homme nommé Pierre;"—"I readily acknowledge that, in the Greek language, there is no great difference between the word that signifies *a stone*, and that which signifies a man named *Peter.*"

[2] "A fin de monstrer qu'au second lieu il parloit de quelque autre chose que de la personne de Pierre;"—"in order to show that, in the latter clause, he was speaking of something totally different from the person of Peter."

[3] By *Christ's own language* is meant the *Syriac*—a dialect of *Hebrew*—which is supposed to have been the vernacular language of Palestine in the time of our Lord, and consequently to have been spoken by him and his apostles. It is enough for our present purpose that CALVIN adopted this hypothesis, whatever may be the result of a controversy in which the claims of the *Greek* language above the *Syriac*, as familiarly spoken and written in Syria at that period, have been urged with vast learning and ability.—*Ed.*

sacrilege, when the Pope has contrived another *foundation*. And certainly no words can express the detestation with which we ought to regard the tyranny of the Papal system on this single account, that, in order to maintain it, the foundation of the Church has been subverted, that the mouth of hell might be opened and swallow up wretched souls. Besides, as I have already hinted, that part does not refer to Peter's public office, but only assigns to him a distinguished place among the sacred stones of the temple. The commendations that follow relate to the Apostolic office; and hence we conclude that nothing is here said to Peter which does not apply equally to the others who were his companions, for if the rank of apostleship was common to them all, whatever was connected with it must also have been held in common.

But it will be said, Christ addresses Peter alone: he does so, because Peter alone, in the name of all, had confessed Christ to be *the Son of God*, and to him alone is addressed the discourse, which applies equally to the rest. And the reason adduced by Cyprian and others is not to be despised, that Christ spake to all in the person of one man, in order to recommend the unity of the Church. They reply,[1] that he to whom this privilege was granted in a peculiar manner is preferred to all others. But that is equivalent to saying that he was more an apostle than his companions; for the power to *bind* and to *loose* can no more be separated from the office of teaching and the Apostleship than light or heat can be separated from the sun. And even granting that something more was bestowed on Peter than on the rest, that he might hold a distinguished place among the Apostles, it is a foolish inference of the Papists, that he received the primacy, and became the universal head of the whole Church. Rank is a different thing from power, and to be elevated to the highest place of honour among a few persons is a different thing from embracing the whole world under his dominion. And in fact, Christ laid no heavier burden on him than he was able to bear. He is ordered to

---

[1] " Les Romanisques repliquent à l'encontre ;"—" the Romanists reply on the other hand."

be the porter of the kingdom of heaven; he is ordered to dispense the grace of God by *binding* and *loosing;* that is, as far as the power of a mortal man reaches. All that was given to him, therefore, must be limited to the measure of grace which he received for the edification of the Church; and so that vast dominion, which the Papists claim for him, falls to the ground.

But though there were no strife or controversy about Peter,[1] still this passage would not lend countenance to the tyranny of the Pope. For no man in his senses will admit the principle which the Papists take for granted, that what is here granted to Peter was intended to be transmitted by him to posterity by hereditary right; for he does not receive permission to give any thing to his successors. So then the Papists make him bountiful with what is not his own. Finally, though the uninterrupted succession were fully established, still the Pope will gain nothing by it till he has proved himself to be Peter's lawful successor. And how does he prove it? Because Peter died at Rome; as if Rome, by the detestable murder of the Apostle, had procured for herself the primacy. But they allege that he was also bishop there. How frivolous[2] that allegation is, I have made abundantly evident in my *Institutes*, (Book IV. chap. vi.,) to which I would willingly send my reader for a complete discussion of this argument, rather than annoy or weary him by repeating it in this place. Yet I would add a few words. Though the Bishop of Rome had been the lawful successor of Peter, since by his own treachery he has deprived himself of so high an honour, all that Christ bestowed on the successors of Peter avails him nothing. That the Pope's court resides at Rome is sufficiently known, but no mark of a Church there can be pointed out. As to the pastoral office, his eagerness to shun it is equal to the ardour with which he contends for his own dominion. Certainly, if it were true that Christ has left nothing undone to exalt the heirs of Peter, still he was not

---

[1] "Mais mettons le cas que ce qu'ils disent de Pierre soit hors de doute;"—"but let us suppose that what they say about Peter were beyond a doubt."

[2] "Combien cela est faux et frivole;"—"how false and frivolous it is."

so lavish as to part with his own honour to bestow it on apostates.

MATTHEW.	MARK.	LUKE.
XVI. 20. Then he charged his disciples[1] not to tell any one that he was Jesus the Christ. 21. From that time Jesus began to make known to his disciples, that he must go to Jerusalem, and suffer many things from the elders, and the chief priests, and the scribes, and be killed, and be raised again on the third day. 22. And Peter, taking him aside,[2] began to rebuke him, saying, Lord, spare thyself;[3] this shall not happen to thee. 23. But he turning said to Peter, Get thee behind me, Satan, thou art an offence to me; for thou relishest not those things which are of God, but those which are of men. 24. Then Jesus said to his disciples, If any man chooses to come after me, let him deny himself, and take up his cross, and follow me. 25. For whosoever would save his life shall lose it; and on the other hand, whosoever shall lose his life on	VIII. 30. And he threatened and forbade them to tell any one concerning him.[4] 31. And he began to teach them, that the Son of man must suffer many things, and be rejected by the elders, and the chief priests, and the scribes, and be killed, and after three days rise again. 32. And he spoke that saying openly, and Peter took him, and began to rebuke him. 33. But he turning and looking upon his disciples, rebuked Peter, saying, Get thee behind me, Satan; for thou relishest not the things that are of God, but those that are of men. 34. And when he had called the multitude to him along with his disciples, he said to them, Whosoever would follow me, let him deny himself, and take up his cross, and follow me. 35. For whosoever would save his life shall lose it; and whosoever shall lose his life for my sake, and for the sake of the gospel, shall save it. 36. For what will it profit a man, if he shall gain the whole world, and lose his	IX. 21. And he threatening charged them not to tell this to any one,[5] 22. Saying, The Son of man must suffer many things, and be rejected by the elders, and the chief priests, and the scribes, and rise again on the third day. 23. And he said to all, If any man would come after me, let him deny himself, and take up his cross daily,[6] and follow me. 24. For whosoever would save his life shall lose it; and whosoever shall lose his life on my account shall save it. 25. For what doth it profit a man, if he shall gain the whole world, and be ruined and lost? 26.

[1] "Lors il commanda expressément à ses disciples;"—"then he expressly commanded his disciples."

[2] "L'ayant prins à part;"—"having taken him aside."

[3] "Seigneur, aye pitié de toy;"—"Lord, have pity on thyself."

[4] "Et il leur defendit avec menace qu'ils ne dissent [cela] de luy à personne;"—"and he forbade them with threatening to tell [this] concerning him to any one."

[5] "Adonc usant de menaces il leur commanda qu'ils ne le dissent à personne;"—"Then employing threatenings, he commanded them not to tell it to any one."

[6] "De iour en iour;"—"day by day."

MATTHEW.	MARK.	LUKE.
my account shall find it. 26. For what doth it profit a man, if he shall gain the whole world, and lose his own soul? or what shall a man give, that, in exchange for it, he may redeem his soul? 27. For the Son of man will come in the glory of his Father with his angels; and then will he render to every one according to his actions. 28. Verily I say to you, There are some standing here, who will not taste death till they have seen the Son of man coming in his kingdom.	soul? 37. Or what shall a man give as a ransom for his soul? 38. For whosoever shall be ashamed of me and of my words in this adulterous and sinful generation, of him likewise will the Son of man be ashamed, when he shall come in the glory of his Father with the holy angels. IX. 1. And he said to them, Verily, I say to you, There are some among those who stand here[1] that will not taste death, till they have seen the kingdom of God come with power.	For whosoever shall be ashamed of me and of my sayings, of him likewise will the Son of man be ashamed, when he shall come in his own majesty, and in the majesty of his Father, and of the holy angels. 27. And I say to you, There truly are some standing here who will not taste death, till they see the kingdom of God.[2]

Having given a proof of his future glory, Christ reminds his disciples of what *he must suffer*, that they also may be prepared to *bear the cross;* for the time was at hand when they must enter into the contest, to which he knew them to be altogether unequal, if they had not been fortified by fresh courage. And first of all, it was necessary to inform them that Christ must commence his reign, not with gaudy display, not with the magnificence of riches, not with the loud applause of the world, but with an ignominious death. But nothing was harder than to rise superior to such an offence; particularly if we consider the opinion which they firmly entertained respecting their Master; for they imagined that he would procure for them earthly happiness. This unfounded expectation held them in suspense, and they eagerly looked forward to the hour when Christ would suddenly reveal the glory of his reign. So far were they from having ever adverted to the ignominy of the cross, that they considered

---

[1] "Il y en d'aucuns de ceux qui sont ici presens;"—"there are some of those who are here present."

[2] "Iusqu'à tant qu'ils ayent veu le regne de Dieu;"—"till they have seen the kingdom of God."

it to be utterly unsuitable that he should be placed in any circumstances from which he did not receive honour.[1] To them it was a distressing occurrence that he should *be rejected by the elders and the scribes,* who held the government of the Church; and hence we may readily conclude that this admonition was highly necessary. But as the bare mention of the cross must, of necessity, have occasioned heavy distress to their weak minds, he presently heals the wound by saying, that *on the third day he will rise again from the dead.* And certainly, as there is nothing to be seen in the cross but the weakness of the flesh, till we come to his resurrection, in which the power of the Spirit shines brightly, our faith will find no encouragement or support. In like manner, all ministers of the Word, who desire that their preaching may be profitable, ought to be exceedingly careful that the glory of his resurrection should be always exhibited by them in connection with the ignominy of his death.

But we naturally wonder why Christ refuses to accept as witnesses the Apostles, whom he had already appointed to that office; for why were they sent but to be the heralds of that redemption which depended on the coming of Christ? The answer is not difficult, if we keep in mind the explanations which I have given on this subject: first, that they were not appointed teachers for the purpose of bearing full and certain testimony to Christ, but only to procure disciples for their Master; that is, to induce those who were too much the victims of sloth to become teachable and attentive; and, secondly, that their commission was temporary, for it ended when Christ himself began to preach. As the time of his death was now at hand, and as they were not yet fully prepared to testify their faith, but, on the contrary, were so weak in faith, that their confession of it would have exposed them to ridicule, the Lord enjoins them to remain silent till others shall have acknowledged him to be the conqueror of death, and till he shall have endued them with increased firmness.

---

[1] "Que rien luy peust advenir qui ne fust honorable et magnifique;"—"that any thing should happen to him which was not honourable and magnificent."

Matthew XVI. 22. *And Peter, taking him aside, began to rebuke him.* It is a proof of the excessive zeal of Peter, that he reproves his Master; though it would appear that the respect he entertained for him was his reason for *taking him aside,* because he did not venture to reprove him in presence of others. Still, it was highly presumptuous in Peter to advise our Lord to *spare himself,* as if he had been deficient in prudence or self-command. But so completely are men hurried on and driven headlong by inconsiderate zeal, that they do not hesitate to pass judgment on God himself, according to their own fancy. Peter views it as absurd, that the Son of God, who was to be the Redeemer of the nation, should be *crucified by the elders,* and that he who was the Author of life should be condemned to die. He therefore endeavours to restrain Christ from exposing himself to death. The reasoning is plausible; but we ought without hesitation to yield greater deference to the opinion of Christ than to the zeal of Peter, whatever excuse he may plead.

And here we learn what estimation in the sight of God belongs to what are called *good intentions.* So deeply is pride rooted in the hearts of men, that they think wrong is done them, and complain, if God does not comply with every thing that they consider to be right. With what obstinacy do we see the Papists boasting of their devotions! But while they applaud themselves in this daring manner, God not only rejects what they believe to be worthy of the highest praise, but even pronounces a severe censure on its folly and wickedness. Certainly, if the feeling and judgment of the flesh be admitted, Peter's intention was pious, or at least it looked well. And yet Christ could not have conveyed his censure in harsher or more disdainful language. Tell me, what is the meaning of that stern reply? How comes it that he who so mildly on all occasions guarded against *breaking* even *a bruised reed,* (Isa. xlii. 3,) thunders so dismally against a chosen disciple? The reason is obvious, that in the person of one man he intended to restrain all from gratifying their own passions. Though the lusts of the flesh, as they resemble wild beasts, are difficult to be restrained, yet there is no beast more furious than the wisdom of the flesh. It is on this account that Christ reproves it so sharply, and bruises it, as it were, with an iron hammer, to teach us that it is only from the word of God that we ought to be wise.

23. *Get thee behind me, Satan.* It is idle to speculate, as some have done, about the word (ὀπίσω) *behind;* as if Peter were ordered to follow, and not to go before; for, in a passage which we have already considered, Luke (iv. 8) informs us that our Lord used those very words in repelling the attacks of Satan, and the verb ὕπαγε (from which the Latin word *Apage* is derived) signifies to *withdraw*.[1] Christ therefore throws his disciple to a distance from him, because, in his inconsiderate zeal, he acted the part of *Satan;* for he does not simply call him *adversary,* but gives him the name of the devil, as an expression of the greatest abhorrence.

Thou art an offence to me; for thou relishest not those things which are of God, but those which are of men. We must attend to this as the reason assigned by our Lord for sending Peter away from him. Peter was *an offence* to Christ, so long as he opposed his calling; for, when Peter attempted to stop the course of his Master, it was not owing to him that he did not deprive himself and all mankind of eternal salvation. This single word, therefore, shows with what care we ought to avoid every thing that withdraws us from obedience to God. And Christ opens up the original source of the whole evil, when he says that Peter *relishes those things which are of men.*[2] Lest we and our intentions should be sent away by our heavenly Judge to the devil,[3] let us learn not to be too much attached to our own views, but submissively to embrace whatever the Lord approves. Let the Papists now go and extol their notions to the skies. They will one day learn, when they appear before the judgment-

---

[1] "Le mot Grec signifie simplement se reculer et s'en aller;"—"the Greek word simply means *to withdraw and go away.*"

[2] "Que Pierre s'arreste à la sagesse de l'homme;"—"that Peter rests satisfied with the wisdom of man."

[3] "Et pourtant de peur que le Iuge celeste ne nous renvoye au diable avec nos bonnes affections et intentions;"—"and then lest our heavenly Judge should send us away to the devil with our good feelings and intentions."

seat of God, what is the value of their boasting, which Christ declares to be from *Satan*. And with regard to ourselves, if we do not, of our own accord, resolve to shut ourselves out from the way of salvation by deadly obstacles, let us not desire to be wise in any other manner than from the mouth of God.

24. *Then Jesus said to his disciples.* As Christ saw that Peter had a dread of *the cross*, and that all the rest were affected in the same way, he enters into a general discourse about *bearing the cross*, and does not limit his address to the twelve apostles, but lays down the same law for all the godly.[1] We have already met with a statement nearly similar, (Matthew x. 38.)[2] But in that passage the apostles were only reminded of the persecution which awaited them, as soon as they should begin to discharge their office; while a general instruction is here conveyed, and the initiatory lessons, so to speak, inculcated on all who profess to believe the Gospel.

If any man will come after me. These words are used for the express purpose of refuting the false views of Peter.[3] Presenting himself to every one as an example of self-denial and of patience, he first shows that it was necessary for him to endure what Peter reckoned to be inconsistent with his character, and next invites every member of his body to imitate him. The words must be explained in this manner: "If any man would be my disciple, let him *follow me* by *denying himself and taking up his cross*, or, let him conform himself to my example." The meaning is, that none can be reckoned to be the disciples of Christ unless they are true imitators of him, and are willing to pursue the same course.

He lays down a brief rule for our imitation, in order to make us acquainted with the chief points in which he wishes us to resemble him. It consists of two parts, *self-denial* and a voluntary *bearing of the cross*. *Let him deny himself.* This

---

[1] "A tous fideles;"—"to all believers."
[2] Harmony, vol. i. p. 472.
[3] "Pour refuter l'imagination que Pierre avoit en son cerveau;"—"to refute the imagination which Peter had in his brain."

self-denial is very extensive, and implies that we ought to give up our natural inclinations, and part with all the affections of the flesh, and thus give our consent to be reduced to nothing, provided that God lives and reigns in us. We know with what blind love men naturally regard themselves, how much they are devoted to themselves, how highly they estimate themselves. But if we desire to enter into the school of Christ, we must begin with that folly to which Paul (1 Cor. iii. 18) exhorts us, *becoming fools, that we may be wise;* and next we must control and subdue all our affections.

And let him take up his cross. He lays down this injunction, because, though there are common miseries to which the life of men is indiscriminately subjected, yet as God trains his people in a peculiar manner, in order that they may be *conformed to the image of his Son,* we need not wonder that this rule is strictly addressed to them. It may be added that, though God lays both on good and bad men the burden of the cross, yet unless they willingly bend their shoulders to it, they are not said to *bear the cross;* for a wild and refractory horse cannot be said to admit his rider, though he carries him. The patience of the saints, therefore, consists in *bearing* willingly *the cross* which has been laid on them.[1] Luke adds the word *daily—let him take up his cross* DAILY—which is very emphatic; for Christ's meaning is, that there will be no end to our warfare till we leave the world. Let it be the uninterrupted exercise of the godly, that when many afflictions have run their course, they may be prepared to endure fresh afflictions.

25. *For he that would save his life shall lose it.* It is a most appropriate consolation, that they who willingly suffer death for the sake of Christ[2] do actually obtain life; for Mark expressly states this as the motive to believers in dying—*for my sake, and for the sake of the Gospel*—and in the words of Matthew the same thing must be understood. It frequently

---

[1] " A porter la croix que Dieu leur met sur les epaules ;"—" in bearing the cross which God lays on their shoulders."
[2] " Ceux qui meurent alaigrement pour Christ ;"—" those who die cheerfully for Christ."

happens that irreligious men are prompted by ambition or despair to despise life; and to such persons it will be no advantage that they are courageous in meeting death. The threatening, which is contrasted with the promise, has also a powerful tendency to shake off carnal sloth, when he reminds men who are desirous of the present life, that the only advantage which they reap is, to *lose* life. There is a contrast intended here between temporal and eternal death, as we have explained under Matthew x. 39, where the reader will find the rest of this subject.[1]

26. *For what doth it profit a man?* The word *soul* is here used in the strictest sense. Christ reminds them that the *soul* of man was not created merely to enjoy the world for a few days, but to obtain at length its immortality in heaven. What carelessness and what brutal stupidity is this, that men are so strongly attached to the world, and so much occupied with its affairs, as not to consider why they were born, and that God gave them an immortal soul, in order that, when the course of the earthly life was finished, they might live eternally in heaven! And, indeed, it is universally acknowledged, that the *soul* is of higher value than all the riches and enjoyments of the world; but yet men are so blinded by carnal views, that they knowingly and wilfully abandon their souls to destruction. That the world may not fascinate us by its allurements, let us remember the surpassing worth of our *soul;* for if this be seriously considered, it will easily dispel the vain imaginations of earthly happiness.

27. *For the Son of man will come.* That the doctrine which has just been laid down may more deeply affect our minds, Christ places before our eyes the future judgment; for if we would perceive the worthlessness of this fading life, we must be deeply affected by the view of the heavenly life. So tardy and sluggish is our mind, that it needs to be aided by looking towards heaven. Christ summons believers to his judgment-seat, to lead them to reflect at all times that they

[1] Harmony, vol. i. p. 472.

lived for no other object than to long after that blessed redemption, which will be revealed at the proper time. The admonition is intended to inform us, that they do not strive in vain who set a higher value on the confession of faith than on their own life. " Place your lives fearlessly," says he, " in my hand, and under my protection; for I will at length appear as your avenger, and will fully restore you, though for the time you may seem to have perished."

In the glory of the Father, with his angels. These are mentioned to guard his disciples against judging of his kingdom from present appearances; for hitherto he was unknown and despised, being concealed under the form and condition of a servant. He assures them that it will be far otherwise when he shall appear as the Judge of the world. As to the remaining part of the passage in Mark and Luke, the reader will find it explained under the tenth chapter of Matthew.[1]

And then will he render to every one according to his actions. The reward of works has been treated by me as fully as was necessary under another passage.[2] It amounts to this: When a *reward* is promised to good works, their merit is not contrasted with the justification which is freely bestowed on us through faith; nor is it pointed out as the cause of our salvation, but is only held out to excite believers to aim at doing what is right,[3] by assuring them that their labour will not be lost. There is a perfect agreement, therefore, between these two statements, that we are *justified freely*, (Rom. iii. 24,) because we are received into God's favour without any merit;[4] and yet that God, of his own good pleasure, bestows on our works a *reward* which we did not deserve.

28. *Verily, I say to you.* As the disciples might still hesi-

---

[1] Harmony, vol. i. p. 466.
[2] *Alibi* is a general reference, but *en un autre passage* is more specific; and the passage to which he probably refers the reader for a distinct exhibition of his views, and in which, so far as I remember, he handles this subject more fully than in any other part of the Gospels, is John iv. 36. —*Ed.*
[3] " A faire bonnes œuvres ;"—" to do good works."
[4] "Sans que nous en soyons dignes, ou l'ayons merité ;"—" without being worthy of it, or having deserved it."

tate and inquire when that day would be, our Lord animates them by the immediate assurance, that he will presently give them a proof of his future glory. We know the truth of the common proverb, that to one who is in expectation even speed looks like delay; but never does it hold more true, than when we are told to wait for our salvation till the *coming* of Christ. To support his disciples in the meantime, our Lord holds out to them, for confirmation, an intermediate period; as much as to say, " If it seem too long to wait for the day of my coming, I will provide against this in good time; for before you come to die, you will see with your eyes that kingdom of God, of which I bid you entertain a confident hope." This is the natural import of the words; for the notion adopted by some, that they were intended to apply to John, is ridiculous.

Coming in his kingdom. By the *coming of the kingdom of God* we are to understand the manifestation of heavenly glory, which Christ began to make at his resurrection, and which he afterwards made more fully by sending the Holy Spirit, and by the performance of miracles; for by those beginnings he gave his people a taste of the newness of the heavenly life, when they perceived, by certain and undoubted proofs, that he was sitting at the right hand of the Father.

MATTHEW.	MARK.	LUKE.
XVII. 1. And after six days Jesus taketh Peter, and James, and John his brother, and leadeth them to a high mountain apart; 2. And was transfigured before them: and his face shone as the sun, and his garments became white as the light. 3. And, lo, there appeared to them[1] Moses and Elijah talking with him. 4.	IX. 2. And after six days Jesus taketh Peter, and James, and John, and leadeth them to a high mountain apart by themselves, and was transfigured before them. 3. And his garments became shining, exceedingly white as snow, so white as no fuller on earth could make them. 4. And there	IX. 28. And it happened about eight days after these words, and he took Peter, and James, and John, and went up to a mountain to pray. 29. And while he was praying, the appearance of his countenance was changed, and his raiment became white and dazzling.[2] 30. And, lo, two men talked with him, who were Moses and Elijah; 31. Who appeared in a majestic form, and spoke of

[1] " Et voyci, ils veirent Moyse et Elie parlans avec luy ;"—" and, lo, they saw Moses and Elijah talking with him."
[2] " Resplendissant comme un esclair ;"—" dazzling like lightning."

MATTHEW.	MARK.	LUKE.
And Peter answering said to Jesus, Lord, it is good for us to be here: if thou wilt, let us make here three tabernacles; one for thee, and one for Moses, and one for Elijah. 5. While he was speaking, lo, a bright cloud overshadowed them; and, lo, a voice out of the cloud, which said, This is my beloved Son, in whom I am well pleased; hear him. 6. And having heard this, the disciples fell on their face,[1] and were exceedingly afraid. 7. Then Jesus approaching touched them, and said, Arise, and be not afraid. 8. And when they had lifted up their eyes, they saw no man but Jesus only.	appeared to them Elijah with Moses, and they were conversing with Jesus. 5. And Peter answering said to Jesus, Rabbi, it is good for us to be here: and let us make three tabernacles; one for thee, and one for Moses, and one for Elijah. 6. For he knew not what he said; for they were terrified. 7. And there came a cloud that overshadowed them; and a voice came out of the cloud, saying, This is my beloved Son; hear him. 8. And suddenly, when they looked around, they saw no other person, but Jesus alone with them.	the decease which he would accomplish at Jerusalem. 32. And Peter, and they that were with him, were overpowered with sleep; and when they awoke, they saw his glory, and the two men who were with him. 33. And it happened, while they were departing from him,[2] Peter said to Jesus, Master, it is good for us to be here: and let us make three tabernacles; one for thee, and one for Moses, and one for Elijah: not knowing what he said. 34. And while he was speaking these words, a cloud came and overshadowed them; and they were afraid as they entered into the cloud. 35. And a voice came out of the cloud, saying, This is my beloved Son; hear him. 36. And while the voice was uttered, Jesus was found alone.

Matthew XVII. 1. *And after six days.* We must first inquire for what purpose Christ clothed himself with heavenly glory for a short time, and why he did not admit more than three of his disciples to be spectators. Some think that he did so, in order to fortify them against the trial which they were soon to meet with, arising from his death. That does not appear to me to be a probable reason; for why should he have deprived the rest of the same remedy, or rather, why does he expressly forbid them to make known what they had seen till after his resurrection, but because the result of the vision would be later than his death? I have no doubt whatever that Christ intended to show that he was not dragged

---

[1] "Ce qu'ayant ouy les disciples cheurent sur leur face en terre;"—"which the disciples having heard, fell on their face to the earth."

[2] "Et adveint quand ceux-la furent departis d'avec luy;"—"and it happened when those men had departed from him."

unwillingly to death, but that he came forward of his own accord, to offer to the Father the sacrifice of obedience. The disciples were not made aware of this till Christ rose; nor was it even necessary that, at the very moment of his death, they should perceive the divine power of Christ, so as to acknowledge it to be victorious on the cross; but the instruction which they now received was intended to be useful at a future period both to themselves and to us, that no man might take offence at the weakness of Christ, as if it were by force and necessity that he had suffered.[1] It would manifestly have been quite as easy for Christ to protect his body from death as to clothe it with heavenly glory.

We are thus taught that he was subjected to death, because he wished it to be so; that he was crucified, because he offered himself. That same flesh, which was sacrificed on the cross and lay in the grave, might have been exempted from death and the grave; for it had already partaken of the heavenly glory. We are also taught that, so long as Christ remained in the world, bearing the form of a servant, and so long as his majesty was concealed under the weakness of the flesh, nothing had been taken from him, for it was of his own accord that he *emptied himself*, (Philip. ii. 7;) but now his resurrection has drawn aside that veil by which his power had been concealed for a time.

Our Lord reckoned it enough to select *three witnesses,* because that is the number which the Law has laid down for proving any thing; *at the mouth of two witnesses or three witnesses,* (Deut. xvii. 6.) The difference as to time ought not to give us uneasiness. Matthew and Mark reckon *six* entire *days,* which had elapsed between the events. Luke says that *it happened about* EIGHT *days afterwards,* including both *the day* on which Christ spake these words, and *the day* on which he was transfigured. We see then that, under a diversity of expression, there is a perfect agreement as to the meaning.

2. *And was transfigured before them.* Luke says that this happened *while he was praying;* and from the circumstances

[1] " Comme si par force et contreinte il fust venu endurer la mort;"— " as if by force and constraint he had come to suffer death."

of time and place, we may infer that he had prayed for what he now obtained, that in the brightness of an unusual form his Godhead might become visible ; not that he needed to ask by prayer from another what he did not possess, or that he doubted his Father's willingness, but because, during the whole course of his humiliation, he always ascribed to the Father whatever he did as a divine Person, and because he intended to excite us to prayer by his example.

His *transfiguration* did not altogether enable his disciples to see Christ, as he now is in heaven, but gave them a taste of his boundless glory, such as they were able to comprehend. Then *his face shone as the sun;* but now he is far beyond the sun in brightness. In his *raiment* an unusual and dazzling whiteness appeared ; but now without *raiment* a divine majesty shines in his whole body. Thus in ancient times God appeared to the holy fathers, not as He was in Himself, but so far as they could endure the rays of His infinite brightness ; for John declares that not until *they are like him will they see him as he is*, (1 John iii. 2.) There is no necessity for entering here into ingenious inquiries as to the *whiteness* of his *garments,* or the *brightness* of his *countenance;* for this was not a complete exhibition of the heavenly glory of Christ, but, under symbols which were adapted to the capacity of the flesh, he enabled them to taste in part what could not be fully comprehended.

3. *And, lo, there appeared to them Moses and Elijah.* It is asked, Were *Moses and Elijah* actually present? or was it only an apparition that was exhibited to the disciples, as the prophets frequently beheld visions of things that were absent? Though the subject admits, as we say, of arguments on both sides, yet I think it more probable that they were actually brought to that place. There is no absurdity in this supposition ; for God has bodies and souls in his hand, and can restore the dead to life at his pleasure, whenever he sees it to be necessary. *Moses and Elijah* did not then rise on their own account,[1] but in order to wait upon Christ. It will next

---

[1] "Moise et Elie ne sont pas lors ressuscitez pour eux, et pour le regard de la resurrection derniere ;"—"Moses and Elijah did not then rise for themselves, and with respect to the last resurrection."

be asked, How came the apostles to know *Moses and Elijah,* whom they had never seen? The answer is easy. God, who brought them forward, gave also signs and tokens by which they were enabled to know them. It was thus by an extraordinary revelation that they obtained the certain knowledge that they were *Moses and Elijah.*

But why did these two appear rather than others who equally belonged to the company of the holy fathers? It was intended to demonstrate that Christ alone is the end of the Law and of the Prophets; and that single reason ought to satisfy us: for it was of the utmost importance to our faith that Christ did not come into our world without a testimony, but with commendations which God had formerly bestowed. I have no objection, however, to the reason which is commonly adduced, that *Elijah* was selected, in preference to others, as the representative of all the Prophets; because, though he left nothing in writing, yet next to Moses he was the most distinguished of their number, restored the worship of God which had been corrupted, and stood unrivalled in his exertions for vindicating the Law and true godliness, which was at that time almost extinct.

And they conversed with Jesus. When they *appeared* along with Christ, and held *conversation* with him, this was a declaration of their being agreed. The subject on which they conversed is stated by Luke only: they *talked of the decease* which awaited Christ *at Jerusalem.* This must not be understood to refer to them as private individuals, but rather to the commission which they had formerly received. Though it was now a long time since they had died and finished the course of their calling, yet our Lord intended once more to ratify by their voice what they had taught during their life, in order to inform us that the same salvation, through the sacrifice of Christ, is held out to us in common with the holy fathers. At the time when the ancient prophets uttered their predictions concerning the death of Christ, he himself, who was the eternal wisdom of God, was sitting on the invisible throne of his glory. Hence it follows that, when he was clothed in flesh, he was not liable to death any farther than as he submitted to it of his own free will.

4. *Lord, it is good for us to be here.* Luke tells us that Peter uttered these words *while Moses and Elijah were departing;* and hence we infer that he was afraid lest, at their departure, that pleasant and delightful exhibition should vanish away. We need not wonder that Peter was so captivated by the loveliness of what he beheld, as to lose sight of every other person, and rest satisfied with the mere enjoyment of it; as it is said in the psalm, *In thy presence is fulness of joy,* (Ps. xvi. 11.) But his desire was foolish; first, because he did not comprehend the design of the vision; secondly, because he absurdly put the servants on a level with their Lord; and, thirdly, he was mistaken in proposing to build fading tabernacles[1] for men who had been already admitted to the glory of heaven and of the angels.

I have said that he did not understand the design of the vision; for, while he was hearing, from the mouth of *Moses and Elijah,* that the time of Christ's death was at hand, he foolishly dreamed that his present aspect, which was temporary, would endure for ever. And what if the kingdom of Christ had been confined in this way to the narrow limits of twenty or thirty feet? Where would have been the redemption of the whole world? Where would have been the communication of eternal salvation? It was also highly absurd to conceive of *Moses and Elijah* as companions of the Son of God, as if it had not been proper that all should be reduced to a lower rank, that he alone may have the pre-eminence. And if Peter is satisfied with his present condition, why does he suppose that earthly supports were needed by those persons, the very sight of whom, he imagined, was enough to make him happy?

Justly, therefore, is it stated by two of the Evangelists, that he *knew not what he said;* and Mark assigns the reason, that *they were afraid;* for God did not intend that the apostles should, at that time, derive any advantage from it beyond that of beholding for a moment, as in a bright mirror, the divinity of his Son. At a later period, he pointed out to them the fruit of the vision, and corrected the error

---

[1] "Des tabernacles terriens;"—"earthly tabernacles."

of their judgment. What is stated by Mark must therefore mean, that Peter was carried away by frenzy, and spoke like a man who had lost his senses.

5. *Lo, a bright cloud overshadowed them.* Their eyes were covered by *a cloud,* in order to inform them, that they were not yet prepared for beholding the brightness of the heavenly glory. For, when the Lord gave tokens of his presence, he employed, at the same time, some coverings to restrain the arrogance of the human mind. So now, with the view of teaching his disciples a lesson of humility, he withdraws from their eyes the sight of the heavenly glory. This admonition is likewise addressed to us, that we may not seek to pry into the secrets which lie beyond our senses, but, on the contrary, that every man may keep within the limits of sobriety, according to the measure of his faith. In a word, this *cloud* ought to serve us as a bridle, that our curiosity may not indulge in undue wantonness. The disciples, too, were warned that they must return to their former warfare, and therefore must not expect a triumph before the time.

And, lo, a voice from the cloud. It deserves our attention, that the *voice* of God was heard from the *cloud,* but that neither a body nor a face was seen. Let us therefore remember the warning which Moses gives us, that God has no visible shape, lest we should deceive ourselves by imagining that He resembled a man, (Deut. iv. 15.) There were, no doubt, various appearances under which God made himself known to the holy fathers in ancient times; but in all cases he refrained from using signs which might induce them to make for themselves idols. And certainly, as the minds of men are too strongly inclined to foolish imaginations, there was no necessity for throwing oil upon the flame.[1] This manifestation of the glory of God was remarkable above all others. When he makes a cloud to pass between Him and us, and invites us to himself by His voice, what madness is it to attempt to place Him before our eyes by a

---

[1] " Il n'estoit ia besoin de ietter de l'huile au feu pour enflamber davantage le mal;"—" there was no necessity for throwing oil on the fire to inflame the evil still more."

block of wood or of stone? Let us therefore endeavour to enter by faith alone, and not by the eyes of flesh, into that inaccessible light in which God dwells. *The voice came from the cloud,* that the disciples, knowing it to have proceeded from God, might receive it with due reverence.

This is my beloved Son. I willingly concur with those who think that there is an implied contrast of *Moses and Elijah* with Christ, and that the disciples of God's own Son are here charged to seek no other teacher. The word *Son* is emphatic, and raises him above servants. There are two titles here bestowed upon Christ, which are not more fitted to do honour to him than to aid our faith: a *beloved Son,* and a Master. The Father calls him *my beloved Son, in whom I am well pleased,* and thus declares him to be the Mediator, by whom he reconciles the world to himself. When he enjoins us to *hear him,* he appoints him to be the supreme and only teacher of his Church. It was his design to distinguish Christ from all the rest, as we truly and strictly infer from those words, that by nature he was God's *only Son.* In like manner, we learn that he alone is *beloved* by the Father, and that he alone is appointed to be our Teacher, that in him all authority may dwell.

But it will perhaps be objected, Does not God love angels and men? It is easy to reply, that the fatherly love of God, which is spread over angels and men, proceeds from him as its source. The *Son* is *beloved* by the Father, not so as to make other creatures the objects of his hatred, but so that he communicates to them what belongs to himself. There is a difference, no doubt, between our condition and that of the angels; for they never were alienated from God, and therefore needed not that he should reconcile them; while we are enemies on account of sin, till Christ procure for us his favour. Still, it is a fixed principle that God is gracious to both, only so far as he embraces us in Christ; for even the angels would not be firmly united to God if Christ were not their Head. It may also be observed that, since the Father here speaks of himself as different from the Son, there is a distinction of persons; for they are one in essence and alike in glory.

Hear him. I mentioned a little ago, that these words were

intended to draw the attention of the Church to Christ as the only Teacher, that on his mouth alone it may depend. For, though Christ came to maintain the authority of *the Law and the Prophets,* (Matth. v. 17,) yet he holds the highest rank, so that, by the brightness of his gospel, he causes those sparks which shone in the Old Testament to disappear. He is *the Sun of righteousness,* whose arrival brought the full light of day. And this is the reason why the Apostle says (Heb. i. 1) that *God, who at sundry times and in various ways spoke formerly by the Prophets, hath in these last days spoken to us by his beloved Son.* In short, Christ is as truly heard at the present day in the Law and in the Prophets as in his Gospel; so that in him dwells the authority of a *Master,* which he claims for himself alone, saying, *One is your Master, even Christ,* (Matth. xxiii. 8.) But his authority is not fully acknowledged, unless all the tongues of men are silent. If we would submit to his doctrine, all that has been invented by men must be thrown down and destroyed. He is every day, no doubt, sending out teachers, but it is to state purely and honestly what they have learned from him, and not to corrupt the gospel by their own additions. In a word, no man can be regarded a faithful teacher of the Church, unless he be himself a disciple of Christ, and bring others to be taught by him.

6. *And having heard this.* God intended that the disciples should be struck with this terror, in order to impress more fully on their hearts the remembrance of the vision. Yet we see how great is the weakness of our nature, which trembles in this manner at hearing the voice of God. If ungodly men mock at God, or despise him without concern, it is because God does not address them so as to cause his presence to be felt; but the majesty of God, as soon as we perceive him, must unavoidably cast us down.

7. *Then Jesus approaching touched them.* Christ raises them up when they had fallen, and by so doing performs his office; for he came down to us for this very purpose, that by his guidance believers might boldly enter into the presence of

God, and that his majesty, which otherwise would swallow up all flesh, might no longer fill them with terror. Nor is it only by his words that he comforts, but by *touching* also that he encourages them.

8. *They saw no man but Jesus only.* When it is said that in the end they saw Christ *alone*, this means that the Law and the Prophets had a temporary glory, that Christ alone might remain fully in view. If we would properly avail ourselves of the aid of Moses, we must not stop with him, but must endeavour to be conducted by his hand to Christ, of whom both he and all the rest are ministers. This passage may also be applied to condemn the superstitions of those who confound Christ not only with prophets and apostles, but with saints of the lowest rank, in such a manner as to make him nothing more than one of their number. But when the saints of God are eminent in graces, it is for a totally different purpose than that they should defraud Christ of a part of his honour, and appropriate it to themselves. In the disciples themselves we may see the origin of the mistake; for so long as they were terrified by the majesty of God, their minds wandered in search of men, but when Christ gently raised them up, they saw him *alone*. If we are made to experience that consolation by which Christ relieves us of our fears, all those foolish affections, which distract us on every hand, will vanish away.

MATTHEW.	MARK.	LUKE.
XVII. 9. And as they were going down from the mountain, Jesus commanded them, saying, Tell the vision to no man, till the Son of man be risen from the dead. 10. And his disciples asked him, saying, Why then do the scribes say that Elijah must come first? 11. And Jesus answering said to them, Elijah indeed will come first, and restore all things. 12. But I say to you, That Elijah is	IX. 9. And when they were going down from the mountain, he charged them not to tell any man those things which they had seen, till the Son of man had risen from the dead. 10. And they kept this saying among themselves, disputing with each other what was the meaning of the expression which he had used, To rise from the dead. 11 And they asked him, saying, Why do the scribes say that Elijah must come first? 12. And he answering said to them,	IX. 36. And they kept silence, and told no man in those days any of those things which they had seen.

MATTHEW.	MARK.	LUKE.
come already, and they did not know him, but have done to him whatever they pleased : thus also will the Son of man suffer from them. 13. Then the disciples understood that he had spoken to them concerning John the Baptist.[1]	Elijah indeed will come first, and restore all things; and, as it is written, the Son of man must suffer many things and be despised. 13. But I say to you, That Elijah is come, and they have done to him whatever they pleased, as it is written of him.	

Matthew XVII. 9. *And as they were going down from the mountain.* We have said that the time for making known *the vision* was not yet fully come; and, indeed, the disciples would not have believed it, if Christ had not given a more striking proof of his glory in his resurrection. But after that his divine power had been openly displayed, that temporary exhibition of his glory began to be admitted, so as to make it fully evident that, even during the time that he *emptied himself*, (Philip. ii. 7,) he continued to retain his divinity entire, though it was concealed under the veil of the flesh. There are good reasons, therefore, why he enjoins his disciples to keep silence, till he be risen from the dead.

10. *And his disciples asked him, saying.* No sooner is the resurrection mentioned than the disciples imagine that the reign of Christ is commenced;[2] for they explain this word to mean that the world would acknowledge him to be the Messiah. That they imagined the resurrection to be something totally different from what Christ meant, is evident from what is stated by Mark, that *they disputed with each other what was the meaning of that expression which he had used, To rise from the dead.* Perhaps, too, they were already under the influence of that dream which is now held as an undoubted oracle among the Rabbins, that there would be a first and a second coming of the Messiah; that in the first he

---

[1] " Que c'estoit de Iean Baptiste qu'il leur avoit parlé ;"—" that it was of John the Baptist that he had spoken to them."
[2] " Ils imaginent que c'est l'entree du regne de Christ, et leur semble qu'ils y sont desia ;"—" they imagine that it is the commencement of the kingdom of Christ, and think that they are already in it."

would be mean and despised, but that this would be shortly afterwards followed by his royal dignity. And, indeed, there is some plausibility in that error, for it springs from a true principle. The Scripture, too, speaks of a first and a second coming of the Messiah; for it promises that he will be a Redeemer, to expiate by his sacrifice the sins of the world.[1] And such is the import of the following prophecies: *Rejoice, daughter of Zion, behold, thy King cometh, poor, sitting on an ass,* (Zech. ix. 9.) *We beheld him, and he had no form or beauty, and he resembled a leper, so that we had no esteem for him,* (Isa. liii. 3, 4.) Again, Scripture represents him as victorious over death, and as subjecting all things to his dominion. But we see how the Rabbins corrupt the pure word of God by their inventions; and as every thing was greatly corrupted in the time of our Lord, it is probable that the people had also embraced this foolish notion.

Why do the scribes say that Elijah must come first? The gross mistakes which they committed as to the person of *Elijah* have been pointed out on two or three occasions.[2] Perhaps, too, they cunningly and wickedly endeavoured to lessen the authority of Christ by bringing forward *Elijah;* for as it had been promised that *Elijah* would come as the forerunner of Messiah, *to prepare the way before him,* (Mal. iii. 1; iv. 5,) it was easy to excite a prejudice against Christ, by saying that he came unaccompanied by *Elijah.* By a trick closely resembling this, the devil enchants the Papists of the present day not to expect the day of judgment till Elijah and Enoch have appeared.[3] It may not usually be conjectured that this expedient was purposely resorted to by the scribes, in order to represent Christ as unworthy of confidence, because he wanted the legitimate badge of the Messiah.

[1] "Faisant par son sacrifice satisfaction pour les pechez du monde;"—"making satisfaction by his sacrifice for the sins of the world."

[2] Among other passages in which our Author has treated of the erroneous notions entertained by the Jews respecting *Elijah,* the reader may consult his Commentary on John i. 21, 25.—*Ed.*

[3] "Iusques à ce qu'on voye Elie et Henoch retourner en ce monde;"—"till Elijah and Enoch are seen returning to this world."

11. *Elijah indeed will come first.* We have stated elsewhere the origin of that error which prevailed among the Jews. As John the Baptist was to resemble *Elijah* by restoring the fallen condition of the Church, the prophet Malachi (iv. 5, 6) had even given to him the name of *Elijah;* and this had been rashly interpreted by the scribes, as if *Elijah the Tishbite* (1 Kings xvii. 1) were to return a second time to the world. Christ now declares that every thing which Malachi uttered was true, but that his prediction had been misunderstood and distorted from its true meaning. "The promise," says he, "that *Elijah* would come was true, and has been already fulfilled; but the scribes have already rejected Elijah, whose name they idly and falsely plead in opposing me."

And will restore all things. This does not mean that *John the Baptist restored* them perfectly, but that he conveyed and handed them over to Christ, who would complete the work which he had begun. Now as the scribes had shamefully rejected John, Christ reminds his disciples that the impostures of such men ought not to give them uneasiness, and that it ought not to be reckoned strange, if, after having rejected the servant, they should, with equal disdain, reject his Master. And that no one might be distressed by a proceeding so strange, our Lord mentions that the Scripture contained predictions of both events, that the Redeemer of the world, and Elijah his forerunner, would be rejected by false and wicked teachers.

MATTHEW.	MARK.	LUKE.
XVII. 14. And when they were come to the multitude, a man came to him, kneeling before him, 15. And saying, Lord, have compassion on my son, for	IX. 14. And when he came to the disciples, he saw a great multitude around them, and the scribes disputing with them. 15. And the whole multitude, as soon as they saw him, were astonished, and, running to him, saluted him. 16. And he asked the scribes, What do you dispute among yourselves? 17. And one of the multitude answering said, Master, I have brought to thee my son, who hath a dumb spirit; 18. And wheresoever it seizeth him, it teareth him, and he	IX. 37. And it happened on the following day, while they were going down from the mountain, a great multitude met him. 38. And, lo, a man, who was one of the multitude, cried out, saying, Master, I beseech thee,

MATTHEW.	MARK.	LUKE.
he is lunatic, and is grievously distressed; for frequently he falleth into the fire, and frequently into the water. 16. And I brought him to thy disciples, and they could not cure him. 17. And Jesus answering said, O unbelieving and perverse nation, how long shall I be with you? How long shall I suffer you? Bring him hither to me. 18. And Jesus rebuked the devil, who went out of him; and from that instant the child was cured.	foameth, and gnasheth with his teeth, and languisheth: and I spoke to thy disciples to cast him out, and they could not. 19. And he, answering, saith to him, O unbelieving nation, how long shall I be with you? How long shall I suffer you? Bring him to me. 20. And they brought him to him; and as soon as he saw him, the spirit tore him, and he lay on the ground, and rolled about, foaming. 21. And he asked his father, How long is it since this happened to him? And he said, From a child. 22. And frequently it hath thrown him into the fire, and into the water, to destroy him: but if thou canst do any thing, have compassion on us, and help us. 23. And Jesus said, If thou canst believe it, all things are possible to him that believeth. 24. And immediately the father of the child, exclaiming with tears, said, Lord, I believe; aid thou my unbelief. 25. And when Jesus saw that the multitude were crowding upon him, he rebuked the unclean spirit, saying to him, Dumb and deaf spirit, I command thee, go out of him, and enter no more into him. 26. And when the spirit had cried out, and torn him greatly, he went out of him; and he became like a dead person, so that many said, He is dead. 27. But Jesus stretched out his hand, and raised him; and he stood up.	look to my son: for he is my only son. 39. And, lo, a spirit seizeth him, and teareth him foaming, and bruising him, hardly departeth from him. 40. And I besought thy disciples to cast him out, and they could not. 41. And Jesus answering said, O unbelieving and perverse nation, how long shall I be with you, and suffer you? Bring thy son hither. 42. And while he was still approaching, the devil tore him, and threw him down; and Jesus rebuked the unclean spirit, and cured the child, and restored him to his father. 43. And they were all astonished at the mighty power of God.

As Mark is more full, and explains the circumstances very minutely, we shall follow the order of his narrative. And first he points out clearly the reason why Christ uses a harshness so unusual with him, when he exclaims that the Jews, on account of their perverse malice, do not deserve to be any longer endured. We know how gently he was wont to receive them, even when their requests were excessively importunate.[1] A father here entreats in behalf of an only

---

[1] "Encores mesme qu'ils se monstrassent import uns et facheux en leurs requestes;"—"even though they showed themselves to be importunate and troublesome in their requests."

son, the necessity is extremely urgent, and a modest and humble appeal is made to the compassion of Christ. Why then does he, contrary to his custom, break out suddenly into passion, and declare that they can be endured no longer? As the narrative of Matthew and Luke does not enable us to discover the reason of this great severity, some commentators have fallen into the mistake of supposing that this rebuke was directed either against the disciples, or against the father of the afflicted child. But if we duly consider all the circumstances of the case, as they are related by Mark, there will be no difficulty in arriving at the conclusion, that the indignation of Christ was directed against the malice of the scribes, and that he did not intend to treat the ignorant and weak with such harshness.

During Christ's absence, a *lunatic* child had been brought forward. The scribes, regarding this as a plausible occasion for giving annoyance, seized upon it eagerly, and entreated the disciples that, if they had any power, they would exercise it in curing the child. It is probable that the disciples made an attempt, and that their efforts were unavailing; upon which the scribes raise the shout of victory, and not only ridicule the disciples, but break out against Christ, as if in their person his power had been baffled. It was an extraordinary display of outrageous impiety united with equally base ingratitude, maliciously to keep out of view so many miracles, from which they had learned the amazing power of Christ; for they manifestly endeavoured to extinguish the light which was placed before their eyes. With good reason, therefore, does Christ exclaim that they could no longer be endured, and pronounce them to be *an unbelieving and perverse nation;* for the numerous proofs which they had formerly beheld ought at least to have had the effect of preventing them from seeking occasion of disparagement.[1]

Mark IX. 14. *He saw a great multitude around them.* The disciples were, no doubt, held up to public gaze; as the

---

[1] " Qu'ils n'allassent plus chercher des cavillations et moyens obliques pour luy resister;"—" not to resort any more to cavils and indirect methods of opposing him."

enemies of the truth are wont, on occasions of triumph, to assemble a crowd about a trifle. The scribes had made such a noise about it, as to draw down on the disciples the ridicule of many persons. And yet it appears that there were some who were not ill disposed; for, as soon as they see Jesus, they salute him; and even the insolence of the scribes is restrained by his presence, for, when they are asked what is the matter in dispute, they have not a word to say.

17. *Master, I have brought to thee my son.* Matthew describes a different sort of disease from what is described by Mark, for he says that the man was *lunatic.* But both agree as to these two points, that he was *dumb,* and that at certain intervals he became furious. The term *lunatic* is applied to those who, about the waning of the *moon,* are seized with epilepsy, or afflicted with giddiness. I do not admit the fanciful notion of Chrysostom, that the word *lunatic* was invented by a trick of Satan, in order to throw disgrace on the good creatures of God; for we learn from undoubted experience, that the course of the moon affects the increase or decline of these diseases.[1] And yet this does not prevent Satan from mixing up his attacks with natural means. I am of opinion, therefore, that the man was not naturally *deaf* and *dumb,* but that Satan had taken possession of his tongue and ears; and that, as the weakness of his brain and nerves made him liable to epilepsy, Satan availed himself of this for aggravating the disease. The consequence was, that he was exposed to danger on every hand, and was thrown into violent convulsions, which left him lying on the ground, in a fainting state, and like a dead man.

Let us learn from this how many ways Satan has of injuring us, were it not that he is restrained by the hand of God. Our infirmities both of soul and body, which we feel to be innumerable, are so many darts with which Satan is supplied for wounding us. We are worse than stupid, if a

---

[1] On the opinion expressed by CALVIN, as to the influence of the *moon* on these diseases, the reader may consult *Harmony,* vol. i. p. 245, n. 1.—*Ed.*

condition so wretched does not arouse us to prayer. But in this we see also an amazing display of the goodness of God, that, though we are liable to such a variety of dangers,[1] he surrounds us with his protection; particularly if we consider with what eagerness our enemy is bent on our destruction. We ought also to call to remembrance the consoling truth, that Christ has come to bridle his rage, and that we are safe in the midst of so many dangers, because our diseases are effectually counteracted by heavenly medicine.

We must attend also to the circumstance of the time. The father replies, that his son had been subject to this grievous disease from his *infancy.* If Satan was permitted to exert his power, to such an extent, on a person of that tender age, what reason have not we to fear, who are continually exposing ourselves by our crimes to deadly strokes, who even supply our enemy with darts, and on whom he might justly be permitted to spend his rage, if it were not kept under restraint by the astonishing goodness of God?

Matthew XVII. 17. *O unbelieving and rebellious nation.* Though Christ appears to direct his discourse to the father of the *lunatic,* yet there can be no doubt that he refers to the scribes, as I have lately explained; for it is certain that the reproof is directed, not against ignorant and weak persons, but against those who, through inveterate malice, obstinately resist God. This is the reason why Christ declares that they are no longer worthy to be endured, and threatens that ere long he will separate from them. But nothing worse could happen to them than that Christ should leave them, and it was no light reproach that they rejected so disdainfully the grace of their visitation. We must also observe here, that we ought to treat men in various ways, each according to his natural disposition. For, while our Lord attracts to him the teachable by the utmost mildness, supports the weak, and gently arouses even the sluggish, he does not spare those crooked serpents, on whom he perceives that no remedies can effect a cure.

[1] " Combien que nous soyons subiets à mille dangers et inconveniens ;"—" though we are liable to a thousand dangers and inconveniences."

Mark IX. 20. *And as soon as he saw him.* That the devil should rage with more than ordinary cruelty against the man, when he is brought to Christ, ought not to excite surprise; for in proportion as the grace of Christ is seen to be nearer at hand, and acts more powerfully, the fury of Satan is the more highly excited. The presence of Christ awakens him like the sound of a trumpet. He raises as violent a storm as he can, and contends with all his might. We ought to be prepared beforehand with such meditations, that our faith may not be disturbed, when the approach of the grace of Christ is met by more than ordinary violence on the part of our enemy. Nor ought we to lose sight of another point, that the true commencement of our cure is, when our affliction is so heavy that we are almost at the point of death. It must also be taken into account that, by means of the furious attack of Satan, our Lord lights a torch to cause his grace to be seen; for, when the spectators were appalled at the dreadful spectacle, the display of the power of Christ, which immediately followed, was more distinctly perceived.

21. *From a child.* Hence we infer that this punishment was not inflicted on account of the sins of the individual, but was a secret judgment of God. True indeed, even infants, as soon as they have come out of the womb, are not innocent in the sight of God, or free from guilt; but God's chastisements have sometimes hidden causes, and are intended to try our obedience. We do not render to God the honour which is due to Him, unless with reverence and modesty we adore His justice, when it is concealed from us. Whoever wishes to obtain more full information on this point, may consult my *Commentary* on these words, *Neither hath this man sinned, nor his parents,* (John ix. 3.)

22. *If thou canst do any thing, have compassion on us, and help us.* We see how little honour he renders to Christ; for, supposing him to be some prophet, whose power was limited, he approaches to him with hesitation. On the other hand, the first foundation of faith is, to embrace the boundless power of God; and the first step to prayer is, to raise it

above all opposition by the firm belief that our prayers are not in vain. As this man did not suppose Christ to be at all different from other men, his false opinion is corrected; for our faith must be so formed as to be capable and prepared for receiving the desired favour. In his reply Christ does not administer a direct reproof, but indirectly reminding the man of what he had said amiss, points out to him his fault, and informs him how a remedy may be obtained.

23. *If thou canst believe.* "You ask me," says he, "to aid you as far as I can; but you will find in me an inexhaustible fountain of power, provided that the faith which you bring be sufficiently large." Hence may be learned a useful doctrine, which will apply equally to all of us, that it is not the Lord that prevents his benefits from flowing to us in large abundance, but that it must be attributed to the narrowness of our faith, that it comes to us only in drops, and that frequently we do not feel even a drop, because unbelief shuts up our heart. It is an idle exercise of ingenuity to prove Christ's meaning to be, that a man can believe of himself: for nothing more was intended than to throw back on men the blame of their poverty, whenever they disparage the power of God by their unbelief.

All things are possible to him that believeth. Christ undoubtedly intended to teach that the fulness of all blessings has been given to us by the Father, and that every kind of assistance must be expected from him alone in the same manner as we expect it from the hand of God. "Only exercise," says he, "a firm belief, and you will obtain." In what manner faith obtains any thing for us we shall immediately see.

24. *Lord, I believe.* He declares that he *believes*, and yet acknowledges himself to have *unbelief*. These two statements may appear to contradict each other, but there is none of us that does not experience both of them in himself. As our *faith* is never perfect, it follows that we are partly *unbelievers;* but God forgives us, and exercises such forbearance towards us, as to reckon us believers on account of

a small portion of faith. It is our duty, in the meantime, carefully to shake off the remains of infidelity which adhere to us, to strive against them, and to pray to God to correct them, and, as often as we are engaged in this conflict, to fly to him for aid. If we duly inquire what portion has been bestowed on each, it will evidently appear that there are very few who are eminent in faith, few who have a moderate portion, and very many who have but a small measure.

MATTHEW.	MARK.	LUKE.
XVII. 19. Then the disciples, coming to Jesus apart, said, Why could not we cast it out? 20. And Jesus said to them, On account of your unbelief; for verily I say to you, If you have faith as a grain of mustard-seed, you shall say to this mountain, Remove thou hence, and it shall remove; and nothing shall be impossible to you. 21. But this kind[1] goeth not out but by prayer and fasting.	IX. 28. And when he had entered into the house, his disciples asked him apart, Why could not we cast him out? 29. And he said to them, This kind[2] cannot go out in any other way than by prayer and fasting.	XVII. 5. And the apostles said to the Lord, Increase our faith. 6. And the Lord said, If you had faith as a grain of mustard-seed, you might say to this sycamore tree, Be thou rooted up and planted in the sea; and it would obey you.

Matthew XVII. 19. *Then the disciples coming.* The disciples wonder that the power which they once possessed has been taken from them; but they had lost it by their own fault. Christ therefore attributes this want of ability to their unbelief, and repeats and illustrates more largely the statement which he had previously made, that *nothing is impossible to faith.* It is a hyperbolical mode of expression, no doubt, when he declares that faith *removes trees and mountains;* but the meaning amounts to this, that God will never forsake us, if we keep the door open for receiving his grace. He does not mean that God will give us every thing that we may mention, or that may strike our minds at random. On the contrary, as nothing is more at variance with faith

---

[1] "Mais ceste sorte [de diables] ne sort point;"—"but this kind [of devils] goeth not out."

[2] "Ceste espece [de diables] ne sort point;"—"this kind [ot devils] goeth not out."

than the foolish and irregular desires of our flesh, it follows that those in whom faith reigns do not desire every thing without discrimination, but only that which the Lord promises to give. Let us therefore maintain such moderation as to desire nothing beyond what he has promised to us, and to confine our prayers within that rule which he has laid down.

But it may be objected, that the disciples did not know whether or not the Lord was pleased to cure the *lunatic*. It is easy to reply, that it was their own fault if they did not know; for Christ is now speaking expressly about special *faith*, which had its secret instincts, as the circumstances of the case required. And this is the *faith* of which Paul speaks, (1 Cor. xii. 9.) How then came it that the apostles were deprived of the power of the Spirit, which they had formerly exercised in working miracles, but because they had quenched it by their indolence? But what Christ said about special *faith*, in reference to this particular event, may be extended to the common *faith* of the whole Church.

21. *This kind goeth not out.*[1] By this expression Christ reproved the negligence of certain persons, in order to inform them that it was not an ordinary *faith* which was required; for otherwise they might have replied that they were not altogether destitute of *faith*. The meaning therefore is, that it is not every kind of *faith* that will suffice, when we have to enter into a serious conflict with Satan, but that vigorous efforts are indispensably necessary. For the weakness of *faith* he prescribes *prayer* as a remedy, to which he adds *fasting* by way of an auxiliary. "You are effeminate exorcists," said he, "and seem as if you were engaged in a mock-battle got up for amusement;[2] but you have to deal with a powerful adversary, who will not yield till the battle has been fought out. Your *faith* must therefore be

---

[1] "Cest espece [de diables] ne sort point;"—"this kind [of devils] goeth not out."
[2] "Vous y venez ainsi qu'à un combat de petits enfans, et comme s'il n'estoit question que de s'escarmoucher pour passe-temps."—"You come to it as if it were to a fight of little children, and as if you had nothing to do but to skirmish for amusement."

excited by *prayer*, and as you are slow and languid in *prayer*, you must resort to *fasting* as an assistance."[1] Hence it is very evident how absurdly the Papists represent *fasting* to be the specific method of driving away devils, since our Lord refers to it for no other reason than to stimulate the earnestness of prayer. When he says that *this kind* of devils *cannot be cast out in any other way than by prayer and fasting*, he means that, when Satan has taken deep root in any one, and has been confirmed by long possession, or when he rages with unbridled fury, the victory is difficult and painful, and therefore the contest must be maintained with all our might.

MATTHEW.	MARK.	LUKE.
XVII. 22. And while they remained in Galilee, Jesus said to them, The Son of man will be delivered into the hands of men: 23. And they will kill him, and on the third day he will rise again. And they were deeply grieved. XVIII. 1. At that time the disciples came to Jesus, saying, Who is the greatest in the kingdom of heaven? 2. And Jesus, having called a little child to him, placed him in the midst of them, 3. And said, Verily I say to you, Unless you be converted, and become as little children, you shall not enter into the kingdom of heaven. 4.	IX. 30. And departing thence, they passed through Galilee, and he was desirous that nobody should know it. 31. For he taught his disciples, and said to them, The Son of man is delivered into the hands of men, and they will kill him; and, after being killed, he will rise on the third day. 32. But they knew not what he said, and were afraid to ask him. 33. And he came to Capernaum;[2] and when he was come into the house, he asked them, What were you disputing about among yourselves on the road? 34. But they were silent; for they had disputed among themselves by the way who was the greatest. 35. And when he had sat down, he called the twelve, and said to them, If any man choose to be first, he shall be last of all,[3] and servant of all. 36. And he took a child, and placed him	IX. 43. But while all were wondering at every thing that he did, he said to his disciples, 44. Put these words in your ears; for the Son of man shall be delivered into the hands of men. 45. But they understood not that saying, and it was hidden from them, so that they did not perceive it, and they were afraid to ask him concerning this saying. 46. And a dispute arose among them, which of them was the greatest. 47. But Jesus, seeing the thought of their heart, took a child, and placed him near him, 48. And said to them, Whoso-

---

[1] " Comme une aide pour vous exciter et enflamber;"—" as an assistance to excite and inflame you."

[2] " Apres ces choses il veint en Capernaum;"—" after these things he came to Capernaum."

[3] " Il sera (*ou, qu'il soit*) le dernier de tous;"—" he shall be (*or, let him be*) servant of all."

MATTHEW.	MARK.	LUKE.
Whosoever then shall humble himself like this little child, he is the greatest in the kingdom of heaven. 5. And whosoever shall receive such a little child in my name receiveth me.	in the midst of them; and when he had taken him in his arms, he said to them, 37. Whosoever shall receive one of such children in my name receiveth me; and whosoever receiveth me receiveth not me, but him that sent me.	ever shall receive this child in my name receiveth me; and whosoever shall receive me receiveth him that sent me; for he that is least among you all shall be great.

Matthew XVII. 22. *And while they remained in Galilee.* The nearer that the time of his death approached, the more frequently did Christ warn his disciples, lest that melancholy spectacle might give a violent shock to their faith. It was shortly after the miracle had been performed that this discourse was delivered; for Mark says that he went from that place to Galilee, in order to spend there the intervening time in privacy; for he had resolved to come to Jerusalem on the day of the annual sacrifice, because he was to be sacrificed at the approaching Passover.

The disciples had previously received several intimations on this subject, and yet they are as much alarmed as if nothing relating to it had ever reached their ears. So great is the influence of preconceived opinion, that it brings darkness over the mind in the midst of the clearest light. The apostles had imagined that the state of Christ's kingdom would be prosperous and delightful, and that, as soon as he made himself known, he would be universally received with the highest approbation. They never thought it possible that the priests, and scribes, and other rulers of the Church, would oppose him. Under the influence of this prejudice, they admit nothing that is said on the other side; for Mark says that they *understood not* what our Lord meant. Whence came it that a discourse so clear and distinct was not understood, but because their minds were covered by the thick veil of a foolish imagination?

They did not venture to make any farther inquiry. This must have been owing, in part, to their reverence for their Master; but I have no doubt that their grief and astonishment at what they had heard kept them silent. Such bashfulness was not altogether commendable; for it kept them in doubt, and hesitation, and sinful grief. In the meantime, a confused principle of piety, rather than a clear knowledge of the truth, kept them attached to Christ, and prevented them from leaving his school. A certain commencement of faith and right understanding had been implanted in their hearts, which made their zeal in following Christ not very different from the *implicit faith* of the Papists; but as they had not yet made such progress as to become acquainted with the nature of the kingdom of God and of the renewal which had been promised in Christ, I say that they were guided by zeal for piety rather than by distinct knowledge.

In this way we come to see what there was in them that deserved praise or blame. But though their stupidity could not entirely be excused, we have no reason to wonder that a plain and distinct announcement of the cross of their Master, and of the ignominy to which he would be subjected, appeared to them a riddle; not only because they reckoned it to be inconsistent with the glory of the Son of God that he should be rejected and condemned, but because it appeared to them to be highly improbable that the grace which was promised in a peculiar manner to the Jews should be set at nought by the rulers of the nation. But as the immoderate dread of the cross, which had suddenly seized upon them, shut the door against the consolation which was immediately added, arising out of the hope of the resurrection, let us learn that, when the death of Christ is mentioned, we ought always to take into view at once the whole of the three days, that his death and burial may lead us to a blessed triumph and to a new life.

Matthew XVIII. 1. *At that time the disciples came to Jesus.* It is evident from the other two Evangelists, that the disciples did not come to Christ of their own accord, but that, having secretly *disputed on the road,* they were brought out of their lurking-places, and dragged forth to light. There is nothing inconsistent with this in the account given by Matthew, who hastens to Christ's reply, and does not relate all the circumstances of the case, but passes over the commencement, and relates in a summary manner the reason why Christ rebuked the foolish ambition of his disciples for the highest rank. When Christ makes inquiry about a secret conversation, and forces the disciples to acknowledge what they would willingly have kept back, this teaches us that we ought to beware of all ambition, however carefully it may be concealed. We must also attend to the time at which this occurred. The prediction of his death had made them sad and perplexed; but as if they had received from it unmingled delight, as if they had tasted of the nectar which the poets feign,[1] they immediately enter into a dispute about the highest rank.[2] How was it possible that their distress of mind vanished in a moment, but because the minds of men are so devoted to ambition, that, forgetful of their present state of warfare, they continually rush forward, under the delusive influence of a false imagination, to obtain a triumph? And if the apostles so soon forgot a discourse which they had lately heard, what will become of us if, dismissing for a long period meditation on the cross, we give ourselves up to indifference and sloth, or to idle speculations?

But it is asked, what occasioned the dispute among the disciples? I reply, as the flesh willingly shakes off all uneasiness, they left out of view every thing that had given rise to grief, and fixed on what had been said about the resurrection; and out of this a debate sprung up among idle persons. And as they refuse the first part of the doctrine, for which the flesh has no relish, God permits them to fall into a mistake about the resurrection, and to dream of what would never take place, that, by mere preaching, Christ would obtain a kingdom, an earthly kingdom, and would immediately rise to the highest prosperity and wealth.

There were two faults in this debate. First, the apostles were to blame for laying aside anxiety about the warfare to which they had been called, and for demanding beforehand repose, and wages, and honours, as if they had been soldiers

---

[1] "Comme si tout alloit à souhait et comme si ce qu'on leur a dit estoit aussi doux à avaller que sucre;"—"as if every thing went to their wish, and as if what was said to them were as pleasant to swallow as sugar."
[2] "De la primauté;"—"about the primacy."

that had served their time. The second fault is, that, instead of labouring with one consent, as they ought to have done, to render mutual assistance, and to secure for their brethren as large a share of honours as for themselves, they strove with wicked ambition to excel each other. If we wish that our manner of life should receive the approbation of the Lord, we must learn to bear patiently the burden of the cross that has been laid on us, till the proper time arrive for obtaining the crown, and, as Paul exhorts, *in honour preferring one another*, (Rom. xii. 10.) To the first of these faults is closely allied the vain curiosity of those persons in the present day, who, leaving the proper duties of their calling, eagerly attempt to fly above the clouds. The Lord, who in the Gospel invites us to his kingdom, points out to us the road by which we are to reach it. Fickle persons, who give themselves no concern about faith, patience, calling on God, and other exercises of religion, dispute about what is going on in heaven; as if a man who was about to commence a journey made inquiry where a lodging-place was situated, but did not move a step. Since we are commanded by the Lord to walk on the earth, those who make the condition of departed saints in heaven the subject of eager debate will be found, in so doing, to retard their own progress towards heaven.

2. *And Jesus called a child to him.* The general meaning is, that those who desire to obtain greatness by rising above their brethren, will be so far from gaining their object that they do not even deserve to occupy the lowest corner. He reasons from contraries, because it is humility alone that exalts us. As we are more powerfully affected by appearances presented to the eyes, he holds up to them *a little child* as an emblem of humility. When he enjoins his followers to become *like a child*, this does not extend indiscriminately to all points. We know that in children there are many things faulty; and accordingly Paul bids us be *children*, not *in understanding*, but *in malice*, (1 Cor. xiv. 20;) and in another passage he exhorts us to strive to reach the state of *a perfect man*, (Eph. iv. 13.) But as *children* know nothing about being preferred to each other, or about contending for the

highest rank, Christ desires that their example should banish from the minds of his followers those eager longings after distinction, which wicked men and the children of the world continually indulge, that they may not be allured by any kind of ambition.

It will perhaps be objected, that children, even from the womb, have a native pride, which leads them to desire the highest honour and distinction; but the reply is obvious, that comparisons must not be too closely or too exactly carried out, so as to apply at all points. The tender age of little children is distinguished by simplicity to such an extent, that they are unacquainted with the degrees of honour, and with all the incentives to pride; so that they are properly and justly held out by Christ as an example.

3. *Unless you are converted.* To the example of *little children* must be referred the *conversion* of which he now speaks. Hitherto they had been too much habituated to the ordinary customs of men; and if they would gain their object, they must pursue a totally different course.[1] Every one wished for himself the first or the second rank; but Christ does not allot even the lowest place to any man who does not lose sight of distinctions and *humble himself.* On the contrary, he says,

4. *Whosoever shall humble himself like this little child, he is the greatest in the kingdom of heaven.* This is intended to guard us against supposing that we degrade ourselves in any measure by freely surrendering every kind of distinction. And hence we may obtain a short definition[2] of humility. That man is truly humble who neither claims any personal merit in the sight of God, nor proudly despises brethren, or aims at being thought superior to them, but reckons it enough that he is one of the members of Christ, and desires nothing more than that the Head alone should be exalted.

5. *And he that shall receive such a child.* The term *children*

---

[1] "Il leur est besoin de tourner bride, et de s'accoustumer à tout cela;"—"they must wheel round, and get accustomed to all this."
[2] "La vraye definition;"—"the true definition."

is now applied metaphorically by Christ to those who have laid aside lofty looks, and who conduct themselves with modesty and humility. This is added by way of consolation, that we may not account it troublesome or disagreeable to exercise humility, by means of which Christ not only receives us under his protection, but likewise recommends us to the favour of men. And thus believers are taught in what way they ought to esteem each other: it is by every one *humbling himself.* How is mutual friendship usually maintained among the children of the world but by every man complying with the wishes of another? The more desirous a man is to obtain renown, the more insolently does he grasp at power, that he may be raised to a lofty station, and that others may be ridiculed or despised; but Christ enjoins that the more a man abases himself, the more highly shall he be honoured. Such, too, is the import of the words given by Luke, *he that is least among you shall be great;* for our Lord does not enjoin us to think more highly of those who justly deserve to be despised, but of those who divest themselves of all pride, and are perfectly willing to occupy the lowest place.

MATTHEW.	MARK.	LUKE.
XVIII. 6. But whosoever shall offend one of those little ones who believe in me, it were better for him that a millstone were hanged about his neck, and that he were sunk to the bottom of the sea. 7. Woe to the world on account of offences! for offences must come; but woe to the man by whom the offence cometh! 8. But if thy hand or thy foot offend thee, cut it off, and cast it from thee;[1] for it is better for thee to enter lame or maimed into life, than that, having two hands or two	IX. 42. And whosoever shall offend one of the little ones who believe in me, it were better for him that a millstone were hung around his neck, and that he were thrown into the sea. 43. And if thy hand shall offend thee, cut it off; for it were better for thee to enter lame into life, than that, having two hands, thou shouldst go into hell, into the unquenchable fire:[2] 44. Where their worm dieth not, and their fire is not quenched. 45. And if thy foot shall offend thee, cut it off; for it were better for thee to enter lame	XVII. 1. And he said to his disciples, It is impossible but that offences will come; but woe to him by whom they come! 2. It were better for him that a millstone were hung around his neck, and that he were

[1] "Et le iette [arriere] de toy;"—"and cast it behind thee."
[2] "Au feu qui ne s'esteint point;"—"into the fire which is not quenched."

MATTHEW.	MARK.	LUKE.
feet, thou shouldst be cast into the everlasting fire. 9. And if thine eye offend thee, pluck it out, and cast it from thee;[1] for it is better that thou shouldst enter into life having one eye, than that, having two eyes, thou shouldst be cast into hell-fire. 10. Beware of despising one of these little ones; for I say to you, That their angels always behold the face of my Father who is in heaven.	into life, than that, having two feet, thou shouldst be cast into hell, into the unquenchable fire: 46. Where their worm dieth not, and their fire is not quenched. 47. And if thine eye offend thee, pluck it out; for it were better for thee to enter with one eye into the kingdom of God, than that, having two eyes, thou shouldst be cast into hell-fire: 48. Where their worm dieth not, and their fire is not quenched.	thrown into the sea, than that he should offend one of these little ones.

Matthew XVIII. 6. *But whosoever shall offend one of those little ones.* This appears to be added for the consolation of the godly, that they may not be rendered uneasy by their condition, if they are despised by the world. It is a powerful obstruction to the voluntary exercise of modesty, when they imagine, that by so doing they expose themselves to contempt; and it is hard to be not only treated disdainfully, but almost trodden under foot, by haughty men. Christ therefore encourages his disciples by the consoling truth, that, if their mean condition draws upon them the insults of the world, God does not despise them.

But he appears to have had likewise another object in view; for a dispute had arisen amongst them as to the first place of honour, from which it might naturally have been inferred that the Apostles were tainted with sinful ambition. Every man who thinks too highly of himself, or desires to be preferred to others, must necessarily treat his brethren with disdain. To cure this disease, Christ threatens a dreadful punishment, if any man in his pride shall throw down those who are oppressed with poverty, or who in heart are already humbled.

Under the word *offend* he includes more than if he had forbidden them to *despise* their brethren; though the man who gives himself no concern about *offending* the weak, does

---

[1] "Et le iette [arriere] de toy;"—"and cast it behind thee."

so for no other reason, than because he does not render to them the honour to which they are entitled. Now as there are various kinds of *offences*, it will be proper to explain generally what is meant by *offending*. If any man through our fault either stumbles, or is drawn aside from the right course, or retarded in it, we are said to *offend* him.[1] Whoever then desires to escape that fearful punishment which Christ denounces, let him stretch out his hand to the *little ones* who are despised by the world, and let him kindly assist them in keeping the path of duty; for Christ recommends them to our notice, that they may lead us to exercise voluntary humility; as Paul enjoins the children of God to *condescend to men of low estate*, (Rom. xii. 16,) and again says that *we ought not to please ourselves*, (Rom. xv. 1.) To *hang a millstone about* a man's *neck, and drown him in the sea*, was the punishment then reckoned the most appalling, and which was inflicted on the most atrocious malefactors. When our Lord alludes to this punishment, we are enabled to perceive how dear and precious those persons are in the sight of God, who are mean and despised in the eyes of the world.

7. *Woe to the world on account of offences!* This passage may be explained in two ways. It may be taken *actively*, as meaning that Christ pronounces a curse on the authors of *offences;* and then by the term *world*, we must understand all unbelievers. Or it may be taken *passively*, as meaning that Christ deplores the evils which he perceives to be rapidly coming on *the world on account of offences;* as if he had said, that no plague will be more destructive, or attended by more fearful calamities, than the alarm or desertion of many *on account of offences.* The latter meaning is more appropriate; for I have no doubt that our Lord, who had spoken on another occasion about offences, proceeded to discourse more largely on this subject; in order to make his disciples more attentive and watchful in guarding against them. That Satan may not gain advantage over us through our sluggishness, our Lord breaks out into an exclamation, that there is

[1] "L'Escriture dit que nous offensons ou scandalizons cestuy là."—"Scripture says that we give *offence* or *scandal* to that man."

nothing which we ought to dread more than *offences;* for as Satan has innumerable kinds of them in his hand, he constantly, and at almost every step, throws new difficulties in our way; while we, through excessive tenderness or sloth, are too ready to yield. The consequence is, that there are few who make tolerable progress in the faith of Christ; and of the few who have begun to walk in the way of salvation, there is scarcely one in ten who has the courage to persevere till he reaches the goal.[1] Now since Christ intended to strike his disciples with terror *on account of offences,* and thus to arouse them to exertion, *woe* to our indifference, if each of us does not earnestly apply himself to overcome those *offences.*

For offences must come. To awaken more powerfully their care and anxiety, our Lord reminds his disciples that there is no possibility of walking but in the midst of various *offences;* as much as to say, that this is an evil which cannot be avoided. Thus he confirms the former statement; for Christ shows us how great are the inconveniences which arise from *offences,* since the Church never will be, and indeed never can be, free from this evil. But he does not state the reason of this necessity, as Paul does, when, speaking of heresies, he says that they arise, *that the good may be made manifest,* (1 Cor. xi. 19.) It must be held by us as a fixed principle, that it is the will of God to leave his people exposed to *offences,* in order to exercise their faith, and to separate believers, as the refuse and the chaff, from the pure wheat. Does any one object or complain, that blame attaches to our Lord for giving loose reins to Satan, to accomplish the destruction of wretched men? It is our duty to think and speak with the deepest reverence of the secret purposes of God, of which this is one, that *the world* must be disturbed by *offences.*

But woe to the man by whom the offence cometh. After having exhorted his disciples to beware of *offences,* he again breaks out against those who occasion them. To impart the greater vehemence to the threatening, he adds, that neither a

---

[1] " Qui persevere courageusement iusqu'à la fin ;"—" who perseveres courageously to the end."

right eye nor a *right hand* ought to be spared, if they occasion *offence* to us; for I explain these words as added for the purpose of amplification. Their meaning is, that we ought to be so constant and so zealous in opposing *offences*, that we would rather choose to *pluck out our eyes, or cut off our hands,* than give encouragement to *offences;* for if any man hesitate to incur the loss of his limbs, he spares them at the risk of throwing himself into eternal perdition. What dreadful vengeance then awaits those who by *offences* shall bring ruin on their brethren![1] As those two verses have been already explained[2] under Matthew v. 29, 30, it was sufficient, on the present occasion, to glance at the reason why Christ repeats here the same statement.

10. *Beware of despising one of these little ones.* As pride is the mother of disdain, and as contempt hardens men in giving *offence,* our Lord, for the purpose of applying an appropriate remedy for curing this disease, forbids his disciples to *despise the little ones.* And certainly, as we have already hinted, no man who has a proper care for his brethren will ever allow himself, on light grounds, to give them *offence.* This conclusion of our Lord's discourse has the same tendency as the commencement of it, to remind us that we ought to strive with each other who shall be most submissive and modest; for God embraces with wonderful love the *little ones.* It would be strange indeed that a mortal man should *despise,* or treat as of no account, those whom God holds in such high esteem. He proves this love from the fact, that angels, who are ministers of their salvation, enjoy intimately the presence of God. Yet I do not think that he intended merely to show what honour God confers on them by appointing *angels* to be their guardians, but likewise to threaten those who *despise* them; as if he had said, that it is no light matter to *despise* those who have *angels* for their companions and friends, to take vengeance in their behalf. We ought therefore to *be-*

---

[1] "Lesquels par scandales auront donné occasion de faire perdre et damner leurs freres;"—"who by offences shall have given occasion to bring ruin and damnation on their brethren."
[2] Harmony, vol. i. p. 291.

ware of despising their salvation, which even angels have been commissioned to advance.

The interpretation given to this passage by some commentators, as if God assigned to each believer his own *angel*, does not rest on solid grounds. For the words of Christ do not mean that a single *angel* is continually occupied with this or the other person;[1] and such an idea is inconsistent with the whole doctrine of Scripture, which declares that *the angels encamp around* (Ps. xxxiv. 7) the godly, and that not one *angel* only, but many, have been commissioned to guard every one of the faithful. Away, then, with the fanciful notion of a good and evil angel, and let us rest satisfied with holding that the care of the whole Church is committed to *angels*, to assist each member as his necessities shall require. It will perhaps be asked, Do the angels occupy a station inferior to ours, because they have been appointed to be our ministers? I reply, Though by nature they take rank above us, this does not prevent them from rendering service to God[2] in dispensing the favour which he freely bestows upon us. For this reason they are called *our angels*, because their labours are bestowed on us.

MATTHEW.	LUKE.
XVIII. 11. For the Son of man is come to save that which was lost. 12. What think you? If a man shall have a hundred sheep, and one of them shall go astray, doth he not leave the ninety-nine, and go to the mountains, and seek that which had gone astray? 13. And if he happen to find it, verily, I say to you,	XV. 1. And all the publicans and sinners drew near to him to hear him. 2. And the Pharisees and scribes murmured, saying, This man receiveth sinners, and eateth with them. 3. And he spoke to them a parable, saying, 4. What man is there among you, who hath a hundred sheep, and, if he shall lose one of them, doth not leave the ninety-nine in the wilderness, and go after that which was lost, till he find it? 5. And when he hath found it, he layeth it on his shoulders, rejoicing: 6. And coming home, he calleth his friends and neighbours, saying to them, Rejoice with me; for I have found the sheep which was lost. 7. I say to you, that in like manner there will be greater joy in heaven over one repenting sinner, than over

[1] " Les mots n'emportent pas qu'un Ange n'ait autre charge que de veiller tousiours sur cestuy-ci ou sur cestuy-là;"—" the words do not bear that one Angel has nothing else to do than to watch continually over this or that man."

[2] " Cela n'empesche point que Dieu n'use de leur service;"—" that does not hinder God from employing their services."

MATTHEW.	LUKE.
he rejoiceth more on account of that sheep than on account of the ninety-nine which had not gone astray. 14. So it is not the will of your Father who is in heaven, that one of those little ones should perish.	ninety-nine righteous persons who do not need repentance. 8. Or what woman having ten pieces of money,[1] if she shall lose one piece, doth not light a candle, and sweep the house, and seek diligently till she find it? 9. And when she hath found it, she calleth together her friends and neighbours, saying, Rejoice with me, for I have found the piece which I had lost. 10. In like manner, I tell you, there will be joy in the presence of the angels of God over one repenting sinner.

Matthew XVIII. 11. *For the Son of man cometh.* Christ now employs his own example in persuading his disciples to honour even weak and despised brethren; for he came down from heaven to save not them only, but even the dead who were *lost*. It is in the highest degree unreasonable that we should disdainfully reject those whom the Son of God has so highly esteemed. And even if the weak labour under imperfections which may expose them to contempt, our pride is not on that account to be excused; for we ought to esteem them not for the value of their virtues, but for the sake of Christ; and he who will not conform himself to Christ's example is too saucy and proud.

12. *What think you?* Luke carries the occasion of this parable still farther back, as having arisen from the *murmurings* of the *Pharisees and scribes* against our Lord, whom they saw conversing daily with sinners. Christ therefore intended to show that a good teacher ought not to labour less to recover those that are *lost*, than to preserve those which are in his possession; though according to Matthew the comparison proceeds farther, and teaches us not only that we ought to treat with kindness the disciples of Christ, but that we ought to bear with their imperfections, and endeavour, when they wander, to bring them back to the road. For, though they happen sometimes to wander, yet as they are *sheep* over which God has appointed his Son to be shepherd, so far are we from having a right to chase or drive

---

[1] "Dix drachmes;"—"ten drachmas."

them away roughly, that we ought to gather them from their wanderings; for the object of the discourse is to lead us to beware of *losing* what God wishes to be *saved*. The narrative of Luke presents to us a somewhat different object. It is, that the whole human race belongs to God, and that therefore we ought to gather those that have gone astray, and that we ought to rejoice as much, when they that are *lost* return to the path of duty, as a man would do who, beyond his expectation, recovered something the loss of which had grieved him.

Luke XV. 10. *There will be joy in the presence of the angels.* If *angels* mutually rejoice with each other in heaven, when they see that what had wandered is restored to the fold, we too, who have the same cause in common with them, ought to be partakers of the same *joy*. But how does he say that the *repentance* of one ungodly man yields greater joy than the perseverance of many *righteous* men to *angels*, whose highest delight is in a continued and uninterrupted course of righteousness? I reply, though it would be more agreeable to the wishes of *angels* (as it is also more desirable) that men should always remain in perfect integrity, yet as in the deliverance of a sinner, who had been already devoted to destruction, and had been cut off as a rotten member from the body, the mercy of God shines more brightly, he attributes to *angels*, after the manner of men, a *greater joy* arising out of an unexpected good.

Over one repenting sinner. The word *repentance* is specially limited to the conversion of those who, having altogether turned aside from God, rise as it were from death to life; for otherwise the exercise of repentance ought to be uninterrupted throughout our whole life,[1] and no man is exempted from this necessity, since every one is reminded by his imperfections that he ought to aim at daily progress. But it is one thing, when a man, who has already entered upon the right course, though he stumble, or fall, or even go astray, endeavours to reach the goal; and another thing, when a man

[1] "Tant que nous sommes en ce monde;"—"as long as we are in this world."

leaves a road which was entirely wrong, or only starts in the right course.[1] Those who have already begun to regulate their life by the standard of the divine law, do not need that kind of *repentance* which consists in beginning to lead a holy and pious life, though they must groan[2] under the infirmities of the flesh, and labour to correct them.

Luke.

XV. 11. And he said,[3] A certain man had two sons: 12. And the younger of them said to his father, Father, give me the portion of property which falls to me. And he divided between them the property. 13. And not many days afterwards,[4] the younger son, having gathered all together, set out on a journey to a distant country, and there wasted his property by living extravagantly. 14. But when he had spent all, a sore famine arose in that country; and he began to be in want. 15. And he went and entered into the service of one of the inhabitants of that country; and he sent him into his field to feed swine. 16. And he was desirous to fill his belly with the husks on which the swine were feeding: and no man gave to him.[5] 17. And when he came to himself, he said, How many hirelings of my father have abundance of bread,[6] while I perish with hunger! 18. I will arise, and go to my father,[7] and will say to him, Father, I have sinned against heaven, and before thee, 19. And am no longer worthy to be called thy son: make me as one of thy hirelings. 20. And he arose, and came to his father. And while he was yet afar off, his father saw him, and was moved with compassion, and ran, and fell on his neck, and kissed him. 21. And the son said to him, Father, I have sinned against heaven, and before thee, and am no longer worthy to be called thy son. 22. And the father said to his servants, Bring out the best robe, and put it on him; and put a ring on his hand, and shoes on his feet: 23. And bring the fatted calf, and kill it; and let us feast, and be merry: 24. For this my son was dead, and is alive again; he was lost, and is found.[8] And they began to be merry.

---

[1] "Quand celuy qui estoit du tout esgaré tourne bride pour commencer à bien faire;"—"when he who had altogether gone astray turns round to begin to do well."

[2] "Combien qu'il soit tousiours necessaire de gemir;"—"though it be necessary for them always to groan."

[3] "Il dit aussi;"—"he said also."

[4] "Et peu de iours apres;"—"and a few days after."

[5] "Et (*ou, mais*) personne ne luy donnoit;"—"and (*or, but*) nobody gave to him."

[6] "Combien y-a-il de mercenaires en la maison de mon pere, qui ont force pain;"—"how many hirelings are there in my father's house, who have plenty of bread."

[7] "Ie partiray d'icy, et m'en iray à mon pere;"—"I will depart hence, and will go away to my father."

[8] "Car mon fils que voyci estoit mort, et il est retourné a vie: il estoit perdu, mais il est retrouvé;"—"for this is my son who was dead, and he is returned to life; he was lost, but he is found again."

This parable is nothing else than a confirmation of the preceding doctrine.[1] In the first part is shown how readily God is disposed to pardon our sins, and in the second part (which we shall afterwards treat in the proper place) is shown the great malignity and obstinacy of those who murmur at his compassion. In the person of a young prodigal who, after having been reduced to the deepest poverty by luxury and extravagance, returns as a suppliant to his father,[2] to whom he had been disobedient and rebellious, Christ describes all sinners who, wearied of their folly, apply to the grace of God. To the kind father,[3] on the other hand, who not only pardons the crimes of his son, but of his own accord meets him when returning, he compares God, who is not satisfied with pardoning those who pray to him, but even advances to meet them with the compassion of a father.[4] Let us now examine the parable in detail.

Luke XV. 12. *And the younger of them said to his father.* The parable opens by describing a mark of wicked arrogance in the youth, which appears in his being desirous to leave his father, and in thinking that he cannot be right without being permitted to indulge in debauchery, free from his father's control. There is also ingratitude in leaving the old man,[5] and not only withholding the performance of the duties which he owed to him, but crippling and diminishing the wealth of his house.[6] This is at length followed by wasteful luxury and wicked extravagance, by which he squanders all

---

[1] " De la doctrine que nous venons de voir ;"—" of the doctrine which we have just now seen."
[2] " Retourne pour demander pardon à son pere ;"—" returns to ask pardon from his father."
[3] " Aussi en la personne de ce bon pere il nous propose l'affection de Dieu ;"—" also in the person of this good father he holds out to us the affection of God."
[4] " Mais les previent par sa bonté et misericorde paternelle ;"—" but anticipates them by his fatherly goodness and compassion."
[5] " Delaissant le bon vieil homme de pere ;"—" leaving the good old man his father."
[6] " Mais aussi diminue le bien de la maison, et en emporte une bonne partie ;"—" but also diminishes the wealth of the house, and carries off a good part of it."

that he had.¹ After so many offences he deserved to find his father implacable.²

Under this image our Lord unquestionably depicts to us the boundless goodness and inestimable forbearance of God, that no crimes, however aggravated, may deter us from the hope of obtaining pardon. There would be some foundation for the analogy, if we were to say that this foolish and insolent youth resembles those persons who, enjoying at the hand of God a great abundance of good things, are moved by a blind and mad ambition to be separated from Him, that they may enjoy perfect freedom; as if it were not more desirable than all the kingdoms of the world to live under the fatherly care and government of God. But as I am afraid that this allusion may be thought overstrained, I shall satisfy myself with the literal meaning; not that I disapprove of the opinion, that under this figure is reproved the madness of those who imagine that it will be advantageous for them to have something of their own, and to be rich apart from the heavenly Father; but that I now confine myself within the limits of a Commentator.³

Christ here describes what usually happens with young men, when they are carried away by their natural disposition. Destitute of sound judgment, and maddened by passion, they are ill fitted for governing themselves, and are not restrained by fear or shame. It is therefore impossible but that they shall abandon themselves to every thing to which their sinful inclination prompts them, and rush on in a disgraceful course, till they are involved in shameful poverty. He afterwards describes the punishment which, in the righteous judgment of God, generally overtakes spendthrifts and prodigals. After having wickedly squandered their means, they are left to pine in hunger, and not

---

[1] "Tout ce qu'il avoit eu du pere;"—"all that he had got from his father."

[2] "Il avoit bien merité de trouver puis apres un pere rigoreux, et qui teint son cœur contre luy iusqu'au bout;"—"he had well deserved to find afterwards a father who was severe, and who kept his heart shut against him to the end."

[3] "Pource que ie me tien maintenant dans mes limites, et ne veux point passer l'office d'expositeur;"—"because I now keep myself within my limits, and do not wish to go beyond the duty of an expositor."

having known how to use in moderation an abundant supply of the best bread, they are reduced to eat acorns and *husks.* In short, they become the companions of *swine,* and are made to feel that they are unworthy to partake of human food; for it is swinish gluttony[1] to squander wickedly what was given for the support of life.[2] As to the ingenious exposition which some have brought forward, that it is the just punishment of wicked scorn, when those who have rejected delicious bread in the house of our heavenly Father are driven by hunger to eat *husks,* it is a true and useful doctrine; but in the meantime, we must bear in mind the difference that exists between allegories and the natural meaning.[3]

16. *And was desirous to fill his belly.* This means that, in consequence of hunger, he no longer thought of his former luxuries, but greedily devoured *husks;* for of that kind of food he could not be in want, when he was giving it to the *swine.* There is a well-known saying of Cyrus who, having for a long time suffered hunger during a flight, and having been slightly refreshed by eating coarse black bread, declared that he had never tasted savoury bread till now; so the young man who is here mentioned was compelled by necessity to betake himself with appetite to *husks.* The reason is added, BECAUSE *no man gave to him;* for the copulative conjunction *and* (καὶ) must, in my opinion, signify *because,*[4] and what is here said does not refer to *husks,* which he had at hand, but I understand the meaning to be, that no man pitied his poverty; for prodigals who throw away the whole of their property are persons whom no man thinks himself bound to relieve,—nay more, as they have been accustomed

---

[1] " C'est une gourmandise plustost convenable à des porceaux qu'à des hommes ;"—" it is a gluttony more suitable to swine than to men."
[2] " Pour subvenir aux necessitez de ceste vie ;"—" to supply the necessities of this life."
[3] " Mais cependant il faut tousiours aviser quelle difference il y a entre les allegories et le vray sens naturel d'un passage ;"—" but yet we must always consider what difference there is between allegories and the true natural meaning of a passage."
[4] " Car selon mon avis ce mot ET se doit resoudre en Car, ou Pource que ;"—" for in my opinion this word AND must mean *For,* or *Because.*"

to squander every thing, men think that nothing ought to be given to them.[1]

17. *And when he came to himself.* Here is described to us the way in which God invites men to repentance. If of their own accord they were wise, and became submissive, he would draw them more gently; but as they never stoop to obedience, till they have been subdued by the rod, he chastises them severely. Accordingly, to this young man, whom abundance[2] rendered fierce and rebellious, hunger proved to be the best teacher. Instructed by this example, let us not imagine that God deals cruelly with us, if at any time he visits us with heavy afflictions; for in this manner those who were obstinate and intoxicated with mirth are taught by him to be obedient. In short, all the miseries which we endure are a profitable invitation to repentance.[3] But as we are slow, we scarcely ever regain *a sound mind,* unless when we are forced by extreme distress; for until we are pressed by difficulties on every hand, and shut up to despair, the flesh always indulges in gaiety, or at least recoils. Hence we infer, that there is no reason to wonder, if the Lord often uses violent and even repeated strokes, in order to subdue our obstinacy, and, as the proverb runs, applies hard wedges to hard knots. It must also be observed, that the hope of bettering his condition, if he returned to his father, gave this young man courage to repent; for no severity of punishment will soften our depravity, or make us displeased with our sins, till we perceive some advantage. As this young man, therefore, is induced by confidence in his father's kindness to seek reconciliation, so the beginning of our repentance must be an acknowledgment of the mercy of God to excite in us favourable hopes.

---

[1] "Il semble que ce qu'on leur donne soit autant de perdu;"—"what is given to them appears to be as good as thrown away."

[2] "L'aise et la trop grande abondance;"—"ease and too great abundance."

[3] "Ce sont autant d'avertissemens proufitables, par lequel Dieu nous convie à repentance;"—"they are so many profitable warnings, by which God invites us to repentance."

20. *And while he was still afar off.* This is the main point of the parable. If men, who are by nature prone to revenge, and too tenacious of their own rights, are moved by fatherly love kindly to forgive their children, and freely to bring them back, when they are sunk in wretchedness, God, whose boundless goodness exceeds all the affection of parents,[1] will not treat us more harshly.[2] And certainly nothing is here attributed to an earthly father which God does not promise with respect to himself. *Before they call,* says he, *I will answer,* (Isa. lxv. 24.) That passage too of David is well known, *I said, I will acknowledge against me my unrighteousness to the Lord, and thou forgavest the iniquity of my sin,* (Ps. xxxii. 5.) As this father, therefore, is not merely pacified by the entreaties of his son, but meets him when he is coming, and before he has heard a word, embraces him, filthy and ugly as he is, so God does not wait for a long prayer, but of his own free will meets the sinner as soon as he proposes to confess his fault.

It is wretched sophistry to infer from this, that the grace of God is not exhibited to sinners until they anticipate it by their repentance. "Here," say they, "is held out to us a father ready to pardon, but it is after that his son has begun to return to him; and therefore God does not look, and does not bestow his grace, on any but those who begin to seek him." It is, no doubt, true that, in order to his obtaining pardon, the sinner is required to have grief of conscience, and to be dissatisfied with himself; but it is wrong to infer from this, that repentance, which is the gift of God, is yielded by men from their own movement of their heart. And in this respect it would be improper to compare a mortal man to God; for it is not in the power of an earthly father to renew the stubborn heart of his son, as God changes hearts of stone into hearts of flesh. In short, the question here is not, whether a man is converted by himself,

---

[1] "L'amour de tous les peres de ce monde;"—"the love of all the fathers in the world."
[2] "Sera bien pour le moins aussi debonnaire envers nous;"—"will be at least as gentle towards us."

and returns to him; but only under the figure of a man is commended the fatherly gentleness of God, and his readiness to grant forgiveness.

21. *Father, I have sinned against heaven.* Here is pointed out another branch of repentance, namely, such a conviction of sin as is accompanied by grief and shame. For he who is not grieved for having sinned, and whose offence is not placed before his eyes, will sooner attempt any thing than think of returning to the path of duty. Displeasure with sin must therefore go before repentance. And there is great emphasis in this expression, that the young man is said to have *come to* himself, as one whom the wanderings of wild desires had hurried away into forgetfulness of himself. And certainly so far astray are the impulses of the flesh, that any one who gives himself up to them may be said to have *gone out of himself*, and to have lost his senses. For this reason transgressors are commanded to *return to the heart*,[1] (Isa. xlvi. 8.) Next follows a confession,[2] not such a one as the Pope has contrived, but one by which the son appeases his offended *father;* for this humility is absolutely necessary in order to obtain forgiveness of sins. This mode of expression, *I have sinned against heaven, and before thee*, is of the same import as if he had said, that God was offended in the person of an earthly father. And certainly this is the dictate of nature, that every one who rebels against a *father* rises wickedly also against God, who has placed children in subjection to parents.

22. *Bring out the best robe.* Although in parables (as we have frequently observed) it would be idle to follow out every minute circumstance, yet it will be no violence to the literal meaning, if we say, that our heavenly Father not only pardons our sins in such a manner as to bury the remem-

---

[1] "A ceste cause en l'Escriture Dieu commande aux transgresseurs de retourner à leur cœur;"—"For this reason, in Scripture God commands transgressors to return to their heart." In the authorized version the passage runs thus: *Bring it again to mind, O ye transgressors.—Ed.*

[2] "Apres la cognoissance du peché s'ensuit aussi la confession;"—"after the knowledge of sin there follows also confession."

brance of them, but even restores those gifts of which we had been deprived; as, on the other hand, by taking them from us, he chastises our ingratitude in order to make us feel ashamed at the reproach and disgrace of our nakedness.

LUKE.

XV. 25. Now his elder son was in the field; and when he came and drew near to the house, he heard music and dancing. 26. And he called one of his servants, and asked what those things were.[1] 27. And he said to him, Thy brother is come; and thy father hath killed the fatted calf, because he hath received him safe and sound.[2] 28. And he was angry, and would not go in: therefore his father went out, and entreated him. 29. But he answering said to his father, Behold, during so many years I serve thee, and never have I transgressed thy commandment; and thou never gavest me a kid, that I might be merry with my friends: 30. But after that this thy son, who hath devoured thy property with harlots, is come, thou hast killed for him the fatted calf. 31. But he said to him, Son,[3] thou art always with me, and all my property is thine. 32. But it was proper that we should be merry and rejoice; because this thy brother was dead, and is alive again; he was lost, and is found.

This latter portion of the parable charges those persons with cruelty, who would wickedly choose to set limits to the grace of God, as if they envied the salvation of wretched sinners. For we know that this is pointed at the haughtiness of the scribes,[4] who did not think that they received the reward due to their merits, if Christ admitted publicans and the common people to the hope of the eternal inheritance. The substance of it therefore is, that, if we are desirous to be reckoned the children of God, we must forgive in a brotherly manner the faults of brethren, which He forgives with fatherly kindness.

25. *And his elder son was in the field.* Those who think that, under the figure of *the first-born son*, the Jewish nation is described, have indeed some argument on their side; but I

---

[1] " Et l'interroga que c'estoit;"—" and asked him what it was."

[2] The two adjectives, *safe and sound,* which occur in the authorized version, are here retained as the translation of " *incolumem,*" which conveys both ideas; and this is fully justified by our author's vernacular, " *pourtant qu'il l'a recouvré* SAIN ET SAUF ;"—" *because he hath received him back* SOUND AND SAFE."—*Ed.*

[3] " Mon enfant ;"—" my child."

[4] " L'orgueil et la presomption des Scribes ;"—" the pride and presumption of the Scribes."

do not think that they attend sufficiently to the whole of the passage. For the discourse was occasioned by *the murmuring of the scribes,* who took offence at the kindness of Christ towards wretched persons who had led a wicked life. He therefore compares the scribes, who were swelled with presumption, to good and modest men, who had always lived with decency and sobriety, and had honourably supported their family; nay, even to obedient children, who throughout their whole life had patiently submitted to their father's control. And though they were utterly unworthy of this commendation, yet Christ, speaking according to their belief, attributes to them, by way of concession, their pretended holiness, as if it had been virtue; as if he had said, Though I were to grant to you what you falsely boast of, that you have always been obedient children to God, still you ought not so haughtily and cruelly to reject your brethren, when they repent of their wicked life.

28. *Therefore his father went out.* By these words he reproaches hypocrites with intolerable pride, which makes it necessary that the Father should entreat them not to envy the compassion manifested to their brethren. Now though God does not entreat, yet by his example he exhorts us to bear with the faults of our brethren. And in order to take away every excuse from wicked severity, he not only introduces hypocrites as speaking, whose false boasting might be confuted, but even affirms that, though any man had discharged, in the most perfect manner, all the duties of piety towards the Father, yet he has no just reason to complain because his brother obtains pardon. It is certain, indeed, that the sincere worshippers of God are always pure and free from this malignant disposition; but the design of Christ is, to show that it would be unjust in any man to murmur on account of his brother having been received into favour, even though he were not inferior in holiness to the angels.

31. *Son,*[1] *thou art always with me.* This answer consists of two parts. The first is, that the *first-born son* has no reason

---

[1] "Mon enfant;"—"my child."

to be angry, when he sees his brother kindly received without any loss to himself;[1] and the second is, that, without paying any regard to his brother's safety, he is grieved on account of the rejoicing occasioned by his return. *All my property,* says he, *is thine :* that is, " Though thou hast hitherto carried nothing away out of my house, it has been no loss to thee, for all is reserved for thee undiminished."[2] Besides, why art thou offended at our joy, in which thou oughtest to have shared? for it was proper that thy brother, who we thought had been lost, should now be congratulated on his safety and return. Those two reasons deserve our attention; for, on the one hand, it is no loss to us,[3] if God graciously receives into favour those who had been at variance with him on account of their sins; and, on the other hand, it is wicked hardness of heart not to rejoice, when we see our brethren returned from death to life.[4]

MATTHEW.

XVIII. 15. But if thy brother hath sinned against thee, go and reprove him between thee and him alone : if he shall hear thee, thou hast gained thy brother. 16. But if he shall not hear thee, take with thee one or two more, that in the mouth of two or three witnesses every word may be confirmed : and if he shall not hear them, tell the church. 17. And if he shall not hear the church, let him be to thee as a heathen and a publican. 18. Verily, I say to thee, What things soever you shall bind on earth[5] shall be bound also in heaven; and what things soever you shall loose on earth shall be loosed also in heaven. 19. Again, I say to you, That if two of you shall agree on earth as to every thing which they shall ask,[6] it will be done to them by my Father who is in heaven. 20. For where two or three are assembled[7] in my name, there am I in the midst of them.

LUKE.

XVII. 3. Be on your guard. If thy brother shall sin against thee, reprove him; and if he shall repent, forgive him.

---

[1] " Veu qu'il n'y perd rien ;"—" since he loses nothing by it."

[2] " Ta condition n'en est pas pire ; car ie te garde tousiours ton droict entier ;"—" thy condition is not the worse for it; for I always preserve thy rights entire."

[3] " Nous n'y perdons rien ;"—" we lose nothing by it."

[4] " Voyans nos freres estre tirez de la mort, et ramenez au chemin de vie ;"—" perceiving our brethren to be drawn from death, and led into the way of life."

[5] " Toutes choses que vous lierez sur la terre ;"—" all things which you shall bind on earth."

[6] " De toutes choses qu'ils demanderont ;"—" of all things which they shall ask."

[7] " Ou il y en a deux ou trois assemblez ;"—" where there are two or three of them assembled."

Matthew XVIII. 15. *But if thy brother shall sin against thee.* As he had discoursed about bearing the infirmities of brethren, he now shows more clearly in what manner, and for what purpose, and to what extent, we ought to bear with them. For otherwise it would have been easy to reply, that there is no other way of avoiding offences, than by every man winking at the faults of others, and thus what is evil would be encouraged by forbearance. Christ therefore prescribes a middle course, which does not give too great offence to the weak, and yet is adapted to cure their diseases; for that severity which is employed as a medicine is profitable and worthy of praise. In short, Christ enjoins his disciples to forgive one another, but to do so in such a manner as to endeavour to correct their faults. It is necessary that this be wisely observed; for nothing is more difficult than to exercise forbearance towards men, and, at the same time, not to neglect the freedom necessary in reproving them.[1] Almost all lean to the one side or to the other, either to deceive themselves mutually by deadly flatteries, or to pursue with excessive bitterness those whom they ought to cure. But Christ recommends to his disciples a mutual love, which is widely distant from flattery; only he enjoins them to season their admonitions with moderation, lest, by excessive severity and harshness, they discourage the weak.

Now he distinctly lays down three steps of brotherly correction. The first is, to give a private advice to the person who has offended. The second is, if he shall give any sign of obstinacy, to advise him again in presence of *witnesses.* The third is, if no advantage shall be obtained in that way, to deliver him up to the public decision of *the Church.* The design of this, as I have said, is, to hinder charity from being violated under the pretence of fervent zeal. As the greater part of men are driven by ambition to publish with excessive eagerness the faults of their brethren, Christ seasonably meets this fault by enjoining us to cover the faults of brethren, as far as lies in our power; for those who take

---

[1] " Que toutesfois on retiene tousiours ceste liberté de reprendre ce qui est à condamner;"—"so as at the same time to reserve always that liberty of reproving what is worthy of condemnation."

pleasure in the disgrace and infamy of brethren are unquestionably carried away by hatred and malice, since, if they were under the influence of charity, they would endeavour to prevent the shame of their brethren.

But it is asked, Ought this rule to be extended indiscriminately to every kind of offence? For there are very many who do not allow any public censures, till the *offender* has been privately admonished. But there is an obvious limitation in the words of Christ; for he does not simply, and without exception, order us to advise or reprove privately, and in the absence of witnesses, all who have *offended*, but bids us attempt this method, when we have been *offended* in private; by which is meant, not that it is a business of our own, but that we ought to be wounded and grieved whenever God is *offended*. And Christ does not now speak about bearing injuries, but teaches us in general to cultivate such meekness towards each other, as not to ruin by harsh treatment those whom we ought to save.[1]

Against thee. This expression, as is evident from what we have said, does not denote an injury committed against any one, but distinguishes between secret and open sins.[2] For if any man shall *offend* against the whole Church, Paul enjoins that he be publicly reproved, so that even *elders* shall not be spared; for it is in reference to them that he expressly enjoins Timothy, to *rebuke them publicly in presence of all, and thus to make them a general example to others,* (1 Tim. v. 20.) And certainly it would be absurd that he who has committed a public offence, so that the disgrace of it is generally known, should be admonished by individuals; for if a thousand persons are aware of it, he ought to receive a thousand admonitions. The distinction, therefore, which Christ expressly lays down, ought to be kept in mind, that no man may bring disgrace upon *his brother*, by rashly, and without necessity, divulging secret offences.

---

[1] "Lesquels nous devions plustost tascher d'amener à salut;"—"whom we ought rather to attempt to lead to salvation."

[2] "Mais pour distinguer et mettre différence entre les pechez secrets, et les offenses manifestes;"—"but to distinguish and put a difference between secret sins and open offences."

If he shall hear thee, thou hast gained thy brother. Christ confirms his doctrine by its usefulness and advantage; for it is no small matter to *gain* to God a soul which had been the slave of Satan. And how comes it that those who have fallen do not often repent, but because they are regarded with hatred, and treated as enemies, and thus acquire a character of hardened obstinacy? Nothing, therefore, is more appropriate than meekness, which reconciles to God those who had departed from him. On the other hand, he who inconsiderately indulges in foolish flattery willingly places in jeopardy the salvation of a *brother,* which he had in his hand.

According to *Luke,* Christ expressly enjoins us to be satisfied with a private reproof, if the *brother* be brought to *repentance.* Hence, too, we infer how necessary it is that mutual freedom of reproof should subsist among believers. For, since each of us in many ways commits daily offences, it would be outrageous cruelty to betray, by our silence and concealment, the salvation of those whom we might, by mild reproof, rescue from perdition. Though it does not always succeed, yet he is chargeable with heinous guilt, who has neglected the remedy which the Lord prescribes for promoting the salvation of the brethren. It is also worthy of notice, that the Lord, in order to render us more zealous in performing our duty, ascribes to us that honour which is his own; for to him alone, and to no other, does it belong to convert a man; and yet he bestows on us this applause, though we did not deserve it, that we *gain a brother* who was lost.

16. *But if he shall not hear thee.* The second step is, that he who displayed obstinacy, or refused to yield to one man, should be again admonished in presence of *witnesses.* Here some object, that it will serve no purpose to call *witnesses,* if we have to deal with an obstinate and rebellious man, because their presence will be so far from leading him to acknowledge his guilt, that he will only make a more wicked denial. But this difficulty will be speedily removed, if we distinguish between *denial* and *evasion.* He who

explicitly denies the fact, and declares that he is falsely and calumniously accused, must be left alone; for it would be in vain to press him by calling *witnesses.* But as, in most cases, men shamelessly evade, or impudently excuse, the improper and unjust actions which they have committed, till greater authority is employed, towards such persons it is useful to observe this method.

That Christ's discourse ought to be understood in this sense is evident from the word used, ἔλεγξον, *reprove*, or *argue;* for to argue is to convince by demonstration.[1] And how could I *argue* with a man[2] who boldly denies the whole matter? for he who has the effrontery to deny the crime which he has committed shuts the door against a second admonition.

We now perceive for what purpose Christ proposes to call *witnesses.* It is, to give greater weight and impressiveness to the admonition. As to the slightly different meaning to which he has turned the words of Moses, it involves no absurdity. Moses forbids sentence to be pronounced on a matter that is unknown, and defines this to be the lawful mode of proving, that it be *established* by the testimony of *two or three witnesses. At the mouth of two witnesses, or at the mouth of three witnesses, shall the matter be established,* (Deut. xix. 15.) Alluding to that law, Christ says that, when two or three witnesses shall rise up to condemn the obstinacy of the man, the case will be clear, at least till the Church be prepared to take cognizance of it; for he who refuses to hear *two or three witnesses*[3] will have no reason to complain that he is dragged forth to light.

Tell it to the Church. It is asked, what does he mean by the term *Church?* For Paul orders (1 Cor. v. 5) that the incestuous Corinthian shall be excommunicated, not by a

[1] "Car arguer signifie convaincre par argumens, et remonstrer par bonnes raisons;"—"for *to argue* signifies to convince by arguments, and to show by good reasons."
[2] "Or comment pourroit on *arguer* ou convaincre un homme, que ce qu'il a fait est mauvais?"—"Now how could we *argue* or convince a man that what he has done is wrong?"
[3] "Veu qu'il n'a pas voulu recevoir l'admonition qui luy a este faite en privé par deux ou trois;"—"since he did not choose to receive the admonition which was given to him in private by two or three."

certain chosen number, but by the whole assembly of the godly; and therefore it might appear to be probable that the power of judging is bestowed on the whole of the people. But as at that time no *Church* as yet was in existence, which acknowledged the authority of Christ, and no such order had been established, and as our Lord employs the ordinary and received forms of expression, there can be no doubt that he alludes to the order of the ancient *Church*, as in other places also he accommodates his modes of expression to what was known and customary.¹ When he commands that *the offering, which we intend to present, shall be left at the altar, till we are reconciled to an offended brother,* (Matth. v. 23,) he unquestionably intends, by means of that form of the worship of God which was then in existence and in force, to teach us, that we cannot in a right manner either pray, or offer any thing to God, so long as we are at variance with our brethren. So then he now looked at the form of discipline which was observed among the Jews; for it would have been absurd to propose an appeal to the judgment of a *Church* which was not yet in existence.

Now since among the Jews the power of excommunication belonged to the elders, who held the government of the whole *Church,* Christ speaks appropriately when he says that they who sinned must at length be brought forward publicly to *the Church*, if they either despise haughtily, or ridicule and evade, the private admonitions. We know that, after the Jews returned from the Babylonish captivity, a council was formed, which they called *Sanhedrim*, and in Greek *Synedrion*, (συνέδριον,) and that to this council was committed the superintendence of morals and of doctrine. This government was lawful and approved by God, and was a bridle to restrain within their duty the dissolute and incorrigible.

It will perhaps be objected that, in the time of Christ, every thing was corrupt and perverted, so that this tyranny was very far from deserving to be accounted the judgment of

¹ " Comme aussi en d'autres passages il s'accomodi à ce qui estoit lors ordinaire, et use des termes communes ;"—" as also in other passages he adapts himself to what was then customary, and employs common terms."

the Church. But the reply is easy. Though the method of procedure was at that time depraved and perverted, yet Christ justly praises that order, such as it had been handed down to them from the fathers. And when, shortly afterwards, he erected a *Church,* while he removed the abuse, he restored the proper use of excommunication. Yet there is no reason to doubt that the form of discipline, which prevailed in the kingdom of Christ, succeeded in the room of that ancient discipline. And certainly, since even heathen nations maintained a shadowy form of excommunication, it appears that, from the beginning, this was impressed by God on the minds of men, that those who were impure and polluted ought to be excluded from religious services.[1] It would therefore have been highly disgraceful to the people of God to have been altogether destitute of that discipline, some trace of which remained among the Gentiles. But what had been preserved under the Law Christ has conveyed to us, because we hold the same rank with the ancient fathers. For it was not the intention of Christ to send his disciples to the synagogue, which, while it willingly cherished in its bosom disgraceful filth, excommunicated the true and sincere worshippers of God; but he reminded us that the order, which had been formerly established in a holy manner under the Law, must be maintained in his *Church.*

Let him be to thee as a heathen and a publican. What is here added as to *heathens and publicans* confirms the interpretation which I have given. For *heathens and publicans* having been at that time regarded by the Jews with the greatest hatred and detestation, he compares to them unholy and irreclaimable men, who yield to no admonitions. Certainly he did not intend to enjoin them to avoid the society of *heathens,* of whom *the Church* was afterwards composed; nor is there any reason at the present day why believers should shrink from associating with *publicans.* But in order that he might be more easily understood by the ignorant, Christ borrowed a mode of expression from what was then

[1] "Ne devoyent estre receus à participer aux choses sacrees appartenantes au sarvice de Dieu;"—" ought not to be admitted to take part in the sacred things belonging to the service of God."

customary among his nation;[1] and the meaning is, that we ought to have no intercourse with the despisers of *the Church* till they repent.

18. *What things soever you shall bind.* He now repeats the same words which he had formerly used, (Matth. xvi. 19,) but in a different sense; for there he intended to maintain their authority in doctrine, but here he appoints discipline, which is an appendage to doctrine. There Christ declared that the preaching of the Gospel would not be without effect, but that the *odour* of it would either be *life-giving* or *deadly*, (2 Cor. ii. 15, 16:) here he affirms that, though wicked men ridicule the judgment of *the Church*, it will not be ineffectual. We must attend to this distinction, that *there* our Lord's discourse relates to the preached word, but *here* to public censures and discipline. Let the reader go to that passage for the import of the metaphor, *binding and loosing*.[2]

The substance of it is this: Whoever, after committing a crime, humbly confesses his fault, and entreats *the Church* to forgive him, is absolved not only by men, but by God himself; and, on the other hand, whoever treats with ridicule the reproofs and threatenings of *the Church*, if he is condemned by her, the decision which men have given will be ratified in heaven. If it be objected, that in this way God is made a sort of petty judge, who concurs in the sentence of mortal men, the reply is at hand. For when Christ maintains the authority of his Church, he does not diminish his own power or that of his Father, but, on the contrary, supports the majesty of his word. As in the former case (Matth. xvi. 19) he did not intend to confirm indiscriminately every kind of doctrine, but only that which had proceeded out of his mouth, so neither does he say in this place that every kind of decision will be approved and ratified, but only that in which he presides, and that too not only by his Spirit, but by his word. Hence it follows, that men do no injury to the authority of God, when they pronounce nothing but what comes from his

---

[1] " A usé d'un terme convenable à la coustume du pays;"—" used a term in accordance with the custom of the country."

[2] See page 293 of this volume.

mouth, and only endeavour faithfully to execute what he has commanded. For, though Christ alone is the Judge of the world, yet he chooses to have ministers to proclaim his word.[1] Besides, he wishes that his own decision should be pronounced by the Church; and thus he takes nothing from his own authority by employing the ministry of men, but it is Himself alone that *looses and binds.*

But here a question arises. Since the Church endures many hypocrites, and likewise *absolves* (or *looses*) many whose professions of repentance are hypocritical, does it follow that such persons will be *absolved* (or *loosed*) in heaven? I reply, the discourse is addressed to those only who are truly and sincerely reconciled to the Church. For Christ, wishing to administer comfort to trembling consciences, and to relieve them from fear, declares that any who may have offended are freed from guilt in the sight of God, provided that they be reconciled to *the Church.* For he has appointed this as the pledge of heavenly grace, which has no reference to hypocrites, who pervert the proper use of reconciliation, but awakens in the godly no ordinary confidence, when they hear that their sins are blotted out before God and angels, as soon as they have obtained forgiveness from *the Church.*

In the other clause, Christ's meaning is not at all ambiguous; for, since obstinate and haughty men are strongly inclined to despise the decision of the Church on this pretence, that they refuse to be subject to men—as wicked profligates often make bold appeals to the heavenly tribunal[2]—Christ, in order to subdue this obstinacy by terror, threatens that the condemnation, which is now despised by them, will be ratified in heaven. He encourages his followers, at the same time, to maintain proper severity, and not to yield to the wicked obstinacy of those who reject or shake off discipline.[3]

---

[1] "Il veut toutesfois cependant que les ministres soyent ambassadeurs pour porter et publier sa parole;"—"yet he wishes that ministers should be ambassadors to carry and publish his word."

[2] "Comme souventesfois on verra de meschans garnemens sans crainte de Dieu, qui diront tout haut et hardiment qu'ils appellent au jugement celeste;"—"as we shall often see wicked profligates without the fear of God, who will quite loudly and boldly say that they appeal to the heavenly tribunal."

[3] "Qui reietteront la discipline, et n'y voudront ployer le col;"—"who will reject discipline, and will refuse to bend the neck to it."

Hence, too, we may see how absurdly the Papists torture this passage to cloak every species of tyranny. That the right of excommunication is granted to the Church is certain, and is acknowledged by every person of sound judgment; but does it follow that any individual, even though not called by the *Church*, but elected[1] by a mitred and disguised beast, shall at his own caprice throw out the useless squibs of excommunications?[2] On the contrary, it is evident that the lawful government of the Church is committed to elders, and not only to the ministers of the word, but to those also who, taken from among the people, have been added to them for the superintendence of morals. And yet, not satisfied with this impudence, they endeavour even to prove from this passage that we must bear all the burdens which they shall impose. I do not mention that the power which has been granted to the Church is basely seized and carried off by those outrageous enemies of the Church; and I only mention that, since Christ speaks only about correcting *offenders*, those who by their laws ensnare souls are chargeable with not less folly than wickedness in abusing this passage. Of the same stamp is their defence of their auricular confession on this pretence; for if Christ intended that those who by their own fault had been brought even to a public sentence should be reconciled to the Church, he does not therefore lay an obligation[3] on every individual to pour his sins into the ear of the priest. But their fooleries are so ridiculous, that it is unnecessary to spend any longer time in refuting them.

19. *Again I say to you.* He confirms the former statement; for not only will God bestow the spirit of wisdom and prudence on those who ask it, but he will also provide that not one thing which they shall do according to his word shall want its power and effect. By uniting *agreement* with *prayer*, he reminds us with what moderation and humility believers ought to conduct themselves in all religious

---

[1] " Mais estant crée et ordonné ;"—" but being created and appointed."
[2] " Et les face peter pour faire peur a qui bon luy semble ;"—" and make them crack to frighten whomsoever he pleases."
[3] " Il ne s'ensuit pas pourtant qu'il ait imposé loy."

acts.¹ The *offender* must be admonished, and, if he does not receive correction, he must be excommunicated. Here it is not only necessary to ask counsel at the sacred mouth of God, so that nothing may be determined but by his word, but it is proper at the same time to begin with prayer. Hence appears more clearly what I have formerly stated, that men are not allowed the liberty of doing whatever they please,² but that God is declared to have the sole claim to the government of the *Church,* so that he approves and ratifies the decisions of which he is himself the Author. Meanwhile, when believers assemble, they are taught to unite their prayers and to pray in common, not only to testify the unity of faith, but that God may listen to the *agreement* of them all. So then, as God frequently promises in other passages that he will graciously listen to the private requests of each individual, so here Christ makes a remarkable promise to public prayers, in order to invite us more earnestly to the practice of them.

20. *For where two or three are assembled in my name.* This promise is more extensive than the former; for the Lord declares that he will be present, *wherever two or three are met together in his name,* to *guide them by his counsel,* (Ps. lxxiii. 24,) and to conduct to a prosperous result whatever they shall undertake. There is therefore no reason to doubt that those who give themselves up to his direction will derive most desirable advantage from his presence. And since it is an invaluable blessing to have Christ for our director in all our affairs, to bless our deliberations and their results; and since, on the other hand, nothing can be more miserable than to be deprived of his grace, this promise ought to add no small excitement to us to unite with each other in piety and holiness.³ For whoever either disregards the holy assemblies, or separates himself from brethren, and takes little interest in

---

[1] " En tous actes concernans la service et la parolle de Dieu ;"—" *in all acts relating to the service and the word of God.*"
[2] " Tout ce que bon leur semble ;"—" whatever they think right."
[3] " A nous lier les uns avec les autres en toute sainctete et crainte de Dieu ;"—" to link ourselves with each other in all holiness and fear of God."

the cultivation of unity, by this alone makes it evident that he sets no value on the presence of Christ.

But we must take care, first of all, that those who are desirous to have Christ present with them shall *assemble in his name;* and we must likewise understand what is the meaning of this expression; for we perceive how ungodly men falsely and impudently, as well as wickedly, cover their conspiracies with his sacred name. If therefore we do not wish to expose Christ to their ridicule, and at the same time to overturn what he has here promised, we must know first of all what is meant by this phrase. It means that those who are *assembled together*, laying aside every thing that hinders them from approaching to Christ, shall sincerely raise their desires to him, shall yield obedience to his word, and allow themselves to be governed by the Spirit. Where this simplicity prevails, there is no reason to fear that Christ will not make it manifest that it was not in vain for *the assembly to meet in his name.*

In this is displayed the gross ignorance of the Papists, who exclaim that Councils could not err, and that all ought to abide by their decisions, because, *as often as two or three are assembled in the name of Christ, he is in the midst of them.* But we ought first of all to inquire whether those persons, as to whose faith, and doctrine, and dispositions, we are in doubt, were *assembled in the name of Christ.* When the Papists leave out or perplex this matter, who does not see that they dexterously confound the distinction between holy and profane assemblies, so that the power of doing any thing is taken from the Church and conveyed to the sworn enemies of Christ? Let us therefore know that none but the pious worshippers of God, who sincerely seek Christ, are encouraged to entertain the confident hope that he will never leave them. Disregarding the bastard and abortive Councils, which out of their own head have woven a web, let Christ alone, with the doctrine of his Gospel, be always exalted amongst us.

Matthew.

XVIII. 21. Then Peter approaching him said, Lord, how often shall my brother offend against me, and I forgive him? Till seven times? 22. Jesus saith to him, I say not to thee till seven times, but till seventy times seven. 23. Therefore the kingdom of heaven is compared to a king, who wished to make a reckoning with his servants. 24. And when he had begun to reckon, one was brought to him who owed ten thousand talents. 25. But as he was unable to pay, his master commanded him to be sold, and his wife and children, and all that he had, and payment to be made. 26. And that servant falling down, entreated him, saying, Master, have patience with me, and I will pay thee all. 27. And his master, pitying that servant, forgave him, and acquitted him of the debt. 28. But that servant, having gone out, found one of his fellow-servants, who owed him a hundred pence : and laying hands on him, and seizing him by the throat, he dragged him, saying, Pay me what thou owest. 29. And his fellow-servant, falling down, entreated him, saying, Have patience with me, and I will pay thee all. 30. But he would not, but went out, and threw him into prison, till he should pay the debt. 31. And when his fellow-servants saw what was done, they were deeply grieved, and came, and related to their master all that had been done. 32. Then his master called him, and said to him, Wicked servant, I forgave thee all that debt, because thou didst implore me : 33. Oughtest not thou also to pity thy fellow-servant, even as I pitied thee? 34. And his master, being enraged, delivered him to the tormentors, till he should pay all that he owed him. 35. So likewise shall my heavenly Father do to you, if you forgive not every one his brother from your hearts their offences.

Luke.

XVII. 4. And if seven times in a day he shall offend against thee, and seven times in a day he shall turn to thee, saying, I repent, forgive him.

Matthew XVIII. 21. *Lord, how often shall my brother offend against me?* Peter made this objection according to the natural feelings and disposition of the flesh. It is natural to all men to wish to be forgiven; and, therefore, if any man does not immediately obtain forgiveness, he complains that he is treated with sternness and cruelty. But those who demand to be treated gently are far from being equally gentle towards others; and therefore, when our Lord exhorted his disciples to meekness, this doubt occurred to Peter : " If we be so strongly disposed to grant forgiveness, what will be the consequence, but that our lenity shall be an inducement to *offend?*"[1] He asks, therefore, if it be proper frequently to forgive offenders; for, since the number *seven* is taken for a

---

[1] " Incitera les autres à mal faire, et à nous offenser ;"—" shall induce others to do ill, and to offend us."

large number, the force of the adverb, (ἑπτάκις,) *seven times*, is the same as if he had said, "How long, Lord, dost thou wish that offenders be received into favour? for it is unreasonable, and by no means advantageous, that they should, in every case, find us willing to be reconciled." But Christ is so far from yielding to this objection, that he expressly declares that there ought to be no limit to forgiving;[1] for he did not intend to lay down a fixed number, but rather to enjoin us never to become wearied.

Luke differs somewhat from *Matthew;* for he states the command of Christ to be simply, that we should be prepared to *forgive seven times;* but the meaning is the same, that we ought to be ready and prepared to grant forgiveness not once or twice, but as often as the sinner *shall repent.* There is only this difference between them, that, according to Matthew, our Lord, in reproving Peter for taking too limited a view, employs hyperbolically a larger number, which of itself is sufficient to point out the substance of what is intended. For when Peter asked if he should *forgive seven times*, it was not because he did not choose to go any farther, but, by presenting the appearance of a great absurdity, to withdraw Christ from his opinion, as I have lately hinted. So then he who shall be prepared to *forgive seven times* will be willing to be reconciled as far as to the *seventieth* offence.

But the words of Luke give rise to another question; for Christ does not order us to grant *forgiveness*, till *the offender turn* to us and give evidence of *repentance*.[2] I reply, there are two ways in which offences are *forgiven*. If a man shall do me an injury, and I, laying aside the desire of revenge, do not cease to love him, but even repay kindness in place of injury, though I entertain an unfavourable opinion of him,

---

[1] "Mais tant s'en faut que Christ ait esgard à ceste obiection pour lascher quelque chose de son dire, que mesmes il dit notamment et expressement que sans fin ne terme on doit tousiours pardonner;"—"but so far was Christ from paying regard to that objection, to extenuate any thing that he had said, that he even says plainly and expressly, that without end or limit we must always forgive."

[2] In the French copy he adds:—"Car il semble par ce moyen qu'il commande aux siens de tenir leur cœur contre les pervers, et leur refuser pardon;"—"for it appears in this way that he commands his followers to shut their heart against the obstinate, and to refuse them pardon."

as he deserves, still I am said to *forgive him*. For when God commands us to wish well to our enemies, He does not therefore demand that we approve in them what He condemns, but only desires that our minds shall be purified from all hatred. In this kind of pardon, so far are we from having any right to wait till he who has offended shall return of his own accord to be reconciled to us, that we ought to love those who deliberately provoke us, who spurn reconciliation, and add to the load of former offences. A second kind of *forgiving* is, when we receive a *brother* into favour, so as to think favourably respecting him, and to be convinced that the remembrance of his offence is blotted out in the sight of God. And this is what I have formerly remarked, that in this passage Christ does not speak only of injuries which have been done to us, but of every kind of offences; for he desires that, by our compassion, we shall raise up those who have fallen.[1] This doctrine is very necessary, because naturally almost all of us are peevish beyond measure; and Satan, under the pretence of severity, drives us to cruel rigour, so that wretched men, to whom pardon is refused, are swallowed up by grief and despair.

But here another question arises. As soon as a man by words makes profession of *repentance*, are we bound to believe him? Were this done, we must of necessity go willingly and knowingly into mistake; for where will be discretion, if any man may freely impose on us, even to the hundredth offence? I answer, *first*, the discourse relates here to daily faults, in which every man, even the best, needs forgiveness.[2] Since, then, amidst such infirmity of the flesh, our road is so slippery, and snares and attacks so numerous, what will be the consequence if, at the second or third fall, the hope of *forgiveness* is cut off? We must add, *secondly*, that Christ does not deprive believers of the exercise of judgment, so as to yield a foolish readiness of belief to every

---

[1] " Ceux qui sont cheus et ont failli;"—" those who are fallen and have transgressed."
[2] " Esquelles les plus parfaits mesmes ont besoin d'estre supportez, et qu'on leur pardonner;"—"in which even the most perfect need to be borne with and forgiven."

slight expression, but only desires us to be so candid and merciful, as to stretch out the hand to *offenders*, provided there be evidence that they are sincerely dissatisfied with their sins. For repentance is a sacred thing, and therefore needs careful examination; but as soon as the offender gives probable evidence of conversion, Christ desires that he shall be admitted to reconciliation, lest, on being repulsed, he lose courage and fall back.

Thirdly, It must be observed that, when any man, through his light and unsteady behaviour, has exposed himself to suspicion, we may grant pardon when he asks it, and yet may do so in such a manner as to watch over his conduct for the future, that our forbearance and meekness, which proceed from the Spirit of Christ, may not become the subject of his ridicule. For we must observe the design of our Lord himself, that we ought, by our gentleness, to assist those who have fallen to rise again. And certainly we ought to imitate the goodness of our heavenly Father, who meets sinners at a distance to invite them to salvation. Besides, as repentance is a wonderful work of the Spirit, and is the creation of the new man, if we despise it, we offer an insult to God himself.

23. *The kingdom of heaven is compared.* As it is difficult to bend us to mercy, and as we are quickly seized with weariness, particularly when we have to bear with many faults of brethren, our Lord confirms this doctrine by a most appropriate parable, the substance of which is, that those who will not yield to pardon the faults of brethren judge very ill for themselves, and subject themselves to a very hard and severe law; for they will find God to be equally stern and inexorable towards themselves. There are three parts in which the resemblance mainly consists; for the *master* is contrasted with the *servant,* the large sum of money with small or ordinary sums, and extraordinary kindness with extreme cruelty. By attending to these three points, it will be easy to ascertain Christ's meaning; for what are we, if we are compared with God? And how large is the sum which every one of us owes to God? Lastly, how inconsiderable are the offences,

with which brethren are chargeable towards us, if we take into account our obligation to God? How ill then does that man deserve the compassion of God, who, though oppressed with an immense load, implacably refuses to forgive even the smallest offences to men like himself? So far as regards the words, *the kingdom of heaven* here denotes the spiritual condition of the Church; as if Christ had said, that the state of matters between God and men, in regard to the soul and the nature of spiritual life, is the same as between an ordinary or earthly *master* and his *servants,* in regard to money and the affairs of the present life.

25. *His master ordered him to be sold.* It would be an idle exercise of ingenuity to examine here every minute clause. For God does not always display severity at first, till, constrained to pray, we implore pardon, but rather meets us with undeserved goodness. But Christ only shows what will become of us, if God shall treat us with the utmost severity; and again, if He shall choose to demand from us what we owe, how necessary it is for us to betake ourselves to prayer, because this is the only refuge that remains for transgressors. We must also attend to the wide difference of the sums; for, since one *talent* is worth more than *a hundred pence,* what proportion will *a hundred pence* bear to *ten thousand talents?*

31. *When his fellow-servants saw what was done.* Though we ought not to search for mystery in these words—because they contain nothing but what nature teaches, and what we learn by daily experience—we ought to know that the men who live among us will be so many witnesses against us before God; for it is impossible but that cruelty shall excite in them displeasure and hatred, more especially, since every man is afraid that what he sees done to others will fall upon his own head. As to the clause which immediately follows, it is foolish to inquire how God punishes those sins[1] which he has already forgiven; for the simple meaning is this: though he offers mercy to all, yet severe creditors, from

[1] "Comment il est possible que Dieu punisse;"—"how it is possible for God to punish."

whom no forgiveness can be obtained, are unworthy of enjoying it.

34. *Delivered him to the tormentors, till he should pay all that he owed.* The Papists are very ridiculous in endeavouring to light the fire of purgatory by the word *till;* for it is certain that Christ here points out not temporal death, by which the judgment of God may be satisfied, but eternal death.

MATTHEW.

XVII. 24. And when they came to Capernaum, those who received the didrachma came to Peter, and said, Does not your Master pay the didrachma? 25. He saith, Yes. And when he came into the house, Jesus anticipated him, saying, What thinkest thou, Simon? From whom do the kings of the earth receive tribute or custom? From their own children, or from strangers? 26. Peter saith to him, From strangers. Jesus saith to him, Then are the children free. 27. But that we may not offend them, go thou to the sea, throw a hook, and take that fish which cometh first up; and when thou hast opened its mouth, thou wilt find a stater: take that, and give it for me and for thee.

Matthew XVII. 24. *And when they came to Capernaum.* We must attend, first of all, to the design of this narrative; which is, that Christ, by paying tribute of his own accord, declared his subjection, as he had *taken upon him the form of a servant,* (Philip. ii. 7,) but at the same time showed, both by words and by the miracle, that it was not by obligation or necessity, but by a free and voluntary submission, that he had reduced himself so low that the world looked upon him as nothing more than one of the common people. This was not a tax which was wont to be demanded on crossing the sea,[1] but an annual tribute laid individually on every man among the Jews, so that they paid to tyrants what they were formerly in the habit of paying to God alone. For we know that this tax was imposed on them by the Law, that, by paying every year half a *stater,* (Exod. xxx. 13,) they might acknowledge that God, by whom they had been redeemed,

---

[1] "LES DIDRACHMES, dont est yci parlé, n'estoit pas un peage qu'on payast à passer d'un costé en autre de la mer;"—"*The didrachma,* which are here spoken of, were not a *custom* paid on crossing from one side of the sea to the other."

was their supreme King. When the kings of Asia appropriated this to themselves, the Romans followed their example. Thus the Jews, as if they had disowned the government of God, paid to profane tyrants the sacred tax required by the Law. But it might appear unreasonable that Christ, when he appeared as the Redeemer of his people, should not himself be exempted from *paying tribute.* To remove that offence, he taught by words, that it was only by his will that he was bound; and he proved the same thing by a miracle, for he who had dominion over the sea and the fishes might have released himself from earthly government.[1]

Doth not your Master pay? Some think that the collectors of the *tribute* intended to throw blame on Christ, as if he were claiming exemption from the common law. For my own part, as men of that class are insolent and abusive, I interpret these words as having been spoken by way of reproach. It was customary for every man to be enrolled in his own city; but we know that Christ had no fixed habitation in one place. Those people therefore inquire if he be exempted from the law on the ground of his frequent removals from place to place.[2]

25. *He saith, Yes. Peter's* reply contains a modest excuse[3] to satisfy them: "he will pay,"[4] says he; from which we infer that Christ had formerly been accustomed to pay, for *Peter* promises it as a thing about which there was no doubt. That they address him rather than the other disciples was, as I conjecture, because Christ lived with him; for if all had occupied the same habitation, the demand would have been made on all alike. It is therefore very ridiculous in the Papists, on so frivolous a pretence, to make *Peter* a partner

---

[1] " Pouvoit bien, s'il eust voulu, s'exempter de la suiection des princes terriens ;"—" might easily, if he had chosen, have exempted himself from subjection to earthly princes."
[2] " Si par ce moyen qu'il est maintenant ci, maintenant là, il faudra qu'il eschappe sans rien payer ;"—" if, because he is sometimes here, and sometimes there, he must escape without paying anything."
[3] " Une excuse bien modeste et honneste ;"—" a very modest and civil excuse."
[4] " Oui, (dit-il,) il payera ;"—" *Yes*, (says he,) he will pay."

in the dignity of Christ. "He chose him (they say) to be his *vicar*, and bestowed on him equal honours, by making him equal to himself in the payment of tribute." But in this way they will make all swine-herds *vicars* of Christ, for they paid as much as he did. And if the primacy of *Peter* was manifested in the paying of tribute, whence comes that exemption which they claim for themselves? But this is the necessary result of the shameful trifling of those who corrupt Scripture according to their own fancy.

What thinkest thou, Simon? In this Christ gave a proof of his Divinity, by showing that nothing was unknown to him. But what is the object of his discourse? Is it to exempt himself and his followers from subjection to the laws? Some explain it thus, that Christians have a right to be exempted, but that they voluntarily subject themselves to the ordinary government, because otherwise human society cannot be maintained. To me, however, the meaning appears to be more simple; for there was danger lest the disciples might think that Christ had come in vain, because, by paying tribute, he cut off the hope of deliverance; and therefore he simply affirms that he pays tribute, solely because he voluntarily refrains from exercising his right and power. Hence it is inferred that this takes nothing from his reign. But why does he not openly claim his right? It is because his kingly power was unknown to the collectors of the tribute. For, though his kingdom be spiritual, still we must maintain, that as he is the only Son of God, he is also the heir of the whole world, so that all things ought to be subject to him, and to acknowledge his authority. The meaning, therefore, is, that God has not appointed kings, and established governments over mankind, in such a manner as to place him who is the Son in the same rank indiscriminately with others, but yet that, of his own accord, he will be a servant along with others, till the glory of his kingdom be displayed.

The Pope has not less foolishly than successfully abused this passage to exempt his clergy from the laws; as if the shaving of the head made them sons of God, and exempted them from tributes and taxes. But nothing else was intended by Christ than to claim for himself the honour of a King's

Son, so as to have at least a home privileged and exempted from the common law. And therefore it is also highly foolish in the Anabaptists to torture these words for overturning political order, since it is more than certain, that Christ does not say any thing about a privilege common to believers, but only draws a comparison from the sons of kings, who, together with their domestics, are exempted.[1]

27. *Throw a hook.* Though I acknowledge that Christ had not always full coffers, yet I think that he was not compelled by poverty to give this order to Peter, but that he did so in order to prove by a miracle, that he had a more extensive dominion than all earthly kings, since he had even *fishes* for his tributaries. And we do not read that this was done more than once, because one proof was enough for his whole life. *Thou wilt find a stater.* A stater was of the same value as a shekel, namely, four drachms or two didrachma.[2]

MATTHEW.	MARK.	LUKE.
XIX. 1. And it happened, when Jesus had finished these discourses, he departed from Galilee, and came into the coasts of Judea beyond Jordan. 2. And great multitudes followed him, and he cured them there.	IX. 38. And John answered him, saying, Master, we saw one casting out devils in thy name, and he followeth not us; and we forbade him, because he followeth not us. 39. And Jesus said, Forbid him not; for there is no man who, if he has performed a miracle in my name, can easily speak evil of me. 40. For he who is not against us is for us. X. 1. And when he had risen thence, he came into the coasts	IX. 49. And John answering said, Master, we saw one casting out devils in thy name ; and we forbade him, because he followeth not with us. 50. And Jesus said to him, Forbid him not ; for he who is not against us is for us. 51. And it happened, when the days of his being received up were in course of being fulfilled, and he set his face stedfastly to go to Jerusalem. 52. And he sent messengers before his face ; and they went and entered into a town of the Samaritans, to make ready for him : 53. And they did not receive him, because his face was as if he were going to Jerusalem.[3] 54. And when his disciples James and John saw it, they said, Lord, wilt thou that we command fire to come down from heaven,

[1] "Lesquels sont exempts de tous imposts, eux et leurs domestiques;"—"who are exempted from all taxes, they and their domestics."
[2] The *didrachmon* weighed *two drachms*, and the *stater*, which weighed *two didrachma*, or *four drachms*, was worth about two shillings and sixpence of our money.—*Ed.*
[3] "Pourtant que sa face estoit tournee pour aller en Ierusalem;"—"because his face was turned to go to Jerusalem."

MATTHEW.	MARK.	LUKE.
	of Judea, through the district which is beyond Jordan. And again the multitudes assemble to him, and again he taught them, as he was accustomed.	and consume them, even as Elijah did? 55. And Jesus, turning, rebuked them, saying, You know not of what spirit you are. 56. For the Son of man is not come to destroy men's lives, but to save them. And they went into another village.

Mark IX. 38. *Master, we saw one.* Hence it is evident that the *name* of Christ was at that time so celebrated, that persons who were not of the number of his intimate disciples used that *name*, or perhaps even abused it, for I will not venture to avouch any thing on this point as certain. It is possible that he who is here mentioned had embraced the doctrine of Christ, and betaken himself to the performance of miracles with no bad intention; but as Christ bestowed this power on none but those whom he had chosen to be heralds of his Gospel, I think that he had rashly taken, or rather seized upon, this office. Now though he was wrong in making this attempt, and in venturing to imitate the disciples without receiving a command to do so, yet his boldness was not without success: for the Lord was pleased, in this way also, to throw lustre around his name,[1] as he sometimes does by means of those of whose ministry he does not approve as lawful. It is not inconsistent with this to say, that one who was endued with special faith followed a blind impulse, and thus proceeded inconsiderately to work miracles.

I now come to *John* and his companions. They say that they *forbade* a man to *work miracles.* Why did they not first ask whether or not he was authorised? For now, being in a state of doubt and suspense, they ask the opinion of their Master. Hence it follows, that they had rashly taken on themselves the right to *forbid;* and therefore every man who undertakes more than he knows that he is permitted to do by the word of God is chargeable with rashness. Besides, there is reason to suspect the disciples of Christ of ambition, because they are anxious to maintain their privilege and honour. For how comes it that they all at once *forbid* a

---

[1] "Pour avancer la gloire de son nom;"—"to advance the glory of his name."

man who is unknown to them to work miracles, but because they wish to be the sole possessors of this right? For they assign the reason, that he *followeth not* Christ; as much as to say, "He is not one of thy associates, as we are: why then shall he possess equal honour?"

39. *Forbid him not.* Christ did not wish that he should be *forbidden;* not that he had given him authority, or approved of what he did, or even wished his disciples to approve of it, but because, when by any occurrence God is glorified, we ought to bear with it and rejoice. Thus Paul, (Philip. i. 18,) though he disapproves of the dispositions of those who used the Gospel as a pretence for aggrandizing themselves, yet rejoices that by this occurrence the glory of Christ is advanced. We must attend also to the reason which is added, that *it is impossible for any man who works miracles in the name of Christ to speak evil of Christ,* and therefore this ought to be reckoned as gain; for hence it follows, that if the disciples had not been more devoted to their own glory than anxious and desirous to promote the glory of their Master, they would not have been offended when they saw that glory heightened and enlarged in another direction. And yet Christ declares that we ought to reckon as friends those who are not open enemies.

40. *For he who is not against us is for us.* He does not enjoin us to give a loose rein to rash men, and to be silent while they intermeddle with this and the other matter, according to their own fancy, and disturb the whole order of the Church: for such licentiousness, so far as our calling allows, must be restrained. He only affirms that they act improperly, who unseasonably prevent the kingdom of God from being advanced by any means whatever. And yet he does not acknowledge as his disciples, or reckon as belonging to his flock, those who hold an intermediate place between enemies and friends, but means that, so far as they do no harm, they are useful and profitable: for it is a proverbial saying, which reminds us that we ought not to raise a quarrel till we are constrained.

Luke IX. 51. *While the days of his being received up, &c.* Luke alone relates this narrative, which, however, is highly useful on many accounts. For, first, it describes the divine courage and firmness of Christ[1] in despising death; secondly, what deadly enmities are produced by differences about religion; thirdly, with what headlong ardour the nature of man is hurried on to impatience; next, how ready we are to fall into mistakes in imitating the saints; and, lastly, by the example of Christ we are called to the exercise of meekness. The death of Christ is called his *being received up,* (ἀνάληψις,) not only because he was then withdrawn from the midst of us,[2] but because, leaving the mean prison of the flesh, he ascended on high.

52. *And he sent messengers.* It is probable that our Lord was, at that time, attended by a great multitude of followers; for the *messengers* were not *sent* to prepare a splendid banquet, or to select some magnificent palace, but only to tell that a vast number of guests were approaching. They again, when excluded and repulsed, wait for their Master. Hence, too, we learn, what I remarked in the second place,[3] that when men differ among themselves about the doctrines of religion, they readily break out into hatred of each other; for it was an evidence of very bitter hatred to withhold food from the hungry, and lodging from those who were fatigued. But the Samaritans have such a dislike and enmity at the Jewish religion, that they look upon all who follow it as unworthy of any kindness. Perhaps, too, they were tormented with vexation at being despised; for they knew that their temple was detested by the Jews as profane, and that they were considered to be spurious and corrupt worshippers of God. But as the superstition once admitted kept so firm a hold of them, they strove, with wicked emu-

---

[1] "La magnanimité et constance admirable de Iesus Christ;"—"the wonderful magnanimity and firmness of Jesus Christ."

[2] "Non pas seulement pource qu'il a lors este enlevé et comme retranché du milieu des hommes;"—"not only because he was then raised up, and, as it were, withdrawn from the midst of men."

[3] See our Author's observations above on Luke ix. 51.

lation, to maintain it to the last. At length the contention grew so hot, that it consumed both nations in one conflagration; for Josephus assures us that it was the torch which kindled the Jewish war. Now though Christ might easily have avoided that dislike, he chooses rather to profess himself to be a Jew, than by an indirect denial to procure a lodging.

53. *He stedfastly set his face.* By this expression Luke has informed us that Christ, when he had death before his eyes, rose above the fear of it, and went forward to meet it; but, at the same time, points out that he had a struggle, and that, having vanquished terror,[1] he boldly presented himself to die. For if no dread, no difficulty, no struggle, no anxiety, had been present to his mind, what need was there that he should *set his face stedfastly?*[2] But as he was neither devoid of feeling, nor under the influence of foolish hardihood, he must have been affected by the cruel and bitter death, or rather the shocking and dreadful agony, which he knew would overtake him from the rigorous judgment of God; and so far is this from obscuring or diminishing his glory, that it is a remarkable proof of his unbounded love to us; for laying aside a regard to himself that he might devote himself to our salvation, through the midst of terrors he hastened to death, the time of which he knew to be at hand.

54. *And when his disciples James and John saw it.* The country itself had perhaps suggested to them the desire of thundering immediately against the ungodly; for it was there that *Elijah* had formerly destroyed, by a fire from heaven, the king's soldiers who had been sent to apprehend him, (2 Kings i. 10.) It therefore occurred to them that the Samaritans, who so basely rejected the Son of God, were at that time devoted to a similar destruction. And

---

[1] "Estans victorieux par dessus ceste frayeur naturelle;"—"being victorious over that natural dread."
[2] "Quel besoin estoit il qu'il prinst sa resolution, et par maniere de dire s'obstinast en soy-mesme?"—"What need was there that he should take his resolution, and, so to speak, persist in his own mind?"

here we see to what we are driven by a foolish imitation[1] of the holy fathers. *James and John* plead the example of *Elijah,* but they do not consider how far they differ from *Elijah ;* they do not examine properly their own intemperate zeal, nor do they look at the calling of God. Under a pretext equally plausible did the Samaritans cloak their idolatry, *our fathers worshipped in this mountain,* (John iv. 20.) But both were in the wrong; for, neglecting the exercise of judgment, they were apes rather than imitators of the holy fathers. Now though it is doubtful whether they think that they have the power in their own hand, or ask Christ to give it to them, I think it more probable that, elated with foolish confidence, they entertain no doubt that they are able to execute vengeance, provided that Christ give his consent.

55. *You know not of what spirit you are.* By this reply he not only restrained the unbridled fury of the two disciples, but laid down a rule to all of us not to indulge our temper. For whoever undertakes any thing, ought to be fully aware that he has the authority and guidance of the Spirit of God, and that he is actuated by proper and holy dispositions. Many will be impelled by the warmth of their zeal, but if the spirit of prudence be wanting, their ebullitions end in foam. Frequently, too, it happens, that the impure feelings of the flesh are mingled with their zeal, and that those who appear to be the keenest zealots for the glory of God are blinded by the private feelings of the flesh. And therefore, unless our zeal be directed by the Spirit of God, it will be of no avail to plead in our behalf, that we undertook nothing but from proper zeal. But the Spirit himself will guide us by wisdom and prudence, that we may do nothing contrary to our duty, or beyond our calling, nothing, in short, but what is prudent and seasonable ; and, by removing all the filth of the flesh, he may impart to our minds proper feelings, that we may desire nothing but what God shall suggest. Christ likewise blames his disciples because, though they

[1] " Une folle et inconsideree imitation des saincts peres ;"—" a foolish and ill-considered imitation of the holy fathers."

are widely distant from the *spirit* of *Elijah*,[1] they rashly take upon themselves to do what he did. For *Elijah* executed the judgment of God, which had been committed to him by the Spirit; but they rush to vengeance, not by the command of God, but by the movement of the flesh. And therefore the examples of the saints are no defence to us, unless the same Spirit that directed them dwell in us.

MATTHEW.

XIX. 3. And the Pharisees came to him, tempting him, and saying to him, Is it lawful for a man to divorce his wife for any cause whatever? 4. Who answering said to them, Have you not read, that he who made them at first,[2] made them male and female? 5. And he said, Therefore shall a man leave his father and mother, and be joined to his wife; and they shall be one flesh. 6. Therefore now they are not two, but one flesh: what God therefore hath joined, let not man separate. 7. They say to him, Why then did Moses order to give a letter of divorcement, and send her away? 8. He said to them, Moses, for the hardness of your heart, permitted you to divorce your wives; but at the beginning it was not so. 9. And I say to you, That whosoever shall divorce his wife, except for fornication, and shall marry another, committeth adultery; and whosoever shall marry her that is divorced committeth adultery.

MARK.

X. 2. And the Pharisees, coming to him, asked him, Is it lawful for a man to divorce his wife? tempting him. 3. But he answering said to them, What did Moses command you? 4. And they said, Moses permitted to write a letter of divorcement, and to send her away. 5. And Jesus answering said to them, For the hardness of your heart he wrote to you this commandment. 6. But at the beginning of the creation God made them male and female. 7. For this reason shall a man leave his father and mother, and cleave to his wife; 8. And they shall be one flesh: therefore now they are not two, but one flesh. 9. What therefore God hath joined together let not man separate. 10. And in the house his disciples again asked him about the same subject. 11. And he saith to them, Whosoever shall divorce his wife, and marry another, committeth adultery against her. 12. And if a woman shall divorce her husband, and shall be married to another, she committeth adultery.

Matthew XIX. 3. *And the Pharisees came to him, tempting him.* Though the Pharisees lay snares for Christ, and cunningly endeavour to impose upon him, yet their malice proves to be highly useful to us; as the Lord knows how to turn, in a wonderful manner, to the advantage of his people all

---

[1] "De l'esprit et affection d'Elie;"—"from the spirit and disposition of Elijah."
[2] "Qui feit *l'homme* dès le commencement;"—"who made *man* from the beginning."

the contrivances of wicked men to overthrow sound doctrine. For, by means of this occurrence, a question arising out of the liberty of divorce was settled, and a fixed law was laid down as to the sacred and indissoluble bond of marriage. The occasion of this quibbling was, that the reply, in whatever way it were given, could not, as they thought, fail to be offensive.

They ask, *Is it lawful for a man to divorce his wife for any cause whatever?* If Christ reply in the negative, they will exclaim that he wickedly abolishes the Law; and if in the affirmative, they will give out that he is not a prophet of God, but rather a pander, who lends such countenance to the lust of men. Such were the calculations which they had made in their own minds; but the Son of God, who knew how to *take the wise in their own craftiness*, (Job v. 13,) disappointed them, sternly opposing unlawful divorces, and at the same time showing that he brings forward nothing which is inconsistent with the Law. For he includes the whole question under two heads: that the order of creation ought to serve for a law, that the husband should maintain conjugal fidelity during the whole of life; and that *divorces* were *permitted*, not because they were lawful, but because Moses had to deal with a rebellious and intractable nation.

4. *Have you not read?* Christ does not indeed reply directly to what was asked, but he fully meets the question which was proposed; just as if a person now interrogated about the Mass were to explain faithfully the mystery of the Holy Supper, and at length to conclude, that they are guilty of sacrilege and forgery who venture either to add or to take away any thing from the pure institution of the Lord, he would plainly overturn the pretended sacrifice of the Mass. Now Christ assumes as an admitted principle, that at the beginning God *joined the male to the female*, so that the two made an entire man; and therefore he who *divorces his wife* tears from him, as it were, the half of himself. But nature does not allow any man to tear in pieces his own body.

He adds another argument drawn from the less to the greater. The bond of marriage is more sacred than that which binds children to their parents. But piety binds children to their parents by a link which cannot be broken. Much less then can the husband renounce his wife. Hence it follows, that a chain which God made is burst asunder, if the husband divorce his wife.[1]

Now the meaning of the words is this: God, who created the human race, *made them male and female,* so that every man might be satisfied with his own wife, and might not desire more. For he insists on the number *two,* as the prophet Malachi, (ii. 15,) when he remonstrates against polygamy, employs the same argument, that God, whose *Spirit was so abundant* that He had it in His power to create more, yet *made but one man,* that is, such a man as Christ here describes. And thus from the order of creation is proved the inviolable union of one husband with one wife. If it be objected, that in this way it will not be lawful, after the first wife is dead, to take another, the reply is easy, that not only is the bond dissolved by death, but the second wife is substituted by God in the room of the first, as if she had been one and the same woman.

5. *Therefore shall a man leave his father and mother.* It is uncertain whether Moses represents Adam or God as speaking these words; but it is of little consequence to the present passage which of these meanings you choose, for it was enough to quote the decision which God had pronounced, though it might have been uttered by the mouth of Adam. Now he who marries a wife is not commanded absolutely to *leave his father;* for God would contradict himself, if by marriage He set aside those duties which He enjoins on children towards their parents; but when a comparison is made between the claims, the *wife* is preferred to the *father and mother.* But if any man abandon his father, and shake off the yoke by which he is bound, no man will own such a monster;[2] much less will he be at liberty to dissolve a marriage.

---

[1] " Que le mari qui se separe d'avecques sa femme rompt le lien duquel Dieu estoit autheur;"—" that the husband, who separates from his wife, bursts the chain of which God was the author."

[2] " Il n'y a celuy qui ne fust estonné d'un tel monstre;"—" there is no man who would not be astonished at such a monster."

And the two shall be one flesh. This expression condemns polygamy not less than it condemns unrestrained liberty in divorcing wives; for, if the mutual union of two persons was consecrated by the Lord, the mixture of three or four persons is unauthorised.[1] But Christ, as I stated a little ago, applies it in a different manner to his purpose; namely, to show that whoever divorces his wife tears himself in pieces, because such is the force of holy marriage, that the husband and wife become one man. For it was not the design of Christ to introduce the impure and filthy speculation of Plato, but he spoke with reverence of the order which God has established. Let the husband and wife, therefore, live together in such a manner, that each shall cherish the other in the same manner as if they were the half of themselves. Let the husband rule, so as to be the head, and not the tyrant, of his wife; and let the woman, on the other hand, yield modestly to his commands.

6. *What God therefore hath joined.* By this sentence Christ restrains the caprice of husbands, that they may not, by divorcing their wives, burst asunder the sacred knot. And as he declares that it is not in the power of the husband to dissolve the marriage, so likewise he forbids all others to confirm by their authority unlawful divorces; for the magistrate abuses his power when he grants permission to the husband to divorce his wife. But the object which Christ had directly in view was, that every man should sacredly observe the promise which he has given, and that those who are tempted, by wantonness or wicked dispositions, to divorce, may reflect thus with themselves: "Who art thou that allowest thyself to *burst asunder what God hath joined?*" But this doctrine may be still farther extended. The Papists, contriving for us a church separated from Christ the Head, leave us an imperfect and mutilated body. In the Holy Supper, Christ joined the bread and the wine; but they have dared to withhold from all the people the use of the cup. To

---

[1] " C'est un meslinge faux et pervers ;"—" it is a false and wicked mixture."

these diabolical corruptions we shall be at liberty to oppose these words, *What God hath joined let not man separate.*

7. *Why then did Moses order?* They had thought of this calumny,[1] if, which was more probable, Christ should demand a proper cause to be shown in cases of divorce; for it appears that whatever God permits by his law, whose will alone establishes the distinction between what is good or evil, is lawful. But Christ disarms the falsehood and slander by the appropriate reply, that Moses permitted it on account of their obstinacy, and not because he approved of it as lawful. And he confirms his opinion by the best argument, *because it was not so at the beginning.* He takes for granted that, when God at first instituted marriage, he established a perpetual law, which ought to remain in force till the end of the world. And if the institution of marriage is to be reckoned an inviolable law, it follows that whatever swerves from it does not arise from its pure nature, but from the depravity of men.

But it is asked, Ought Moses to have permitted what was in itself bad and sinful? I reply, That, in an unusual sense of the word, he is said to have *permitted* what he did not severely forbid;[2] for he did not lay down a law about divorces, so as to give them the seal of his approbation, but as the wickedness of men could not be restrained in any other way, he applied what was the most admissible remedy, that the husband should, at least, attest the chastity of his wife. For the law was made solely for the protection of the women, that they might not suffer any disgrace after they had been unjustly rejected. Hence we infer, that it was rather a punishment inflicted on the husbands, than an indulgence or *permission* fitted to inflame their lust. Besides, political and

---

[1] "Ils avoyent songé ceste calomnie pour l'avoir toute preste;"—"they had thought of this calumny, to have it all ready."

[2] "Ie repond, Qu'à parler proprement, il ne l'a pas permis: mais d'autant qu'il ne l'a pas defendu estroittement, il est dit qu'il l'a permis;" —"I reply, That, strictly speaking, he did not *permit* it; but in so far as he did not strictly forbid it, he is said to have *permitted* it."

outward order is widely different from spiritual government. What is lawful and proper the Lord has comprehended under the *ten words*.¹ Now as it is possible that many things, for which every man's conscience reproves and charges him, may not be called in question at a human tribunal, it is not wonderful if those things are connived at by political laws.

Let us take a familiar instance. The laws grant to us a greater liberty of litigation than the law of charity allows. Why is this? Because the right cannot be conferred on individuals, unless there be an open door for demanding it; and yet the inward law of God declares that we ought to follow what charity shall dictate. And yet there is no reason why magistrates should make this an excuse for their indolence, if they voluntarily abstain from correcting vices, or neglect what the nature of their office demands. But let men in a private station beware of doubling the criminality of the magistrates, by screening their own vices under the protection of the laws. For here the Lord indirectly reproves the Jews for not reckoning it enough that their stubbornness was allowed to pass unpunished, if they did not implicate God as defending their iniquity. And if the rule of a holy and pious life is not always, or in all places, to be sought from political laws, much less ought we to seek it from custom.

9. *But I say to you.* *Mark* relates that this was spoken to the disciples apart, when they had come *into the house;* but *Matthew*, leaving out this circumstance, gives it as a part of the discourse, as the Evangelists frequently leave out some intermediate occurrence, because they reckon it enough to sum up the leading points. There is therefore no difference, except that the one explains the matter more distinctly than the other. The substance of it is: though the Law does not punish divorces, which are at variance with God's first institution, yet he is an adulterer who rejects his wife and takes another. For it is not in the power of a man to

¹ Where the English version gives the words, *ten commandments*, the phrase in the original Hebrew is. עשרת הדברים, *the ten words*, (Exod. xxxiv. 28; Deut. iv. 13; x. 4.)—*Ed.*

dissolve the engagement of marriage, which the Lord wishes to remain inviolate; and so the woman who occupies the bed of a lawful wife is a concubine.

But an exception is added; for the woman, by *fornication*, cuts herself off, as a rotten member, from her husband, and sets him at liberty. Those who search for other reasons ought justly to be set at nought, because they choose to be wise above the heavenly teacher. They say that *leprosy* is a proper ground for divorce, because the contagion of the disease affects not only the husband, but likewise the children. For my own part, while I advise a religious man not to touch a woman afflicted with leprosy, I do not pronounce him to be at liberty to divorce her. If it be objected, that they who cannot live unmarried need a remedy, that they may not be *burned*, I answer, that what is sought in opposition to the word of God is not a remedy. I add too, that if they give themselves up to be guided by the Lord, they will never want continence, for they follow what he has prescribed. One man shall contract such a dislike of his wife, that he cannot endure to keep company with her: will polygamy cure this evil? Another man's wife shall fall into palsy or apoplexy, or be afflicted with some other incurable disease, shall the husband reject her under the pretence of incontinency? We know, on the contrary, that none of those who walk in their ways are ever left destitute of the assistance of the Spirit.

For the sake of avoiding fornication, says Paul, *let every man marry a wife,* (1 Cor. vii. 2.) He who has done so, though he may not succeed to his wish, has done his duty; and, therefore, if any thing be wanting, he will be supported by divine aid. To go beyond this is nothing else than to tempt God. When Paul mentions another reason, namely, that when, through a dislike of godliness, wives happen to be rejected by unbelievers, a godly *brother or sister* is not, in such a case, liable to *bondage,* (1 Cor. vii. 12, 15,) this is not inconsistent with Christ's meaning. For he does not there inquire into the proper grounds of divorce, but only whether a woman continues to be bound to an unbelieving husband, after that, through hatred of God, she has been wickedly rejected, and cannot be reconciled to him in any other way than by forsaking God; and therefore we need not wonder if Paul think it better that she should part with a mortal man than that she should be at variance with God.

But the exception which Christ states appears to be superfluous. For, if the adulteress deserve to be punished with death, what purpose does it serve to talk of divorces? But as it was the duty of the husband to prosecute his wife for adultery, in order to purge his house from infamy, whatever might be the result, the husband, who convicts his wife of uncleanness, is here freed by Christ from the bond. It is even possible that, among a corrupt and degenerate people, this crime remained to a great extent unpunished; as, in our own day, the wicked forbearance of magistrates makes it necessary for husbands to put away unchaste wives, because adulterers are not punished. It must also be observed, that the right belongs equally and mutually to both sides, as there is a mutual and equal obligation to fidelity. For, though in other matters the husband holds the superiority, as to the marriage bed, the wife has an equal right: for he is not the lord of his body; and therefore when, by committing adultery, he has dissolved the marriage, the wife is set at liberty.

And whosoever shall marry her that is divorced. This clause has been very ill explained by many commentators; for they have thought that generally, and without exception, celibacy is enjoined in all cases when a divorce has taken place; and, therefore, if a husband should put away an adulteress, both would be laid under the necessity of remaining unmarried. As if this liberty of divorce meant only not to lie with his wife; and as if Christ did not evidently grant permission in this case to do what the Jews were wont indiscriminately to do at their pleasure. It was therefore a gross error; for, though Christ condemns as an adulterer the man *who shall marry a wife that has been divorced,* this is undoubtedly restricted to unlawful and frivolous divorces. In like manner, Paul enjoins those who have been so dismissed *to remain unmarried, or to be reconciled to their husbands,* (1 Cor. vii. 11;) that is, because quarrels and differences do not dissolve a marriage. This is clearly made out from the passage in

Mark, where express mention is made of the wife who has left her husband : *and if the wife shall divorce her husband.* Not that wives were permitted to give their husbands a letter of divorcement, unless so far as the Jews had been contaminated by foreign customs; but Mark intended to show that our Lord condemned the corruption which was at that time universal, that, after voluntary divorces, they entered on both sides into new marriages; and therefore he makes no mention of adultery.

MATTHEW.

XIX. 10. His disciples say to him, If such be the case of the man with his wife,[1] it is not expedient to enter into marriage. 11. Who said to them,[2] All are not capable of receiving this saying, but those to whom it is given. 12. For there are eunuchs, who were so born from their mother's womb; and there are eunuchs, who have been made eunuchs by men; and there are eunuchs, who have castrated themselves for the sake of the kingdom of heaven. He who can receive it,[3] let him receive it.

10. *His disciples say to him.* As if it were a hard condition for husbands to be so bound to their wives, that, so long as they remain chaste, they are compelled to endure every thing rather than leave them, the disciples, roused by this answer of Christ, reply, that it is better to want wives than to submit to a knot of this kind.[4] But why do they not, on the other hand, consider how hard is the bondage of wives,[5] but because, devoted to themselves and their own convenience, they are driven by the feeling of the flesh to disregard others, and to think only of what is advantageous for themselves? Meanwhile, it is a display of base ingratitude that, from the dread or dislike of a single inconvenience, they reject a wonderful gift of God. It is better, according to them, to avoid marriage than to bind one's self by the bond of living always together.[6] But if God has ordained marriage for the general advantage of mankind, though it

---

[1] " Avec sa femme."
[2] " Il leur dit;"—" he said to them."
[3] " Qui peut comprendre *ceci* ;"—" he who can receive *this*."
[4] " Que de se mettre en une telle necessité et suiection;"—" than to place one's self under such restraint and subjection."
[5] " La servitude que les femmes ont à porter;"—" the bondage of which wives have to endure."
[6] " De vivre tousiours avec une femme;"—" of living always with one wife."

may be attended by some things that are disagreeable, it is not on that account to be despised. Let us therefore learn not to be delicate and saucy, but to use with reverence the gifts of God, even if there be something in them that does not please us. Above all, let us guard against this wickedness in reference to holy marriage; for, in consequence of its being attended by many annoyances, Satan has always endeavoured to make it an object of hatred and detestation, in order to withdraw men from it. And Jerome has given too manifest a proof of a malicious and wicked disposition, in not only loading with calumnies that sacred and divinely appointed condition of life, but in collecting as many terms of reproach (λοιδορίας) as he could from profane authors, in order to take away its respectability. But let us recollect that whatever annoyances belong to marriage are accidental, for they arise out of the depravity of man. Let us remember that, since our nature was corrupted, marriage began to be a medicine, and therefore we need not wonder if it have a bitter taste mixed with its sweetness. But we must see how our Lord confutes this folly.

11. *All are not capable of receiving this saying.* By this he means, that the choice is not placed in our hands, as if we were to deliberate on a matter submitted to us. If any man thinks it advantageous for him to want a wife, and, without making any inquiry, lays upon himself an obligation to celibacy,[1] he is widely mistaken. God, who has declared it to be good that a man should have a woman to be his helper, will punish the contempt of his own appointment; for mortals take too much on themselves, when they endeavour to exempt themselves from the heavenly calling. But Christ proves that it is not free to all to make what choice they please, because the gift of continence is a special gift; for when he says that *all are not capable of receiving it, but those to whom it is given*, he plainly shows that it was not given to all. And this reproves the pride of those who do not hesitate to claim for themselves what Christ so manifestly refuses to them.

[1] " S'il s'astreigne à n'estre point marié ;"—" if he bind himself not to be married."

12. *For there are eunuchs.* Christ distinguishes three kinds of *eunuchs.* Those who are so by nature, or who have been castrated by men, are debarred from marriage by this defect, for they are not men. He says that there are other *eunuchs,* who have castrated themselves, that they may be more at liberty to serve God; and these he exempts from the obligation to marry. Hence it follows, that all others who avoid marriage fight against God with sacrilegious hardihood, after the manner of the giants. When Papists urge the word *castrate,* (εὐνούχισαν,) as if at their own pleasure men might lay themselves under obligation to continence, it is too frivolous. For Christ has already declared, that God gives it to whom he chooses; and, a little afterwards, we shall find him maintaining, that it is folly in any man to choose to live unmarried, when he has not received this special gift. This castration, therefore, is not left to free will; but the plain meaning is, while some men are by nature fit to marry, though they abstain, they do not tempt God, because God grants them exemption.[1]

For the sake of the kingdom of heaven. Many foolishly explain this as meaning, *in order to deserve eternal life;* as if celibacy contained within itself some meritorious service, as the Papists imagine that it is an angelical state. But Christ meant nothing more than that persons unmarried ought to have this for their object, that, being freed from all cares, they may apply themselves more readily to the duties of piety. It is, therefore, a foolish imagination, that celibacy is a virtue; for it is not in itself more pleasing to God than fasting, and is not entitled to be reckoned among the duties which he requires from us, but ought to have a reference to another object. Nay more, Christ expressly intended to declare that, though a man be pure from fornication, yet his celibacy is not approved by God, if he only consults his own ease and comfort, but that he is excused on this single ground, that he aims at a free and unrestrained meditation on the heavenly life. In short, Christ teaches us, that it is

---

[1] " Pource qu'il leur permet de s'en passer, et leur baille un privilege par dessus les autres ;"—" because he allows them to abstain from it, and grants them a privilege above others."

not enough, if unmarried men live chastely, unless they abstain from having wives, for the express purpose of devoting themselves to better employments.[1]

He that can receive it, let him receive it. By this conclusion Christ warns them, that the use of marriage is not to be despised, unless we intend, with blind rashness, to rush headlong to destruction: for it became necessary to restrain the disciples, whom he saw acting inconsiderately and without judgment. But the warning is useful to all; for, in selecting a manner of life, few consider what has been given to them, but men rush forward, without discrimination, in whatever direction inconsiderate zeal prompts them. And I wish that the warning had been attended to in past times; but men's ears are stopped by I know not what enchantments of Satan, so that, contrary to nature, and, at it were, in spite of God, those whom God called to marriage have bound themselves by the cord of *perpetual virginity.*[2] Next came the deadly cord of a vow, by which wretched souls were bound,[3] so that they never rose out of the ditch.

MATTHEW.	MARK.	LUKE.
XIX. 13. Then were presented to him children, that he might lay hands on them and pray; but the disciples rebuked them. 14. And Jesus said to them, Suffer children, and forbid them not, to come to me; for of such is the kingdom of heaven. 15. And when he had laid hands on them, he departed thence.	X. 13. And they brought to him children, that he might touch them; but the disciples rebuked those who presented them. 14. And when Jesus saw it, he was displeased, and said to them, Suffer children to come to me, and do not forbid them; for of such is the kingdom of heaven. 15. Verily I say to you, Whosoever shall not receive the kingdom of God as a child shall not enter into it. 16. And when he had taken them in his arms, he laid hands on them, and blessed them.	XVIII. 15. And they presented to him also infants, that he might touch them; which, when the disciples saw, they rebuked them. 16. But Jesus, when he had called them to him, said, Suffer children to come to me, and do not forbid them; for of such is the kingdom of God. 17. Verily I say to you, Whosoever shall not receive the kingdom of God as a child shall not enter into it.

[1] "Afin d'estre plus libres pour s'employer à meilleures choses à la gloire de Dieu;"—" in order to be more free for being employed in better things for the glory of God."

[2] "De perpetuelle virginité, comme on dit;"—" of perpetual virginity, as it is called."

[3] "Le voeu qui a este comme un licol pour tenir les poures ames enserrees de court;"—" the vow, which was like a halter to keep poor souls firmly bound."

This narrative is highly useful; for it shows that Christ receives not only those who, moved by holy desire and faith, freely approach to him, but those who are not yet of age to know how much they need his grace. Those *little children* have not yet any understanding to desire his blessing; but when they are presented to him, he gently and kindly receives them, and dedicates them to the Father[1] by a solemn act of blessing. We must observe the intention of those who presented the children; for if there had not been a deep-rooted conviction in their minds, that the power of the Spirit was at his disposal, that he might pour it out on the people of God, it would have been unreasonable to present their children. There is no room, therefore, to doubt, that they ask for them a participation of his grace; and so, by way of amplification, Luke adds the particle *also;* as if he had said that, after they had experienced the various ways in which he assisted adults, they formed an expectation likewise in regard to *children*, that, if he *laid hands on them*, they would not leave him without having received some of the gifts of the Spirit. The *laying on of hands* (as we have said on a former occasion) was an ancient and well known sign of *blessing;* and so there is no reason to wonder, if they desire that Christ, while employing that solemn ceremony, should pray for the *children*. At the same time, as *the inferior are blessed by the better*, (Heb. vii. 7,) they ascribe to him the power and honour of the highest Prophet.

Matthew XIX. 13. *But the disciples rebuked them.* If a crown[2] had been put on his head, they would have admitted it willingly, and with approbation; for they did not yet comprehend his actual office. But they reckon it unworthy of his character to receive *children;* and their error wanted not plausibility; for what has the highest Prophet and the Son of God to do with *infants?* But hence we learn, that they who judge of Christ according to the feeling of their flesh are unfair judges; for they constantly deprive him of his peculiar excellencies, and, on the other hand, ascribe,

---

[1] " A Dieu son Pere ;"—" to God his Father."
[2] " Une couronne royale ;"—" a royal crown."

under the appearance of honour, what does not at all belong to him. Hence arose an immense mass of superstitions, which presented to the world a fancied Christ.[1] And therefore let us learn not to think of him otherwise than what himself teaches, and not to assign to him a character different from what he has received from the Father. We see what happened with Popery. They thought that they were conferring a great honour on Christ, if they bowed down before a small piece of bread; but in the sight of God it was an offensive abomination. Again, because they did not think it sufficiently honourable to him to perform the office of an Advocate for us, they made for themselves innumerable intercessors; but in this way they deprived him of the honour of Mediator

14. *Suffer children.* He declares that he wishes to receive *children;* and at length, *taking them in his arms,* he not only embraces, but *blesses* them by the *laying on of hands;* from which we infer that his grace is extended even to those who are of that age. And no wonder; for since the whole race of Adam is shut up under the sentence of death, all from the least even to the greatest must perish, except those who are rescued by the only Redeemer. To exclude from the grace of redemption those who are of that age would be too cruel; and therefore it is not without reason that we employ this passage as a shield against the Anabaptists. They refuse baptism to *infants,* because infants are incapable of understanding that mystery which is denoted by it. We, on the other hand, maintain that, since baptism is the pledge and figure of the forgiveness of sins, and likewise of adoption by God, it ought not to be denied to *infants,* whom God adopts and washes with the blood of his Son. Their objection, that repentance and newness of life are also denoted by it, is easily answered. *Infants* are renewed by the Spirit of God, according to the capacity of their age, till that power which was concealed within them grows by degrees, and becomes fully manifest at the proper time. Again, when they argue that

[1] " Un Christ faict à la fantasie des hommes;"—" a Christ made according to the fancy of men."

there is no other way in which we are reconciled to God, and become heirs of adoption, than by faith, we admit this as to adults, but, with respect to *infants,* this passage demonstrates it to be false. Certainly, the *laying on of hands* was not a trifling or empty sign, and the prayers of Christ were not idly wasted in air. But he could not present the infants solemnly to God without giving them purity. And for what did he pray for them, but that they might be received into the number of the children of God? Hence it follows, that they were renewed by the Spirit to the hope of salvation. In short, by embracing them, he testified that they were reckoned by Christ among his flock. And if they were partakers of the spiritual gifts, which are represented by Baptism, it is unreasonable that they should be deprived of the outward sign. But it is presumption and sacrilege to drive far from the fold of Christ those whom he cherishes in his bosom, and to shut the door, and exclude as strangers those whom he does not wish to be *forbidden to come to him.*

For of such is the kingdom of heaven. Under this term he includes both *little children* and those who resemble them; for the Anabaptists foolishly exclude children, with whom the subject must have commenced; but at the same time, taking occasion from the present occurrence, he intended to exhort his disciples to lay aside malice and pride, and put on the nature of *children.* Accordingly, it is added by Mark and Luke, that no man *can enter into the kingdom of heaven* unless he be made to resemble a child. But we must attend to Paul's admonition, *not to be children in understanding, but in malice,* (1 Cor. xiv. 20.)

MATTHEW.	MARK.	LUKE.
XIX. 16. And, lo, one came and said to him, Good Master, what good thing shall I do, that I may have eternal life? 17. Who said to him, Why callest thou me good? There is none good but God alone;[1]	X. 17. And as he was going out into the road, one ran, and, when he had kneeled down, asked him, Good Master, what shall I do, that I may obtain eternal life? 18. And Jesus said to him, Why callest thou	XVIII. 18. And a certain ruler asked him, saying, Good Master, what shall I do, that I may obtain eternal life? 19. And Jesus said to him, Why callest thou me good?

[1] " Il n'y a nul bon, sinon un seul, c'est Dieu :"—" There is none good but one only, it is God."

MATTHEW.	MARK.	LUKE.
but if thou wilt enter into life, keep the commandments. 18. He saith to him, Which? And Jesus said, Thou shalt not murder, Thou shalt not commit adultery, Thou shalt not steal, Thou shalt not bear false witness, 19. Honour thy father and mother: and, Thou shalt love thy neighbour as thyself. 20. The young man saith to him, All these things have I kept from my youth: what do I still want? 21. Jesus saith to him, If thou wilt be perfect, go sell what thou hast, and give to the poor, and thou shalt have a treasure in heaven; and come, follow me. 22. And when the young man heard that saying, he went away sorrowful; for he had many possessions.[1]	me good? There is none good but God alone. 19. Thou knowest the commandments, Do not commit adultery, Do not kill, Do not steal, Do not bear false witness, Defraud not, Honour thy father and mother. 20. But he answering said to him, Master, all these things have I kept from my youth. 21. And Jesus, beholding him, loved him, and said to him, Thou art in want of one thing, go sell what thou hast, and give to the poor, and thou shalt have a treasure in heaven; and come, follow me, taking the cross on thy shoulders. 22. But he, affected with uneasiness on account of the saying, went away sorrowful; for he had many possessions.	None is good but God alone. 20. Thou knowest the commandments, Thou shalt not commit adultery, Thou shalt not kill, Thou shalt not steal, Thou shalt not bear false witness, Honour thy father and thy mother. 21. And he said, All these things have I kept from my youth. 22. Having heard this, Jesus said to him, Yet one thing thou wantest; sell all that thou hast, and give to the poor, and thou shalt have a treasure in heaven; and come, follow me. 23. Having heard these things, he was grieved; for he was very rich.

Matthew XIX. 16. *And, lo, one.* Luke says that he was *a ruler*, (ἄρχων,) that is, a man of very high authority, not one of the common people.[2] And though riches procure respect,[3] yet he appears to be here represented to have been held in high estimation as a good man. For my own part, after weighing all the circumstances, I have no doubt that, though he is called a *young man*, he belonged to the class of those who upheld the integrity of the *Elders*, by a sober and regular life.[4] He did not come treacherously, as the scribes were wont to do, but from a desire of instruction; and, accordingly,

---

[1] " Car il avoit beaucoup de richesses ;"—" for he had much wealth."
[2] " Que c'estoit un PRINCE ou seigneur ; c'est à dire, un homme d'estat et de grande authorité ;"—" that he was a PRINCE or lord ; that is to say, a man of rank and of great authority."
[3] " Combien que les richesses rendent un homme honorable au monde ;" —" though riches render a man honourable in the world."
[4] " Non point par trahison, et pour surprendre Christ ;"—" not by treachery, and to take Christ by surprise."

both by words and by *kneeling*, he testifies his reverence for Christ as a faithful teacher. But, on the other hand, a blind confidence in his works hindered him from profiting under Christ, to whom, in other respects, he wished to be submissive. Thus, in our own day, we find some who are not ill-disposed, but who, under the influence of I know not what shadowy holiness,[1] hardly relish the doctrine of the Gospel.

But, in order to form a more correct judgment of the meaning of the answer, we must attend to the form of the question. He does not simply ask how and by what means he shall reach *life*, but *what good thing he shall do, in order to obtain it*. He therefore dreams of merits, on account of which he may receive *eternal life* as a reward due; and therefore Christ appropriately sends him to the keeping of the law, which unquestionably is the way of *life*, as I shall explain more fully afterwards.

17. *Why callest thou me good?* I do not understand this correction in so refined a sense as is given by a good part of interpreters, as if Christ intended to suggest his Divinity; for they imagine that these words mean, " If thou perceivest in me nothing more exalted than human nature, thou falsely appliest to me the epithet *good*, which belongs to *God alone*." I do acknowledge that, strictly speaking, men and even angels do not deserve so honourable a title; because they have not a drop of goodness in themselves, but borrowed from God; and because in the former, goodness is only begun, and is not perfect. But Christ had no other intention than to maintain the truth of his doctrine; as if he had said, " Thou falsely *callest me a good Master*, unless thou acknowledgest that I have come from God." The essence of his Godhead, therefore, is not here maintained, but the *young man* is directed to admit the truth of the doctrine. He had already felt some disposition to obey; but Christ wishes him to rise higher, that he may hear God speaking. For—as it is customary with men to make angels of those who are devils—they indiscriminately give the appellation of *good teachers* to those in whom they

---

[1] " Pource qu'ils sont enveloppez de ie ne scay quelle ombre de sainctete;"—" because they are covered by I know not what shadow of holiness."

perceive nothing divine; but those modes of speaking are only profanations of the gifts of God. We need not wonder, therefore, if Christ, in order to maintain the authority of his doctrine, directs the *young man* to God.

Keep the commandments. This passage was erroneously interpreted by some of the ancients, whom the Papists have followed, as if Christ taught that, by *keeping* the law, we may merit *eternal life.* On the contrary, Christ did not take into consideration what men can do, but replied to the question, What is the righteousness of works? or, What does the Law require? And certainly we ought to believe that God comprehended in his law the way of living holily and righteously, in which righteousness is included; for not without reason did Moses make this statement, *He that doeth these things shall live in them,* (Lev. xviii. 5;) and again, *I call heaven and earth to witness that I have this day showed you life,* (Deut. xxx. 19.) We have no right, therefore, to deny that the keeping of the law is righteousness, by which any man who kept the law perfectly—if there were such a man—would obtain life for himself. But as we are *all destitute of the glory of God,* (Rom. iii. 23,) nothing but cursing will be found in the law; and nothing remains for us but to betake ourselves to the undeserved gift of righteousness. And therefore Paul lays down a twofold righteousness, *the righteousness of the law,* (Rom. x. 5,) and the righteousness of faith, (Rom. x. 6.) He makes the first to consist in works, and the second, in the free grace of Christ.

Hence we infer, that this reply of Christ is legal, because it was proper that the *young man* who inquired about the righteousness of works should first be taught that no man is accounted righteous before God unless he has fulfilled the law,[1] (which is impossible,) that, convinced of his weakness, he might betake himself to the assistance of faith. I acknowledge, therefore, that, as God has promised the reward of *eternal life* to those who keep his law, we ought to hold by this way, if the weakness of our flesh did not prevent; but Scripture teaches us, that it is through our own fault that it becomes necessary for us to receive as a gift

---

[1] "Sinon qu'il ait accompli toute la loy de poinct en poinct;"—"unless he has fulfilled all the law in every point."

what we cannot obtain by works. If it be objected, that it is in vain to hold out to us *the righteousness which is in the law,* (Rom. x. 5,) which no man will ever be able to reach, I reply, since it is the first part of instruction, by which we are led to the righteousness which is obtained by prayer, it is far from being superfluous; and, therefore, when Paul says, that *the doers of the law are justified,* (Rom. ii. 13,) he excludes all from *the righteousness of the law.*

This passage sets aside all the inventions which the Papists have contrived in order to obtain salvation. For not only are they mistaken in wishing to lay God under obligation to them by their good works, to bestow salvation as a debt; but when they apply themselves to do what is right, they leave out of view the doctrine of the law, and attend chiefly to their pretended *devotions,* as they call them, not that they openly reject the law of God, but that they greatly prefer human traditions.[1] But what does Christ say? That the only worship of which God approves is that which he has prescribed; because *obedience is better to him than all sacrifices,*[2] (1 Sam. xv. 22.) So then, while the Papists are employed in frivolous traditions, let every man who endeavours to regulate his life by obedience to Christ direct his whole attention to *keep the commandments* of the law.

18. *Thou shalt not murder.* It is surprising that, though Christ intended to show that we are bound to obey the whole law, he should mention the second table only; but he did so, because from the duties of charity the disposition of every man is better ascertained. Piety towards God holds, no doubt, a higher rank;[3] but as the observation of the first

---

[1] "D'autant qu'ils font bien plus grand cas de leurs traditions humaines, que des commandemens de Dieu;"—" because they set far higher value on their human traditions than on the commandments of God."

[2] "Pource qu'il estime plus obeissance que tous les sacrifices du monde;"—" because he esteems obedience more than all the sacrifices in the world."

[3] "Vray est qu'entre les commandemens ceux qui parlent de la recognoissance que nous devons à Dieu tiennent le premier degre;"—" it is

table is often feigned by hypocrites, the second table is better adapted for making a scrutiny.[1] Let us know, therefore, that Christ selected those commandments in which is contained a proof of true righteousness; but by a *synecdoche* he takes a part for the whole. As to the circumstance of his placing that commandment last which speaks of *honouring* parents, it is of no consequence, for he paid no attention to the regular order. Yet it is worthy of notice, that this commandment is declared to belong to the second table, that no one may be led astray by the error of Josephus, who thought that it belonged to the first table.[2] What is added at the end, *Thou shalt love thy neighbour*, contains nothing different from the former commandments, but is a general explanation of them all.

The young man saith to him. The law must have been dead to him, when he vainly imagined that he was so righteous; for if he had not flattered himself through hypocrisy, it was an excellent advice to him to learn humility, to contemplate his spots and blemishes in the mirror of the law. But, intoxicated with foolish confidence, he fearlessly boasts that he has discharged his duty properly from his childhood. Paul acknowledges that the same thing happened to himself, that, so long as the power of *the law* was unknown to him, he believed that he *was alive;* but that, after he knew what *the law* could do, a deadly wound was inflicted on him, (Rom. vii. 9.) So the reply of Christ, which follows, was suited to the man's disposition. And yet Christ does not demand any thing beyond the commandments of the law, but, as the bare recital had not affected him, Christ employed other words for detecting the hidden disease of avarice.

I confess that we are nowhere commanded in the law to *sell all;* but as the design of the law is, to bring men to self-denial,

---

true that, among the commandments, those which speak of the acknowledgment which we owe to God hold the first rank."

[1] "*A faire examen pour cognoistre les personnes;*"—"to make a scrutiny for knowing persons."

[2] Josephus says that there were *five on each table*, from which it must be inferred, that he considered the Fifth commandment as belonging to the First Table. His words are: *He showed them the two tables, with the ten commandments engraven upon them,* FIVE UPON EACH TABLE; *and the writing was by the hand of God.*—(Ant. iii. 6, 8.)—*Ed.*

and as it expressly condemns covetousness, we see that Christ had no other object in view than to correct the false conviction of the *young man*.[1] For if he had known himself thoroughly, as soon as he heard the mention of *the law*, he would have acknowledged that he was liable to the judgment of God; but now, when the bare words of the law do not sufficiently convince him of his guilt, the inward meaning is expressed by other words. If Christ now demanded any thing beyond the commandments of the law, he would be at variance with himself. He just now taught that perfect righteousness is comprehended in *the commandments* of the law: how then will it agree with this to charge the law with deficiency? Besides, the protestation of Moses, (Deut. xxx. 15,) which I formerly quoted, would be false.

Mark X. 21. *One thing thou wantest.* Christ therefore does not mean that the *young man wanted* ONE THING beyond the keeping of the law, but in the very keeping of the law. For though the law nowhere obliges us to *sell all*, yet as it represses all sinful desires, and teaches us to *bear the cross*, as it bids us be prepared for hunger and poverty, the *young man* is very far from keeping it fully, so long as he is attached to his riches, and burns with covetousness. And he says that *one thing is wanting*, because he does not need to preach to him about fornication and murder, but to point out a particular disease, as if he were laying his finger on the sore.

It ought also to be observed, that he does not only enjoin him to *sell*, but likewise to *give to the poor*; for to part with riches would not be in itself a virtue, but rather a vain ambition. Profane historians applaud Crates, a Theban, because he threw into the sea his money and all that he reckoned valuable; for he did not think that he could save himself unless his wealth were lost; as if it would not have been better to bestow on others what he imagined to be more than he needed. Certainly, as *charity is the bond of perfection*, (Col. iii. 14,) he who deprives others, along with himself, of the use of money, de-

---

[1] "La fausse persuasion et presomption de ce ieune homme;"—"the false conviction and presumption of this young man."

serves no praise; and therefore Christ applauds not simply the *selling*, but liberality in assisting *the poor*.

The mortification of the flesh is still more strongly urged by Christ, when he says, *Follow me.* For he enjoins him not only to become his disciple, but to submit his shoulders to *bear the cross*, as Mark expressly states. And it was necessary that such an excitement should be applied; for, having been accustomed to the ease, and leisure, and conveniences, of home, he had never experienced, in the smallest degree, what it was to crucify the old man, and to subdue the desires of the flesh. But it is excessively ridiculous in the monks, under the pretence of this passage, to claim for themselves a state of perfection. First, it is easy to infer, that Christ does not command all without exception to *sell all that they have;* for the husbandman, who had been accustomed to live by his labour, and to support his children, would do wrong in selling his possession, if he were not constrained to it by any necessity. To keep what God has put in our power, provided that, by maintaining ourselves and our family in a sober and frugal manner, we bestow some portion on the poor, is a greater virtue than to squander all. But what sort of thing is that famous *selling*, on which the monks plume themselves? A good part of them, finding no provision at home, plunge themselves into monasteries as well-stocked hog-styes. All take such good care of themselves, that they feed in idleness on the bread of others. A rare exchange truly, when those who are ordered to give to the poor what they justly possess are not satisfied with their own, but seize on the property of others.

Jesus beholding him, loved him. The inference which the Papists draw from this, that works morally good—that is, works which are not performed by the impulse of the Spirit, but go before regeneration—have *the merit of congruity*, is an excessively childish contrivance. For if *merit* be alleged to be the consequence of the love of God, we must then say that frogs and fleas have merit, because all the creatures of God, without exception, are the objects of his love. To distinguish the degrees of love is, therefore, a matter of importance.[1] As to the present passage, it may be enough to state briefly, that God embraces in fatherly love none but his children, whom he has regenerated with the Spirit of adoption, and that it is in consequence of this love that they are accepted at his tribunal. In this sense, to be loved by God, and to be justified in his sight, are synonymous terms.[2]

But God is sometimes said to *love* those whom he does not approve or justify; for, since the preservation of the human race is agreeable to Him—which consists in justice, uprightness, moderation, prudence, fidelity, and temperance—he is said to *love* the political virtues; not that they are meritorious of salvation or of grace, but that they have reference to an end of which he approves. In this sense, under various points of view, God *loved* Aristides and Fabricius, and also *hated* them; for, in so far as he had bestowed on them outward righteousness, and that for the general advantage, he *loved* his own work in them; but as their heart was impure, the outward semblance of righteousness was of no avail for obtaining righteousness. For we know that by faith alone hearts are purified, and that the Spirit of uprightness is given to the members of Christ alone. Thus the question is answered, How was it possible that Christ should *love* a man who was proud and a hypocrite, while nothing is more hateful to God than these two vices? For it is not inconsistent, that the good seed, which God has implanted in some natures, shall be *loved* by Him, and yet that He should reject their persons and works on account of corruption.

Matthew XIX. 22. *He went away sorrowful.* The result at length showed how widely distant the *young man* was from that perfection to which Christ had called him; for how comes it that he withdraws from the school of Christ, but because he finds it uneasy to be stripped of his riches? But if we are not prepared to endure poverty, it is manifest that covetousness reigns in us. And this is what I said at the

---

[1] " Parquoy il est besoin de mettre quelque distinction, et recognoistre qu'il y a divers degrez d'amour en Dieu;"—" wherefore it is necessary to state some distinction, and to observe that there are various degrees of love in God."

[2] " Signifient du tout une mesme chose;"—" mean entirely the same thing."

outset, that the order which Christ gave, to *sell all that he had,* was not an addition to the law, but the scrutiny of a concealed vice.¹ For the more deeply a man is tainted by this or the other vice, the more strikingly will it be dragged forth to light by being reproved. We are reminded also by this example that, if we would persevere steadily in the school of Christ, we must renounce the flesh. This *young man*, who had brought both a desire to learn and modesty, withdrew from Christ, because it was hard to part with a darling vice. The same thing will happen to us, unless the sweetness of the grace of Christ render all the allurements of the flesh distasteful to us. Whether or not this temptation was temporary, so that the *young man* afterwards repented, we know not; but it may be conjectured with probability, that his covetousness kept him back from making any proficiency.

MATTHEW.	MARK.	LUKE.
XIX. 23. And Jesus said to his disciples, Verily I say to you, A rich man will with difficulty enter into the kingdom of heaven. 24. Again I say to you, It is easier for a camel² to pass through the eye of a needle, than for a rich man to enter into the kingdom of God. 25. And his disciples, when they had heard these things, were greatly amazed,³ saying, Who then can be saved? 26. And Jesus, beholding them, said to them, With men this is impossible; but with God all things are possible.	X. 23. And when Jesus had looked around, he said to his disciples, With what difficulty shall they who have riches enter into the kingdom of God! 24. And the disciples were astonished at his words. But Jesus again replying, said to them, Children, how difficult is it for those who have confidence in riches to enter into the kingdom of God! 25. It is easier for a camel to pass through the eye of a needle, than for a rich man to enter into the kingdom of God. 26. And they wondered beyond measure, saying within themselves, And who can be saved? 27. And Jesus beholding them saith, With men it is impossible, but not with God: for all things are possible with God.	XVIII. 24. And Jesus, perceiving that he was sorrowful, said, With what difficulty shall they who have riches enter into the kingdom of God! 25. For it is easier for a camel to pass through the eye of a needle, than for a rich man to enter into the kingdom of God. 26. And they that heard it said, And who can be saved?⁴ 27. But he said, The things which are impossible with men are possible with God.

¹ " Que ç'a este pour sonder et descouvrir un vice caché ;"—" that it was to search and discover a concealed vice."
² " Il est plus facile qu'un CHABLE passe ;"—" it is easier for a CABLE to pass."
³ " S'estonnerent grandement ;"—" were greatly astonished."
⁴ " Qui peut donc estre sauvé ?"—" Who can then be saved ?"

Matthew XIX. 23. *A rich man will with difficulty enter.* Christ warns them, not only how dangerous and how deadly a plague avarice is, but also how great an obstacle is presented by riches. In Mark, indeed, he mitigates the harshness of his expression, by restricting it to those only *who place confidence in riches.* But these words are, I think, intended to confirm, rather than correct, the former statement, as if he had affirmed that they ought not to think it strange, that he made the *entrance into the kingdom of heaven* so *difficult* for *the rich,* because it is an evil almost common to all to *trust in their riches.* Yet this doctrine is highly useful to all; to *the rich,* that, being warned of their danger, they may be on their guard; to the poor, that, satisfied with their lot, they may not so eagerly desire what would bring more damage than gain. It is true, indeed, that *riches* do not, in their own nature, hinder us from following God; but, in consequence of the depravity of the human mind, it is scarcely possible for those who have a great abundance to avoid being intoxicated by them. So they who are exceedingly *rich* are held by Satan bound, as it were, in chains, that they may not raise their thoughts to heaven; nay more, they bury and entangle themselves, and become utter slaves to the earth. The comparison of the *camel,* which is soon after added, is intended to amplify the *difficulty;* for it means that *the rich* are so swelled with pride and presumption, that they cannot endure to be reduced to the straits through which God makes his people to pass. The word *camel* denotes, I think, a rope used by sailors, rather than the animal so named.[1]

[1] "Vray est que le mot CAMELUS, dont a usé l'Evangeliste, signifie tant un chameau qu'un chable : mais i'aime mieux le prendre en la derniere signitication pour une grosse corde de navire."—"It is true that the word κάμηλος, which the Evangelist has employed, means both a *camel* and a *cable;* but I prefer taking it in the latter signification for *a large rope used by sailors.*" The two English words *camel* and *cable* closely resemble each other, and the corresponding Greek words differ only by a single vowel; κάμηλος denoting a *camel,* and κάμιλος a *cable* or *rope.* It does not appear that CALVIN relied on certain Manuscripts of no good authority, which substitute καμίλον for καμήλον. But he adopted the notion equally unfounded, that Greek writers sometimes used κάμηλος in the sense of κάμιλος. Had due allowance been made for the boldness of Eastern imagery, the supposed difficulty would have disappeared, and the

25. *And his disciples, when they heard these things, were greatly amazed.* The *disciples are astonished*, because it ought to awaken in us no little anxiety, that *riches* obstruct the *entrance into the kingdom of God;* for, wherever we turn our eyes, a thousand obstacles will present themselves. But let us observe that, while they were struck with astonishment, they did not shrink from the doctrines of Christ. The case was different with him who was lately mentioned; for he was so much alarmed by the severity of the commandment, that he separated from Christ; while they, though trembling, and inquiring, *who can be saved?* do not break off in an opposite direction, but are desirous to conquer despair. Thus it will be of service to us to tremble at the threatenings of God, whenever he denounces any thing that is gloomy or dreadful, provided that our minds are not discouraged, but rather aroused.

26. *With men this is impossible.* Christ does not entirely free the minds of his disciples from all anxiety; for it is proper that they should perceive how difficult it is to ascend to heaven; first, that they may direct all their efforts to this object; and next, that, distrusting themselves, they may implore strength from heaven. We see how great is our indolence and carelessness; and what the consequence would be if believers thought that they had to walk at ease, for pastime, along a smooth and cheerful plain. Such is the reason why Christ does not extenuate the danger—though he perceives the terror which it excited in his disciples—but

most refined taste would have been fully gratified. The poet Southey has seized the true spirit of the passage:—

" *S.* The *camel* and the *needle*,—
Is that then in your mind?
" *T.* Even so. The text
Is gospel wisdom. I would ride the *camel*,—
Yea leap him flying, through the *needle's eye*,
As easily as such a pampered soul
Could pass the narrow gate."

At one period, critics showed a strong leaning to the idea of *cable*, which our Author favours, but have now very generally abandoned it, and returned to the true reading.—*Ed.*

rather increases it; for though formerly he said only that it was *difficult,* he now affirms it to be *impossible.* Hence it is evident, that those teachers are guilty of gross impropriety, who are so much afraid to speak harshly, that they give indulgence to the slothfulness of the flesh. They ought to follow, on the contrary, the rule of Christ, who so regulates his style that, after men have been bowed down within themselves, he teaches them to rely on the grace of God alone, and, at the same time, excites them to prayer. In this manner, the weakness of men is seasonably relieved, not by ascribing anything to them, but by arousing their minds to expect the grace of God. By this reply of Christ is also refuted that widely embraced principle—which the Papists have borrowed from Jerome—"Whoever shall say that it is impossible to keep the law, let him be accursed." For Christ plainly declares, that it is not possible for men to keep the way of salvation, except so far as the grace of God assists them.

MATTHEW.	MARK.	LUKE.
XIX. 27. Then Peter answering said to him, Lo, we have left all, and have followed thee: what therefore shall we have? 28. And Jesus said to them, Verily I say to you, That you who have followed me in the regeneration, when the Son of man shall sit on the throne of his majesty, you also shall sit on twelve thrones, judging the twelve tribes of Israel. 29. And whosoever shall leave houses, or brothers, or sisters, or father, or mother, or wife,	X. 28. And Peter began to say to him, Lo, we have left all, and have followed thee. 29. And Jesus answering said, Verily I say to you, There is no man that hath left house, or brothers, or sisters, or father, or mother, or wife, or children, or fields, for my sake, and (for the sake) of the Gospel,[1] 30. But shall receive a hundred-fold now at this time, houses, and brothers, and sisters, and mothers, and children, and	XVIII. 28. And Peter said, Lo, we have left all, and have followed thee. 29. Who said to them, Verily I say to you, There is no man who hath left house, or parents, or brothers, or wife, or children, on account of the kingdom of God, 30. Who shall not receive much more at this time, and in the world to come eternal life. XXII. 28. You are they that have continued with me in my temptations:[2] 29. And I appoint to you the

[1] "Pour l'amour de moy et de l'Evangile;"—"for the love of me and of the Gospel."
[2] "Qui avez persévéré avec moy;"—"who have persevered with me."

MATTHEW.	MARK.	LUKE.
or children, or fields, for the sake of my name, shall receive a hundred-fold, and shall obtain eternal life. 30. And many that are first shall be last, and the last first.[1]	fields, with persecution, and in the world to come eternal life. 31. But many that are first shall be last, and the last first.[1]	kingdom,[2] as my Father hath appointed it to me; 30. That you may eat and drink at my table in my kingdom, and may sit on thrones, judging the twelve tribes of Israel.

Matthew XIX. 27. *Then Peter answering said to him.* *Peter* tacitly compares himself and the other disciples to the *rich* man, whom the world had turned aside from Christ. As they had led a poor and wandering[3] life, which was not unaccompanied by disgrace and by annoyances, and as no better condition for the future presented itself, he properly inquires if it be to no purpose that they have *left all* their property, and devoted themselves to Christ; for it would be unreasonable if, after having been stripped of their property by the Lord, they should not be restored to a better condition.

Lo, we have left all. But what were those *all things?* for, being mean and very poor men, they scarcely had a home to leave, and therefore this boasting might appear to be ridiculous. And certainly experience shows how large an estimate men commonly form of their duties towards God, as at this day, among the Papists, those who were little else than beggars make it a subject of haughty reproach that they have sustained great damage for the sake of the Gospel. But the disciples may be excused on this ground, that, though their wealth was not magnificent, they subsisted at home, by their manual labours, not less cheerfully than the richest man. And we know that men of humble condition, who have been accustomed to a quiet and modest life, reckon it a greater hardship to be torn from their wives and children than those who are led by ambition, or who are carried in various directions by the gale of prosperity. Certainly, if some reward

---

[1] "Et les derniers seront premiers;"—"and the last shall be first."
[2] "Le royaume."
[3] "Et suiete à changer souvent de demeurance;"—"and liable to change their residence frequently."

had not been reserved for the disciples, it would have been foolish in them to have changed their course of life.[1] But though on that ground they might be excused, they err in this respect, that they demand a triumph to be given them, before they have finished their warfare. If we ever experience such uneasiness at delay, and if we are tempted by impatience, let us learn first to reflect on the comforts by which the Lord soothes the bitterness of the cup in this world, and next elevate our minds to the hope of the heavenly life; for these two points embrace the answer of Christ.

28. *Verily I say to you.* That the disciples may not think that they have lost their pains, and repent of having begun the course, Christ warns them that the glory of his kingdom, which at that time was still hidden, was about to be revealed. As if he had said, "There is no reason why that mean condition should discourage you; for I, who am scarcely equal to the lowest, will at length ascend to my throne of majesty. Endure then for a little, till the time arrive for revealing my glory." And what does he then promise to them? That they shall be partakers of the same glory.

You also shall sit on twelve thrones. By assigning to them *thrones,* from which they may *judge the twelve tribes of Israel,* he compares them to assessors, or first councillors and judges, who occupy the highest seats in the royal council. We know that the number of those who were chosen to be apostles was *twelve,* in order to testify that, by the agency of Christ, God purposed to collect the remnant of his people which was scattered. This was a very high rank, but hitherto was concealed; and therefore Christ holds their wishes in suspense till the latest revelation of his kingdom, when they will fully receive the fruit of their election. And though the kingdom of Christ is, in some respects, manifested by the preaching of the Gospel, there is no doubt that Christ here speaks of the last day.

---

[1] "D'avoir changé d'estat et de façon de vivre;"—"for having changed their condition and their way of living."

In the regeneration. Some connect this term with the following clause. In this sense, *regeneration* would be nothing else than the renovation which shall follow our restoration, when life shall swallow up what is mortal, and when our mean body shall be transformed into the heavenly glory of Christ. But I rather explain *regeneration* as referring to the first coming of Christ; for then the world began to be renewed, and arose out of the darkness of death into the light of life. And this way of speaking occurs frequently in the Prophets, and is exceedingly adapted to the connection of this passage. For the renovation of the Church, which had been so frequently promised, had raised an expectation of wonderful happiness, as soon as the Messiah should appear; and therefore, in order to guard against that error, Christ distinguishes between the beginning and the completion of his reign.

Luke XXII. 28. *You are they who have continued with me.* Although Luke appears to relate a different discourse of Christ, and one which was delivered at a different time, yet I have no doubt that it refers to the same time. For it is not a continued discourse of Christ that is here related, but detached sentences, without any regard to the order of time, as we shall shortly afterwards have occasion to state. But he employs more words than Matthew; for he declares that, as the apostles had accompanied him, and had *remained stedfastly in his temptations*, they would also be partakers of his glory. It is asked, in what sense does he call them *his temptations?* I think that he means the contests by which God tried him and the apostles in common. And properly did he use the word *temptations;* for, according to the feeling of human nature, his faith and patience were actually tried.

29. *And I appoint to you the kingdom.* Here he makes them not only judges, but *kings;* for he shares with them *the kingdom* which he received from *the Father.* There is an emphasis in the word *appoint,* that they may not, by warmth and vehemence of desire, hasten too eagerly to possess *the kingdom,* of which he alone has the lawful right to dispose. By his own example, also, he exhorts them to patience; for,

though he was ordained by *the Father* to be a King, yet he was not immediately raised to his glory, but even *emptied himself,* (Philip. ii. 7,) and by the ignominy of the cross obtained kingly honour. To *eat and drink at his table* is put metaphorically for being made partakers of the same glory.

Matthew XIX. 29. *And whosoever shall forsake.* After having raised the expectation of his followers to the hope of a future life, he supports them by immediate consolations,[1] and strengthens them for bearing the cross. For though God permit his people to be severely afflicted, he never abandons them, so as not to recompense their distresses by his assistance. And here he does not merely address the apostles, but takes occasion to direct his discourse generally to all the godly. The substance of it is this: Those who shall willingly *lose all* for the sake of Christ, will be more happy even in this life than if they had retained the full possession of them; but the chief reward is laid up for them in heaven.

But what he promises about recompensing them *a hundredfold* appears not at all to agree with experience; for in the greater number of cases, those who have been deprived of their parents, or children, and other relatives—who have been reduced to widowhood, and stripped of their wealth, for the testimony of Christ—are so far from recovering their property, that in exile, solitude, and desertion, they have a hard struggle with severe poverty. I reply, if any man estimate aright the immediate grace of God, by which he relieves the sorrows of his people, he will acknowledge that it is justly preferred to all the riches of the world. For though unbelievers *flourish,* (Ps. xcii. 7,) yet as they *know not what awaits them on the morrow,* (James iv. 14,) they must be always tossed about in perplexity and terror, and it is only by stupifying themselves in some sort that they can at all enjoy prosperity.[2] Yet God

---

[1] "De consolations de la vie presente;"—" by consolations of the present life."

[2] "Ils ne peuvent iouir à leur aise des biens qu'ils ont, sinon qu'ils entrent comme en une stupidite, et effacent tout sentiment de leur conscience;"—"they cannot enjoy at their ease the good things which they possess, unless they become, as it were, stupid, and destroy every feeling of their conscience."

gladdens his people, so that the small portion of good which they enjoy is more highly valued by them, and far sweeter, than if out of Christ they had enjoyed an unlimited abundance of good things. In this sense I interpret the expression used by Mark, *with persecutions;* as if Christ had said, Though *persecutions* always await the godly in this world, and though the cross, as it were, is attached to their back, yet so sweet is the seasoning of the grace of God, which gladdens them, that their condition is more desirable than the luxuries of kings.

30. *And many that are first shall be last.* This sentence was added in order to shake off the indolence of the flesh. The apostles, though they had scarcely begun the course, were hastening to demand the prize. And such is the disposition of almost all of us, that, when a month has elapsed, we ask, like soldiers who have served their time, to receive a discharge. But Christ exhorts those who have *begun well* (Gal. iii. 3; v. 7) to vigorous perseverance, and at the same time gives warning, that it will be of no avail to *runners* to have begun with alacrity, if they lose courage in the midst of the course. In like manner Paul also warns us, that *not all who run obtain the prize,* (1 Cor. ix. 24;) and in another passage he exhorts believers, by referring to his own example, to *forget those things which are behind, and press forward to the remaining portion of their course,* (Philip. iii. 13, 14.) As often, therefore, as we call to mind the heavenly crown, we ought, as it were, to feel the application of fresh spurs, that we may not be more indolent for the future.

MATTHEW.

XX. 1. For the kingdom of heaven is like a householder, who went out at break of day to hire labourers into his vineyard. 2. And having made an agreement with the labourers for a penny a day, he sent them into his vineyard. 3. And having gone out about the third hour, he saw others standing idle in the market-place. 4. And he said to them, Go you also into the vineyard, and whatever shall be right I will give you. 5. And they went away. And again he went out about the sixth and ninth hour, and acted in the same manner. 6. And about the eleventh hour he went out, and found others standing idle, and said to them, Why stand you here all the day idle? 7. They say to him, Because nobody hath hired us. He saith to them, Go you also into the vineyard, and you

MATTHEW.

will receive what shall be right. 8. And when the evening was come, the master of the vineyard saith to his steward, Call the labourers, and pay them their hire, beginning with the last even to the first. 9. And when they came who had come about the eleventh hour, they received every man a penny. 10. And they who had come first thought that they would receive more, and they also received every man a penny. 11. And when they had received it, they murmured against the householder, 12. Saying, These last have been but one hour at work, and thou hast made them equal to us, who have endured the burden of the day and the heat. 13. But he answering one of them, said, Friend, I do thee no wrong : didst not thou agree with me for a penny ? 14. Take what is thine, and go away : and I intend to give to this last as much as to thee. 15. Is it not lawful for me to do what I will with my own property ? Is thy eye evil, because I am good ? 16. So the last shall be first, and the first shall be last : for many are called, but few are chosen.

As this parable is nothing else than a confirmation of the preceding sentence, *the last shall be first,* it now remains to see in what manner it ought to be applied. Some commentators reduce it to this general proposition, that the glory of all will be equal, because the heavenly inheritance is not obtained by the merits of works, but is bestowed freely. But Christ does not here argue either about the equality of the heavenly glory, or about the future condition of the godly. He only declares that those who were first in point of time have no right to boast or to insult others; because the Lord, whenever he pleases, may call those whom he appeared for a time to disregard, and may make them equal, or even superior, to the first. If any man should resolve to sift out with exactness every portion of this parable, his curiosity would be useless; and therefore we have nothing more to inquire than what was the design of Christ to teach. Now we have already said that he had no other object in view than to excite his people by continual spurs to make progress. We know that indolence almost always springs from excessive confidence; and this is the reason why many, as if they had reached the goal, stop short in the middle of the course. Thus Paul enjoins us to *forget the things which are behind,* (Philip. iii. 13,) that, reflecting on what yet remains for us, we may arouse ourselves to persevere in running. But there will be no harm in examining the words, that the doctrine may be more clearly evinced.

Matthew XX. 1. *For the kingdom of heaven is like a householder.* The meaning is, that such is the nature of the divine calling, as if a man were, early in the morning, to hire labourers for the cultivation of his vineyard at a fixed price, and were afterwards to employ others without an agreement, but to give them an equal hire. He uses the phrase, *kingdom of heaven,* because he compares the spiritual life to the earthly life, and the reward of eternal life to money which men pay in return for work that has been done for them. There are some who give an ingenious interpretation to this passage, as if Christ were distinguishing between Jews and Gentiles. The Jews, they tell us, were called *at the first hour,* with an agreement as to the hire; for the Lord promised to them eternal life, on the condition that they should fulfil the law; while, in calling the Gentiles, no bargain was made, at least as to works, for salvation was freely offered to them in Christ. But all subtleties of that sort are unseasonable; for the Lord makes no distinction in the bargain, but only in the time; because those who entered *last,* and in the evening, *into the vineyard,* receive the same hire with *the first.* Though, in the Law, God formerly promised to the Jews the hire of works, (Lev. xviii. 5,) yet we know that this was without effect, because no man ever obtained salvation by his merits.

Why then, it will be said, does Christ expressly mention a bargain[1] in reference to *the first,* but make no mention of it in reference to the others? It was in order to show that, without doing injury to any one, as much honour is conferred on *the last,* as if they had been called at the beginning. For, strictly speaking, he owes no man any thing, and from us, who are devoted to his service, he demands, as a matter of right, all the duties which are incumbent on us. But as he freely offers to us a *reward,* he is said to *hire* the labours which, on other grounds, were due to him. This is also the reason why he gives the name of *a hire* to the crown which he bestows freely. Again, in order to show that we have no right to complain of God, if he make us companions in honour

---

[1] "Un pris convenu;"—"a price agreed upon."

with those who followed us after a long interval, he borrowed a comparison from the ordinary custom of men, who bargain about the *hire*, before they send labourers to their work.

If any man infer from this, that men are created for the purpose of doing something, and that every man has his province assigned him by God, that they may not sit down in idleness, he will offer no violence to the words of Christ.[1] We are also at liberty to infer, that our whole life is unprofitable, and that we are justly accused of indolence, until each of us regulate his life by the command and calling of God. Hence it follows, that they labour to no purpose, who rashly undertake this or that course of life, and do not wait for the intimation of the call of God. Lastly, we learn from the words of Christ, that those only are pleasing to God who labour for the advantage of their brethren.

A *penny* (which was rather more than four times the value of a French *carolus*[2]) was probably the ordinary hire for a day's work. The *third, sixth,* and *ninth hour*, are expressly mentioned, because, while the ancients were wont to divide the day into twelve hours, from sunrise to sunset, there was another division of the day into every three hours; as, again, the night was divided into four *watches;* and so *the eleventh hour* means the close of the day.

8. *And when the evening was come.* It would be improper to look for a mystery in the injunction of the *householder* to *begin with the last*, as if God crowned those *first* who were last in the order of time; for such a notion would not at all agree with the doctrine of Paul. They *that are alive*, he says, *at the coming of Christ, will not come before those who previously fell asleep in Christ,* but will follow, (1 Thess. iv. 15.) But Christ observes a different order in this passage, because he could not otherwise have expressed—what he afterwards adds —that *the first murmured,* because they did not *receive more.*[3]

[1] " Cela ne sera point tirer trop loin les parolles de Christ;"—" this will not be straining too far the words of Christ."
[2] *A penny* (δηνάριον) was worth about *sevenpence-halfpenny* of our money.—*Ed.*
[3] " Pource qu'on ne leur donnoit non plus qu'aux derniers;"—"because no more was given to them than to the last."

Besides, he did not intend to say that this *murmuring* will take place at the last day, but merely to affirm that there will be no occasion for *murmuring*. The *personification* (προ- σωποποιία) which he employs throws no small light on this doctrine, that men have no right to complain of the bounty of God, when he honours unworthy persons by large rewards beyond what they deserve. There is no foundation, therefore, for what some have imagined, that these words are directed against the Jews, who were full of malice and envy towards the Gentiles; for it would be absurd to say that such persons receive an equal *hire* with the children of God, and this malignity, which leads men to exclaim against God, does not apply to believers. But the plain meaning is, that, since God defrauds no man of a just *hire*, He is at liberty to bestow on those whom He has lately called an undeserved reward.

16. *So the first shall be last.* He does not now compare the Jews to the Gentiles, (as in another passage,) nor the reprobate, who swerve from the faith, to the elect who persevere; and therefore the sentence which is introduced by some interpreters, *many are called, but few are chosen,* does not apply to that point. Christ only meant to say that every one who has been called before others ought to run with so much the greater alacrity, and, next, to exhort all men to be modest, not to give themselves the preference above others, but willingly to share with them a common prize. As the apostles were the first-fruits of the whole church, they appeared to possess some superiority; and Christ did not deny that they would *sit as judges to govern the twelve tribes of Israel.* But that they might not be carried away by ambition or vain confidence in themselves, it was necessary also to remind them that others, who would long afterwards be called, would be partakers of the same glory, because God is not limited to any person, but calls freely whomsoever He pleases, and bestows on those who are called whatever rewards He thinks fit.

MATTHEW.	MARK.	LUKE.
XX. 17. And Jesus, going up to Jerusalem, took the twelve disciples apart in the way, and said to them, 18, Lo, we go up to Jerusalem; and the Son of man will be delivered to the chief priests and scribes; and they will condemn him to death, 19. And they will deliver him to the Gentiles to mock, and to scourge, and to crucify him;[1] and on the third day he will rise again.	X. 32. And they were in the way going up to Jerusalem; and Jesus went before them: and they were amazed; and, while they followed him, were afraid. And having again taken aside the twelve, he began to tell them what things would happen to him: 33. Lo, we go up to Jerusalem; and the Son of man will be delivered to the chief priests and scribes; and they will condemn him to death, and will deliver him to the Gentiles: 34. And will mock him, and scourge him, and spit upon him, and kill him; and on the third day he will rise again.	XVIII. 31. And Jesus took the twelve, and said to them, Lo, we go up to Jerusalem, and all things which have been written by the prophets concerning the Son of man will be accomplished. 32. For he will be delivered to the Gentiles, and mocked, and insulted, and spat on; 33. And after having scourged, they will kill him; and on the third day he will rise again. 34. And they understood none of these things; and this saying was hidden from them, and they understood not the things which were spoken.[2]

Though the apostles had been previously informed what kind of death awaited our Lord, yet as they had not sufficiently profited by it, he now repeats anew what he had frequently said. He sees that the day of his death is at hand; nay more, he is already in a state of readiness to offer himself to be sacrificed; and, on the other hand, he sees the disciples not only afraid, but overwhelmed by blind alarm. He therefore exhorts them to steadiness, that they may not immediately yield to temptation. Now there are two methods by which he confirms them; for, by foretelling what would happen, he not only fortifies them, that they may not give way, when a calamity, which has arisen suddenly and contrary to expectation, takes them by surprise, but meets the offence of the cross by a proof of his Divinity, that they may not lose courage at beholding his short abasement, when they are convinced that he is the Son of God, and therefore

---

[1] "Pour estre mocqué, et flagellé, et crucifié;"—"to be mocked, and scourged, and crucified."

[2] "Et ne pouvoyent entendre ce qu'il leur disoit;"—"and they could not understand what he said to them."

will be victorious over death. The second method of confirmation is taken from his approaching resurrection.

But it will be proper to look more closely at the words. *Mark* states—what is omitted by the other two Evangelists—that, before our Lord explained to his disciples in private that he was going straight to the sacrifice of death, not only they, but also the rest of his followers, were sorrowful and *trembling.* Now why they were seized with this fear it is not easy to say, if it was not because they had already learned that they had dangerous adversaries at *Jerusalem,* and would therefore have wished that Christ should remain in some quiet retreat beyond the reach of the darts, rather than voluntarily expose himself to such inveterate enemies. Although this fear was in many respects improper, yet the circumstance of their following Christ is a proof of no ordinary respect and obedience. It would indeed have been far better to hasten cheerfully and without regret, wheresoever the Son of God chose to lead them; but commendation is due to their reverence for his person, which appears in choosing to do violence to their own feelings rather than to forsake him.

Matthew XX. 17. *Took the twelve disciples apart in the way.* It may appear surprising that he makes *the twelve* alone acquainted with his secret, since all have need of consolation, for all had been alike seized with fear. I consider the reason why he did not publish his death to have been, that the report might not spread too widely before the time. Besides, as he did not expect that the warning would be of immediate advantage, he reckoned it enough to entrust it to a few, who were afterwards to be his witnesses. For, as the seed thrown into the earth does not immediately spring up, so we know that Christ said many things to the apostles which did not immediately yield fruit. And if he had admitted all indiscriminately to this discourse, it was possible that many persons, seized with alarm, might flee, and fill the ears of the public with this report; and thus the death of Christ would have lost its glory, because he would have appeared to have rashly brought it on himself. Secretly, therefore, he addresses the apostles, and does not even select them as qualified to receive profit by it, but, as I lately hinted, that they may afterwards be witnesses.

On this subject Luke is more full than the others; for he relates not only that Christ predicted the events which were near at hand, but also that he added the doctrine, that *those things which had been written by the prophets would be accomplished in the Son of man.* It was an excellent remedy for overcoming temptation, to perceive in the very ignominy of the cross the marks by which the Prophets had pointed out the promised Author of salvation. There can be no doubt that our Lord pointed out also from the Prophets what kind of fruit they ought to expect from his death; for the Prophets do not only teach that Christ must suffer, but add the reason, that he may reconcile the world to God.

18. *Lo, we go up to Jerusalem.* Hence we perceive that Christ was endued with divine fortitude for overcoming the terrors of death, for he knowingly and willingly hastens to undergo it.[1] For why does he, without any constraint, march forward to suffer a shocking murder, but because the invincible power of the Spirit enabled him to subdue fear, and raised him above all human feelings? By a minute detail of the circumstances, he gives a still more evident proof of his Divinity. For he could not—*as man*—have foreseen that, after having been *condemned by the chief priests and scribes,* he would be *delivered up to the Gentiles,* and *spat on,* and *mocked* in various ways, and *scourged,* and at length dragged to the punishment of the *cross.* Yet it must be observed that, though our Lord was fully acquainted with the weakness of his disciples, he does not conceal from them a very grievous offence. For—as we have said on a former occasion[2]—nothing could at that time have happened more powerfully calculated to shake the minds of the godly, than to see the whole of the sacred order of the Church opposed to Christ.

---

[1] "Veu qu'il se haste pour s'y presenter de son bon gre, et scachant bien ce qu'il avoit à endurer;"—"since he hastens to present himself to it of his own accord, and knowing well what he had to endure."

[2] See p. 301 of this volume.

And yet he does not spare their weakness by deceiving them, but, candidly declaring the whole matter, points out the way to overcome temptation; namely, by looking forward with certainty to his resurrection. But as it was necessary that his death should go before, he makes their triumph, in the meantime, to consist in hope.

Luke XVIII. 34. *And they understood none of these things.* What stupidity was this, not to understand what Christ said to them in a plain and familiar manner, on a subject not too lofty or intricate, but of which they had, at their own suggestion, entertained some suspicion! But it is proper also to bear in mind—what I have formerly observed—the reason why they were held in such gross ignorance, which was, that they had formed the expectation of a joyful and prosperous advancement, and therefore reckoned it to be in the highest degree absurd, that Christ should be ignominiously crucified. Hence we infer with what madness the minds of men are seized through a false imagination; and therefore we ought to be the more careful not to yield to any foolish thoughts, and shut our eyes against the light.

Matthew.	Mark.
XX. 20. Then came to him the mother of Zebedee's children with her sons, worshipping,[1] and asking something from him. 21. And he said to her, What wilt thou? She saith to him, Grant that these my two sons may sit, one at thy right hand, and the other at the left, in thy kingdom. 22. And Jesus answering said, You know not what you ask. Can you drink the cup which I shall drink, and be baptized with the baptism with which I am baptized? They say to him, We can. 23. He saith to them, You shall indeed drink my cup, and you shall be baptized with the baptism with which I am baptized; but to sit at my right hand, and at	X. 35. And James and John, sons of Zebedee, came to him, saying, Master, we desire that thou shouldest do for us whatsoever we shall ask. 36. And he said to them, What do you wish that I should do for you? 37. And they said, Grant to us that we may sit, one at thy right hand, and the other at thy left, in thy glory. 38. And Jesus said to them, You know not what you ask. Can you drink the cup which I drink, and be baptized with the baptism with which I am baptized? 39. And they said to him, We can. And Jesus said to them, You shall indeed drink the cup which I drink, and you shall be baptized with the baptism with which I am baptized: 40. But to sit

[1] "S'enclinant a luy;"—"bowing down to him."

MATTHEW.	MARK.
my left, is not mine to give; but it shall fall to those for whom it is prepared by my Father.[1]	at my right hand, and at my left, is not mine to give; but it shall fall to those for whom it is prepared.[2]

Matthew XX. 20. *Then came to him the mother of Zebedee's children.* This narrative contains a bright mirror of human vanity; for it shows that proper and holy zeal is often accompanied by ambition, or some other vice of the flesh, so that they who follow Christ have a different object in view from what they ought to have. They who are not satisfied with himself alone, but seek this or the other thing apart from him and his promises, wander egregiously from the right path. Nor is it enough that, at the commencement, we sincerely apply our minds to Christ, if we do not stedfastly maintain the same purity; for frequently, in the midst of the course, there spring up sinful affections by which we are led astray. In this way it is probable that the *two sons of Zebedee* were, at first, sincere in their adherence to Christ; but when they see that they have no ordinary share of his favour, and hear his reign spoken of as near at hand, their minds are immediately led to wicked ambition, and they are greatly distressed at the thought of remaining in their present situation. If this happens to two excellent disciples, with what care ought we to walk, if we do not wish to turn aside from the right path! More especially, when any plausible occasion presents itself, we ought to be on our guard, lest the desire of honours corrupt the feeling of piety.

Though *Matthew* and *Mark* differ somewhat in the words, yet they agree as to the substance of the matter. *Matthew* says that the wife of *Zebedee* came, and *asked for her sons* that they might hold the highest places *in the kingdom* of Christ. *Mark* represents themselves as making the request. But it is probable that, being restrained by bashfulness, they had the dexterity to employ their mother, who would pre-

---

[1] "Mais ceux ausquels il est appareillé de mon Pere [l'auront];"—"but those for whom it is prepared by my Father [shall have it.]"

[2] "Mais il sera [donné] a ceux ausquels il est preparé;"—"but it shall be given to those for whom it is prepared."

sent the request with greater boldness. That the wish came originally from themselves may be inferred from this circumstance, that Christ replied to them, and not to their mother. Besides, when their mother, *bowing down*, states that she has something to ask, and when themselves, according to Mark, apply for a general engagement, *that whatever they ask shall be granted to them*, this timid insinuation proves that they were conscious of something wrong.[1]

21. *In thy kingdom.* It was worthy of commendation in the *sons of Zebedee*, that they expected some *kingdom* of Christ, of which not even the slightest trace was then visible. They see Christ exposed to contempt under the mean aspect of a servant; nay more, they see him despised and loaded with many reproaches by the world; but they are convinced that he will soon become a magnificent king, for so he had taught them. It is unquestionably a noble specimen of faith; but hence we perceive how easily the pure seed is no sooner implanted in our hearts than it becomes degenerate and corrupted; for they imagined to themselves a *kingdom* which had no existence, and presently committed the folly of desiring the highest places. Since, therefore, this wicked ambition flowed from a general principle of faith, which in itself was highly commendable, we ought to pray, not only that the Lord would open the eyes of our mind, but that he would give us continual direction, and keep our minds fixed on the proper object. We ought also to pray, not only that he would bestow faith upon us, but that he would keep it pure from all mixture.

22. *You know not what you ask.* Their ignorance was worthy of blame on two accounts; first, because their ambition led them to desire more than was proper; and, secondly, because, instead of the heavenly kingdom of Christ, they had formed the idea of a phantom in the air. As to the first of those reasons, whoever is not satisfied with the free adoption of God, and desires to raise himself, such a person

[1] "Monstre que leur conscience les redarguoit;"—"shows that their conscience was reproving them."

wanders beyond his limits, and, by unseasonably pressing himself forward beyond what was proper for him to do, is ungrateful to God. Now to estimate the spiritual kingdom of Christ according to the feeling of our flesh is highly perverse. And, indeed, the greater the delight which the mind of man takes in idle speculations, the more carefully ought we to guard against them; as we see that the books of the sophists are stuffed with useless notions of this sort.

Can you drink the cup which I shall drink? To correct their ambition, and to withdraw them from this wicked desire, he holds out to them the cross, and all the annoyances which the children of God must endure. As if he had said, " Does your present warfare allow you so much leisure, that you are now making arrangements for a triumphal procession?" For if they had been earnestly employed in the duties of their calling, they would never have given way to this wicked imagination. In these words, therefore, those who are desirous to obtain the prize before the proper time are enjoined by Christ to employ themselves in attending to the duties of piety. And certainly this is an excellent bridle for restraining ambition; for, so long as we are pilgrims in this world, our condition is such as ought to banish vain luxuries. We are surrounded by a thousand dangers. Sometimes the enemy assails us by ambush, and that in a variety of ways; and sometimes he attacks us by open violence. Is he not worse than stupid who, amidst so many deaths, entertains himself at his ease by drawing pictures of a triumph?

Our Lord enjoins his followers, indeed, to feel assured of victory, and to sing a triumphal song in the midst of death; for otherwise they would not have courage to fight valiantly. But it is one thing to advance manfully to the battle, in reliance on the reward which God has promised to them, and to labour with their whole might for this object; and it is another thing to forget the contest, to turn aside from the enemy, to lose sight of dangers, and to rush forward to a triumph, for which they ought to wait till the proper time. Besides, this foolish speed, for the most part, draws men aside from their calling; for as in battle the greatest coward is the keenest to seize the booty, so in the kingdom of Christ none are more eager to obtain the superiority than those who shrink from all the annoyance which attends toil. Most properly, therefore, does Christ enjoin those who were puffed up with vain glory to keep by their post.[1] The sum of the whole is, that for none but him who has fought lawfully is the crown prepared ; and especially, that none will be a partaker of the life and the kingdom of Christ who has not previously shared in his sufferings and death.

In the word *baptism* the force of the metaphor is very evident; for we know that by *baptism* believers are instructed to *deny themselves,* (Matth. xvi. 24 ;) to *crucify the old man,* (Rom. vi. 6 ;) and, in short, to *bear the cross.* It is uncertain if, by the word *cup,* (ποτήριον,) our Lord alluded to the mystery of the Holy Supper; but as it had not yet come into use, I choose to interpret it more simply as denoting the measure of afflictions which God appoints to every one. For as it is his right to lay on every one his own burden according to his pleasure, in the same manner as a householder distributes and allots the portions of the members of his family, so He is said to *give them a cup to drink.*[2]

These words contain no ordinary consolation for alleviating the bitterness of *the cross,* when in *the cross* Christ associates himself with us. And what could be more desirable than to have every thing in common with the Son of God ? for thus are those things which at first sight appear to be deadly made to yield to us salvation and life. On the other hand, how shall he be reckoned among the disciples of Christ, who desires to be wholly exempted from the cross? For such a person refuses to submit to the baptism of Christ, which is nothing else than to withdraw from the earliest lessons.[3]

---

[1] "A bon droict donc Christ voyant ses deux disciples eslevez d'une vaine gloire, les arreste à penser aux choses qui concernent le devoir de leur vocation ;"—" with good reason, then, does Christ, seeing his two disciples carried away by vain glory, make them stop to consider the things which belong to the duty of their calling."

[2] "Il est dit pour ceste cause, que Dieu donne la coupe à boire ;"—"for this reason it is said that God gives the cup to drink."

[3] "Car cela n'est proprement autre chose que se retirer des commencemens, et ne vouloir entrer à la premiere leçon de son eschole ;"—" for that is properly nothing else than to withdraw at the beginning, and to refuse to enter into the first lesson of his school."

Now whenever baptism is mentioned, let us recollect that we were baptized on this condition, and for this purpose, that the cross may be attached to our shoulders.

The boast made with so much confidence by John and James, that they are prepared *to drink the cup,* manifests the presumption of the flesh; for, when we are beyond the reach of darts, we think nothing impossible. And not long afterwards, the melancholy result exposed their rashness; but in so far it was good in them that, when they were free to make a choice, they presented themselves to bear the cross.

23. *You shall indeed drink my cup.* As they were disciples, it was proper that they should be assimilated to their Master. Christ warns them of what will take place, that they may be prepared to endure it with patience; and, in the persons of two men, he addresses all his followers. For though many believers die a natural death, and without violence or shedding of blood, yet it is common to all of them, as Paul informs us, (Rom. viii. 29; 2 Cor. iii. 18,) *to be conformed to the image of Christ;* and, therefore, *during their whole life, they are sheep appointed to the slaughter,* (Rom. viii. 36.)

Is not mine to give.[1] By this reply Christ surrenders nothing, but only states that the Father had not assigned to him this office of appointing to each person his own peculiar place in the kingdom of heaven. He came, indeed, in order to bring all his people to eternal life; but we ought to reckon it enough that the inheritance obtained by his blood awaits us. As to the degree in which some men rise above others, it is not our business to inquire, and God did not intend that it should be revealed to us by Christ, but that it should be reserved till the latest revelation. We have now ascertained Christ's meaning; for he does not here reason as to his power, but only desires us to consider for what purpose he was sent by the Father, and what corresponds to his calling, and therefore distinguishes between the secret purpose of God and the nature of that teaching which had been enjoined

---

[1] " *Ce n'est pas à moy à le donner;*"—" *it does not belong to me to give it.*"

on him. It is a useful warning, that we may learn to be wise with sobriety, and may not attempt to force our way into the hidden mysteries of God, and more especially, that we may not indulge excessive curiosity in our inquiries about the future state; for *it hath not yet appeared what we shall be, till God shall make us like himself,* (1 John iii. 2.) It is also worthy of our notice, that these words do not imply that there will be equality among the children of God, after they have been admitted to the heavenly glory, but rather that to each is promised that degree of honour to which he has been set apart by the eternal purpose of God.

Matthew.	Mark.	Luke.
XX. 24. And when the ten heard it,[1] they were displeased with the two brethren. 25. And Jesus called them to him, and said, You know that the princes of the Gentiles rule over them, and they who are great exercise authority over them. 26. It shall not be so among you: but whoever wishes to be great among you, let him be your minister; 27. And he that wishes to be chief among you, let him be your servant: 28. Even as the Son of man came not that he might be served, but that he might serve, and that he might give his life a ransom for many.	X. 41. And when the ten heard it, they began to be displeased with James and John. 42. And Jesus, when he had called them to him, saith to them, You know that they who appear to rule over the Gentiles exercise dominion over them; and they who are princes among them exercise power over them. 43. But it shall not be so among you; but whoever wishes to become great among you, shall be your minister; 44. And whoever wishes to be the chief among you, shall be your servant. 45. For even the Son of man came not that he might be served, but that he might serve, and that he might give his life a ransom for many.	XXII. 24. And there arose also a dispute among them, which of them appeared to be greatest. 25. And he said to them, The kings of the Gentiles rule over them; and they that have power over them are called benefactors. 26. But you are not so: but he that is greatest among you, let him become as the younger; and he that is ruler, as he that serves. 27. For which is greater, he that sitteth at table, or he that serveth? Is it not he that sitteth at table? But I am in the midst of you as he that serveth.

Matthew XX. 24. *And when the ten heard it.*[1] Luke appears to refer this dispute to a different time. But any

---

[1] "*Les dix* autres *ayans ouy cela;*"—"*the* other ten *having heard that.*"

one who shall carefully examine that twenty-second chapter will plainly see that discourses delivered at different times are there brought together, without any regard to order. The dispute about the primacy, therefore, which Luke mentions, flowed from this source, that *the sons of Zebedee* aspired to the first places in the kingdom of Christ. And yet the displeasure of the rest was far from being well-founded; for, while the foolish ambition of the *two disciples* was so severely blamed, that they retired from Christ with disgrace, what injury was it to the other *ten*, that those disciples foolishly wished what they did not obtain?[1] For though they had a good right to be offended at the ambition of those disciples, yet when it was put down they ought to have been satisfied. But our Lord intended to seize on this occasion for laying open a disease which was lurking within them; for there was not one of them who would willingly yield to others, but every one secretly cherished within himself the expectation of the primacy; in consequence of which, they envy and dispute with one another, and yet in all there reigns wicked ambition. And if this fault was found to be natural to uneducated men of ordinary rank, and if it broke out on a slight occasion, and almost without any occasion at all, how much more ought we to be on our guard, when there is abundance of fuel to feed a concealed flame? We see then how ambition springs up in any man who has great power and honours, and sends out its flames far and wide, unless the spirit of modesty, coming from heaven, extinguish the pride which has a firm hold of the nature of man.

25. *You know that the princes of the Gentiles rule over them.* It is first said that Christ *called them to him*, that he might reprove them in private; and next we learn from it that, being ashamed of their ambition, they did not openly complain, but that a sort of hollow murmur arose, and every one secretly preferred himself to the rest. He does not explain generally how deadly a plague ambition is, but simply warns them, that nothing is more foolish than to fight about no-

[1] "Avoyent follement désiré une chose qu'ils n'ont peu obtenir;"—"had foolishly desired a thing which they could not obtain."

thing.[1] He shows that the primacy, which was the occasion of dispute among them, has no existence in his kingdom. Those persons, therefore, who extend this saying indiscriminately to all the godly are mistaken; for Christ only takes occasion from the present occurrence to show that it is absurd in the apostles to dispute about the degree of power and honour in their own rank, because the office of teaching, to which they were appointed, has no resemblance to the governments of the world. I do acknowledge that this doctrine applies both to private persons and to kings and magistrates; for no man deserves to be reckoned one of Christ's flock, unless he has made such proficiency under the teacher of humility, as to claim nothing for himself, but condescend to cultivate brotherly love. This is, no doubt, true; but the design of Christ was, as I have said, to distinguish between the spiritual government of his Church and the empires of the world, that the apostles might not look for the favours of a court; for in proportion as any of the nobles is loved by kings, he rises to wealth and distinction. But Christ appoints pastors of his Church, not to *rule*, but to *serve*.

This refutes the error of the Anabaptists, who exclude kings and magistrates from the Church of God, because Christ declares[2] that they are not like his disciples; though the comparison is here made not between Christians and ungodly men, but between the nature of their offices. Besides, Christ did not look so much at the persons of men as at the condition of his Church. For it was possible that one who was governor of a village or of a city might, in a case of urgent necessity, discharge also the office of teaching; but Christ satisfied himself with explaining what belongs to the apostolic office, and what is at variance with it.

But a question arises, Why does Christ, who appointed separate orders in his Church, disown in this passage all degrees? For he appears to throw them all down, or, at least,

---

[1] " Qu'il n'y a point de folie plus grande, que de debattre d'une chose qui n'est point ;"—" that there is no greater folly than to debate about a thing which does not exist."
[2] " Sous couleur de ce que Christ dit ;"—" under the pretence of what Christ says."

to place them on a level, so that not one rises above the rest. But natural reason prescribes a very different method; and Paul, when describing the government of the Church, (Eph. iv. 11,) enumerates the various departments of the ministry, in such a manner as to make the rank of apostleship higher than the office of pastors. Timothy and Titus, also, are unquestionably enjoined by him to exercise authoritative superintendence over others, according to the command of God. I reply, if we carefully examine the whole, it will be found that even kings do not rule justly or lawfully, unless they serve; but that the apostolic office differs from earthly government in this respect, that the manner in which kings and magistrates serve does not prevent them from governing, or indeed from rising above their subjects in magnificent pomp and splendour. Thus David, Hezekiah, and others of the same class, while they were the willing servants of all, used a sceptre, a crown, a throne, and other emblems of royalty. But the government of the Church admits nothing of this sort; for Christ allowed the pastors nothing more than to be ministers, and to abstain entirely from the exercise of authority. Here, too, it ought to be observed, that the discourse relates to the thing itself rather than to the disposition. Christ distinguishes between the apostles and the rank of kings, not because kings have a right to act haughtily, but because the station of royalty is different from the apostolic office. While, therefore, both ought to be humble, it is the duty of the apostles always to consider what form of government the Lord has appointed for his Church.

As to the words which Matthew employs, *the princes of the Gentiles rule over them*, Luke conveys the same import by saying, *they are called benefactors;* which means, that kings possess great wealth and abundance, in order that they may be generous and bountiful. For though kings have greater delight in their power, and a stronger desire that it should be formidable, than that it should be founded in the consent of the people, still they desire the praise of munificence.[1] Hence,

---

[1] "Toutesfois ils appetent d'avoir la louange d'estre magnifiques et liberaux;"—" yet they desire to have the praise of being sumptuous and liberal."

too, they take the name in the Hebrew language, נדיבים, (*nedibim.*) They are so called from *bestowing gifts;*[1] for taxes and tributes are paid to them for no other purpose than to furnish the expense necessary to the magnificence of their rank.

26. *It shall not be so among you.* There can be no doubt that Christ refers to the foolish imagination by which he saw that the apostles were deceived. "It is foolish and improper in you," he says, "to imagine a kingdom, which is unsuitable to me; and therefore, if you desire to serve me faithfully, you must resort to a different method, which is, that each of you may strive to serve others."[2] *But whoever wishes to be great among you, let him be your servant.* These words are employed in an unusual sense; for ambition does not allow a man to be *devoted,* or, rather, to be *subject* to his brethren. Abject flattery, I do acknowledge, is practised by those who aspire to honours, but nothing is farther from their intention than to *serve.* But Christ's meaning is not difficult to be perceived. As every man is carried away by a love of himself, he declares that this passion ought to be directed to a different object. Let the only greatness, eminence, and rank, which you desire, be, to submit to your brethren; and let this be your primacy, to be the *servants* of all.

28. *As the Son of man.* Christ confirms the preceding doctrine by his own example; for he voluntarily *took upon himself the form of a servant, and emptied himself,* as Paul also informs us, (Philip. ii. 7.) To prove more clearly how far he was from indulging in lofty views, he reminds them of his death. "Because I have chosen you to the honour of being near me, you are seized by a wicked ambition to reign. But I—by whose example you ought to regulate your life— came not to exalt myself, or to claim any royal dignity. On

---

[1] נדיב, (*nadib,*) *a prince,* which is derived from נדב, (*nadab,*) *to be bountiful,* is the very word to which allusion is supposed to be made in the passage, (Luke xxii. 25,) where it is said that the name *princes* (נדיבים, *nedibim*) signifies *benefactors.—Ed.*

[2] "De se rendre serviteur à ses compagnons;"—"to become a servant to his companions."

the contrary, I took upon me, along with the mean and despised form of the flesh, the ignominy of the cross." If it be objected, that Christ was *exalted by the Father, in order that every knee might bow to him,* (Philip. ii. 9, 10,) it is easy to reply, that what he now says refers to the period of his humiliation. Accordingly, Luke adds, that he lived among them, *as if he were a servant:* not that in appearance, or in name, or in reality, he was inferior to them, (for he always wished to be acknowledged as their Master and Lord,) but because from the heavenly glory he descended to such meekness, that he submitted to bear their infirmities. Besides, it ought to be remembered that a comparison is here made between the greater and the less, as in that passage, *If I, who am your Master and Lord, have washed your feet, much more ought you to perform this service to one another,* (John xiii. 14.)

And to give his life a ransom for many. Christ mentioned his death, as we have said, in order to withdraw his disciples from the foolish imagination of an earthly kingdom. But it is a just and appropriate statement of its power and results, when he declares that his life is the price of our redemption; whence it follows, that we obtain an undeserved reconciliation with God, the price of which is to be found nowhere else than in the death of Christ. Wherefore, this single word overturns all the idle talk of the Papists about their abominable *satisfactions.* Again, while Christ has purchased us by his death to be his property, this submission, of which he speaks, is so far from diminishing his boundless glory, that it greatly increases its splendour. The word *many* ($\pi o\lambda\lambda\tilde{\omega}\nu$) is not put definitely for a fixed number, but for a large number; for he contrasts himself with all others.[1] And in this sense it is used in Romans v. 15, where Paul does not speak of any part of men, but embraces the whole human race.

---

[1] "Il prend PLUSIEURS, non pas pour quelque certain nombre, mais pour les autres : car il fait une comparaison de sa personne à tout le reste des hommes ;"—"He takes MANY, not for any fixed number, but for the others ; for he makes a comparison of his person with all the rest of men."

MATTHEW.	MARK.	LUKE.
XX. 29. And while they were departing from Jericho, a great multitude followed him. 30. And, lo, two blind men sitting near the road, when they heard that Jesus was passing by, cried aloud, saying, Have mercy on us, O Lord, thou Son of David. 31. And the multitude rebuked them, that they might be silent; but they cried out the more, saying, Have mercy on us, O Lord, thou Son of David. 32. And Jesus stood, and called them, and said, What do you wish that I should do to you? 33. They say to him, Lord, that our eyes may be opened. 34. And Jesus, moved with compassion, touched their eyes; and immediately their eyes received sight, and they followed him.	X. 46. And they come to Jericho: and while he was departing from the city Jericho, and his disciples, and a great multitude, Bartimeus, son of Timeus, a blind man, was sitting near the road begging. 47. And when he heard that it was Jesus of Nazareth, he began to cry aloud, and to say, Jesus, Son of David, have mercy on me. 48. And many rebuked him, that he might be silent: but he cried out so much the more, Son of David, have mercy on me. 49. And Jesus stood, and commanded him to be called. And they call the blind man, saying to him, Be of good courage, rise; he calleth thee. 50. And he, throwing away his mantle, arose, and came to Jesus. 51. And Jesus answering, saith to him, What dost thou wish that I should do to thee? And the blind man said to him, Master,[1] that I may receive sight. 52. And Jesus said to him, Go away; thy faith hath cured thee. And immediately he received sight, and followed Jesus in the way.	XVIII. 35. And it happened that, while he was approaching Jericho, a certain blind man was sitting near the road begging: 36. And when he heard a multitude passing by, he asked what it was. 37. And they said to him, that Jesus of Nazareth was passing by. 38. And he cried out, saying, Jesus, Son of David, have mercy on me. 39. And they that were going before rebuked him, that he might be silent: but he cried out so much the more, Son of David, have mercy on me. 40. And Jesus, standing still, commanded him to be brought to him: and while he was approaching, he asked him, 41. Saying, What dost thou wish that I should do to thee? And he said, Lord, that I may receive sight. 42. Then Jesus said to him, Receive sight: thy faith hath cured thee. 43. And immediately he received sight, and followed him, glorifying God: and all the people, when they saw it, gave praise to God.

Matthew XX. 29. *And while they were departing from Jericho.* Osiander has resolved to display his ingenuity by making four blind men out of one. But nothing can be more frivolous than this supposition. Having observed that the Evangelists differ in a few expressions, he imagined that *one blind man received sight* when they were entering into the city, and that the second, and other two, *received sight* when

---

[1] "Rabboni;"—"Maistre."

Christ *was departing from it.* But all the circumstances agree so completely, that no person of sound judgment will believe them to be different narratives. Not to mention other matters, when Christ's followers had endeavoured to put the first to silence, and saw him cured contrary to their expectation, would they immediately have made the same attempt with the other three? But it is unnecessary to go into particulars, from which any man may easily infer that it is one and the same event which is related.

But there is a puzzling contradiction in this respect, that *Matthew* and *Mark* say that the miracle was performed on *one* or on *two blind men,* when Christ had already *departed from the city;* while *Luke* relates that it was done before he came to the city. Besides, *Mark* and *Luke* speak of not more than *one blind man,* while *Matthew* mentions *two.* But as we know that it frequently occurs in the Evangelists, that in the same narrative one passes by what is mentioned by the others, and, on the other hand, states more clearly what they have omitted, it ought not to be looked upon as strange or unusual in the present passage. My conjecture is, that, while Christ was approaching to the city, the *blind man cried out,* but that, as he was not heard on account of the noise, he placed himself in the way, *as they were departing from the city,*[1] and then was at length called by Christ. And so *Luke,* commencing with what was true, does not follow out the whole narrative, but passes over Christ's stay in the city; while the other Evangelists attend only to the time which was nearer to the miracle. There is probability in the conjecture that, as Christ frequently, when he wished to try the faith of men, delayed for a short time to relieve them, so he subjected this *blind man* to the same scrutiny.

The second difficulty may be speedily removed; for we have seen, on a former occasion, that *Mark* and *Luke* speak of *one* demoniac as having been cured, while *Matthew,* as in

---

[1] "Mais pource qu'il ne peut estre ouy à cause du bruit du peuple, qu'il s'en alla à l'autre porte de la ville par laquelle Christ devoit sortir, pour l'attendre là au chemin;"—" but, because he could not be heard on account of the noise of the people, that he went away to the other gate by which Christ was to go out, to wait for him there on the road."

the present instance, mentions *two*, (Matth. viii. 28; Mark v. 2; Luke viii. 27.[1]) And yet this involves no contradiction between them; but it may rather be conjectured with probability, that at first *one blind man* implored the favour of Christ, and that another was excited by his example, and that in this way *two* persons *received sight*. *Mark* and *Luke* speak of *one* only, either because he was better known, or because in him the demonstration of Christ's power was not less remarkable than it was in both. It certainly appears to have been on account of his having been extensively known that he was selected by *Mark*, who gives both his own name and that of his father: *Bartimeus, son of Timeus*. By doing so, he does not claim for him either illustrious descent or wealth; for he was a beggar of the lowest class. Hence it appears that the miracle was more remarkable in his person, because his calamity had been generally known. This appears to me to be the reason why *Mark* and *Luke* mention him only, and say nothing about the other, who was a sort of inferior appendage. But *Matthew*, who was an eye-witness,[2] did not choose to pass by even this person, though less known.

30. *Have mercy on me, O Lord.* I stated, a little ago, that there was at first but *one* who *cried out*, but the other was induced by a similar necessity to join him. They confer on Christ no ordinary honour, when they request him to *have mercy*, and relieve them; for they must have been convinced that he had in his power the assistance or remedy which they needed. But their faith is still more clearly exhibited by their acknowledgment of him as Messiah, to whom we know that the Jews gave this designation, *Son of David*. They therefore apply to Christ, not only as some Prophet, but as that person whom God had promised to be the only Author of salvation. The *cry* proved the ardour of the desire; for, though they knew that what they said exposed them to the hatred of many, who were highly dis-

---

[1] See *Harmony*, vol. i. p. 428.
[2] "Qui avoit este present au miracle;"—"who had been present at the miracle."

pleased with the honour done to Christ, their fear was overcome by the ardour of desire, so that they did not refrain, on this account, from raising their voice aloud.

31. *And the multitude reproved them.* It is surprising that the disciples of Christ, who follow him through a sense of duty and of respect, should wish to drive wretched men from the favour of Christ, and, so far as lies in them, to prevent the exercise of his power. But it frequently happens that the greater part of those who profess the name of Christ, instead of inviting us to him, rather hinder or delay our approach. If Satan endeavoured to throw obstacles in the way of *two blind men,* by means of pious and simple persons, who were induced by some sentiments of religion to follow Christ, how much more will he succeed in accomplishing it by means of hypocrites and traitors, if we be not strictly on our guard. Perseverance is therefore necessary to overcome every difficulty, and the more numerous the obstacles are which Satan throws in the way, the more powerfully ought we to be excited to earnestness in prayer, as we see that the *blind men* redoubled their *cry.*

32. *What do you wish that I should do to you?* He gently and kindly asks what they desire; for he had determined to grant their requests. There is no reason to doubt that they prayed by a special movement of the Holy Spirit; for, as the Lord does not intend to grant to all persons deliverance from bodily diseases, so neither does he permit them simply to pray for it. A rule has been prescribed for us what we ought to ask, and in what manner, and to what extent; and we are not at liberty to depart from that rule, unless the Lord, by a secret movement of the Spirit, suggest to us some special prayer, which rarely happens. Christ puts the question to them, not for their sake as individuals, but for the sake of all the people; for we know how the world swallows God's benefits without perceiving them, unless they are stimulated and aroused. Christ, therefore, by his voice, awakens the assembled crowd to observe the miracle, as he awakens them

shortly afterwards by a visible sign, when he opens their eyes by touching them.

34. *And Jesus, moved with compassion, &c.* Σπλαγχνισθείς, *moved with compassion,* is not the participle of the same verb which Matthew had just now employed in reference to the *blind man,* ἐλέησον, *have mercy.*[1] They implored the *mercy* of Christ, that he might relieve their wretchedness; but now the Evangelist expresses that Christ was induced to cure them, not only by undeserved goodness, but because he pitied their distress. For the metaphor is taken from the *bowels*, (σπλάγχνα,) in which dwells that kindness and mutual compassion which prompts us to assist our neighbours.

Mark X. 52. *Thy faith hath saved thee.* By the word *faith* is meant not only a confident hope of recovering sight, but a loftier conviction, which was, that this *blind man* had acknowledged Jesus to be the Messiah whom God had promised. Nor must we imagine that it was only some confused knowledge; for we have already seen that this confession was taken from the Law and the Prophets. For the *blind man* did not at random bestow on Christ the name of *Son of David*, but embraced him as that person whose coming he had been taught by the divine predictions to expect. Now Christ attributes it to faith that *the blind man received sight;* for, though the power and grace of God sometimes extend even to unbelievers, yet no man enjoys His benefits in a right and profitable manner, unless he receive them by faith; nay, the use of the gifts of God is so far from being advantageous to unbelievers, that it is even hurtful. And therefore, when Christ says, *thy faith hath saved thee,* the word *saved* is not limited to an outward *cure*, but includes also the *health* and *safety* of the soul; as if Christ had said, that by *faith* the blind man obtained that God was gracious to him, and granted his wish. And if it was in regard to *faith* that God bestowed his favour on the blind man, it follows that he was justified by *faith*.

[1] " Quand ils disoyent, *Fils de David, aye misericorde de nous;*"—" when they said, *Son of David, have mercy on us.*"

Matthew XX. 34. *And followed him.* This was an expression of gratitude,[1] when the blind men became *followers* of Christ; for, though it is uncertain how long they discharged this duty, yet it showed a grateful mind, that they presented themselves to many, in that journey, as mirrors of the grace of Christ. Luke adds, that *the people gave praise to God,* which tends to prove the certainty of the miracle.

LUKE.

XIX. 1. And having entered, he passeth through Jericho.[2] 2. And, lo, a man named Zaccheus, and he was chief of the publicans, and was rich. 3. And he sought to see Jesus who he was,[3] and could not on account of the multitude; for he was of small stature. 4. And running before, he climbed up into a sycamore tree to see him; for he was to pass that way. 5. And when Jesus came to the place, he looked up, and saw him, and said to him, Zaccheus, make haste, and come down; for to-day I must abide at thy house. 6. And he made haste, and came down, and received him joyfully. 7. And when they saw it, they all murmured, saying, That he had gone to lodge with a man who is a sinner. 8. And Zaccheus stood, and said to the Lord, Lo, O Lord, the half of my goods I give to the poor; and if I have defrauded any man in any thing, I restore fourfold.[4] 9. Jesus said to him, To-day is salvation come to this house, inasmuch as he also is a son of Abraham.[5] 10. For the Son of man came to seek and save what was lost.

This shows how little attention Luke paid to observing the order of dates; for, after having detailed the miracle, he now relates what happened in the city of *Jericho*. He tells us that, while Christ presented himself to the view of all, as he went along the streets, *Zaccheus* alone was very desirous to see him. For it was an evidence of intense desire that he *climbed up a tree;* since *rich* men are, for the most part, haughty, and plume themselves on affected gravity. It is possible, indeed, that others entertained the same wish, but this man was most properly singled out by Luke, both on account of his rank, and on account of his wonderful conversion, which took place suddenly. Now, though faith was not

---

[1] "Ceci a este un signe de recognoissance du bien receu de Christ;"—"this was an expression of gratitude for the favour received from Christ."

[2] "Estant entré en Iericho, il alloit par la ville;"—"having entered into Jericho, he went through the town."

[3] "Et taschoit a veoir lequel estoit Iesus;"—"and endeavoured to see who Jesus was."

[4] "I'en rend quatre fois autant;"—"I restore four times as much for it."

[5] "*Pourtant que ceste-ci aussi est fille d'Abraham,* ou, *cestuy-ci aussi est fils d'Abraham;*"—"*because this also is a daughter of Abraham,* or, *this also is a son of Abraham.*"

yet formed in *Zaccheus*, yet this was a sort of preparation for it; for it was not without a heavenly inspiration that he desired so earnestly to get a sight of Christ; I mean, in reference to that design which immediately appeared. Some were led, no doubt, by vain curiosity to run even from distant places, for the purpose of seeing Christ, but the event showed that the mind of *Zaccheus* contained some seed of piety. In this manner, before revealing himself to men, the Lord frequently communicates to them a secret desire, by which they are led to Him, while He is still concealed and unknown; and, though they have no fixed object in view, He does not disappoint them, but manifests Himself in due time.

5. *Zaccheus, make haste, and come down.* It is a remarkable instance of favour, that the Lord anticipates *Zaccheus*, and does not wait for his invitation, but of his own accord asks lodging at his house. We know how hateful, nay, how detestable the name of *publican* at that time was; and we shall find that this is shortly afterwards mentioned by Luke. It is therefore astonishing kindness in the Son of God to approach a man, from whom the great body of men recoil, and that before he is requested to do so. But we need not wonder, if he bestows this honour on one who was already drawn to him by a secret movement of the Spirit; for it was a more valuable gift to dwell in his heart than to enter his house. But by this expression he made it evident, that he is never sought in vain by those who sincerely desire to know him; for *Zaccheus* obtained vastly more than he had expected. Besides, the great readiness of *Zaccheus* to obey, his *hastening to come down* from the tree, and his *joy* in *receiving* Christ, exhibit still more clearly the power and guidance of the Holy Spirit; for, though he did not yet possess a pure faith, yet this submissiveness and obedience must be regarded as the beginning of faith.

7. *And when they saw it, they all murmured.* The inhabitants of the town—and, perhaps, some of Christ's followers—*murmur* that *he goes to lodge with a man* who is looked upon as wicked and infamous, even though nobody invited him. It is thus that the world disregards the offer of the grace of

God, but complains bitterly [1] when it is conveyed to others. But let us consider how unjust this *murmuring* was. They think it unreasonable that Christ should bestow so great an honour on a wicked man; for in this passage, as in many others, the word *sinner* is not taken in the ordinary sense,[2] but denotes a man of disgraceful and scandalous life. Let us suppose that *Zaccheus* was a person of this description. Still, we ought first to inquire for what purpose Christ chose to become his guest; for, while out of doors men are *murmuring*, *within* the house God displays magnificently the glory of His name, and refutes their wicked calumny.

The conversion of *Zaccheus* was an astonishing work of God, and yet there was no good reason why *Zaccheus* should be marked with infamy. He had the charge of collecting the taxes. Now to collect taxes was no crime in itself, but men of that class were exceedingly despised and hated by the Jews, because they reckoned it to be in the highest degree unjust that they should pay tribute. But whatever might be the character of *Zaccheus*, still the kindness of Christ ought not to be blamed, but commended, in not refusing his assistance to a wretched man, to rescue him from destruction, and bring him to salvation. And therefore the offence which was wickedly taken did not hinder him from proceeding to execute his Father's command. With such magnanimity ought all his ministers to be endued, as to think more highly of the salvation of one soul than of the murmurs which all ignorant persons may utter, and not to desist from their duty, even though all their actions and words may expose them to reproaches.

8. *And Zaccheus stood, and said.* From this result they ought to have formed their opinion of what Christ did; but men are so hasty and precipitate, that they do not take time to wait for God.[3] The conversion of Zaccheus is described

[1] "Et cependant est envieux et marri;"—" and yet is envious and offended."
[2] "Et ne signifie pas ce que communeement nous appelons *pecheur*;"—" and does not mean what we usually call *a sinner*."
[3] "Qu'ils n'ont pas la patience d'attendre que Dieu monstre ce qu'il veut faire;"—" that they have not patience to wait till God show what he intends to do."

by fruits and outward signs. As it was probable that he had enriched himself to the injury of others, *if he had wronged any man*, he was ready to *restore fourfold.* Besides, *the half of his goods* he dedicates *to the poor.* A man might indeed *bestow all his goods on the poor,* (1 Cor. xiii. 3,) and yet his generosity might be of no value in the sight of God; but, though no mention is here made of inward repentance, yet Luke means that the godly zeal, which he commends in *Zaccheus,* proceeded from that living root. In like manner, Paul, when treating of repentance, exhorts us to those duties, by which men may learn that we are changed for the better. *Let him that stole steal no more ; but rather let him labour with his hands, that he may assist the poor and needy,* (Eph. iv. 28.) We ought therefore to begin with the heart, but our repentance ought also to be evinced by works.

Now let us observe that *Zaccheus* does not make a present to God out of his extortions, as many rich men give to God a portion of what they have obtained by dishonesty, that they may the more freely pillage in future, and that they may be acquitted of the wrongs which they have formerly done. But *Zaccheus* devotes *the half of his goods* to God in such a manner, as to give, at the same time, compensation for whatever wrongs he has done ; and hence we infer that the riches which he possessed were not the fruit of dishonest gain. Thus *Zaccheus* is not only ready to give satisfaction, *if he has taken any thing by fraud,* but shares his lawful possessions with the poor; by which he shows that he is changed from a wolf not only into a sheep, but even into a shepherd. And while he corrects the faults which had been formerly committed, he renounces wicked practices for the future, as God demands from his people, first of all, that they abstain from doing any act of injury. *Zaccheus* has not laid others under obligation, by his example, to strip themselves of *the half of their goods ;* but we have only to observe the rule which the Lord prescribes, that we dedicate ourselves, and all that we have, to holy and lawful purposes.

9. *To-day is salvation come to this house.* Christ, bearing testimony to Zaccheus, declares that his professions were not hypocritical. And yet he does not ascribe to the good works

of Zaccheus the cause of *salvation;* but, as that conversion was an undoubted pledge of the divine adoption, he justly concludes from it that *this house* is a possessor of *salvation.* Such, too, is the import of the words; for, since Zaccheus is one of the *children of Abraham,* he argues that his *house* is saved. In order that any man may be reckoned among the *children of Abraham,* it is necessary for him to imitate *Abraham's* faith; nay, Scripture expressly bestows on faith this commendation, that it distinguishes the genuine *children of Abraham* from strangers. Let us therefore know that in Zaccheus faith is chiefly commended, on account of which his good works were acceptable to God. Nor is there reason to doubt that the doctrine of Christ went before the conversion of Zaccheus; and, consequently, the commencement of his salvation was, to hear Christ discoursing on the undeserved mercy of God, and on the reconciliation of men to Him, and on the redemption of the Church, and to embrace this doctrine by faith.

In consequence of the Greek word οἶκος *(house)* being of the masculine gender, this passage is explained in two ways. The old translator[1] has made the reference to be to Zaccheus, which I also prefer.[2] *Erasmus* has chosen to render it, *inasmuch as* THE HOUSE *itself is a* DAUGHTER *of Abraham;*[3] and although I do not disapprove of this, I think it more natural to explain it as referring to *Zaccheus.* For, since God, when he adopts the head of a family, promises that He will be a God even to his whole house, *salvation* is, with propriety, extended from the head to the whole body. Now the particle καί *(also)* is emphatic; for Christ means, that *Zaccheus,* not less than the other Jews who haughtily detested him, is *a son of Abraham.* And that his former life may not seem to have shut against him the gate of salvation, Christ argues from his own office, that there is nothing in this change

---

[1] "Le translateur Latin ancien;"—"the old Latin translator."
[2] The question is, whether the antecedent to αὐτός be Ζακχαῖος or ὁ οἶκος. On the former supposition, our English version will be approved: HE *also* (namely, *Zaccheus) is a son of Abraham.* On the latter supposition, the translation will run thus: IT *also* (namely, *the house) is a child of Abraham;* or—carrying out the metaphor as *Erasmus* has done—IT *also is a* DAUGHTER *of Abraham.*—*Ed.*
[3] "*Eo quod ipsa domus sit filia Abrahae.*"

at which any man ought to take offence, since he was sent by the Father to *save those who were lost.*

MATTHEW.

XXV. 14. For as a certain man, setting out on a journey, called his servants, and delivered to them his goods. 15. And to one he gave five talents, and to another two, and to another one; to every one according to his own ability; and immediately set out. 16. And he who had received five talents went away and traded with them, and amassed other five talents. 17. And likewise he who had received two, he also gained other two. 18. But he who had received one went away, and dug in the earth, and hid his master's money. 19. And after a long time the master of those servants cometh, and reckoneth with them. 20. And he who had received five talents came, and brought other five talents, saying, Master, thou deliveredst to me five talents: lo, I have gained by them other five talents. 21. His master saith to him, Well done, good and faithful servant; thou hast been faithful over a few things, I will place thee over many things: enter thou into the joy of thy master. 22. And he also who had received two talents came, and said, Master, thou deliveredst to me two talents: lo, I have gained by them other two. 23. His master saith to him, Well done, good and faithful servant; thou hast been faithful over a few things, I will place thee over many things: enter thou into the joy of thy master. 24. But he who had received one talent came and said, Master, I knew thee that thou art a harsh man, reaping where thou didst not sow, and gathering where thou didst not scatter: 25. And, being afraid, I went away, and hid thy talent in the earth: lo, thou hast what is thine. 26. And his master answering said to him, Wicked and slothful servant, thou knewest

LUKE.

XIX. 11. While they were hearing these things, he added, and spoke a parable, because he was near Jerusalem, and because they thought that the kingdom of God would immediately be revealed. 12. He said therefore, A certain nobleman set out for a distant country, to receive for himself a kingdom,[1] and to return. 13. And, having called his ten servants, he gave to them ten pounds, and said to them, Trade till I come. 14. And his citizens hated him, and sent a message after him, saying, We will not have this man to reign over us. 15. And it happened that he returned, after having obtained the kingdom,[2] and commanded those servants to be called to him, to whom he had given money, that he might know how much every one had gained by trading. 16. And the first came, saying, Master, thy pound hath gained ten pounds. 17. And he said to him, Well done, good servant; because thou hast been faithful in a very small matter, have thou power over ten cities. 18. And another came, saying, Master, thy pound hath gained five pounds. 19. And he said to him, And be thou also ruler over five cities. 20. And another came, saying, Master, lo, thy pound, which I have kept laid up in a napkin: 21. For I feared thee, because thou art a harsh man: thou takest up what thou didst not lay down, and reapest what thou didst not sow. 22. He saith to him, Out of thy mouth will I judge thee, wicked servant. Thou knewest that I am a harsh man, taking up what I did not lay down, and reaping what I did not sow: 23. And why didst not

---

[1] "Pour conquester un royaume;"—"to conquer a kingdom."

[2] "Apres avoir conquesté le royaume;"—"after having conquered the kingdom."

MATTHEW.

that I reap where I sowed not, and gather where I did not scatter: 27. Thou oughtest therefore to have given my money to the bankers, and, when I came, I would have received my own with usury. 28. Take away then from him the talent, and give it to him who hath ten talents. 29. For to every one that hath shall be given, and he shall abound; but he that hath not, even that which he hath shall be taken from him. 30. And cast out the unprofitable servant into outer darkness, where shall be weeping and gnashing of teeth.

LUKE.

thou give my money to the bank, and, when I came, I would have demanded it with usury? 24. And to those who stood by he said, Take from him the pound, and give it to him who hath ten pounds. 25. And they said to him, Master, he hath ten pounds. 26. For I say to you, That to him that hath it shall be given; but from him who hath not, even what he hath shall be taken away. 27. But bring hither those my enemies, who refused that I should reign over them, and slay them before me. 28. And, having said these things, he went before, to go up to Jerusalem.

Luke XIX. 11. *While they were hearing these things.* It was next to a prodigy that the disciples, after having been so frequently warned as to the approaching death of Christ, flew aside from it to think of his kingdom. There were two mistakes; first, that they pictured to themselves rest and happiness without the cross; secondly, that they judged of *the kingdom of God* according to their own carnal sense. Hence it appears how slight and obscure their faith was; for though they had entertained a hope of the resurrection, yet the taste was too slight for forming a fixed and decided opinion about Christ. They believe him to be the Redeemer who had been formerly promised, and hence they conceive a hope that the Church will be renewed; but that knowledge immediately degenerates into vain imaginations, which either overturn or obscure the power of his kingdom. But the strangest thing of all was, that so many warnings should have passed away from their recollection without yielding any advantage. At least, it was brutal stupidity that, though Christ had lately declared, in express terms, that he was just about to undergo a bitter and ignominious death, they not only remained unconcerned, but rushed forward, as if to a joyful triumph.

12. *A certain nobleman.* Matthew interweaves this parable with others, without attending to the order of time; but, as

his intention was, in the twenty-second chapter, to make a collection of Christ's latest discourses, readers ought not to trouble themselves greatly with the inquiry which of them was delivered on the first, or the second, or the third day within that short period. But it is proper to observe the difference between *Matthew* and *Luke;* for, while the former touches only on one point, the latter embraces two. This point is common to both, that Christ resembles *a nobleman,* who, undertaking a *long journey* for the sake of *obtaining a kingdom,* has entrusted his *money* to the management of *his servants,* and so on. The other point is peculiar to Luke, that the subjects abused the absence of the prince, and raised a tumult in order to shake off his yoke. In both parts Christ intended to show, that the disciples were greatly mistaken in supposing that his royal authority was already established, and that he was coming *to Jerusalem,* in order to commence immediately a course of prosperity. Thus by taking away the expectation of an immediate *kingdom,* he exhorts them to hope and patience; for he tells them that they must long and steadily endure many toils, before they enjoy that glory for which they pant too earnestly.

Into a distant country. As the disciples thought that Christ was now about to enter into the possession of his kingdom, he first corrects this mistake by informing them, that he must undertake a *long journey,* in order *to obtain the kingdom.*[1] As to what is meant by the *distant country,* I leave it to the ingenious expositions of those who are fond of subtleties. For my own part, I think that Christ expresses nothing more than his long absence, which would extend from the time of his death to his last coming. For, though he sits at the right hand of the Father, and holds the government of heaven and earth, and though, from the time that he ascended to heaven, *all power was given to him,* (Matth. xxviii. 18,) *that every knee might bow before him,* (Philip. ii. 10;) yet as he has not yet subdued his enemies—has not yet appeared as Judge of the world, or revealed his majesty—it is not without propriety that he is said to be absent from his people, till he return again, clothed with his

---

[1] " Pour conquester ce royaume ;"—" to conquer this kingdom.'

new sovereignty. It is true, indeed, that he now reigns, while he regenerates his people to the heavenly life, forms them anew to the image of God, and associates them with angels; while he governs the Church by his word, guards it by his protection, enriches it with the gifts of the Spirit, nourishes it by his grace, and maintains it by his power, and, in short, supplies it with all that is necessary for salvation; while he restrains the fury of Satan and of all the ungodly, and defeats all their schemes. But as this way of reigning is concealed from the flesh, his manifestation is properly said to be delayed till the last day. Since, therefore, the apostles foolishly aimed at the shadow of a kingdom, our Lord declares that he must go to seek a *distant* kingdom, that they may learn to endure delay.[1]

13. *And having called his ten servants.* We must not inquire anxiously into the number of the servants, or into the sums of money. For Matthew, by expressing various sums, includes a more extensive doctrine, namely, that Christ does not lay on all an equal charge of trafficking, but commits to one a small, and to another a larger sum of money. Both agree in this, that till the last day of the resurrection Christ, in some respects, goes to a distance from his people, but yet that it would be highly improper for them to sit down in idleness and do no good; for each has a certain office enjoined him, in which he ought to be employed, and, therefore, they ought to be diligent in *trading*, that they may be careful to increase their Lord's property.

Luke says simply, that to each he gave *a pound;* because, whether more or less may be committed to us by our Lord, every man must equally give account for himself. Matthew, as I have said, is more full and copious; for he states various degrees. Let us know that the Lord does not bestow on all indiscriminately the same *measure of gifts,* (Eph. iv. 7,) but *distributes them variously as he thinks proper,* (1 Cor. xii. 11,) so that some excel others. But whatever gifts the Lord has bestowed upon us, let us know that it is committed to us as so much money, that it may yield some gain; for

---

[1] "Qu'ils apprenent de porter patiemment la longue attente;"— "that they may learn to endure patiently the long delay."

nothing could be more unreasonable than that we should allow to remain buried, or should apply to no use, God's favours, the value of which consists in yielding fruit.

Matthew XXV. 15. *To every one according to his own ability.* By this term Christ does not distinguish between natural gifts and the gifts of the Spirit; for we have neither power nor skill[1] which ought not to be acknowledged as having been received from God; and, therefore, whoever shall determine to give God his share will leave nothing for himself. What then is meant by saying, that the master of the house gives to each person more or less, *according to his own ability?* It is because God, as he has assigned to every one his place, and has bestowed on him natural gifts, gives him also this or the other injunction, employs him in the management of affairs, raises him to various offices, furnishes him with abundant means of eminent usefulness, and presents to him the opportunity.

It is absurd, however, in the Papists to infer from this, that the gifts of God are conferred on every man according to the measure which he deserves. For, though the old translator[2] employed the word *virtus*,[3] he did not mean that God bestows his gifts, according as men have acquitted themselves well, and obtained the praise of *virtue*, but only so far as the master of the house has judged them to be suitable. Now we know that no man is found by God to be suitable till He has made him so; and the Greek word δύναμις, (*power, ability,*) which Christ employed, is free from all ambiguity.

[1] "Il n'y a ne puissance, ne industrie, ou dexterité;"—"there is neither power, nor industry, nor skill."

[2] "Le translateur Latin ancien;"—"the old Latin translator."

[3] An interpreter who was willing to twist a passage, so as to bring out of it any meaning that he chose, would find the vagueness of the Latin word *virtus* to be well suited to his purpose. Its derivation from *vir, a man*, shows that it originally signified *manliness*, from which it easily passed to denote *courage*, and, from the high estimation in which *courage* was held among warlike nations, became the general expression for *moral excellence*, out of which arose the application of it to other kinds of *excellence*, as in the phrase, *virtutes orationis, the ornaments of style.* Again, from denoting *manly vigour* it came naturally to denote *ability*; and it is undoubtedly in this sense, with which our English version accords, that *virtus* is employed by the Vulgate in this passage.—*Ed.*

20. *And he who had received five talents.* Those who employ usefully whatever God has committed to them are said to be engaged in *trading*. The life of the godly[1] is justly compared to *trading*, for they ought naturally to exchange and barter with each other, in order to maintain intercourse; and the industry with which every man discharges the office assigned him, the calling itself, the power of acting properly, and other gifts, are reckoned to be so many kinds of *merchandise;* because the use or object which they have in view is, to promote mutual intercourse among men.

Now the *gain* which Christ mentions is general usefulness,[2] which illustrates the glory of God. For, though God is not enriched, and makes no *gain,* by our labours, yet when every one is highly profitable to his brethren, and applies advantageously, for their salvation, the gifts which he has received from God, he is said to yield *profit,* or *gain,* to God himself. So highly does our heavenly Father value the salvation of men, that whatever contributes to it he chooses to place to his own account. That we may not *become weary in doing well,* (Gal. vi. 9,) Christ declares that the labour of those who are faithfully employed in their calling will not be useless.

According to *Luke,* he says that *he who gained five pounds obtains the government of five cities;* by which words he informs them, that the glory of his kingdom will be very different at his last coming from what it now appears. For now[3] we have labour and anxiety in managing, as it were, the affairs of an absent master; but then he will have at his command an ample and copious supply of honours, to ennoble and enrich us. The form of expression employed by *Matthew* is more simple, *Enter thou into the joy of thy master;* by which he means that faithful servants, whose discharge of duty shall meet with his approbation, will share with himself a blessed abundance of all good things.

---

[1] " Des fideles;"—" of believers."
[2] " C'est le profit ou l'avancement de toute la compagnie des fideles en commun;"—" it is the profit or advancement of the whole company of believers in common."
[3] " En ce monde;"—" in this world."

But it is asked, What is meant by what is added, *Take from him the talent, and give it to him who hath ten talents?* For every kind of *trading* will then be at an end. I reply, We ought to keep in remembrance what I formerly mentioned, that those who insist on explaining, with exactness, every minute phrase, are mistaken. The true meaning is, though slothful and unprofitable servants are now endued with the gifts of the Spirit, yet they will at length be deprived of them all, that their wretched and shameful poverty may redound to the glory of the good. Now these slothful persons, Christ tells us, *hide* either the *talent* or the *pound* in the earth; because, while they consult their own ease and gratifications, they refuse to submit to any uneasiness; as we see very many who, while they are privately devoted to themselves and to their own advantage, avoid all the duties of charity, and have no regard to the general edification. When it is said that the master of the house, after his return, called the servants to account; as this ought to impart courage to the good, when they understand that they do not lose their pains, so the indolent and careless, on the other hand, ought to be struck with no small terror. Let us therefore learn to call ourselves daily to account, before the Lord come, and *make a reckoning* with us.

24. *I knew thee, that thou art a harsh man.* This *harshness* has nothing to do with the substance of the parable; and it is an idle speculation in which those indulge, who reason from this passage, how severely and rigorously God deals with his own people. For Christ did not intend to describe such *rigour*, any more than to applaud *usury*, when he represents the master of the house as saying, that the money ought to have been deposited with a *banker*, that it might, at least, *gain interest*. Christ only means, that there will be no excuse for the indolence of those who both conceal the gifts of God, and waste their time in idleness. Hence also we infer that no manner of life is more praiseworthy in the sight of God, than that which yields some advantage to human society.

29. *To every one that hath shall be given.* This sentence has been explained[1] under Matthew xiii. 12.

30. *And cast the unprofitable servant into outer darkness.* We have also explained,[2] under Matthew viii. 12, that *outer darkness* is contrasted with the light which is within the house;[3] for, as banquets were anciently held, for the most part, at night, and were illuminated by numerous torches and lamps, of those who are banished from the kingdom of God, Christ says, that they are cast *without into darkness.*

Luke XIX. 27. *But those my enemies.* In this second part, he appears to glance principally at the Jews, but includes all who, in the absence of their master, determine to revolt. Now Christ's intention was, not only to terrify such persons by threatening an awful punishment, but also to keep his own people in faithful subjection; for it was no small temptation to see the kingdom of God scattered by the treachery and rebellion of many. In order then that we may preserve our composure in the midst of troubles, Christ informs us that he will return, and that at his coming he will punish wicked rebellion.[4]

MATTHEW.	MARK.	LUKE.
XXI. 1. And when they approached Jerusalem, and were come to Bethphage, to the mountain of Olives, then Jesus sent two disciples,[5] 2. Saying to them, Go into the village which is opposite to you, and immediately you will find an ass tied, and a colt with her: loose them, and	XI. 1. And as they approach Jerusalem, at Bethphage and Bethany, near the mountain of Olives, he sendeth two of his disciples, 2. And saith to them, Go away into the village which is opposite to you, and, just as you are entering into it, you will find a colt tied, on which no man ever	XIX. 29. And it happened, when he approached Bethphage and Bethany, near the mountain which is called the mountain of Olives, he sent two of his disciples, 30. Saying, Go into the village which is opposite; and, as you enter into it, you will find a colt tied, on which no man ever sat; loose

[1] See p. 104 of this volume.
[2] *Harmony*, vol. i. p. 384.
[3] "*De la lumiere et clarte qui est en la maison;*"—"with the light and brightness that is within the house."
[4] "*Il se vengera contre les traistres, et les punira de leur rebellion;*"—"he will take vengeance on traitors, and will punish them for their rebellion."
[5] "*Deux* de ses *disciples;*"—"*two* of his *disciples.*"

MATTHEW.	MARK.	LUKE.
bring them to me. 3. And if any man shall say any thing to you, say, The Lord hath need of them; and immediately he will send them.[1] 4. Now all this was done, that it might be fulfilled which was spoken by the prophet, saying, 5. Say to the daughter of Zion, Lo, thy King cometh to thee, meek, and sitting on an ass, and on a colt, the foal of one that is under the yoke.[2] 6. And the disciples went, and did as Jesus had commanded them. 7. And they brought the ass and the colt, and laid on them their garments, and placed him upon them.[3] 8. And a very great multitude spread their garments in the way; and others cut down branches from the trees, and strawed them in the way. 9. And the multitudes that went before, and that followed, cried, saying, Hosanna to the Son of David: Blessed be he[4] that cometh in the name of the Lord; Hosanna in the highest.[5]	sat; loose him, and bring him. 3. And if any man shall say to you, Why do you this? say, Because the Lord hath need of him; and immediately he will send him hither. 4. And they went away, and found a colt tied near a door where two ways meet, and they loose him. 5 And some of those who stood there said to them, What do you,[6] loosing the colt? 6. And they said to them as Jesus had commanded, and they allowed them.[7] 7. And they brought the colt to Jesus, and threw their garments on him, and he sat upon him. 8. And many spread their garments in the way; and others cut down branches from the trees, and strawed them in the way. 9. And they that went before, and that followed, cried, saying, Blessed be he[4] that cometh in the name of the Lord: 10. Blessed be the kingdom of our father David, that cometh in the name of the Lord; Hosanna in the highest.[5]	him, and bring him. 31. And if any man shall ask you, Why do you loose him? thus shall you say to him, Because the Lord hath need of him. 32. And they that were sent went away, and found as he had said to them. 33. And while they were loosing the colt, its owners[8] said to them, Why do you loose the colt? 34. And they said, The Lord hath need of him. 35. And they brought him to Jesus; and, having thrown their garments on the colt, they set Jesus upon it. 36. And while he was going, they strawed their garments in the way. 37. And when he was already approaching the descent of the mountain of Olives, the whole multitude of the disciples, rejoicing, began to praise God with a loud voice, for all the miracles which they had seen, 38. Saying, Blessed be the King that cometh in the name of the Lord; peace in heaven, and glory in the highest.[5]

[1] " Et incontinent les laissera aller;"—" and immediately he will allow them to go."

[2] " Et la petit asnon de celle qui est sous le ioug;"—" and the young ass-colt of her that is under the yoke."—*Campbell* brings out, in the same manner, the force of ὑποζύγιον, " *even the colt of a labouring beast.*"—*Ed.*

[3] " Et le feirent asseoir sur iceux vestemens;"—" *and made him sit on those* garments."

[4] " *Benit soit celuy;*"—" *blessed be he.*"

[5] " *Es tres-hauts lieux;*"—" *in the very high places.*"

[6] " *Que voulez-vous faire?*"—" *What do you wish to do?*"

[7] " *Et ceux-la les laisserent aller;*"—" *and* those men *allowed them to go.*"

[8] " *Ceux à qui il estoit;*"—" those to whom it belonged."

Matthew XXI. 1. *Then Jesus sent two disciples.* Jesus *sends* his *disciples* to bring *an ass* to him, not because he was wearied with the journey, but for a different reason; for, in consequence of the time of his death being at hand, he intended to show, by a solemn performance, what was the nature of his kingdom. He had begun, indeed, to do this at his baptism, but it remained that this demonstration should be given by him towards the end of his calling: for why did he hitherto refrain from the title of *King,* and now at length openly declare himself to be a *King,* but because he is not far from the end of his course?[1] So then, as his removal to heaven was at hand, he intended to commence his reign openly on earth.

This would have been a ridiculous display, if it had not been in accordance with the prediction of Zechariah, (ix. 9.) In order to lay claim to the honours of royalty, he enters Jerusalem, *riding on an ass.* A magnificent display, truly! more especially when *the ass* was borrowed from some person, and when the want of a saddle and of accoutrements compelled the disciples to *throw their garments on it,* which was a mark of mean and disgraceful poverty. He is attended, I admit, by a large retinue; but of what sort of people? Of those who had hastily assembled from the neighbouring villages. Sounds of loud and joyful welcome are heard;[2] but from whom? From the very poorest, and from those who belong to the despised multitude. One might think, therefore, that he intentionally exposed himself to the ridicule of all. But as he had two things to do at the same time,—as he had to exhibit some proof of his kingdom, and to show that it does not resemble earthly kingdoms, and does not consist of the fading riches of this world, it was altogether necessary for him to take this method.

To wicked men, no doubt, this might be very unacceptable, had not God long before testified by his Prophet that such would be the king who would come to restore the salvation

---

[1] "Pource qu'il se voit estre bien pres du but de sa course;"—"because he sees that he is very near the end of his course."
[2] "Les voix retentissent pour luy faire honneur, et le recevoir en grande ioye et triomphe;"—"voices resound to do him honour, and to receive him in great joy and triumph."

of his people. In order, therefore, that the mean aspect of Christ may not hinder us from perceiving in this exhibition[1] his spiritual kingdom, let us keep before our eyes the heavenly prediction, by which God conferred more honour on his Son under the revolting aspect of a beggar, than if he had been decorated with all the dazzling ornaments of kings. Without this seasoning, we shall never have any relish for this history; and therefore there is great weight in the words of Matthew, when he says, that *the prediction of the Prophet was fulfilled*.[2] Perceiving that it was hardly possible that men, who are too much devoted to wealth and splendour, should derive any advantage from this narrative, when viewed according to the feeling of the flesh, he leads them away from the simple contemplation of the fact to the consideration of the prophecy.

2. *Go into the village.* As he was *at Bethany*, he did not ask for *an ass* to relieve the fatigue of travelling; for he could easily have performed the rest of the journey on foot.[3] But as kings are wont to ascend their chariots, from which they may be easily seen, so the Lord intended to turn the eyes of the people on himself, and to place some mark of approbation on the applauses of his followers, lest any might think that he unwillingly received the honour of a king.[4]

From what place he ordered *the ass* to be brought is uncertain, except what may naturally be inferred, that it was some village adjoining to the city; for the allegorical exposition of it, which some give, as applying to Jerusalem, is ridiculous. Not a whit more admissible is the allegory which certain persons have contrived about the *ass* and the *colt*. " The *she-ass*," they tell us, " is a figure of the Jewish nation,

---

[1] " Sous la couverture des choses yci recitees;"—" under the disguise of the things here related."
[2] " Quand il dit que *tout cela se faisoit afin que ce qui avoit este dit par le Prophete fust accompli*;"—" when he says that *all this was done, in order that what had been said by the Prophet might be fulfilled.*"
[3] " Car il y avoit si peu de là iusques en Ierusalem, qu'il y fust aisee-ment allé à pied;"—" for it was so short a distance from that place to Jerusalem, that he would easily have gone thither on foot."
[4] " Afin qu'on ne pensast point qu'il prinst cela a desplaisir, et qu'on lui attribuast l'honneur de Roy contre son vouloir;"—" that it might not be thought that he took offence at this, and that the honour of King was given to him in opposition to his will."

which had been long subdued, and accustomed to the yoke of the Law. The Gentiles, again, are represented by the *colt, on which no man ever sat.* Christ sat first on the *ass* for this reason, that it was proper for him to begin with the Jews; and afterwards he passed over to the *colt,* because he was appointed to govern the Gentiles also in the second place." And indeed Matthew appears to say that he rode on both of them; but as instances of *Synecdoche* occur frequently in Scripture, we need not wonder if he mentions two instead of one. From the other Evangelists it appears manifestly that the *colt* only was used by Christ; and all doubt is removed by Zechariah, (ix. 9,) who twice repeats the same thing, according to the ordinary custom of the Hebrew language.[1]

And immediately you will find. That the disciples may feel no hesitation about immediate compliance, our Lord anticipates and replies to their questions. First, he explains that he does not send them away at random, and this he does by saying that, at the very entrance into the village, they will find an *ass-colt with its mother;* and, secondly, that nobody will hinder them from leading him away, if they only reply that He *hath need of him.* In this way he proved his Divinity; for both to know absent matters, and to bend the hearts of men to compliance,[2] belonged to God alone. It was, no doubt, possible that the owner of the ass, entertaining no unfavourable opinion of Christ, would cheerfully grant it; but to foresee if he would be at home, if it would then be convenient for him, or if he would place confidence in unknown persons, was not in the power of a mortal man. Again, as Christ strengthens the disciples, that they may be more ready to obey, so we see how they, on the other hand, yield submission. The result shows that the whole of this affair was directed by God.

5. *Say to the daughter of Zion.* This is not found, word

---

[1] " Car voyla ses mots, *Estant monté sur an asne, et sur un asnon poullain d'asnesse;*"—"for his words are these, *Sitting on an ass, and on an ass-colt, the foal of an ass.*"
[2] " Et de faire flechir les cœurs des hommes, pour accorder ce qu'il luy plaist;"—" and to bend the hearts of men to grant what he pleases."

for word, in Zechariah; but what God commanded one Prophet to proclaim, the Evangelist justly and appropriately applies to all godly teachers; for the only hope, on which the children of God ought both to build and to rely, was, that the Redeemer would at length come. Accordingly, the Prophet shows that the coming of Christ yields to believers a full and complete ground of joy; for, since God is not reconciled to them in any other way than through the agency of the Mediator, and as it is the same Mediator who delivers his people from all evils, what can there be, apart from him, that is fitted to cheer men ruined by their sins, and oppressed by troubles? And as we must be altogether overwhelmed with grief when Christ is absent, so, on the other hand, the Prophet reminds believers that, when the Redeemer is present with them, they ought to be perfectly joyful. Now though he bestows on Christ other commendations—namely, that *he is just, and having salvation*—Matthew has taken but a single portion, which applied to the object he had in view, which is, that Christ will come, *poor* or *meek;* or, in other words, that he will be unlike earthly kings, whose apparel is very magnificent and costly. Another mark of poverty is added, that he will *ride on an ass,* or *the foal of an ass;* for there can be no doubt that the manner of *riding* which belongs to the common people is contrasted with royal splendour.

6. *And the disciples went.* It was just now remarked, that the zeal and readiness of *the disciples* to obey are here mentioned with commendation; for the influence of Christ was not so great, that his name alone would be sufficient to produce an impression on unknown persons; and besides, there was reason to fear that they would be blamed for theft. It is therefore a proof of the deference which they paid to their Master, when they make no reply, but proceed readily towards that place to which he has ordered them to go, relying on his command and promise. Let us also learn by their example to press forward through every kind of difficulty, so as to render to the Lord the obedience which he demands from us; for he will remove obstacles, and open up a path, and will not permit our endeavours to be unavailing.

8. *And a very great multitude.* Here the Evangelists relate that Christ was acknowledged as a king by the people. It might, indeed, appear to be a ludicrous exhibition,[1] that a multitude of obscure persons, by *cutting down trees, and strawing their garments,* bestowed on Christ the empty title of *King;* but as they did this in good earnest, and as they gave an honest testimony of their reverence, so Christ looked upon them as fit heralds of his kingdom. Nor ought we to wonder at such a beginning, when even in the present day, while sitting at the right hand of the Father, he commissions from the heavenly throne obscure men, by whom his majesty is celebrated in a despicable manner. I do not think it probable that the *branches of palm-trees* were cut down, as some interpreters conjecture, in accordance with an ancient and solemn rite appointed for that day. On the contrary, it would seem to have been by a sudden movement of the Spirit that this honour was rendered to Christ, when nothing of this nature had been intended by the disciples, whom the rest of the multitude imitated by doing the same thing; for this also may be inferred from the words of Luke.

9. *Hosanna to the Son of David.* This prayer is taken from Psalm cxviii. 25. Matthew relates expressly the Hebrew words, in order to inform us, that these applauses were not rashly bestowed on Christ, and that the disciples did not utter without consideration the prayers which came to their lips, but that they followed with reverence the form of prayer, which the Holy Spirit had prescribed to the whole Church by the mouth of the Prophet. For, though he speaks there of his own kingdom, yet there is no reason to doubt that he principally looks, and intends others to look, to the eternal succession, which the Lord had promised to him. He drew up a perpetual form of prayer, which would be observed, even when the wealth of the kingdom was decayed; and therefore it was a prevailing custom, that prayers for the promised redemption were generally pre-

---

[1] " Vray est qu'il pouvoit sembler que c'estoit un ieu de petits enfans;" —" true, it might be thought that it was a game of little children."

sented in these words. And the design of Matthew was, as we have just hinted, to quote in Hebrew a well-known psalm, for the purpose of showing that Christ was acknowledged by the multitude as a Redeemer. The pronunciation of the words, indeed, is somewhat changed; for it ought rather to have been written, *Hoshiana*, (הושיע נא) *Save now, we beseech thee;* but we know that it is scarcely possible to take a word from one language into another, without making some alteration in the sound. Nor was it only the ancient people whom God enjoined to pray daily for the kingdom of Christ, but the same rule is now laid down for us. And certainly, as it is the will of God to reign only in the person of his Son, when we say, *May thy kingdom come,* under this petition is conveyed the same thing which is expressed more clearly in the psalm. Besides, when we pray to God to maintain his Son as our King, we acknowledge that this kingdom was not erected by men, and is not upheld by the power of men, but remains invincible through heavenly protection.

In the name of the Lord. He is said to come *in the name of God,* who not only conducts himself, but receives the kingdom, by the command and appointment of God. This may be more certainly inferred from the words of *Mark,* where another exclamation is added, *Blessed be the kingdom of our father David, which cometh in the name of the Lord;* for they speak thus in reference to the promises; because the Lord had testified that he would at length be a deliverer of that nation, and had appointed as the means the restoration of the kingdom of David. We see then that the honour of Mediator, from whom the restoration of all things and of salvation was to be expected, is ascribed to Christ. Now as it was mean and uneducated men by whom the kingdom of Christ was called *the kingdom of David,* let us hence learn that this doctrine was at that time well known, which in the present day appears to many to be forced and harsh, because they are not well acquainted with Scripture.

Luke adds a few words, *Peace in heaven, and glory in the highest;*[1] in which there would be no obscurity, were it not

---

[1] " Es lieux tres-hauts ;"—" in the very high places."

that they do not correspond to the song of the angels, (Luke ii. 14;) for there the angels ascribe to God *glory in heaven,* and to men *peace on earth;* while here both *peace* and *glory* are ascribed to God. But there is no contradiction in the meaning; for, though the angels state more distinctly the reason why we ought to sing, *Glory to God*—namely, because through his mercy men enjoy peace in this world—yet the meaning is the same with what is now declared by the multitude, that there is *peace in heaven;* for we know that there is no other way in which wretched souls find rest in the world, than by God reconciling himself to them out of heaven.

Luke.

XIX. 41. And when he came near, he beheld the city, and wept over it, saying, 42. O if even thou, and at least in this thy day, hadst known and considered the things which belong to thy peace! but now they are hid from thy eyes. 43. For the days will come upon thee, and thy enemies will encompass thee with a rampart;[1] and will enclose thee, and will shut thee in on all sides; 44. And will level thee with the ground, and thy children who are within thee; and will not leave in thee one stone upon another; because thou didst not know the time of thy visitation.

41. *And wept over it.* As there was nothing which Christ more ardently desired than to execute the office which the Father had committed to him, and as he knew that the end of his calling was to gather *the lost sheep of the house of Israel,* (Matth. xv. 24,) he wished that his coming might bring salvation to all. This was the reason why he was moved with compassion, and *wept over* the approaching destruction of the city of Jerusalem. For while he reflected that this was the sacred abode which God had chosen, in which the covenant of eternal salvation should dwell—the sanctuary from which salvation would go forth to the whole world, it was impossible that he should not deeply deplore its ruin. And when he saw the people, who had been adopted to the hope of eternal life, perish miserably through their ingratitude and wickedness, we need not wonder if he could not refrain from tears.

As to those who think it strange that Christ should bewail an evil which he had it in his power to remedy, this difficulty is quickly removed. For as he came down from heaven, that,

---

[1] "T'assiegeront de rempars;"—"will besiege thee with ramparts."

clothed in human flesh, he might be the witness and minister of the salvation which comes from God, so he actually took upon him human feelings, as far as the office which he had undertaken allowed. And it is necessary that we should always give due consideration to the character which he sustains, when he speaks, or when he is employed in accomplishing the salvation of men; as in this passage, in order that he may execute faithfully his Father's commission, he must necessarily desire that the fruit of the redemption should come to the whole body of the elect people. Since, therefore, he was given to this people as a minister for salvation, it is in accordance with the nature of his office that he should deplore its destruction. He was God, I acknowledge; but on all occasions when it was necessary that he should perform the office of teacher, his divinity rested, and was in a manner concealed, that it might not hinder what belonged to him as Mediator. By this *weeping* he proved not only that he loved, like a brother, those for whose sake he became man, but also that God made to flow into human nature the Spirit of fatherly love.

42. *O if even thou hadst known!* The discourse is pathetic, and therefore abrupt; for we know that by those who are under the influence of vehement passion their feelings are not more than half-expressed. Besides, two feelings are here mingled; for not only does Christ bewail the destruction of the city, but he likewise reproaches the ungrateful people with the deepest guilt, in rejecting the salvation which was offered to them, and drawing down on themselves a dreadful judgment of God. The word *even*, which is interwoven with it, is emphatic; for Christ silently contrasts Jerusalem with the other cities of Judea, or rather, of the whole world, and the meaning is: "*If* EVEN *thou*, who art distinguished by a remarkable privilege above the whole world,—*if thou at least*, (I say,) who art a heavenly sanctuary in the earth, *hadst known*." This is immediately followed by another amplification taken from the time: "Though hitherto thou hast wickedly and outrageously rebelled against God, *now at least* there is time for repentance." For he means that the day is now at hand, which had been appointed by the eternal pur-

pose of God for the salvation of Jerusalem, and had been foretold by the prophets. *This* (says Isaiah) *is the accepted time, this is the day of salvation,* (Isa. xlix. 8 ; 2 Cor. vi. 2.) *Seek the Lord while he may be found ; call upon him while he is near,* (Isa. lv. 6.)

The things which belong to thy peace. Under the word *peace* he includes, according to the meaning of the Hebrew phrase, all that is essential to happiness. Nor does he simply say, that Jerusalem did not *know her peace,* but *the things which belonged to her peace;* for it frequently happens that men are far from being unacquainted with their happiness, but they are ignorant of the way and means, (as we say,) because they are blinded by their wickedness. Now since the compassion is mingled with reproach, let us observe, that men deserve the heavier punishment in proportion to the excellence of the gifts which they have received, because to other sins there is added an impious profanation of heavenly grace. Secondly, let us observe, that the nearer God approaches to us, and holds out the light of sound doctrine, the less excusable are we, if we neglect this opportunity. The gate of salvation, indeed, is always open; but as God is sometimes silent, it is no ordinary privilege, when He invites us to himself with a loud voice, and in a familiar manner, and therefore the contempt will be visited by severer punishment.

But now they are hid from thy eyes. This is not said for the purpose of extenuating the guilt of Jerusalem ; for, on the contrary, it marks with disgrace the monstrous stupidity of that city, that, when God is present, it does not perceive him. I do acknowledge that it belongs to God alone to open the eyes of the blind, and that no man is qualified for understanding the mysteries of the heavenly kingdom, unless God enlighten him inwardly by his Spirit; but it does not follow from this that they who perish through their own brutal blindness are excusable. Christ intended also to remove an offence, which might otherwise have perplexed the ignorant and weak; for when the eyes of all were directed to that city, his example might have very great influence in both respects, either for evil or for good. That no man then may be perplexed by its unbelief and proud contempt of the Gospel, *Jerusalem* is condemned for disgraceful blindness.

43. *For the days shall come upon thee.* He now assumes, as it were, the character of a judge, and addresses Jerusalem with greater severity. In like manner, the prophets also, though they shed tears over the destruction of those about whom they ought to feel anxiety, yet they summon up courage to pronounce severe threatenings, because they know that not only are they commanded to watch over the salvation of men, but that they have also been appointed to be the heralds of the judgment of God. Under these terms Jesus declares that Jerusalem will suffer dreadful punishment, *because she did not know the time of her visitation;* that is, because she despised the Redeemer who had been exhibited to her, and did not embrace his grace. Let the fearful nature of the punishments which she endured now alarm us, that we may not, by our carelessness, extinguish the light of salvation, but may be careful to receive the grace of God, and may even run with vigour to meet it.